15 MINUTES

15 MINUTES

GENERAL CURTIS LEMAY
AND THE COUNTDOWN TO
NUCLEAR
ANNIHILATION

L. DOUGLAS KEENEY

ST. MARTIN'S PRESS ⚅ NEW YORK

www.stmartins.com

Design by William Ruoto

ISBN 978-0-312-61156-9

First Edition: February 2011

10   9   8   7   6   5   4   3   2   1

CONTENTS

ACKNOWLEDGMENTS

THE HAPPY CIRCUMSTANCE of finishing a book is occasioned by the opportunity of thanking those who helped. It is important to remember that those who help are in their own ways the silent co-authors. This is a tribute to my silent co-authors.

To Stephen I. Schwartz, who, no less than fourteen years ago, first provided me with declassified records that started my quest to understand the lost bombs referenced in this book.

To Keith R. Whittle of the National Association of Atomic Veterans, Harold Wainscott of the Atomic Veterans, and Boley Caldwell, who arranged interviews with the men of the Bravo shot of Operation Castle and helped tell that story.

To Holly Barker of the embassy of the Republic of the Marshall Islands, who provided me with the oral histories of those who lived in the radioactive fallout of Bravo for nearly three days.

To the late John Kapral and his wife, who shared time in their home with me and kept sending me documents as they rummaged through their files. John was on the island of Rongerik and lived in fallout for thirty-six hours.

To Jeff Gordon, who suffered through no fewer than five of my visits to his offices at the Coordination and Information Center for the Department of Energy archives in North Las Vegas. Jeff patiently corrected my mistakes and narrowed my research to a lengthy but nonetheless manageable forty thousand pages of material unveiling Gerald Scarpino's story, which ricochets through the book.

To Howard Richardson and Bob Lagerstrom, who provided me with their notes from 1958 and spent time with me in person and on the telephone to help me understand SAC procedures and policies. These brilliant pilots brought their bomber home. That the recovery of their bomb was bungled by the air force and the navy tars their heroic flying.

To Mickey Youmans, a master filmmaker with whom I visited the Goldsboro crash site, interviewed the atomic veterans in Portland, and flew above Wassaw Sound in Savannah, my gratitude for directly touching so many of the events in this book and yet remaining throughout an independent critic of my thinking.

To Jim Oppel, who recoiled at the thought of nuclear annihilation and lent me a copy of his favorite book on the subject, *The Fate of the Earth*.

To Don Abbott, who assisted me as I worked my way through the testimony regarding the collapse of Texas Tower Four. Don's father was one of the twenty-eight men who died in the collapse of this radar station-at-sea.

To the countless SAC pilots, bomb-navs, aircrews and ground crews who allowed me to interview them, my appreciation for your time and your insights. Combined with the recent declassification of so many documents, the nation can now see your incredible world of sorties and bombs and alerts in detail that has never before appeared in print.

To Doug Grad at the Doug Grad Literary Agency and to my editor, Marc Resnik, both of whom kept me from losing sight of the human side of this story and who appreciated the possibilities of telling a story in episodic vignettes, my thanks.

Finally, to everyone in the Keeney family, I give my thanks—Alex, Dougo, my brother and sister, and my mother, for whom "the book" has been a daily topic of conversation; and in particular to my wife, Jill, to whom I've always wanted to publicly dedicate something, and now I can: this book.

15 MINUTES

INEXTINGUISHABLE

THE COLD WAR of 1948 to 1992 was a complex ecosystem of nuclear weapons, military intelligence, enemy targeting, air-defense radar stations, air-refueling tankers, ground- and air-alert bombers, overseas bases, fail-safe communication systems, alternate command posts, rockets and missiles, and prerecorded messages, the sole purpose of which was to maintain an uneasy peace through the threat of massive retaliation. This was called deterrence. Deterrence was premised not only on having a striking force so inextinguishably powerful that even after absorbing a devastating first blow it could deliver a strike of nation-killing proportions, but on having the will to pull the trigger. Would the capability be credible, former secretary of defense Robert McNamara once asked rhetorically, meaning did we have it, would we use it, and would it inflict unacceptable damage to the enemy?

The answer to that question fell to General Curtis E. LeMay, a man so uniquely qualified to the task—he led bombers in the defeat of Germany *and* Japan—that one could scarcely imagine anyone else. LeMay's Cold War thinking was heavily influenced by three events whose consequences were impossible to ignore—the surprise attack on Pearl Harbor, the near total destruction of Hiroshima by a single atomic fireball, and the remarkable truth that not once during World War II had a bombing mission once launched ever been turned back or defeated by the enemy. Put all three together and you had an event of terrifying proportions. Thus it was that the Soviet Union and the United States placed all-in bets that they could deter a surprise nuclear attack by maintaining a retaliatory strike power that, no matter how weakened by a first blow, could still deliver a counterstrike that could vanquish a nation.

That LeMay's Strategic Air Command played a dominant role in the evolution of this ecosystem is well known. SAC endlessly pushed for more capabilities, more redundancy, more early warning, more accuracy, more bombs, and more contingencies covered by more bombers and tankers and intelligence-gathering aircraft. It grew in size and scope and lethality. It had a strong voice in the affairs of the air force, the Joint Chiefs of Staff, the Atomic Energy Commission, the CIA, and the many government agencies that it dealt with on a regular basis. SAC had its own tempo, its own timing, its own sense of how things were done. Sometimes that was good. Sometimes that was bad. SAC no doubt acted as an accelerant in the developmental timetables for nuclear bombs, which in turn led to plans that were poorly executed by the Joint task forces charged with testing new weapons. On the other hand, SAC opposed air-defense radar stations and slowed their funding until it was clear that early warning was essential to its own survival. SAC had its own political adviser, its own intelligence directorate, its own alternate command posts, and its own communications networks. Few outside SAC could match their own sense of urgency, as SAC generals would often say—SAC liked to do things themselves, their way, whatever that might require.

That said, there was enormous interconnectivity between disparate events. Operation Castle, for instance, resulted in the worst radiological disaster in American history, but it also produced a new lightweight, high-yielding megaton bomb that SAC so urgently required. Then there was the ever-quickening drumbeat of readiness that in turn led to a fear of being caught with unarmed bombers in the air, which in turn led to the practice of placing bombs on board SAC bombers, which meant that accidents would now involve nuclear weapons and that cover stories would now have to be concocted for accidents. Interconnected.

So, why is this important? A free people must have faith that their government is living up to its promises and conforming to the nation's laws and directives. In those often legitimate but necessarily gray areas, one needs to put the actions of a people or an organization into a perspective, and that perspective can come only from a better understanding of surrounding events. Truman was certainly reluctant to allow the military to control the bomb, but when he saw the necessity for it he quietly sent more than one hundred bombs to Europe to hold the Soviets in check during the Korean War. At that time, this was entirely secret and largely inconsistent with his public policies on the control of nuclear bombs. But now we have context. The bombs were in fact a hedge against the Soviets' opening up a second front in Europe, which indeed was consistent with Truman's public policies on containment. Likewise, during the Vietnam War the nation's stated policy was that we were not in Laos, but in fact we were bombing Laos with ever-increasing regularity. Unlike Truman, there as yet seems to be no evidence of any higher purpose to it, just war run amok.

As more information is declassified, the timeline of events in this nation's history may be moved back or forward a day, a month, or even a year. Some of that is apparent in this book, particularly with respect to bombs, where they were, and when. But more important, when viewed through a properly refracted lens of history, current military practices take on new meaning. Reagan's Strategic Defense Initiative had its roots in the antiballistic-missile systems and the warhead penetration aids described in this book. But in Reagan's time, after countless misses, few could understand the basis for the military's seemingly misplaced faith that one could ever intercept a Soviet warhead, largely because the military's experience with such intercept systems was at that time classified. No longer. Now we know, and we know at least one key ingredient for that faith: we always knew where the Soviets would be aiming.

In declassified documents we oftentimes find things that are subtle stuff indeed—"inside baseball," as it were—but if we want true context we need accurate data. In the last several years, formerly secret facts and figures, such as the number of bombers on alert, the type and size of weapons they carried, the total megatonnage, and the air defense the Soviets had in place, have in one document or another been recently declassified, some even for this book. These data rewrite the footnotes of history but they also let us reconstruct Humpty Dumpty and see a new and larger picture. We *guessed* that SAC had nuclear bombs at its disposal, we *thought* they had too many but now we *know* that they had some three thousand megatons on the alert aircraft, *alone.* Crazy. But not so crazy when you know why. Paraphrasing LeMay, it didn't mean much to say that SAC had too many bombs when inside SAC they were all too aware of the more than six thousand Soviet fighters and some one thousand surface-to-air-missile batteries they had to get past to reach a Soviet target. In truth, SAC knew that very few of those bombs would ever make it to their targets, but they could hardly say so in their own defense. We can now.

On the other hand, we are certainly on firm ground when we object to the obfuscations and wordsmithing of the Cold War. As one air force officer put it in 1954, when it came to how much radiation a soldier could be exposed to, there was "rule safety" and "real safety," whatever that meant to him. Then again, as another historian put it when talking about bombing missions, there was a "press mission" covering a real mission, something we've always suspected but now we see in writing. And then there is the enduring question of what the words *armed* and *unarmed* mean, at least in the sense of a nuclear bomb. As one frustrated senator said, if you are to believe what the military tells you, then a rifle with a bullet chambered would be unarmed if the safety was still on. Semantics. Obfuscations.

Most of the official documents referenced in this book were declassified after 1995 and thus represent the first appearance in print of many new and fascinating details. For instance, the 2009 declassification of interviews with former Soviet military officials revealed detail about a faintly known Soviet "dead hand" system that could be used to launch missiles after almost everyone was dead. This revelation in turn illuminated a series of references to an American system that would use timers and rockets to release our own missiles. In that happy coincidence of facts, it appears that there was more truth than science fiction to the *Terminator* notion that machines would end the world. Or at least have the last say.

One would be justified to criticize me for going into depth on certain events and brushing over others. To them I say that there are many books on the lost bomb of Palomares, many books on the emergence of the air force, and many books on the broad issues of nuclear weapons and their development. I have taken just one story from nuclear testing, one from SAC, and one from Air Defense Command to characterize the enormity of the entire Cold War machinery. Each of these events was a complicated affair about which something was known to the public, and much was not. I have selected them to illustrate the consequences of complicated process, the consequences of hubris, but in the end, because they have one thing in common—*15 minutes.* Deterrence was no doubt the riskiest military gambit in world history, but to work, it *all* had to work. To absorb a first punch, SAC needed to keep a portion of its forces on alert so that they would survive, but to launch those forces it needed warning, and that meant radar stations. To be certain that the retaliatory punch was never weakened, alert bombers had to be armed with live bombs, and that created risks. To pack as much punch for the bombers that made it through the Soviet defenses, the H-bomb was needed, and that meant testing in the Pacific. To get past Soviet defenses, low-level training corridors were established, mission folders were modified, attrition factors were calculated, bombs were assigned targets, and targets were given sorties. It was complicated. But it was interrelated and it all went hand in glove and was folded into that precious span of 15 minutes in which the existence of two societies was held in perfect balance for nearly fifty tense years.

WAR

WROTE *TIME* MAGAZINE: "SAC has keyed its 3,700 combat crews so tautly to what SAC Commanding General Thomas Power calls 'the compression of time in the Atomic Age' that SAC is even designing a new type of slip-on shoe to save alert crews the few seconds spent on fumbling with shoelaces."

It was November 1958.

HOW TO DETERMINE which country won a nuclear exchange was a riddle few attempted to solve save for Harvard Professor of Economics Dr. Carl Kaysen. Working with McGeorge Bundy, President Kennedy's special assistant for National Security, Kaysen prepared a briefing on the current war plan in which he presented a set of calculations. Said Kaysen, no matter what war scenario played out, both the United States and the Soviet Union would be horribly devastated by the nuclear exchange. How then was a winner to be determined? "Accompanying these assumptions is the notion that prevailing in general war means coming out *relatively* ahead of the enemy. As an example, if the U.S. has lost 20 percent of its industrial capacity and 30 percent of its people, but the Sino-Soviet Bloc has lost 40 percent of its industrial capacity and 60 percent of its people, then the U.S., somehow or other, has won the war."

Percentages.

WROTE JONATHAN SCHELL in his book *The Fate of the Earth*: "Now we are sitting at the breakfast table drinking our coffee and reading the newspaper, but in a moment we may be inside a fireball whose temperature is tens of thousands of degrees. Now we are on our way to work, walking through city streets, but in a moment we may be standing on an empty plain under a darkened sky looking for the charred remnants of our children. Now we are alive, but in a moment we may be dead. Now there is human life on Earth, but in a moment it may be gone."

This was the Cold War.

NECESSITIES

IN 1945, A special committee of the Manhattan Project headed by Nobel Prize–winning physicist James Franck was asked to examine the political consequences of atomic bombs. In their final report they reduced to one sentence the essence of combat for those armed with atomic weapons. Wrote Franck: "In no other type of warfare does the advantage lie so heavily with the aggressor."

The committee, which had no military training whatsoever, thus summed up what would come to be known as the Cold War.

IN 1907, AN engineer with the J. M. Guffey Petroleum Company slipped into a canoe and paddled across a swamp to Caddo Lake, Louisiana. He halted, pulled in his paddles, leaned over the gunwales, and, near the surface of the water, lit a match. The match promptly went *poof!* into a blossom of fire, proving that gas, and certainly oil, lay beneath this otherwise forlorn backwater of Louisiana. Gulf Oil Company promptly bought the rights to drill through the lake, and within years a cobweb of wooden trestles and walkways had spread across the surface of the lake, connecting an eerie landscape of wooden derricks. One after the other, the rigs found oil and gas, and soon Caddo Lake was forested with derricks standing in twelve feet of water, all of it sheltered, all of it calm.

Oil exploration would now take to the seas.

WELL BEFORE THE Battle of Britain, the British Air Ministry wanted to evaluate the offensive capabilities of a new thing known as electromagnetic radiation. Could an electromagnetic wave of sufficient power melt the skin of a German bomber or, absent that, could it in some way incapacitate or kill the enemy pilot? they asked. They turned to Sir Robert Watson-Watt, superintendent of the Radio Research Station in Slough, England. Watson-Watt passed the question along and reported that there was no possibility of developing a radio "Death Ray," as one historian wrote, but there was an excellent possibility of tracking the reflected energy of such a ray and using it to detect enemy bombers. Asked to prove it, Watson-Watt set up a demonstration so simple that a school-age child could have understood it. He tuned a receiver to the frequency of a common signal used by the BBC and set up an oscilloscope to display what he called "the bounce." He had a Royal Air Force Handley Page Heyford bomber fly a predetermined route some miles away and pointed his antenna to the sky. He turned on the scope and watched with amusement as the eyes of his observers snapped open wide as the line on the scope flared.

Radar.

Watson-Watt's first radio-wave-bouncing device would in time become Britain's Chain Home radar stations. In 1940, the Germans launched the air invasion of Great Britain but the warnings from the Chain Home radar stations gave the RAF time to launch their fighters. The British never blocked the German raids—that was beyond the capability of radar and certainly more than their small cadre of RAF pilots might hope to accomplish—but they exacted enough in German losses to win the Battle of Britain.

THE BATTLE FOR the Marshall Islands began on January 31, 1944, and ended February 21. More than 40,000 American soldiers and marines took part in the invasion at a cost of more than 3,000 injured and 372 fatalities. The soldiers secured the islands and promptly moved forward, while behind them the construction battalions of the Seabees arrived. By March 1944, Kwajalein had been transformed into an island of barracks, Quonset huts, sheds, fuel farms, airfield, runways, maintenance sheds, docks, dust, and ammo dumps that, taken together, would become the primary advance resupply base supporting what would be known as the Pacific campaign. Twenty-two thousand men were based on Kwajalein, twelve thousand on Enewetak. Their sheltered lagoons would be dotted by ships that numbered in the hundreds. Said Don Whitman, who went to Enewetak to man a weather station: "I had these images of the South Pacific but when I arrived here, it was just another base. All of the trees had been blasted away in the war and what was left of them, bulldozed. It was barren except for buildings and people and telephone poles."

Barren and more. About these islands an air force historian would write: "It was doubtful that searchers would find a more remote region on this planet outside the polar regions."

In the years to come, even *remote* would be relative.

* * *

IN 1941, GERMANY invaded the Soviet Union, thus putting at war Adolf Hitler's Third Reich against Joseph Stalin's Communist Russia. Senator Harry Truman made no effort to hide his contempt for both nations when he spoke of this sudden turn of events. "If we see that Germany is winning the war, we ought to help Russia," said Truman, "and if Russia is winning we ought to help Germany and in that way let them kill as many as possible."

President Franklin D. Roosevelt said more or less the same thing even as he forged an alliance with the Russians. "My children," said Roosevelt, paraphrasing an old Balkan proverb, "it is permitted you in time of grave danger to walk with the devil until you have crossed the bridge."

The bridge Americans wanted to cross was the one that led from the beaches of Normandy to Berlin. The devil they would walk with was Stalin.

FORECASTING THE HEIGHT of waves created by storms took on a sense of urgency in 1938 when the Pure Oil Company joined with the Superior Oil Company to explore a leased tract of land one mile offshore near Cameron, Louisiana. The plan was to build a freestanding platform in the Gulf of Mexico and drill in fourteen feet of water. The question was this: how high should the platform be elevated to allow free passage of waves between its legs?

I. W. Alcorn, an engineer with Pure Oil, had ample experience building derricks on land but had no experience at sea. However, he had the cunning of a poker player. Alcorn consulted wave experts who assured him that in the Gulf of Mexico waves could grow no higher than fifteen feet.

Alcorn didn't believe them for a moment. Instead, he had his own ideas.

The name of Alcorn's platform would be taken from the tract leased from the state of Louisiana called the Creole tract and would be called the Creole platform. I. W. Alcorn's Creole platform would go into the history books as the first real freestanding structure built in the open seas but more infamously as the first freestanding structure to be hit by a hurricane and washed away. But for Alcorn's cunning, the offshore-oil industry might well have retreated to land, but in fact Alcorn *expected* his platform to be struck by waves; what he endeavored to do was to preserve the piles, the legs under the platform. Alcorn knew that the driving of piles was by far the most difficult and certainly the most costly part of an offshore rig, so instead of *hoping* that waves would never top fifteen feet, he simply designed a platform that would break away in a storm if the waves hit it. Alcorn placed his platform on a swarm of three hundred legs, only a handful of which moved when a hurricane finally swept the Creole platform into the sea.

The waves, of course, topped fifteen feet.

Still, the experts ran thriving businesses.

IN THE FALL of 1943, Major General Leslie R. Groves, head of the Manhattan Project, met with General Henry H. "Hap" Arnold, commanding general of the army air forces, to ask for help. Groves needed to test the ballistics of a bomb casing that would in time hold an atomic bomb. Practice bombs' shapes needed to be modified based on the flight characteristics they exhibited. Groves asked Arnold to streamline the testing, but he also needed a guarantee of absolute secrecy. Arnold obliged on both parts, an act of cooperation that cut through countless weeks of senseless red tape. That Arnold did so had as much to do with the demands of the war effort as with Arnold's personal witness to the rapid changes in aeronautics. Arnold, the man who would usher in the era of the intercontinental nuclear bomber, had been trained to fly an airplane by the Wright brothers themselves.

HARRY DAGHLIAN FUMBLED. After an evening lecture at the Los Alamos labs, Daghlian decided to continue a criticality experiment he'd started during the day. Daghlian had been "tickling the dragon's tail," as the scientists called it, building a critical assembly with a ball of plutonium and thirteen-pound tamper bricks made of tungsten carbide. At some point the assembly would go "critical" and a chain reaction would start, essentially a small atomic bomb; the trick was to contain it, to contain the fire of the dragon, so to speak.

The sweet smell of piñons no doubt drifted on the cool New Mexico air as Daghlian readied the final brick, but he fumbled and the tamper brick dropped into the pile, and with that, a bright, bluish light swelled between his hands. Daghlian hurriedly tore the pile apart but the spears of gamma had already pierced the flesh of his body and bathed his right hand in intense, deadly radiation.

Daghlian was rushed to the infirmary. For twenty-five days he wasted away. The incessant sweats and the onset of delirium reverberated down the halls and marked the hours as surely as the ticking of a clock. His hand swelled to nearly twice its normal size. His skin died, first the hands, then the abdomen. The desquamation continued up his arms to his neck and face. They debrided the necrotic skin. He was given shots of morphine and was bathed in cool water but no doubt his organs shut down and the walls of his abdominal tract sloughed. Daghlian died.

Three months later, as General Groves was testifying before the Special Senate Committee on Atomic Energy, he was asked to explain his understanding of radiation and death. With a sufficiently powerful dose of radiation, Groves said, death could be nearly instantaneous. In cases of minor exposure, death might well result, too, but without undue suffering. "In fact," said Groves, "they say it is a very pleasant way to die."

AN AMERICAN AIR-DEFENSE radar station was put into operation near Kahuku Point on Oahu, Hawaii, famously detecting (only to be dismissed as a flight of B-17s) the inbound flight of Japanese aircraft on December 7, 1941. Despite this inauspicious start, ninety-five radar stations soon dotted the East and West coasts of the United States, the radar operators intently watching for the blip that would be the sign of a second attack.

All this, however, was short-lived. The 1942 naval victory against the Japanese at Midway and the 1943 defeat of the Germans in North Africa pushed back the front lines far enough for one to conclude that radar stations were a needless drain of precious war assets. In 1943, the War Department disbanded the Air Defense Command.

The oceans, it was thought, were defense enough.

WELL BEFORE THE United States entered World War II, the army air forces issued a design specification for a bomber that could fly the unheard-of distance of five thousand miles with ten thousand pounds of bombs, bomb a target, then return to base without refueling. That such an aircraft would even be considered had much to do with the deteriorating situation in Europe. Washington feared that Great Britain would fall to the Germans and, as a result, bombing missions to liberate Europe would have to be staged from Upstate New York.

On August 8, 1946, the prototype for the B-36 intercontinental bomber rolled off the production lines and began its preliminary flight tests. In every dimension, it was an aircraft of staggering proportions. It was 162 feet long and 230 feet from wingtip to wingtip. Its fuselage was so long that a trolley had been installed in a tunnel that the crew used to pull themselves from the nose to the tail. If you put a B-36 at the center of a football field its wingtips would touch the ten-yard lines on both sides. It could stay aloft so long that it often carried backup pilots and had bunk beds fore and aft. So thick were the wings that a man could enter them nearly upright and crawl inside to work on the engines.

The bomber was in all respects built in accordance with the original 1941 design specifications except for the bomb bay. In the aftermath of Hiroshima, it would be modified to carry Fat Boy.

* * *

THE D-DAY BEACHES were alive with construction equipment, tracked vehicles, traffic marshals with whistles, and a steady stream of men wading ashore, marred only by the occasional thump of a distant enemy shell. Ships dotted the horizon; tethered blimps soared into the sky to snare unwary enemy fighters. It was June 8, 1944, two days after D-day. Omaha Beach had become a small port city with its own protected harbor. Enormous concrete caissons— two hundred feet long by sixty feet wide and sixty feet tall—called Phoenixes had been fabricated in Great Britain and then carefully pulled across the English Channel. They were positioned off Omaha Beach and Gold Beach and sunk to create a pair of one-mile-long breakwaters called Mulberries. The Mulberries stood thirty feet above the water at low tide and ten feet above it at high tide. So impressively large were they that seven Liberty ships could tie up on them at the same time.

The Mulberries, however, lasted mere days. On June 19, 1944, a powerful Atlantic storm pummeled the caissons with pounding waves and tossed them about as if they were cork. As the skies cleared, the harbor, such as it was, was gone. The concrete caissons dotted the ocean helter-skelter, most turned over, sunken or breached. There was no breakwater, the port was in shambles, but there was an inspiration.

Colonel Leon B. DeLong, an engineer, saw the destruction and pictured a better way to handle the seas. DeLong envisioned a type of pier that could be jacked up or down according to the height of the waves. In his mind he saw piers that would inch above the cresting waves and be impervious to the seas.

In 1949, Colonel DeLong established the DeLong Engineering Company and promptly won a government contract to build a pier that would extend into North Star Bay, a finger of the Atlantic that adjoined a small air force base located in Thule, Greenland, 695 miles north of the arctic circle. Because North Star Bay was frozen for all but a few precious months, DeLong decided to use surplus landing ships as the frame for the pier. These 250-foot-long flat-bottom barges, as they were called, were filled with concrete, through which six legs to a side were drilled and prepositioned. DeLong fabricated those parts in a shipyard in the Gulf of Mexico and then, like bugs on their back, towed them up the Atlantic to Greenland, where he lowered the legs into the seabed and jacked up the barges above the waterline to become an instant pier including a concrete roadway on top.

DeLong's "jack-up" was an instant success and DeLong's name quickly became synonymous with portable maritime structures, including his jack-up oil rigs that could be implanted in the ocean, jacked up, and then moved to another spot if the well was dry.

DeLong's name, too, would become synonymous with an air force plan to use jack-ups to elevate the platform for a radar station that would be built in the Atlantic Ocean, although not because he built the largest of these stations but because he did not.

T H E R E W E R E N O more cloudy days, not the way bomb-weary Germans had come to relish days when the skies were overcast and the bombers were forced to give them rest. On November 13, 1943, iron bombs unexpectedly pierced a solid cloud deck over the city of Bremen and, impossibly, the unwelcome sound of bombs exploding punctured the morning quiet. Little known to the Germans, the Americans were now using a British radar-bombing system that made the thickest of clouds seem as invisible as air and displayed the otherwise hidden city on a radar-bomb scope as if it were a sunny day.

Thus began radar bombing, an invention of war that in coming years would be refined and improved and for which tactics would be developed until radar bombing became the rule and not the exception, and cities unseen to the naked eye of a bombardier would be destroyed in the flash of an atomic bomb.

All using radar.

I N 1 9 4 4 , T H E United States Navy contracted with the Massachusetts Institute of Technology to create a computing device that would speed up the calculations required to display how aircraft stability would be affected by human inputs delivered through flight controls. The project was called Whirlwind. Whirlwind was expected to become the brains inside a flight simulator that would react to a pilot's actions in real time and in this manner dramatically improve flight training.

Whirlwind, however, moved in fits and starts and was fast becoming something quite apart from the flight simulator originally envisaged. Whirlwind was a machine with possibilities and complexities, the sum of which was slowly overwhelming the resources of MIT and exhausting the navy's budget but attracting the interest of a new user that saw it not as a flight simulator but as a nerve center for a global network of radar stations that had not yet been designed.

Whirlwind was fast becoming the world's first mainframe computer, not that such words had yet been coined.

* * *

A DRAMATIC CHANGE in the concept of warfare was unfolding in the Central Pacific. From the Northern Mariana Islands of Saipan, Guam, and Tinian, long-range B-29 bombers were systematically destroying Japan, although no one back in Washington seemed to understand what was under way. With tactics of his own design, Major General Curtis E. LeMay had been sending streams of bombers, which numbered in the hundreds, seventeen hundred miles across the Pacific to attack Japanese targets at altitudes low enough to avoid the jet stream yet high enough to avoid the burst points of the antiaircraft shells fired from the ground. He had experimented with bomb loads and, unhappy with conventional bombs, had switched to incendiary bombs to trigger secondary fires on the ground. Because bad weather had been the cause of too many aborts, he trained his crews in the new radar so that they could bomb in any weather.

LeMay bombed with an increasing sense of urgency. He bombed Tokyo, Nagoya, Osaka, Kobe, Kawasaki, and Yokohama. He attacked when and where he was ordered to, but when he was finished he pulled names out of almanacs or off maps and bombed some more. In his view, the only reason runways had been built on Tinian and the only reason the B-29s were fueled up and loaded with bombs—*the only reason he was in the Marianas*—was to bomb Japan. Five hundred bombers against one city, eight hundred against another. Nine hundred bombers today, a thousand bombers tomorrow—the only point was to end the war, one factory, one city at a time.

So intense were his operations that by the end of May LeMay eventually exceeded the supply of bombs the United States Navy could deliver to him and was forced to take a break. "I feel that the destruction of Japan's ability to wage war lies within the capacity of this command," LeMay wrote of the bomber forces he commanded.

Yet, few comprehended any of this. On a trip to the Pacific, General Arnold landed on Tinian and asked LeMay when he thought the war would be over. LeMay said he hadn't given the topic much thought. He excused himself. Thirty minutes later, LeMay returned and, much to Arnold's surprise, said, ever so matter-of-factly, that it would probably be September before he could complete the destruction of Japan's industry. LeMay no doubt displayed aerial photographs of the cities he had firebombed and the utter destruction of so many of Japan's factories. He no doubt reminded Arnold that his B-29s had dropped thousands of mines in Japan's harbors, thus making resupply nearly impossible, which meant that unlike Germany, there was little chance that Japan could rebuild any of its industrial capacity. All things considered, said LeMay, Japan would have nothing left to fight with by September 1945.

A somewhat startled but impressed Arnold asked LeMay to fly back to Washington and tell the Joint Chiefs what he had just said. LeMay promptly pulled a B-29 off the flight line.

Back in Washington, LeMay's assessment was met with skepticism. It seemed impossible that a bomber command on a tiny island in the Pacific, thousands of miles from American shores, could single-handedly bring a nation as powerful as Japan to its knees. Wars were ended with soldiers and a million would invade Japan in November 1945. So unbelievable was it that General George C. Marshall, chief of staff of the U.S. Army, fell asleep. "I don't blame the old boy for sleeping through a dull presentation," LeMay later said. "Here were these dumb kids coming in saying they were going to end the war for him."

While indeed LeMay failed to get his point across, the trip was not without its rewards. General Groves managed to get an hour with the general and briefed him on the atomic bomb and how it would be delivered by air. While LeMay didn't completely understand the physics of the weapon, he did know Japan's air defenses and promptly recommended a change in the bombing strategy. Rather than nest a queen among a cluster of worker bees and unnecessarily attract attention, LeMay suggested that they use a lone aircraft to drop the bomb. The Japanese were too weak and had too many problems to worry about one plane, LeMay said. A single bomber would look like just another reconnaissance flight, and reconnaissance flights were a waste of precious Japanese resources and were unlikely to meet any fighter resistance whatsoever.

Groves saw LeMay's point and ordered the change. The first intercontinental-atomic-bombing mission would be as simple as any bombing mission LeMay had designed. One bomber, one bomb, planned in one casual meeting that would indeed end the war in September.

As to Marshall's skepticism, there is no record of a subsequent conversation with LeMay about strategic bombing, but the truth was evident. "The fact that Japan while still in possession of a formidable and intact land army, surrendered without having her homeland invaded by enemy land forces, represents a unique and significant event in military history," LeMay would later say. General James H. "Jimmy" Doolittle agreed: "The Navy had the transport to make the invasion of Japan possible; the Ground Forces had the power to make it successful; and the B-29 made it unnecessary."

Said Hap Arnold: "The influence of atomic energy on air power can be stated very simply. It has made air power all-important."

And thus it was that in the Pacific, with a bomb, air power entered its primacy.

SEEDS

IN 1942, IRAN signed the Tripartite Treaty of Alliance with the Soviet Union and Great Britain, thus granting the Soviets and the British permission to use Iran as a staging area for World War II military operations against Germany, subject to a clause that required both countries to withdraw their forces within six months of a cease-fire.

On May 19, 1945, less than two weeks after the surrender of Germany, Iran demanded that Britain and Russia withdraw their forces. The British left within ninety days, as stipulated by the treaty. The Soviet military did, too.

But not their civilian secret police.

LITTLE BOY EXPLODED at nineteen hundred feet above Hiroshima and yielded seventeen kilotons of energy, the equivalent of seventeen thousand tons of dynamite. The heat from the fireball vaporized humans; the thermal pulse at ground level was some ten thousand degrees. Charred remains marked the bodies somewhat farther from the flash. Even farther from ground zero, the heat melted away human flesh, revealing limbs and skin hung in sheets from dazed survivors unable to understand what had just happened. Children searched for their parents and parents for their children. One man stood naked in obvious pain, holding his eyeball in the palm of his hand. A baby tenderly tipped a cup of water to the lips of her dead mother. Many walked about utterly dazed and able to do little more than hold their painful, heat-swollen arms in front of them, like "crabs with two claws."

In the days that followed, murmurs of a "strange malady" began to circulate. Those otherwise unaffected by the blast began to bleed from their gums and suffered hair loss and experienced "inexplicable fatigue."

SHORTLY AFTER THE bombing of Hiroshima, but before the bombing of Nagasaki, the United States Army Air Forces handed General Groves a list of new targets. Highlighted were forty "key" or "leading" cities, each assigned a priority for destruction. A map accompanied the chart and on it were drawn lines that showed the likely penetration routes for the A-bomb carriers.

That such a list might be handed to the man who oversaw the production of atomic bombs was in and of itself inconsequential. That the map was centered on the North Pole, was.

The forty cities were in the Soviet Union.

SOON AFTER THE surrender of the Japanese in Tokyo Bay, the 509th Composite Group departed the Pacific island of Tinian and returned to the United States, where it took up permanent residence at Roswell Army Air Base, New Mexico, thus making Roswell the first nuclear-bomber base and making the B-29s of the 509th the first nuclear-strike force in the world.

Although depleted by scientists who returned to their academic posts, the machinery of the Manhattan Project continued to produce atomic cores and bomb assemblies. To facilitate storage of these bombs, construction began on the first of six National Stockpile Sites.

It was in this fashion that the essential elements of aircraft, bombs, and supply channels were put in place, from which would grow the largest air-atomic-bomber force in the world.

TWO RETIRED NAVAL officers, each of whom gained extensive experience forecasting weather during World War II, F. R. Harris and H. G. Knox, sold their formulated wave forecasts to the offshore explorers. Using proprietary methodologies and their own analysis of historical wave data, a practice known as hindcasting, the pair gained the attention of the media when in 1947 they stated categorically that "in 100 feet of water waves will probably seldom, if ever, exceed 20 feet in height." Thus, they advised their oil-company clients to place the decks of their offshore oil rigs no less than "20 feet above the still water line."

A rival service was offered by W. H. Munk, the officer who forecast the weather conditions for D-day. In 1948, Munk released his own report, stating conclusively that the maximum wave height in the gulf was twenty-five feet, and to add a slight margin for variability, he recommended that his clients build their decks thirty-two feet above sea level.

The veracity of their calculations was tested one year later. In October 1949, a hurricane spun toward Freeport, Texas, capsizing a platform that had a twenty-six-foot deck.

The waves were forty feet high.

The old question—would oil be found under the oceans?—was now being replaced by a far more troubling new question; how could oil be recovered safely?

As American and Russian soldiers met one another along the uncomfortable divide of a bombed-out Berlin, there was an uneasiness felt by the general officer and the foot soldier alike. To the Americans, the Russians were noticeably *different*. It was in how they walked, the appraising nods they gave the German refugees, the set of their jaws as they looked across the rubble through the smoke and dust, the look of conquerors, not of weary warriors. In the way that Americans wanted to go home, the Russians seemed to be *at* home.

General Leslie Groves and Lieutenant Colonel Charles E. Rea, medical chief at the Oak Ridge Hospital, which was used by the employees of the Manhattan Project in Oak Ridge, Tennessee, discussed reports of radiation deaths coming out of Japan. Groves, who feared public outrage should the use of atomic weapons appear inhumane, was trying to put a favorable spin on the news. Fragments of that conversation were declassified. The transcript is dated August 25, 1945. It picks up in midsentence. Groves appears to be reading a newspaper account of the postblast situation in Japan.

> GROVES ("G"): . . . which fatally burned 30,000 victims during the first two weeks following its explosion.
>
> REA ("R"): Ultra-violet—is that the word?
>
> G: Yes.
>
> R: That's kind of crazy."
>
> G: Of course, its [sic] crazy—a doctor like me can tell that. The death toll at Hiroshima and Nagasaki, the other Japanese city blasted atomically, is still rising, the broadcast said. Radio Tokyo described Hiroshima as a city of death. "90% of its houses, in which 250,000 lived, were instantly crushed." I don't understand the 250,000 because it had such a bigger population a number of years before we started and it was a military city. Now it is populated by "[a] ghost parade, the living doomed to die of radioactivity burns."
>
> R: Let me interrupt you a minute. I would say this: I think it is good propaganda. The thing is people got good and burned—good thermal burns.

G: That's the feeling I have. Let me go on here and give you the rest of the picture. "So painful are these injuries that sufferers plead: 'Please kill me,'" the broadcast said. "No one can ever recover completely."

R: I would say this. You yourself, as far as radioactivity is concerned, it isn't anything immediate, it's a prolonged thing. I think what these people have, they just have a good thermal burn, that's what it is. A lot of these people, first of all, they didn't notice it much. You may get burned and you may have a little redness, but in a couple of days you may have a big blister or a sloughing of the skin, and I think that is what these people have had.

G: That is brought out a little later on. Now it says here: "A special news correspondent of the Japanese said that three days after the bomb fell, there were 30,000 dead, and two weeks later the death toll had mounted to 60,000 and it is continuing to rise." One thing is they are finding bodies.

R: They are getting the delayed action of the burn. For instance, at the Coconut Grove, they didn't die all at once, you know—they were dying for a month afterward.*

G: Now then, he says—this is the thing I wanted to ask you about particularly—"An examination of soldiers working on reconstruction projects one week after the bombing showed that their white corpuscles had diminished by half and had a severe deficiency of red corpuscles."

R: I read that too—I think there is something hookum about that.

G: Would they both go down?

R: They may, yes—they may, but that's awfully quick, pretty terrifically quick. Of course, it depends—but I wonder if you aren't getting a good dose of propaganda.

And there the transcript ends.

AMERICAN RIFLES, MORTAR shells, jeeps, canteens, bedrolls, and countless other items were tossed into boxes and piled in the streets of Germany until stacks of surplus war materials reached as high as a two-story building and as long as ten blocks. Things that the soldiers and airmen had so desperately needed before, in war, now lay about here and there, including

---

* ʻ On November 29, 1942, fire broke out in the overcrowded Coconut Grove nightclub in Boston. A total of 492 perished.

freshly manufactured parts strapped to pallets stamped MADE IN THE UNITED STATES. P-47s and P-51s and B-17s by the hundredfold were towed into farm fields, where they were parked until they could be chopped into scrap. In less than two years, America's armed forces would be reduced from more than 12 million men and women in uniform to just 1.6 million, with a scant 221 B-29s, of which a mere 46 were modified to carry the A-bomb.

Not so the Russians. Such piles of bedrolls and discarded war materiel were not to be found on the Soviet side of Germany. Quite the contrary. The Soviet Union retained nearly 4.5 million men and women in their postwar armed forces, including 113 divisions in the Red Army and as many as 15,500 combat aircraft, including 4,500 combat aircraft based in occupied Germany alone. To the Soviets, the end of the war was not so much a time to demobilize as an opportunity to modernize its forces without the distraction of war.

The Allies could do little more than watch.

GENERAL LeMAY'S RETURN from the Pacific Theater created an opportunity to make a statement of sorts. No doubt to underscore the global reach of American bombers, LeMay was asked to lead a formation of three B-29s on a nonstop flight from Japan to Washington, D.C. It was the sort of thing LeMay relished. Years earlier, on February 3, 1938, the Department of State announced that six army air corps B-17 bombers would fly from Miami to Buenos Aires to attend the inauguration of Argentina's newly elected president, Dr. Roberto M. Ortiz. The first leg of this historic trip would be a nonstop flight to Lima, Peru, a then-unheard flight time of fourteen hours and thirty-five minutes.

The mission was nearly flawless—six B-17 Flying Fortresses, as the new bombers were called, arrived in Argentina as scheduled on February 20, 1938, and landed in near-perfect synchronicity. Curtis LeMay was the lead navigator. "We had demonstrated that a flight of heavy bombers could proceed across land and water masses to visit an objective successfully at even as great a distance as twenty-eight hundred miles," LeMay would later write. And now he would nearly double that distance.

The three B-29s were stripped of nonessential gear and loaded with extra fuel. They departed from an airfield in Hokkaido, in northern Japan, and flew a nonstop route 5,553 miles. Although unexpected headwinds and severe storms forced the bombers to land in Chicago, the point had been made. Said army air forces general Carl A. "Tooey" Spaatz in testimony before a congressional appropriations hearing: "We must visualize the launching of heavy blows from any point on the globe against any other point."

The long-range heavy bomber, said Spaatz, "makes the airplane at present, and its descendents in the future, the greatest offensive weapon of all times."

And America had the only long-range bombers in the world. For now.

A S O V I E T   D E M A N D for military bases in the Bosphorus Strait, inside the borders of Turkey, as well as their continued presence in Iran proved correct those who had argued that postwar Russia intended to enlarge her sphere of influence through unilateral aggression. It also proved correct the thinking of diplomat and statesman George Kennan, who wrote that "Soviet power is impervious to the logic of reason and is highly sensitive to the logic of force."

President Truman dispatched written demands that the Soviets withdraw from Iran and withdraw their demands for bases in Turkey, and to underscore his seriousness he added a measure of Kennan's logic of force by sending to the Mediterranean the battleship *Missouri* and then the aircraft carrier *Franklin D. Roosevelt.*

The threat of military action prompted the Soviets to back down, but the die was cast, and to those in the military, there was no doubt about who America's new enemy was, and it had nothing to do with the foes of World War II.

I N   T H E   A F T E R M A T H of World War II, Britain's former prime minister Winston Churchill arrived in Florida for some well-deserved rest. During his visit, he spoke to a class at Westminster College, in Fulton, Missouri.

It would be remembered as his "iron curtain" speech. Eastern Europe, said Churchill, was fast disappearing behind the iron curtain of communism.

Nations were closing their borders.

Totalitarianism was replacing democracies.

It was March 5, 1946.

A drum was beating.

I N   T H E   S P R I N G of 1946, any pretense of cooperation between the Soviet Union and the United States was set aside and a neat divide was cleaved between Russia and the West. In a February 1946 speech before the Supreme Soviet, Joseph Stalin presented the first postwar five-year plan, setting capitalism and communism on a collision course when he stated that capitalism was hostile to communism. World War II had been caused in part by capitalism, said Stalin, adding that while the Soviets had joined with the West to eliminate fascism, the postwar landscape was "hostile" to Russia and that the ever-growing "capitalist encirclement" of the Soviet Union might very well pit communism and capitalism in a war in the not-too-distant future. The five-year plan called for a surge of industrial and scientific investment by the state to advance technology and further the development of essential resources so that the Soviet Union would match the accomplishments of any nation in any field of their choosing, most certainly in building and owning the atomic bomb. The Soviets would not again be beaten.

Said Eric Sevareid of this speech: "If you can brush aside Stalin's speech of February ninth you are a braver man than I." Supreme Court Justice William O. Douglas called it "the declaration of World War III."

IN TRUTH, STALIN'S language was scarcely different from the harsh language used by President Truman. "Soviet leaders profess to believe that the downfall of capitalism and the world triumph of Communism is a historical necessity that will inevitably result from the workings of the immutable laws of social science," said Truman. "The avowed basic intention of the USSR is to engage in 'competition' with the U.S. until the U.S. is destroyed." Peaceful coexistence with capitalist countries, said a Joint Chiefs of Staff historian, was "in the long run, impossible."

It was the age-old argument written in black-and-white: you're either with us or against us. It was an argument that in the years to come would spawn the growth of two global nuclear powers, each willing to place all-or-nothing bets that neither would attack the other first—but if one did, each was willing to accept that, in fact, it was all over.

UNDERSTANDING HIROSHIMA

IN THE AFTERMATH of World War II, army general Omar Bradley responded to those who criticized mass bombing as immoral with his now-famous retort that "all war is immoral." But Bradley also had strong feelings about the use of the atomic bomb. "Strategic bombing has a high priority in our military planning because we cannot hope to keep forces in being of sufficient size to meet Russia in the early stages of war. This is particularly true since we are never going to start the war." Said General Bradley: "Lacking such forces in being our greatest strength lies in the threat of quick retaliation in the event we are attacked."

Retaliation, said Bradley, would require the atomic bomb. "The A-bomb is the most powerfully destructive weapon known today. As a believer in humanity I deplore its use, and as a soldier I respect it. And as an American citizen I believe we should be prepared to use its full psychological and military effect toward preventing war, and if we are attacked, toward winning with it."

TO SOME, THE atomic bomb made future wars too horrid to contemplate. As General Groves would later say, the atomic bomb made war "unendurable—it's very existence makes war unthinkable."* But unendurable and unthinkable hardly seemed to matter. Rather, how best to use the atomic bomb in the next war was a far more domineering line of thinking. Indeed, said one early war analyst, by subjecting multiple cities simultaneously to the devastation suffered at Hiroshima, one could write a battle plan that would essentially amount to "killing a nation."

Said another: "Of primary military concern will be the bomb's potentiality

---

* Groves may well have picked up this thought from Robert Oppenheimer, who often couched the A-bomb in terms of making "the prospect of future wars unendurable."

to break the will of nations and peoples by the stimulation of man's primordial fears, those of the unknown, the invisible, the mysterious."

Primordial fears aside, it was a weapon, and when used simultaneously in air attacks, it was likened to a bullet to the heart. Wrote air force colonel Dale O. Smith in *Air University Quarterly Review,* the publication of the Air University at Maxwell Air Force Base: "The most effective air siege will result by concurrently attacking every critical element of an enemy's economy at the same time . . . If all critical systems could be destroyed at one blow, so that recuperation were impossible within any foreseeable time, there seems little question but that a nation would die just as surely as a man will die if a bullet pierces his heart and his circulating system has stopped."

THE CONCEPT THAT atomic war was unthinkable was in fact the first strategy that governments proposed to control the spread of the bomb, a strategy simply to ban war altogether, although no one had the slightest idea how to accomplish that. Sharing the secret of the bomb under tightly regulated powers of inspection and control was another idea, an equilibrium of sorts, but that, too, failed the test of pragmatic implementation.

What did gain traction was the concept of deterrence. In a 1942 speech to an assemblage of civilian scientists, General Groves used the phrase *fear of counteremployment* to explain why other nations would not seek the atomic bomb. This concept seemed to resonate with some and it quickly started to gain ground, although with a slightly different emphasis. General Lauris Norstad, assistant chief of staff for plans of the army air forces, in testimony before the House of Representatives described how a "ready force" able to strike quickly and decisively would in fact control the spread of the bomb because the consequences of being bombed in return were unthinkable. Norstad said that the mere existence of a ready force would by nature "act as a deterrent" to those who had designs on the atomic bomb.

In a 1945 letter Hap Arnold expanded on Norstad's comments and explained that the underpinnings of deterrence were in fact weapons, forces, and techniques. Said Arnold: "We must therefore secure our nation by developing and maintaining those weapons, forces, and techniques required to pose a warning to aggressors in order to deter them from launching a modern devastating war."

A modern devastating war of course would be atomic.

WHILE MATTERS REGARDING deterrence were being refined, so, too, were the planks that would become the platform for modern air power and its place in war strategy. "Pearl Harbor demonstrated the swiftness with which devastating results could be achieved in the age of air power," wrote one air force historian, speaking of the devastating consequences of a surprise nuclear attack in the new atomic age.

According to an air force general: "The air force that is superior in its capability of destruction plays the dominant role and has the power of decision. The inferior air force has no role. Before it can be built up the war will be over."

Said another general: "With the character of modern warfare changed so radically in this last war, particularly by new weapons, in the next war we will be in the midst of an all-out war from the start." Said another: "[T]he blessing of time lag which we enjoyed in the two World Wars is gone, perhaps forever. As top dog, America becomes Target Number 1."

And then there was the memory of America's awkward entry into World War II, when unprepared pilots flying with poorly thought-out tactics had led to countless mistakes and the loss of numerous bomber crews during the early months of the war. Said one air force general: "In jet-atomic warfare, there will be no room for gross errors of judgment. There will be no time, should hostilities start, to correct mistakes in the types of forces that we have provided, the manner in which they have been organized and trained, or the way we fight."

Such were the consequences of the atomic bomb.

GENERAL GROVES CODE-NAMED it "Water Supply." Water Supply was the blueprint for a postwar distribution system that would send atomic bombs from Los Alamos to highly secret and heavily guarded storage facilities called National Stockpile Sites. Each National Stockpile Site would operate within a current military base but with its own people and its own guards, and in the center of each compound each would have a highly secured zone called the "Q" area.

Inside the Q area would be acres of underground storage vaults for atomic bombs, above-ground reinforced buildings, blast-proof igloos, and weapons magazines, some with concrete walls seventeen feet thick. There would be buildings where atomic bombs would undergo maintenance, areas where the electronics of a bomb could be upgraded, and highly secured vaults where the precious plutonium capsules would be individually stored in a spindly, hourglass-shaped device called a birdcage.

A Q area, so named because it required an FBI "Q" clearance to enter, would be nearly impenetrable.* Each would be surrounded by three rings of barbed-wire fencing, including one ring that was electrified. There would be soft loam dirt between the fences, with concrete barricades pushed underground to prevent tunneling. Searchlights, armed patrols, sentries, and pillboxes manned with guns would secure the area when bombs were moved.

In 1946, General Groves presided over the groundbreaking for the first National Stockpile Site, thus setting into motion the Water Supply distribution network, a network that in time would pre-position atomic bombs across the nation and around the globe. At an ever-increasing tempo, bombs would arrive, be stored, be removed for maintenance and transported to waiting bombers for training missions, and then stockpiled yet again. Remembered a technician who worked in a Q area: "On occasion, [we] would receive shipments of nuclear devices from the Army, Navy or the labs at Sandia, New Mexico, aboard specially designed steel railcars that arrived at a small railhead just outside the main gate. An overhead crane would lift the devices from the railcar onto the railhead. The sight of two dozen nukes arranged in a group on that railhead was rather sobering in light of the briefings we'd received on the potential devastation each of these weapons could wreak on an entire city."

IN THE AFTERMATH of World War II, members of the Strategic Bombing Survey questioned the validity of bombing German population centers in an attempt to break that nation's will to continue the war. Rather than break their will, a counter-cities approach, as this was called, tended to intensify a nation's resolve. And even so, how did one measure a broken will? Far more effective were strikes against petroleum refineries, airplane factories, and power plants, the loss of which "ravaged" the Germans' war-making capabilities and "destroyed" their economy. This led to postwar air-atomic planning that emphasized Soviet industry as targets for nuclear strikes, key targets that if destroyed would have an effect far larger than the facilities' mere destruction. These plants, however, were often located in major urban areas and that circled back around to targeting population centers, the counter-cities approach. Said

---

* The etymology of "Q" eluded historians for many years. John Taylor of Sandia National Labs believes it comes from a government document called a PSQ form used by applicants for a nuclear security clearance. The PSQ, or Personal Service Questionnaire, contributed the "P" in its name to the P clearance given to contractors, the "S" to frequent visitors, and the "Q" for clearances given to government employees with access to restricted data (nuclear weapons data) and security exclusion areas. (Correspondence from Steven Aftergood, Federation of American Scientists, to author, December 3, 2009.)

one air force general of this conundrum: "I think it was sort of a shock to people when a few began to talk about the bonus effects and industrial capital and particularly when some began to ask what was a city but a collection of industry."

Thus it was that the term *bonus effect* entered the language of atomic war.

GENERAL SPAATZ MET with his British counterpart in July 1946 and secured two airfields in Great Britain that would, according to the painfully oblique language of the memo written by an American military attaché summarizing the meeting, have "certain facilities" to be used by "some very special purpose VLR [very long range] aircraft."

It was with this first baby step that American atomic bombs and American bombers would spread across the globe. In a matter of years, American atomic bombers and bombs would be based at or would have permissions to use air bases in as many as twenty-four countries, including Cuba, Labrador, Spain, Great Britain, Netherlands, Belgium, West Germany, Morocco, Greenland, and Guam.

And Bermuda.

As IT IS often said among military people, one seldom finishes a war with the same weapons that one started a war. If proof were needed, one needed to look no further than World War II. A war that began with bullets, torpedoes, and bombs had ended with an atomic device that was powered by uranium and plutonium. That said, rare was the case when the weapon of the future, the weapon that would end the next war, was envisaged so early. Within months of the end of World War II, the very futuristic idea of a guided ICBM—a guided intercontinental ballistic missile—came forth. In the final report of the Strategic Bombing Survey, titled *Air Campaigns of the Pacific War,* a new concept of air superiority materialized. In a time when rockets were rudimentary and had largely been used by the Germans as a weapon of terror, the authors saw a future that was in fact defined by the ICBM. Said the report: "If science and technology produce an air weapon which can, unaided, penetrate enemy defenses and accurately deposit its bombs, it may not be necessary to fight the conventional air battle and obtain conventional air superiority before the decisive attacks on an enemy's economy are mounted."

The author of this report said in a later lecture, "You will reach the point in the distant future when you won't even think of opposing air in the air . . . You'll fight them at the launching site or you won't fight them."

Launching sites would indeed soon dot the Soviet landscape, although in truth they were called "no show" targets by SAC bombardiers because these enormous "air weapons" would be buried in underground silos that would be largely invisible even when using the most advanced radar-bombing sights.

PRESIDENT TRUMAN CREATED the Air Policy Commission and asked it to examine advances in aviation and to determine what America should do to fully capitalize on them. The final report was no less than a playbook for fighting a war against the United States. In it, they included the knockout blow that would bring America to its knees. Or any country, for that matter, what with the atomic bomb.

Said the commission: "Heretofore the United States has been able to make most of its preparations for war after war began. In World War I and World War II the oceans lay between us and the enemy. Protected by the Navy, and by the land, sea and air forces of our Allies, we were able to convert our great industrial machine and our manpower for war after war had begun. No enemy action interfered with us as we got our factories going. Our army was trained in peaceful areas. Our cities were untouched."

No more, said the commission: "We can no longer count on having our cities and the rest of our mainland untouched in future wars . . . we must assume that if future aggressors will have learned anything from World Wars I and II it will be that they must never let [the] United States industrial power get underway; they must destroy it at the outset if they are to win."

Destroy its industrial capacity from the onset.

It was a truth that applied equally to American and Soviet targeting.

EMERGENCY WAR PLANS were theoretical models of political situations that could result in hostilities that would lead to a war that would require intervention by, or war with, the United States. The Emergency War Plan concept was created at the end of World War II by the Joint Chiefs of Staff as a tool to help evaluate American military capabilities against possible world situations. A war plan, when approved by the Joint Chiefs, would be handed to the army, navy, and air force for their own planning purposes.

Not surprisingly, from 1945 on, virtually every approved war plan started with the preassumption that the Russians had taken some unilateral action that drew America into a war. In most cases this was a land grab of sorts, usually into the Middle East to secure valuable oil fields. In so doing, the Red Army would overrun the British positions in the region and America would be at war.

The earliest plans assumed that American B-29s would be mobilized. They would be flown to forward bases in the Middle East or North Africa, from which they would launch conventional air attacks against Russia's industrial heartland. The first approved version of this plan, a plan code-named Pincher, hinted at the use of atomic weapons but largely relied on conventional bombs to bring hostilities to a halt. Subsequent versions were scarcely so hesitant. A revised Pincher made no effort to underplay the overpowering strength of the Red Army. With more than one hundred divisions on the ground against perhaps five or so combined Allied divisions, there would be no way to force a cessation of hostilities save by using the atomic bomb. Within sixty days of American mobilization, said the revised plan, a total of thirty-four American atomic bombs would be dropped on twenty-four Soviet cities. Moscow alone would be hit with seven atomic bombs. If this failed to halt the advance and bring the Soviets to the negotiating table, atomic bombs would be dropped continuously until the Soviets sought a cease-fire. The stockpile was projected to total two hundred bombs.

Pincher lasted for less than a year but it established a framework for future war plans, against which bombs and targets would be continuously revised upward but against which the circumstances of war would remain unchanged for fifty years. The next war would be with the Soviet Union. And it would be atomic.

THE AIR POLICY Commission made another recommendation. The safety of the United States, they wrote, depended upon a threat to any aggressor that in the face of hostile acts against the United States, we would "retaliate with utmost violence."

DURING A BRIEF rest with his family, General LeMay mulled over the war he had fought and came to conclusions, some of which would become the touchstones of his career. LeMay knew it was unlikely that bomber formations of eight hundred B-17s or nine hundred B-29s would ever again take to the air; the A-bomb had seen to that. One atomic bomb was equal to the payload of three thousand conventional bombers and the atomic bomb would henceforth be the air weapon of choice.

The long-range bomber, too, had more than proven its worth. As a bomber pilot who flew missions over Germany, and then as the commander of bomb wings in both Germany and the Pacific, LeMay had flown against every air defense imaginable and yet one thing had always been the same. Said LeMay:

"No air attack, once it is launched, can be completely stopped." Said another general: "No bombing mission set in motion by the Army Air Forces in World War II was ever stopped short of its target by enemy opposition."

Which, when considered in the context of the atomic bomb, had sobering implications—and no one was more sobered by them than one of the most experienced bomber commanders in the world.

DISORGANIZATION

I N M A R C H 1 9 4 6, the army air forces performed some much-needed housekeeping when it divided its operations into three distinct commands. Air Defense Command would consist of radar stations and air-defense intercept fighters that would defend the United States in the event of an attack. The second command would be an offensive air force with light bombers and air-superiority fighters but without heavy bombers and would be called Tactical Air Command. The third command was Strategic Air Command and to it would be given the atomic bomb.

In a throwback to the highly structured world of the prewar army air corps, Lieutenant General Curtis LeMay, a young and technically junior officer among postwar air force generals, was not assigned to lead Strategic Air Command. Rather, LeMay would be sent to Europe in the somewhat diminished role of commander of United States Air Forces in Europe. SAC, as it would be called, would instead be given to the well-spoken and entirely photogenic general named George Kenney.

Addressing General Kenney, Major General Carl "Tooey" Spaatz, commanding general of the army air forces, articulated Strategic Air Command's mission: "The Strategic Air Command will be prepared to conduct long range offensive operations in any part of the world . . . capable of intense and sustained combat operations employing the latest and most advanced weapons . . ."

The latest and most advanced weapon was, of course, the bomb.

T H E F I R S T P O S T W A R nuclear test was conducted in 1946 in the Marshall Islands, inside Bikini Atoll. It was called Operation Crossroads. Designed largely as a test to see if naval ships could survive nuclear war, a twenty-one-kiloton atomic bomb called Able would be air-dropped by a B-29 into a target area consisting of more than ninety ships spread across Bikini lagoon in ever-widening distances around a brightly painted ship that was the designated ground zero. A second bomb would be detonated under water.

A sailor aboard a tender ship remembers the uncertainty felt by those who attended the test: "We were quite nervous. We would ask the scientists that were out there. And they said, 'Well, we really don't know ourselves what's really going to happen.' They really kind of unsettled us."

Crossroads was equally unsettling to the Americans back home. As news of the underwater explosion appeared in the press, one Yale professor stated that "the probability that a crack or crevasse or hole might be blasted in the ocean floor is assuredly not zero." Because water is not compressible, others argued that the blast would kill half the fish in the Pacific Ocean and contaminate the rest so thoroughly that humans who ate them would die of radiation poisoning. Still others spoke of a tidal wave so enormous that all ships at sea would be swamped, or, in yet another scenario, that the explosion would ignite the hydrogen in the water and thus end the world.

However improbable each scenario was, there were unknowns, one of which would be encountered head-on in the Pacific. It was a deadly phenomenon called a "base surge."

THE MANDATE TO fly "offensive operations in any part of the world" was easier said than done, a truth not overlooked by General Spaatz. A quick look at any map revealed staggering distances between the United States and Soviet military bases near Moscow, Magnitogorsk, Novosibirsk, and Omsk. The "penetration routes," as they would soon be called, greatly exceeded the round-trip range of a B-29, and this created a problem. The operations chief of the army air forces suggested that if atomic bombs were quickly needed, the best thing might be to "expend the crew, expend the bomb, expend the airplane all at once. Kiss them goodbye and let them go."

General Thomas C. Power, who in years hence would become commander in chief of Strategic Air Command, disagreed, noting that the reliability of the crew might "decline" when it became obvious to them that they were to be "dispatched on one-way missions."

Still, for almost ten years, one-way missions were a fact of life in Strategic Air Command, not that any discussions about them were held in anything above a shared whisper.

THE NEWLY FORMED commands of the army air forces limped into being. Exhausted by war, congressional attention was on demobilization, not on building the postwar military. For example, Air Defense Command found it nearly impossible to gain any meaningful traction in its efforts to create a continental network of air-defense radar stations. For one, while it was all but certain that the Russians would at some point have the bomb, until they did, which could take years, there wasn't any real military threat to America. For another, even if they did have the bomb, they didn't have any long-range bomber.

The ambivalence about air defense was magnified all the more by budgets that were scarcely sufficient to build an offensive air force such as SAC. Thus, despite its name, in 1946 not a single air-defense radar beam swept even the smallest arc of sky over the continental United States.

And so it remained for the entire year.

WHILE AIR DEFENSE Command went begging for funds, Strategic Air Command went largely unattended. General Kenney was an absentee commander in chief, a commander who could more often be found giving speeches than dissecting the thorny requirements of building an atomic-bombing force. This would be evident during Operation Crossroads. The 509th Bomb Group had been selected to drop the test bomb, but it had been ten months since the 509th had dropped any atomic bomb, simulated or otherwise. With Crossroads now approved, the training tempo picked up and a bombing competition was held to determine who would go to the Pacific, but midway through the competition the leading aircrew was killed in an accident.

Once deployed to the Pacific, things fared no better. Bombing accuracy plummeted when test shapes were buffeted by the confusing wind patterns above the Marshall Islands, and the B-29s that arrived were dogged by mechanical failures and breakdowns. During one key dress rehearsal, a radar set failed; during another, a maintenance supervisor walked into a spinning propeller.

Happily, the weather on shot day was nearly perfect. The B-29 with the atomic bomb flew a straight-and-level flight at twenty-eight thousand feet through a blue sky flecked not with enemy flax but with puffy white clouds. The pilot followed a road map made by a series of destroyers laid across the lagoon pointing arrow-straight toward the bull's-eye; the navigator homed in on a beacon placed squarely on the brightly painted target, the USS *Nevada*. In the sky, there were mere whispers of winds.

The Able bomb missed by more than a quarter mile.

The *Nevada* emerged from the smoke as handsome as she'd ever been.*

---

* Despite theories, charges, and countercharges, the error was never satisfactorily explained, but the

* * *

THE PROPAGANDA OF the Cold War began in earnest—propaganda that started at home. "Destruction is just around the corner for any future aggressor against this United States," warned a 1946 press release reprinted in *Air Force Magazine*. "Quick retaliation will be our answer in the form of an aerial knock-out delivered by the Strategic Air Command."

"QUICK" WOULD HARDLY stand the test of any reasonable assessment of the atomic machinery at Los Alamos. Bombs were hardly available, and production-line practices that would result in reliable weapons were entirely absent. The nuclear physicist J. Robert Oppenheimer said that little progress had been made to improve quality. Atomic bombs were "largely the haywire contraptions that were slapped together in 1945." He derisively called them "laboratory objects."

In 1946, the Mark III Fat Man was the sole atomic bomb in the American nuclear inventory and was identical to the Fat Man that was dropped on Nagasaki—an enormous ball of steel ten feet long, five feet in diameter, and weighing an imposing five tons. It took thirty-nine men two days to assemble one bomb, and even then it had to be disassembled routinely to keep it functioning. Said Norris Bradbury, then head of the Los Alamos labs: "We had, to put it bluntly, lousy bombs. I mean, we could make a device that would stay pretty for a week, two weeks, three weeks, a month. Then it began to look like it had the measles."

Researcher and author Chuck Hansen explained the problem: "The Mark III could be maintained in combat-ready status for just a short time. The life span of its lead-acid batteries, once charged and installed, was only nine days. After nine days, the entire bomb had to be disassembled to remove [them] lest they begin to corrode . . . The large amount of plutonium in the weapon radiated so much energy from alpha decay that the pit had to be removed after ten days . . . Like battery change, pit replacement also required complete disassembly and reassembly of the bomb, a procedure that took 40 to 50 men between 56 and 76 hours to complete, depending on the skill and experience of the assembly team."

Still, this haywire contraption of wires, detonators, baroswitches, countdown

---

likely culprit was the egg-shape bomb itself. Absent a sleek aerodynamic profile, even a five-ton object could be blown off course by a shift in winds. Considering a twenty-eight-thousand-foot freefall, in some respects accuracy might have been more a matter of luck than training.

timers, fuses, and radar altimeters—this physics package of fissile material encased in thousands of pounds of chemical high explosives, this complicated device that was prone to measles—was an enormously effective device that was able to burst within a few dozen feet of the altitude specified to destroy a city in one single, blinding fireball of light and heat.

It may have been haywire. But it was a near perfect killing machine.

OPERATION CROSSROADS' UNDERWATER atomic explosion burst through the surface of Bikini lagoon with breathtaking violence. A darkened column of radioactive water rose more than one mile into the sky before it hesitated and collapsed upon itself. The collapse created a second plume, which rose and spread out from ground zero eighteen hundred feet in height and moving at sixty miles per hour. The boiling plume was as eerie as anything yet seen. It would later be called a "base surge." A reporter for the *New York Herald Tribune* wrote: "We saw the most terrifying sight of all. A bank of radioactive cloud and steam some two thousand feet high crept over the target fleet, swallowing the ships from view."

The radioactive cloud promptly triggered new images of atomic destruction and death. Said one analysis of the new possibilities: ". . . the detonation of an a-bomb in a body of water contiguous to a city would vastly enhance its radioactive effect by the creation of a base surge whose mist, contaminated with fission products, and dispersed by wind over [a] great area, would have not only an immediate lethal effect, but would establish a long term hazard through contamination of structures by the deposition of radioactive particles."

Using words that would no doubt delight a saboteur, the report continued: "We can form no adequate mental picture of the multiple disasters which would befall a modern city blasted by one or more atomic bombs and enveloped by radioactive mist. Of the survivors in the contaminated areas, some would be doomed to die of radiation sickness in hours, some in days, and others in years. No survivor could be certain he was not among the doomed and so, added to every terror of the moment, thousands would be stricken with a fear of death and the uncertainty of the time of its arrival."

Fear and uncertainty. Two hallmarks of the emerging Cold War.

ATTEMPTS TO DECONTAMINATE the ships engulfed by the radioactive base surge brought untold numbers of sailors into hot zones with scarcely a hint of restraint from their commanders, and thus a pattern fell into place. Nuclear weapons required testing and testing required explosions of atomic bombs.

As the pace of weapons development accelerated, so, too, would the pace of testing. But testing was done in the atmosphere and radiation could be blown one way or the other, much less carried by the ocean currents, so exposure limits were established, such as they were. The problem was that radiation did not "come out and fight," as one writer put it. Instead of affording radiation the same respect one gave a bullet fired from a gun, there was a "'hairy-chested' approach toward the matter with a disdain for the unseen hazard." This attitude was "contagious" and could be seen in the swagger of the junior officers who determined who went aboard the hot ships and how long they stayed.

Most stayed too long. As sailors hosed down radioactive decks and mopped the contaminants into the sea, their radiation-monitoring film badges recorded their accumulated exposure until their numbers peaked, which, to use a new phrase heard at the tests, meant that they were "burned out." Still, weapons needed to be tested and jobs needed to be completed, so waivers were granted one by one to burned-out sailors, and one by one the Maximum Permissible Exposure limits—the absolute amount of radiation one was allowed to absorb at a test site—were simply increased.

Hairy-chested indeed.

In 1946, the Manhattan Project came to a formal end when President Truman signed into law the Atomic Energy Act, creating the Atomic Energy Commission, commonly referred to as the AEC. The AEC took over substantially all of the assets and responsibilities of the Manhattan Project, including the design and manufacture of bombs. To oversee the AEC, the Joint Committee on Atomic Energy was established, with members appointed from both the House and the Senate.

Separately, the Armed Forces Special Weapons Project was created to take over military-related responsibilities of the Manhattan Project such as weapons testing, aerodynamic ballistics, radiological safety, and matters of weapons employment.

All told, the hundreds of corporations, universities, manufacturers, fabricators, and suppliers of parts, casings, electronics, and components required for the assembly of a single bomb remained entirely intact.

All that was missing was a sense of direction.

In 1946, Yugoslavian fighters twice attacked and shot down army air forces C-47 transport planes flying in what they considered restricted Yugoslavian airspace but which was in fact airspace above disputed territory. The first attack merely forced the plane to the ground, but the second attack was deadly and killed five. In response, the air force alerted Strategic Air Command to prepare B-29s for a transatlantic flight. SAC complied and six B-29s were promptly dispatched to Europe.

The bombers landed at the Rhein-Main Air Base near Frankfurt, Germany, and promptly began a series of flights. Day after day, with engines thundering, the B-29s flew across the European continent in a highly visible show of air power. More to the point, the B-29s made a particularly good effort to be highly visible when flying along the borders of Russia and Yugoslavia.

The official story was that the nuclear bombers were in Europe to evaluate prospective airfields.

Perhaps.

But what was certain was that a sense of direction was now crystallizing.

BECOMING A WEAPON

Remembered one Los Alamos scientist who was calculating the heat and blast pressures of the bomb: "[We were] drawing circles around Moscow and other cities [to] determine the most efficient way to destroy a city with one big bomb using a given quantity of fissionable material and a specific ground zero. . . . I spent a lot of time drawing circles with the ground-zero on the Kremlin and the distance corresponding to various calories per square centimeter and pounds per square inch pressure. I remember a deep sense of disappointment that none of the circles included all of Moscow . . ."

The National Security Act of 1947 created the Department of Defense and established the air force as an independent branch of the military. The wording of U.S. Code, Title 10 best summarized the responsibility handed to the new air branch. The United States Air Force's primary responsibility was to "overcome any nations responsible for aggressive acts that imperil the peace and security of the United States."

Overcome any nation.

It was as simple as a directive could be, albeit one with far-reaching consequences.

If dealing a knockout blow meant an atomic knockout blow, the atomic blow would have to wait. Unknown to all but a handful of people at Los Alamos, the number of bombs in the National Stockpile was a theoretical number based on the availability of components sufficient to make bombs, not on the number of finished bombs themselves. Norris Bradbury complained to General Groves of this method of counting the National Stockpile: "The presence of a stockpile of all weapons components does not [e]nsure a state of readiness." But Groves saw it differently, and parts equaled bombs, at least under his command.

Not so, thought the newly installed commissioners of the Atomic Energy Commission when they visited Los Alamos to see their stockpile in January 1947. They saw what Bradbury had seen—parts, not bombs. Said David Lilienthal, chairman of the commission: "Winston Churchill was declaiming that it was our atomic stockpile that restrained the Soviet Union from moving in on the otherwise defenseless Europe. What we of the new AEC had just discovered . . . was that this defense did not exist. We did not have a stockpile."

One of the commissioners remembered: "We had lots of nuclear capsules—nuclear cores—I guarantee you. But we didn't have weapons, we had lots of pieces. The idea was, if you had a threat, you started putting them together."

IN THE SUMMER of 1947, the Joint Committee on Atomic Energy held hearings to determine how many atomic bombs the military needed. Stating that national defense held the highest priority for the use of the precious resources available for atomic energy, the committee wanted to know how many bombs the military needed the Atomic Energy Commission to manufacture.

The answer, unfortunately, was more complicated than it seemed. Apart from the circles drawn on maps by the Los Alamos physicists, and apart from the destruction of Hiroshima and Nagasaki—which, while devastating, was in fact difficult to translate to concrete-and-steel cities such as Moscow—there was almost no real data on the blast effects of an atomic bomb. While over the course of the next decade bombs would be exploded to measure how effective they were against tanks, trucks, railroads, warehouses, power grids, office buildings, factories, weapons-storage igloos, and the concrete-and-steel doors that would cover underground missile silos, in 1947 there was little or no data to go on. The answer, as it were, would be good guesswork.

Less subject to uncertainty was the target list. The air staff developed a list of forty-nine Russian cities that if destroyed, they said, "would leave [Russia] without military potential." Factoring in bombing error, and considering that destruction of some of the cities might require more than one bomb, they decided that the Atomic Energy Commission should build one hundred bombs, a number they then doubled to account for 50 percent losses during the attack. The stockpile requirement was thus estimated to be two hundred bombs.

While other accounts say that the Joint Chiefs provided this estimate, what is certain is that this was the beginning of an almost endless process of selecting targets and estimating weapons requirements, each revision having an attendant increase in stockpile requirements such that at the peak of the Cold War the plan of attack would call for 840 Soviet targets to be hit by some thirty-four hundred nuclear weapons delivering four thousand megatons of devastation. The master target list itself would grow to four thousand desired ground zeros, while the stockpile would grow to thirty thousand bombs and warheads.

But it would begin here, modestly, with a requirement for two hundred bombs.

HAVING SUFFERED BATTLE damage during World War II bombing raids over Manchuria, shot-up American B-29 bombers on several occasions were forced to divert to Vladivostok for emergency landings. Because the Soviets remained neutral in the Pacific, the bombers and their aircrews were summarily seized but in time the crews were released and the bombers forgotten.

In August 1947, at an air show near Moscow celebrating Soviet aviation, three of the B-29s seized by the Russians seemed to reappear, flying in a formation that soared over the crowds to what no doubt was enthusiastic applause. But then a fourth bomber appeared and with that came the unwelcome realization that these were not American bombers but rather Soviet copies. The Soviets had in production a long-range bomber of their own. That it looked like the B-29 was obvious. To jump-start their own program, the Soviets had reverse-engineered the American bombers.*

More sobering was the realization that the Soviets could now reach America. They lacked only the bomb.

IN 1947, THE Kerr-McGee Corporation ventured over the horizon nine miles into the Gulf of Mexico to explore what was then known as Track 32. On Track 32 they erected a rig called Kermac 16, the first freestanding oil rig built out of sight of land. Kermac 16 stood in twenty feet of water, on sixteen steel legs pile-driven into the ocean floor. Based on the advice of the weather experts, the platform deck was elevated twenty feet above sea level. Docked to the rig was a surplus navy tender 260 feet long, which was used to haul supplies and to allow men to remain overnight in its crude but serviceable quarters.

Kermac 16 was a gusher. Oil had been found under the vast expanse of the Gulf of Mexico and farther from land than ever before. Within four months, twenty oil companies were sinking wells off the Louisiana coast.

ON NOVEMBER 12, 1947, Brigadier General Lewis Brereton, head of the Military Liaison Committee, the policy bridge between the Atomic Energy

---

* Sources differ on the number of American B-29s that diverted during the war.

Commission and the Armed Forces Special Weapons Project, wrote to the chairman of the Atomic Energy Commission and requested that consideration be given to transferring the custody and control of atomic weapons to the military. That this ran afoul of the general interpretations of the Atomic Energy Act mattered not. There was legal ambiguity in the area of custody and for this task the military deserved consideration. Said Brereton: "In order to [e]nsure that all the interested agencies of the Armed Forces are prepared at all times to use the available bombs, it is necessary that they have actual custody of the completed weapons."

The letter ended up on the desk of Norris Bradbury at Los Alamos. Bradbury felt that atomic bombs, and their measles, were too complicated and could barely be managed by the full-time people at Los Alamos, much less the military. Bradbury agreed with the opinion of the AEC and said no.

AT YEAR'S END, Strategic Air Command had 319 B-29s, of which between 32 and 35 were modified to carry the bomb and were certified combat ready. There were six crews fully trained in atomic bombing and fourteen more nearly so. SAC had sixteen air bases in the United States.

The numbers that in the past had defined air power—hundreds of bombers dropping bombs in a single mission—were antiquated and slight in comparison to the yield of just one atomic bomb. In 1947, thirty-five air atomic B-29s in the air with thirty-five Mark III Fat Man bombs was the equivalent of bombing a target in 1945 with the full force of seventy thousand conventional B-29s.

Moreover, the yardsticks for SAC readiness that would in years define it as the most powerful force in the world—quick reaction, massive retaliation, assured destruction—were, on a relative basis, well met by the imperfect system of 1947. Absent a Soviet blue-water navy, a Soviet long-range bomber, or a Soviet atomic bomb, the fact that Strategic Air Command might take weeks to mount an attack in no way lessened the fact that a devastating blow—and a cataclysmic loss of human life—was on the way.

Still, SAC was hardly on a war footing. If one believed those who spoke passionately about future wars—*the theater will be global; the war will be fought in the first exchange; there will be no time to mobilize*—one turned to Strategic Air Command and no doubt wanted more.

BECOMING A WAR COMMAND

ON OCTOBER 23, 1947, the Army Intelligence Division issued an intelligence summary which included a sighting of a flight of at least forty-eight Soviet B-29–type bombers.

It is unclear if the sighting received further attention—the first public flight of the Russian Tu-4s had occurred months earlier and it was well known that the bomber existed. One presumes, however, that someone noted that the Soviet Long-Range Bomber Force, nonexistent prior to World War II, was growing.

And it was growing quickly.

ON DECEMBER 17, 1947, at a Council of Foreign Ministers' meeting in London, the Soviets demanded $10 billion from the Germans in war reparations. Secretary of State General George C. Marshall, frustrated by the largely contentious meetings of the Council, said: "It was difficult to inspire respect for the dignity of the Soviet government."

"I HAVE FELT and held that war was unlikely for at least ten years," said General Lucius C. Clay, military governor of the U.S. Occupation Forces in Berlin. "Within the last few weeks, I have felt a subtle change in Soviet attitude which I cannot define but which now gives me a feeling that it may come with dramatic suddenness."

On February 23, 1948, the government of Czechoslovakia was overthrown in a coup d'état and a pro-Communist regime was seated in its place. President Truman called it a "ruthless course of action" that caused "the tragic death of Czechoslovakia."

On April 1, 1948, the Soviet Union demanded that all rail and roadway traffic entering their occupation zone of Germany stop for an inspection. The movement of goods to West Berlin was thus brought to a mere crawl.

The dramatic suddenness of war seemed more likely with each passing week.

* * *

ON MARCH 18, 1948, a lone B-29 landed at what is now Heathrow Airport and discharged six passengers, who promptly purchased for the air force two sets of an in-flight refueling system developed by the British called the "looped-hose system." The B-29 returned to Wright-Patterson AFB in Dayton, Ohio, and the refueling units were sent to the Boeing factory, where they were promptly installed on two other B-29s. The looped-hose system was awkward at best. It required a tanker to trail a hose behind it and a receiver to hook it by dangling a grapnel and flying a loop over it. But it worked, and with this system bombers could be refueled as they flew to and from Soviet targets, thus extending the range of a B-29 to what amounted to global reach. The air force promptly ordered enough systems to equip eighty B-29s as tankers and receivers, and by the end of June, SAC established its first aerial-refueling units. In a matter of months, air refueling progressed from a simple test to a proficiency requirement for all crews certified to fly A-bomb missions.

Air refueling would henceforth be an integral part of SAC Emergency War Plans.

A SECOND SERIES of atomic tests commenced in the Pacific in 1948, the purpose of which was to test a new core design with the hopes of creating more bombs out of the limited supply of fissile material. The test was code-named Operation Sandstone. Los Alamos scientists theorized that by using a new, levitated composite core, the yield of a bomb could be significantly increased while at the same time reducing the plutonium and uranium required for the blast. The idea was to suspend a ball of fissionable material inside a shell of uranium surrounded by the curved lens of high explosives so that on detonation the shell would be slammed into the core and thus more powerfully compress the capsule. Said a nuclear-weapons designer of the hollow shell: "When you hammer a nail what do you do? Do you put the hammer on the nail and push it?" The levitated core would be hit by the "hammer" of the shell, thus creating a more violent impact and presumably a more efficient and thus higher yield.

On April 14, 1948, the new levitated core rested inside a bomb placed on the top of a steel tower erected on the island of Enewetak. The fissionable material was a combination of uranium and plutonium. The device, code-named X-Ray, yielded thirty-seven kilotons, more than twice that of Fat Man. A second test, code-named Yoke, yielded forty-nine kilotons. The tests were a spectacular success.

Operation Sandstone proved that more bombs could be produced from the same quantities of fissile material yet still generate more than twice the power of the Hiroshima bomb.

In effect, as one historian aptly noted, the size of the nuclear stockpile, and its total explosive yield, had more or less doubled instantly.

Which also meant that one bomber could now deliver twice the devastation in a single attack.

It was the stuff of answered prayers.

THE NATIONAL SECURITY Council issued NSC 20/4 on November 23, 1948. NSC 20/4 assessed threats to the security of the United States posed by the USSR. It contained twenty-three points, the first of which was to state clearly that the USSR was the "single greatest danger to the U.S. within the foreseeable future." The next point explained why. "Communist ideology and Soviet behavior clearly demonstrate that the ultimate objective of the leaders of the USSR is domination of the world. Soviet leaders hold that the Soviet communist party is the militant vanguard of the world proletariat in its rise to political power, and that the USSR, base of the world communist movement, will not be safe until the non-communist nations have been so reduced in strength and numbers that communist influence is dominant throughout the world . . . The resistance of the United States is recognized by the USSR as a major obstacle to the attainment of these goals."

EMERGENCY WAR PLAN Pincher was refined and became Boiler but was promptly revised to become Halfmoon, which was approved by the Joint Chiefs of Staff in May 1948. Halfmoon was notable in that it contained a remarkably detailed plan of attack called Harrow. Harrow was a war plan of sorts developed by the air staff of the air force to achieve the objectives stated in Halfmoon.*

As before, after the beginning of Soviet hostilities, the air force would deploy atomic-capable B-29 bombers to forward bases in the United Kingdom and Egypt ("Cairo-Suez"). Bomb-assembly teams would follow them and set up shop. Atomic bombs would be ferried to them for assembly. As bombs were completed, Strategic Air Command would begin air strikes against twenty Soviet cities on a bomb-as-you-build schedule that would expend fifty atomic bombs over the next thirty days.

---

* The origins of code names for Emergency War Plans are not entirely clear, but code names proliferated through much of the first decade of the air atomic age.

The atomic-bombing strikes would use neither the large bomber streams of World War II nor the lone A-bomb carriers that had dealt the fatal blows to Japan. Instead, small clusters of ten or so bombers would be grouped together and would attack a target. Some of the bombers would carry conventional bombs for their own targets, some were mere decoys; at least one bomber would be equipped with electronic countermeasures and one bomber would be the A-bomb carrier. The attacks would take place at night, or in bad weather, and they would be at a high altitude to stay above Soviet antiaircraft fire. Radar bombing, so effective over Japan, would be used throughout.

Halfmoon and Harrow marked the beginning of a nearly continuous process of developing more-accurate information on Soviet factories and installations with the attendant increase in targets and bombs delivered. With each new plan, the intensity of the counteroffensive increased until bombs and targets alone were not the only considerations. Things like off-continent fallout and deconflicted timelines would soon become the language of the attacks on the Soviet Union.

But for now there was Harrow, and Harrow would be the first tactical description of how the next war would be fought. It was, however, missing one important ingredient.

Harrow was not an SAC plan.

THE B-36 ARRIVED in June 1948. It was "spacious," as one navigator described it. The fuselage held ten men forward and five men aft and could accommodate more if the bomber was configured for reconnaissance. It had ten engines, four of which were jet engines, and it could outclimb most fighters and cruise at altitudes few airplanes could reach. In early tests, one B-36 remained airborne for thirty-two hours; another flew eighty-five hundred miles nonstop.

So long and wide was the fuselage that during one mission while standing near the bunks in the aft compartment one crewman felt "a horrendous thud." Wrote the unit historian: "The intercom went dead and the sound of the engines died away. It seemed to him as if the B-36 had come to an abrupt halt in mid-air." And it had. The bomber had suffered a midair collision but the fuselage was so long that in the back it actually took a moment for the rest of the crew to realize it.

By December 1948 there were thirty-five B-36As on the flight line at Carswell Air Force Base in Fort Worth, Texas, including thirteen B-36Bs, a model that was modified to carry atomic bombs.

Over the course of its service life, 385 of these planes would be built for Strategic Air Command. It would remain the largest bomber ever placed into service, but more infamously, the B-36 would be the first bomber involved in an accident that would destroy an atomic bomb.

AN ATOMIC BOMB once dropped virtually came alive with pulses and energy and electronics. It could sense that it was falling through the sky by using its barometric sensors, detect the onset of G-forces by using its built-in accelerometer, and continuously monitor how high it was above the ground, using the radar altimeter in the nose cone. It could sense all this and put those inputs into a fusing system that would evaluate those data to determine if the bomb should explode.

But therein lay its weakness. A bomb could be tricked. Inside the nose cone, the bounce of the radar signal off the ground was converted into altitude by calculating the wink of time between the sending and the receiving. By surrounding a target area with ground-based radar jammers, a false signal could be broadcast skyward that would either jam the radar altimeter in the bomb's nose cone or feed it a false altitude and cause the bomb to detonate prematurely. This nifty capability was called "spoofing" a bomb. The airspace above a target could be covered by a blizzard of interlaced, frequency-hopping radar signals sufficient to cause the radar altimeter in the bomb to pass the false information into its own circuitry, thereby causing the bomb to burst at the wrong altitude, optimally at a high altitude, and thus protecting the target from destruction. This was considered so effective—and so dangerous—that when the air force sent the AEC a list of improvements in 1948, one of the most important items on it was the "improvement of the bomb firing system so as to offer, with dependable operation, the least practicable chance of being prematurely triggered or jammed."*

Thus began a little-known technology race pitting American and Soviet electronic measures and countermeasures against each other, one country advancing, the other countering the advance with a solution that would then be defeated by a new countermeasure, and so on.

It was a problem that would persist over time and would concern designers of the reentry vehicles that carried nuclear warheads launched by ICBMs.

To this day, it remains largely unsolved.

---

* Similar but simpler measures included using artillery shells to explode electronic chaff in the air to reflect back false altitude to the radar, or simply to shoot down the bomb.

* * *

ON JUNE 24, 1948, the inspections of road and railway traffic into West Berlin were replaced by a total blockade. No trains could come or go; no cars or trucks could bring in new provisions. West Berlin was now an island in a hostile sea with a scant few months' worth of food and fuel. Said General Clay in a sentiment that was entirely befitting the action: "It was one of the most ruthless efforts in modern time to use mass starvation for political purposes . . ."

THE FIRST ALL-JET bomber rolled off the production lines in December 1947. The B-47 Stratojet was atomic-age technology rendered with a dash of verve. The tapered fuselage made the bomber look like a fighter jet and the first-ever swept wings and swept tail gave it some hard-to-define but rakish good looks. It could fly at the unheard of speed of five hundred miles per hour while having a service ceiling of an impossible forty thousand feet with a combat radius of one thousand miles. As if riding a bronco, the pilots sat on top of the bomber under a bubble canopy that gave them a commanding view of the sky above. Six powerful jet engines hung from pods beneath the wings. Even on the tarmac, its looks said it was meant for speed.

Later, some would say that it was the most unforgiving aircraft in SAC's fleet of bombers. True or not, 2,041 would be flown by Strategic Air Command.

WITH THE DETERIORATING situation in Europe, Air Defense Command activated five radar stations in Washington and Oregon, two in New Jersey, and one in New York. Thirteen additional radar stations went live in an arc that stretched from Maine to Michigan. The shortest routes between the Soviet Union and America were now protected. Radar stations were now sweeping the sky with their "strange sinister resources," as Churchill once called the technology.

SEPARATING THE PLUTONIUM capsule from the bomb assembly eliminated any chance that an atomic bomb would explode if, for instance, a bomber crashed on takeoff. On the other hand, unless there was a way to insert the ball of plutonium, the bomb would be just an ordinary bomb. The solution was called "in-flight insertion." To test this concept, a trapdoor was cut into the casing of a dummy bomb that was placed inside the bomb bay of a parked B-29. Nine times a crewman lowered himself into the bomb bay, opened the trapdoor, lifted out portions of the high explosives, pushed in a ball of fissile material, then closed up the bomb. Each test was timed. The entire process took just thirty-one minutes. It was entirely straightforward.

Bombs would immediately be redesigned. Aircrews would learn to insert plutonium capsules into atomic bombs after takeoffs and remove them before landings. That this made flying safer, however, hardly crossed anyone's mind as they crawled into the bomb bay and came face-to-face with an atomic bomb, with just millimeters of aircraft aluminum between their feet and the earth more than ten thousand feet below.

BEHIND THE SCENES of the impressive air-power displays that Strategic Air Command so perfectly executed over New York and Chicago and European capitals was in fact a disheveled command. By 1948, one-third of SAC's B-29s were sitting idle, out of commission but for parts or mechanics to repair them. There were sixty crashes per one hundred thousand hours of flying, an unacceptably high number of accidents in any flying organization, with an equally high number of injuries among ground crews who made mistakes. A total of 408 men were AWOL, a troubling problem of character, a problem the military referred to as "military fitness."

The air force recruited Charles Lindbergh to find out what was wrong. Lindbergh visited the bases and flew with the crews and got to the bottom of the matter. "Accident rates are high, landings are too rough and fast, crew duties are not smoothly coordinated, equipment is not neatly stowed in flight, engine and accessory troubles are excessive and there are not enough training missions which simulate combat missions which would be required in the event of war," wrote Lindbergh. Indeed, bombs dropped from combat altitudes of forty thousand feet were as much as a mile off target. Equally disheartening, the crews with good scores were dropping bombs from unrealistically low altitudes.

Citing a list of problems that were as telling as they were damning, Lindbergh concluded: "The average pilot's proficiency is unsatisfactory, teamwork is not properly developed, and maintenance of aircraft and equipment is inadequate."

But then Lindbergh added a note that caught the eye of the air force chief of staff. Things were bad, yes, but the aircrews knew it, said Lindbergh. They wanted more and they were *ready* to be better, they just needed a leader.

THERE WERE TWO immediate responses to the blockade of Berlin. Curtis LeMay initiated an aerial resupply of Berlin using cargo planes and named LeMay's Feed and Coal Company, which in time became Operation Vittles and would evolve into a nearly continuous airlift of food and supplies into Berlin. At the same time, General Kenney's Strategic Air Command was alerted, and on July 17, 1948, sixty B-29s landed on British soil.

Somehow, however, none of this seemed quite right. LeMay was a bombardment officer, not an air cargo officer, and Kenney was an intellectual and hardly a commander of bombers. Moreover, the best air cargo officer the air force had was General William H. Tunner, a man who had cut his teeth flying supplies over the Hump during World War II—and Tunner was back in Massachusetts.

On July 22, 1948, air force chief of staff Hoyt Vandenberg brought General Tunner over to command LeMay's airlift. Vandenberg then sent General Kenney to become the new commandant of the United States Air Force Air University, and on October 19, 1948, Vandenberg gave LeMay command of SAC. Things suddenly felt right.

"THE WHOLE PURPOSE of the Air Corps was to fly and fight in a war, and to be ready to fly and fight in that war at any given moment," said Curtis LeMay, speaking of the education he received in the 1930s from an early mentor, Lieutenant Colonel Robert Olds. Olds was then the commanding officer of the Second Bomb Group, based in Langley Field, Virginia. When he arrived each morning he tossed off questions to his young staff officer that at first seemed somewhat senseless. If it was raining at Langley Field, Olds wanted to know if it was snowing in Chicago, or, for that matter, what the weather was anywhere his bombers could reach. If a bomber was in the hangar for repairs, Olds wanted to know why, what was being done about it, and when it would be out. So it went, endlessly—the status of fuel stored on base, the upkeep of bombs in storage, training completed or planned, the currency of all navigational charts. "He was the first man that I'd ever come in contact with who really penetrated my thick skull with a sense of urgency in getting things done," said LeMay, a point he never forgot.

In 1942, LeMay was ordered to take a squadron of bombers to Spokane to defend the coastline against a second attack by the Japanese. If Japanese ships appeared offshore, LeMay was ordered to sink them. LeMay flew his unit to Spokane, landed, and with scarcely a nod to protocol promptly scrounged up bombs, bomb racks, and ammunition and started training his crews to drop bombs on ships. Speaking as his mentor Colonel Olds might have, LeMay said: "Everything was primed towards this one possible operation. That was our whole purpose in being in Spokane." And that was that.

During World War II, this single-mindedness was his stock-in-trade. LeMay said that the only point of bombing up and fueling a bomber was to drop "bombs where they would do the most harm to the enemy." His aircrews would die in air battles, that was war; what mattered most was that one concentrated on the mission, planned it as best as one could, and executed it without fear, certain in the knowledge that one was doing the most harm possible to the enemy. LeMay would later remark that if he were to meet one of his crewmen lost on a mission, he felt certain that he would be able to say to him, "You were properly expended, Gus. It was part of the price."

However cold the sentiment seemed, against the landscape of war there was an undeniable soundness to the logic. On October 19, General LeMay arrived at Strategic Air Command's headquarters. He scarcely shook a hand. His first order of business was to see the war plan.

The air force had Harrow.

But SAC had none.

To THE AVERAGE American, the B-36 was little more than a flickering image on a Universal newsreel, but in truth it was an impressive aircraft that dominated the sky in a way that suggested that America was safe. In perhaps one of the fastest publicity tours yet orchestrated, SAC scheduled an air-power display that would fly a B-36 bomber over forty-three major cities in one day. It was September 18, 1948. The day started when two B-36s thundered down the runway at Carswell AFB, Texas, and in formation flew over the cities of El Paso, Tucson, Los Angeles, San Francisco, Seattle, Salt Lake City, and then back to Carswell. A third bomber took off and flew over Kansas City, Omaha, Denver, Abilene, Oklahoma City, and Tulsa, while a fourth bomber covered the Midwest by flying over Des Moines, Minneapolis, Duluth, Chicago, Detroit, Fort Wayne, Indianapolis, and St. Louis.

The fifth bomber flew directly to Boston, then made its way over New York City, Philadelphia, Washington, D.C., Buffalo, Cleveland, Pittsburgh, Cincinnati, Louisville, Nashville, and Memphis, before landing at Carswell. The sixth bomber covered the southern states, flying over Birmingham, Atlanta, Charleston, Jacksonville, Miami, Tampa, Montgomery, New Orleans, Shreveport, Houston, and San Antonio.

And then they were done.

However extraordinary the B-36 was—and it was indeed physically imposing—it wasn't the bomber of the future. That designation would belong to the B-52, an all-jet, eight-engine, swept-wing intercontinental bomber designed from the ground up for nuclear bombing. How the B-52 came into being, however, was the stuff of legend. In October 1948, a team of

Boeing designers arrived at Wright Field, in Dayton, Ohio, to present their latest plans for the prototype of this new bomber, only to be informed that a new jet engine was on the drawing boards that would vastly improve fuel consumption, which in turn would sharply improve the bombers' range. The Boeing engineers instantly recognized that their own engineering plans were now out-of-date. In an act of incredible stamina, the team checked in to the Hotel Van Cleve in Dayton, and after four days of discussions, calculations, and basic re-engineering, they returned to Wright Field with engineering plans and a hand-carved model of a 330,000-pound bomber calculated to have a range of eight thousand miles, a speed of up to 570 miles per hour, and a ceiling of forty-five thousand feet, all while carrying a 10,000-pound nuclear bomb. The aircraft they proposed had eight jet engines hung in pods beneath shoulder-mounted wings. It had swept wings and a swept tail and even in engineering drawings it exuded a certain detachment that made the bomber seem *trustworthy*.

This near-perfect image of the near-perfect bombing machine would undergo design modifications of the cockpit and other engineering changes, but for the most part out of this hotel room would emerge the B-52 Stratofortress, the signature aircraft of Strategic Air Command, of which 744 would be built, and in its peak year in service an imposing 639 would be on the flight line.

HAVING ORCHESTRATED A near-complete reordering of his generals, Vandenberg called his commanders to a three-day meeting at Maxwell Air Force Base, in Montgomery, Alabama. It was December 6, 1948. With Berlin under a Soviet blockade and Czechoslovakia now a satellite, Vandenberg wanted to determine the readiness of his commands for what could unhappily turn into war.

The lights were dimmed in the conference room as Strategic Air Command Plans director Brigadier General John S. Montgomery began his presentation of the SAC war plan. Montgomery used a series of prepared slides to outline the attack and in an instant it was apparent that the Harrow plan was gone. No longer would Strategic Air Command bomb the Soviet Union on a forty-five-day, bomb-as-you-build plan. Rather, said Montgomery, SAC would launch the counteroffensive with every atomic bomb they had and on the very first day they would deliver the *entire* atomic stockpile in a single blow.

To an audience that no doubt needed to catch their breath, Montgomery then spelled out the tactics and the timeline. SAC's A-bomb carriers would be embedded in small cells of bombers consisting of a few decoy bombers and an ECM (electronic countermeasures) jammer. Unlike Harrow, the air strike would come as one overwhelming mass penetration of Soviet air defenses from all directions at once. Montgomery clicked through one slide after another and, in exacting detail, walked through the entire mission, hour by hour, target by target, start to finish, a somber, direct, unflinching presentation of war rendered most vicious. Russia's leadership would be dead or cut off; more than eight million Soviets would have died in a matter of hours. Cities would be cut down as if by a scythe. Remembered one who attended the meeting: "It was the voice of doom."

Perhaps it was, but it was hardly theoretical. That LeMay could execute this plan was a point he wanted to underscore. Unknown to Vandenberg, LeMay had sent a B-50 and a B-36 out of Carswell Air Force Base to drop a load of dummy bombs in the ocean off the island of Hawaii at roughly the same hour as the 1941 attack on Pearl Harbor. Without landing, these bombers would then turn around and fly all the way back to Alabama and land at the conference. It was an impossible distance even with a bomber stripped down to its essentials—seventy-seven hundred miles—but LeMay insisted that the bombers not be stripped down but instead be configured for war. To make that possible, LeMay had the B-50 modified for in-flight refueling. It refueled three times.

That the planes diverted at the last minute had to do with scheduling problems at the conference, but it hardly diminished the impact when the news reached the assembled commanders. LeMay not only presented a plan but backed it up with proof that his bombers could fly a combat mission with an atomic bomb against any target in the world, and could do so today, if ordered, which was entirely his point.*

Said LeMay: "We have our troubles; however, we can carry out our mission. I think we can carry it out very well."

Said Montgomery: ". . . we feel targets can be hit as assigned."

And there wasn't the slightest whisper of disagreement.

As 1948 CAME to an end, the Berlin airlift was working around-the-clock, in good weather or bad. Food, clothing, coal, salt, milk, medicines, and spare parts came in by air with timing down to the minute. As a plane taxied

---

* Because the only aircraft capable of a nonstop flight to and from Pearl Harbor was the B-36, most historians mistakenly concluded that two B-36s flew this mission. Smith (*75 years of Inflight Refueling*) makes clear that a B-50A was modified for in-flight refueling while Moody (*Building a Strategic Air Force*) confirms that a B-36 and a B-50 were the bombers on the mission. Most accounts incorrectly cite this flight as an example of how little progress had been made in air defense since Pearl Harbor when in fact it was a LeMay show-of-force mission.

to a halt, laborers swarmed over it like ants and emptied the cargo into containers; coffee and doughnuts were served on the flight line by women attractive enough to keep the pilots from leaving their planes.

Berliners cheered the cargo planes and children scrambled up piles of rubble to wave as the planes zoomed down the final half-mile. Some pilots tied parachutes to small bundles of candy and pushed them out their windows. These "candy bombers," as they would be called, were soon famous the world over. One pilot was called Uncle Wiggly Wings because he wiggled his wings as he flew in.

Some say that the airlift was the beginning of the unusual friendship that exists today between the British, the Americans, and the Germans. Either way, on December 31, 1948, the one hundred thousandth flight landed.

TRANSFORMATIONS

LeMay gave General Montgomery the job of laying out a simulated bombing mission using Wright Field, in Dayton, Ohio, as the target. It was a stripped-down version of the plan presented at Maxwell Air Force Base, but it served LeMay's purpose, which was to gain a measure of his new command. SAC had more than five hundred bombers and almost fifty-two thousand people.

Montgomery created a mission that was as realistic as possible and as difficult as safety would permit. The bomber crews had to identify their ground zeros by extrapolating what they could from the outdated photos of Wright Field they were purposefully given. They were required to attack at night, from the uncomfortably high altitude of thirty thousand feet, and with radar and radar alone.

The results were poor. A total of just 303 bombers reached the target, with an average bombing error that was a disheartening 10,090 feet.

LeMay went to work. SAC crews lived on a steady diet of radar training, target familiarization, and practice missions, using American cities as stand-ins. They flew, they bombed, they were graded, and they were promoted or demoted. Because they would fly overseas at the start of any war, every crew was required to complete one four-thousand-mile mission every three months.

From a scant 2,499 bomb runs scored by radar-bomb-scoring sites in 1947, SAC scored 29,049 runs in 1949. By July 1950, bombing accuracy had improved to an impressive average circular error of just 2,500 feet. Eighty crews were now designated A-bomb carriers, each with a Soviet target assigned to them. Dayton-styled night radar-bombing missions against Phoenix and against Sacramento had a circular error of just 2,600 feet. In another exercise, B-36s bombed from 40,000 feet. The overall error was just 1,925 feet, near pinpoint accuracy with atomic bombs.

* * *

CHARLES LINDBERGH ACCEPTED an appointment as a consultant to the air force chief of staff. As it happened, Lindbergh was a fierce advocate of early-warning radar stations, but he came at his advocacy with a line of reasoning quite apart from traditional thinking. In his speeches Lindbergh sidestepped the capabilities of an early-warning network as a *defensive* measure, a futile approach that had been used by air-defense advocates in the past, and chose instead to focus on the far more popular topic of Strategic Air Command and radar as an *offensive* measure. SAC, said Lindbergh, needed a realistic radar fence against which to train their pilots. How could they practice radar jamming and penetration techniques without a true radar network? If for no other reason than to strengthen the offensive capabilities of SAC, building early-warning radar stations was more than justified. "The need for a training area of this kind is so vital," said Lindbergh, "that immediate steps should be taken to set it up."

Partly due to Lindbergh's clever advocacy, Air Defense Command received their much-sought-after approval to surround the United States with a radar fence that consisted of seventy-five long-range radar stations and ten control centers, augmented by ten radar stations and one control center in Alaska. In December 1949, fifty million dollars was released for the construction of the first twenty-four stations.

Sinister beams as powerful as any in the world would soon start sweeping the approaches to the United States.

WOULD AN AIR atomic strike lead to the capitulation of the Red Army and force an end to hostilities, as anticipated in the ever-evolving Emergency War Plans being developed by the Joint Chiefs? Was too much reliance being placed on atomic bombs and Strategic Air Command? USAF lieutenant general Hubert R. Harmon was asked to chair a committee to evaluate the bomb as a weapon that could end a war.

The Harmon Committee concluded that the current Emergency War Plan—a plan that now called for air strikes using 133 bombs against 70 Soviet cities—would neither force the USSR to end hostilities nor decimate its industry. The war-making sector of the Soviet industrial base might be reduced by as much as 40 percent, and the petroleum industry severely damaged, but the front lines would scarcely notice the effects. The Red Army was highly self-sufficient, which meant that even as atomic bombs burst above Russian cities the army could continue the fight, thus gaining time for factories to be rebuilt and supply lines to be reestablished.

The committee estimated that atomic bombs would kill 2.7 million Soviets, injure another 4 million, and displace many millions more. Possessing a keen diplomatic ear, they warned that such an attack might do more to stiffen Soviet resolve than to force it to the bargaining table, and would, in any case, be damaging to the world's opinion of America.

That said, the Harmon Committee believed that the atomic bomb was the most effective weapon America had and in fact it argued for more bombs, not fewer. The early use of atomic bombs in war would be "transcending." Said the report: "Every reasonable effort should be devoted to providing the means to be prepared for prompt and effective delivery of the maximum number of atomic bombs to appropriate target systems."

The Harmon Committee released their report on May 12, 1949. The Joint Chiefs of Staff promptly asked the Atomic Energy Commission to triple the nuclear stockpiles.

STRATEGIC AIR COMMAND air bases were dotted with tar-paper shacks and threadbare barracks. To become the bomber force that LeMay envisioned, SAC would have to rid itself of the open barracks and the common latrines typical of World War II bases and build housing that would allow one crew to sleep while another flew, one crew to eat while another prepared a bomber—a base for around-the-clock operations. That meant kitchens that served good food, hobby shops for time off, and clubs for drinks and fellowship.

That LeMay lent his force of personality to facilities no doubt reflected the experiences he'd had when the army air corps took over the postal air routes in 1934. In their haste, the air corps neglected to provide pilots with facilities, food, or even travel money. Pilots forced to remain overnight at remote air terminals were often out of luck. LeMay remembered pilots who "laid planks across a sawhorse in cold hangars" to make impromptu beds.

Rather than planks on sawhorses, LeMay hired an architectural firm to design SAC's new housing. Men would bunk two to a room in dormitories designed for twenty-four-hour operations. Recreation rooms would have plenty of comfortable sofas and meals would be served around the clock. LeMay had his cooks sent to commercial eating establishments to learn how to make more-palatable food. Wrote the Seventh Bomb Wing's historian: "Several airmen assigned to the squadron were attending cooking course[s] . . . in such establishments as The Texas Hotel, Dean and Kroger Wholesale Meat and Provisions, and Milan Cafeteria, Fort Worth. With the knowledge gained from the well-known chiefs of these establishments, the 7th Food Service Squadron expected to create culinary masterpieces."

Perhaps. But what was true was that when his budget ran out, LeMay appealed to the citizens of Omaha, the site of the first redesigned housing facility, to help with his project. The people of Omaha responded by raising the money to furnish every room with beds and linens.

Such was the cachet of Strategic Air Command.

IN ADDITION TO improving the facilities on its old bases, Strategic Air Command was going to build new bases, too. The new bases were to have "sufficient housing, be close to town, and be suitable for B-29 operations, which required sufficiently long and durable runways, adequate parking space, large hangars and adequate shop facilities," wrote a historian of the rather ordinary specifications for choosing a new site. But not all of the specifications were so ordinary. "Permanent SAC bases were to be located at least 250 nautical miles from the seacoasts to reduce their vulnerability to Soviet sea-launched missiles. Bases were also to be located outside of atomic radiation fallout patterns of large industrial targets of over 100,000 population, and at right angles to the prevailing winds."

Right angles to prevailing winds.

THE NIGGLING PROBLEM of radar remained its line-of-sight limitation, which created a low-altitude gap through which a determined Soviet bomber crew could pass unnoticed.

A test in 1949 determined the feasibility of placing volunteers along the Eastern Seaboard to monitor low-altitude approaches. Much like the Ground Observation Corps of World War II, this test led to the permanent low-altitude system called Operation Skywatch. Until low-altitude radar capabilities were developed, the nation that cracked the code on fission would enlist more than three hundred thousand ordinary citizens to scan the skies from more than eight thousand stations and report their sightings to eleven centers, where their results would be passed along to designated military centers that were linked to nearly forty fighter-interceptor squadrons.

Thus it was that for nearly ten years, a significant portion of the nation's early-warning network built to protect against invading Soviet bombers consisted of ground observers clutching mugs of coffee.

Looking at the sky.

* * *

IN 1949, PREPARATIONS for another series of nuclear tests began when an advance party arrived on Enewetak Atoll to build new piers, ramps, buildings, and other structures for the Department of Defense and the Atomic Energy Commission. According to Philip Drake, who arrived on the island of Parry in Enewetak Atoll: "When we first got to Parry we were shocked to find all sorts of ordnance just about anywhere you looked. Dud mortar shells still stuck in trees. Fifty-caliber bullets laying all over the place. Every now and then a phosphorous bomb would explode down along the beach. There were any number of small Japanese tanks along the ocean side of the island. Along the lagoon shoreline and at the north end of the island were Japanese graves with thin wood markers still standing. Near the lagoon shoreline we found parts of Japanese planes that had been shot down. We uncovered full wings with Japanese markings.

"Several of the islands in the atoll were storage places for military equipment left behind when the war was over. One had 50 infantry landing boats stored bow-to-bow on a sand spit at the south end of the island."

Drake added: "The war was not so far removed in 1949."

LCMs were landing craft used for beach assaults during World War II.

IN AUGUST 1949, residues of the by-products of an atomic explosion were detected in the atmosphere by American aircraft. The time-consuming analysis that ensued concluded that the Soviets had detonated an atomic bomb. While the American nuclear stockpile now stood at an impressive 235 bombs, the atomic monopoly was over. On September 23, 1949, President Truman passed the sobering news on to the nation.

THE SOVIET DETONATION created a sense of urgency to speed everything up—more bombers for SAC, more radar stations, and, most important, bigger bombs, including one that would be one thousand times more powerful than the atomic bomb. It would be called the hydrogen bomb, and would be ignited by a small atomic bomb and used elements of hydrogen to create an explosion. While atomic bombs were measured in increments of one thousand tons of TNT equivalent—a kiloton—hydrogen bombs would be measured in one-million-ton equivalents—megatons. Better still, surprisingly large yields might be generated from bombs that would be light in weight. One could see the day when five-thousand-pound H-bombs would replace the behemoths that today inched their way in and out of SAC's bomb bays.

But it was all theoretical. For now.

* * *

ON DECEMBER 8, 1949, the Joint Chiefs of Staff approved yet another new Emergency War Plan, this one called Offtackle. Offtackle reflected Le-May's concept of a massive first strike to achieve the "maximum exploitation of the power of the atomic bomb, at the earliest practicable date."

That said, owing to a change of just one word, Offtackle was a far more brutal strike than its predecessors. No longer was it sufficient to "direct" bombs against Soviet targets; the wording now called for SAC to "destroy" targets. This would be accomplished by dropping 292 atomic bombs against targets in 104 Soviet cities, holding back 72 bombs to strike targets as they were discovered by reconnaissance.*

Because many of the targets were in large population centers, entire cities would be destroyed, wrote one commander, an inevitable "by-product" of the attack.

Offtackle was promptly handed to Strategic Air Command as guidance for their own war plan.

PROVIDING A RARE insight into the behind-the-scenes thinking of what a war would cost in terms of Strategic Air Command casualties, Offtackle was no longer silent on the losses that SAC was expected to suffer. In a raid against the Soviets, 20 to 30 percent of the attacking bombers would be shot down before they reached their targets. Between half and two-thirds of the remaining aircraft would be damaged beyond repair. Casualties would decimate the ranks of pilots and aircrews; the numbers of wounded and dead on the bombers that made it back would be staggering.

All in all, through enemy fire, surface-to-air missiles, casualities, exhaustion, attrition, or by virtue of the staggering psychological toil of watching countless atomic bursts, at the end of the campaign, SAC would have "largely expended itself." There would be no collapse of either militaries, no victor, and no end of hostilities per se but rather just the ragged remnants of two countries that could do little more than survive.

In the aftermath, Strategic Air Command would be reduced to hauling freight.

---

* Emergency War Plans did not directly tie in to the official stockpile numbers. Rather, they provided guidance to the AEC on how many bombs would be needed, given specific scenarios. One version of Off-tackle called for 220 bombs against 104 cities, while another called for 292 against 104 cities.

THE FIRST LOST BOMB

THERE WAS AN inevitability to the first lost bomb. Bill Sheehy, a staff member of the Joint Committee on Atomic Energy, was at an undisclosed National Stockpile Site as two MK-4 atomic bombs were delivered to a pair of B-50s. "I was making an inspection at the time the loading operations were taking place as the initial phase of this Air Force maneuver," said Sheehy, in notes he wrote to himself. "Atomic weapons were being loaded into B-50s from whence they were ferried to Carswell Air Force Base at Ft. Worth, transferred to B-36s, and the actual practice mission or maneuver was planned to fly them from Carswell to Eielson Air Force Base in Alaska and return."

THE MANEUVER UP to Alaska was uneventful; the bombers landed and were turned over to a second crew, who departed for the return leg to Texas. The weather along the route was bitterly cold with squall-like conditions all the way down the coast of Alaska and into British Columbia. It was in this weather and over a jagged and desolate stretch of coastline that the first flickers of flames spit into the night.

The pilot called the scanners and the scanners confirmed that flames were indeed coming from three engines. The pilot feathered the props but the bomber started to lose altitude. The radio operator began broadcasting their position, an effort he knew was largely futile. "We were out of radio range of any ground station," said a crewman during the investigation that followed. "We never knew if our transmissions were heard as we received no response."

In what had to be one of his most unnerving decisions, the pilot elected to lighten the bombers' load by ejecting the atomic bomb. To avoid inhabited areas, he turned the bomber out to sea. The crew readied the bomb for an airburst; the radar altimeter was set for three thousand feet. The bomb jerked free of the plane and the crew reported a flash as they turned back toward land.

* * *

ALTHOUGH LIGHTER, THE bomber continued to sink, so the captain ordered a bailout. "We knew that a water landing would be fatal because of the freezing temperature so [Captain] Barry turned the plane toward land and ordered everyone out as soon as the radar indicated we had land beneath us. The other crew members . . . put on their parachutes and removed the observation blisters from the sides of the plane to provide openings from which to exit."

Cold air no doubt rushed through the fuselage.

AS THEY REACHED land, the pilot put the bomber on autopilot and the bailout commenced. One crewman looked back as he left the plane. "As I jumped I rolled over so I could see the plane pass over me before my chute opened. I saw a brilliant blue white streamer of fire trailing one engine for as far back as the tail of the plane."

Unfortunately, the winds were too strong. "The plane reached the coast, but strong winds were believed to have carried the first men back over the water since their bodies were never found."

BACK IN THE United States, news of the crash reached the press. The air force confirmed that a bomber was down but they would say no more, so, outside the Pentagon, no one knew anything about a bomb—no one except Sheehy. "Upon my return to Washington, and after reading in the Washington *Times Herald* that evening of the crash of a B-36 en route from Eielson Air Force Base to Fort Worth, I became personally as well as officially alarmed," he wrote in his notes. Sheehy believed that this bomber had his bomb.

Unfortunately, the road map forward was entirely unclear.

Sheehy called the Pentagon and asked for information. "Some days later I received a telephone call from Lt. Colonel Wilhoyt and he advised me that they had no official report from the Air Force but had received verbal reports that the B-36 which went down was carrying an atomic weapon."

Sheehy persisted. He decided to make a personal visit to the air force offices, which had the unexpected effect of backing them into a corner. Sheehy would get his information when they were "damn good and ready" to give it to him, said the officer. Sheehy left and promptly put his otherwise informal inquiries into a written query on the letterhead of the Joint Committee on Atomic Energy.

In March 1950 the air force responded in writing, confirming that the MK-4 had been on the plane, that it had been ejected, and that it had detonated. They provided no new details, but they ended their letter with a cautionary note: "Since the B-36 story has died out of the press and apparently diminished from public interest, I recommend no release be made concerning the airplane's bomb load."

Thus it was that the military completed the inevitable but unwelcome passage from a flawless safety record to the first nuclear accident. Accidents were not the catastrophe most feared; the loss of a bomb was not the end of the world, however dire it seemed.

True, too, this would mark the beginning of a practice by the military to neither confirm nor deny the existence of atomic weapons in accidents, a practice that remained to the end of the Cold War.

TRUMAN'S HEDGE

AFTER NO SMALL measure of soul-searching, on January 13, 1950, President Harry Truman signed a presidential directive to develop the thermonuclear bomb. In short order the drawing boards at Los Alamos were filled with specifications, weights, yields, and estimated timetables. It was believed that the first emergency capability H-bomb, as they would be called, could be exploded as early as 1954 in a series of tests that would be called Operation Castle.

But then in February, Klaus Fuchs, a former Los Alamos physicist now working in London, was arrested for selling American atomic secrets to the Soviets and suddenly no one was quite sure who was ahead in the world of nuclear weapons.

"THE PERIOD WHICH we all realized must some day come when intercontinental air warfare would be a possibility is now at hand," said General Muir S. Fairchild, air force vice chief of staff, as he lobbied for better continental air defenses

It was February 1950.

The Soviet Long-Distance Aviation force had grown to between four hundred and eight hundred Tu-4 bombers, all of them capable of one-way missions to virtually any target in America.

And the Soviets now had the bomb.

ON FEBRUARY 9, 1950, Senator Joseph McCarthy leveled charges against the U.S. State Department. McCarthy accused them of harboring hundreds of members of the Communist Party. In time, the hunt for Communists would dominate the media and hearings, and accusations and blacklists would become the language of McCarthyism.

* * *

SOVIET FIGHTERS ATTACKED and shot down a United States Navy PB4Y Privateer reconnaissance plane flying near or in the airspace of Soviet-occupied Latvia. The navy plane crashed into the Baltic Sea and all ten crew members were presumed dead. It was April 8, 1950.

The political reaction was nearly instant. Representative Carl Vinson compared the attack on the Privateer to Japan's brutal 1937 attack on the USS *Panay,* an unarmed navy vessel that was evacuating Americans from the Chinese city of Nanking. While at anchor in the Yangtze River, the *Panay* was strafed and bombed by Japanese aircraft, and sank. Three men died and forty-eight were injured. The attack was caught on film; the footage, which was played in American movie theaters, depicted sustained gunfire and civilians swimming for their lives.

Said Vinson: "Here is the same pattern, the same manner for the same purpose, with the same ruthlessness, with the same contempt for life, for democratic institutions, for international law, for decency—a barbaric attack is made on an unarmed, defenseless American aircraft."

When asked what implication this had in the overall sense of the Cold War, the air force director of intelligence Major General C. P. Cabel was rather nonchalant about it all. "It was probably done as a probing to see what our reaction would be."

On that count there were two. Whatever the average American thought about the Russians was further darkened by the image of the navy aircraft caught in a deadly hail of Soviet bullets, and being as brutally butchered as the *Panay* had been by the Japanese.

On the other hand, the concept of acceptable losses began to take shape.

THAT AMERICAN MEMBERS of the Communist Party might attempt to interfere with Strategic Air Command on the ground was emerging as a serious concern. Not counting the influence the party had within American labor unions, there were now tens of thousands of card-carrying members in the United States. These Communists, the Joint Chiefs worried, could disrupt America's war-making capability through labor strikes, labor slowdowns, and sabotage. American air bases were "fairly easy for almost anyone to visit," said General Kenney, speaking now as the commanding general of Air University. "As recently as last January [1950] leaders of the Communist Party in this country boasted that in the event of war between the United States and Russia our bombers would not take to the air nor would they find a place to land."

Indeed, as one general would later remark, SAC facilities were too vulnerable. A well-aimed bazooka could take out SAC headquarters. Even easier, wrote an SAC historian, would be a bullet fired at a bomber: "A rifle bullet puncture in a fuel cell would require hours to correct and thus effectively accomplish the delaying actions."

As was SAC's penchant, they looked inward for a solution and launched the most extensive base-defense and antisabotage program in the United States military. It divided its air police into two commands, one involved with day-to-day law enforcement and the other with base defense. Soldiers assigned to base defense would become the Combat Defense Squadrons, SAC's elite heavily armed, well-trained, and in every aspect extraordinarily alert internal force.

LeMay used surprise attacks by "adversary" forces and simulated infiltrations to test his defenses. SAC's Combat Defense Squadrons would be as meticulous and unforgiving about access protocols as they would be ready and trained to fire, if fire they must.

IN THE AFTERMATH of the Soviet A-bomb, the eleven member nations of NATO met at The Hague to discuss the defense of Western Europe. While the tone of the meeting was upbeat, it masked a sobering reality: the United States no longer had a monopoly on the atomic bomb. Little could hold back the Soviet Army should the Russians decide to invade the West. The nations represented at the meeting would be the first to be attacked.

The assumption was that at some point they would.

GATHERING ACCURATE TARGET data behind the closed borders of the Soviet Union was taxing American intelligence resources. Said General Cabel: "Although we are searching for, creating, and exploiting every opening in the iron curtain that we can think of, our success leaves much to be desired. At this moment we are seriously deficient in the means to collect the necessary intelligence on existing and potential Soviet air offensive and defensive capabilities."

One exception was a program called Operation Wringer. Cabel described Wringer: "This program provides for the systematic intelligence exploitation of returned German prisoners of war. It is beginning to produce a wealth of material which is significant for air intelligence, particularly for use in Objective Folders." German prisoners of war had been held in gulags located in parts of the Soviet Union that no westerners had ever seen. They spoke about airfields, troop barracks, cities, manufacturing and mining facilities, rail, and other discernible features. Refineries, manufacturing plants, and mining operations were described in regions whose details until then had never been known to outsiders. Others made sketches of rivers, roads, and bridges. Some saw nothing, which eliminated certain areas as targets. One man was sent to the camps near Pevek. His information was far more useful: he identified uranium mines and ore-sorting facilities.

At a time when head-spinning physics were triggering breakthroughs in the labs at Los Alamos and advanced aeronautical engineering was expanding the flight envelopes of some of the most advanced aircraft in the world, some of the best targeting information SAC had was being gathered during interviews with prisoners released from Soviet gulags.

THE SPANISH WORD for "apple tree" is *manzano,* and because early settlers found apple trees in the foothills of a line of mountains near Albuquerque, New Mexico, the mountains were promptly named the Manzano Mountains. The arid Manzanos, however, would in time be far better known for bombs than for apples. As one of the first of three national storage sites, Manzano was laced with storage bunkers, weapons magazines, and hardened igloos both inside and around the mountain.

It was here, however, that the nation's second atomic bomb would be lost. Just seven days after the Manzano Base opened as an official National Stockpile Site, a B-29 arrived to pick up an atomic bomb and capsule. Minutes after it departed, it flew head-on into a ridge of mountains several miles beyond the airfield. Because the crash occurred at dusk, the first indication that something had gone wrong was a smudge of red on the horizon, but then flames boiled skyward and there was a violent explosion. The high explosives inside the atomic bomb had detonated. *The New York Times,* one of the first to report on the accident, said the flames were visible for fifteen miles. Thirteen died.

ON APRIL 25, 1950, Strategic Air Command unveiled their war plan if Offtackle became a reality. A total of 397 bombers and recon aircraft, and more than 80 fighters, would fly forward to bases in the United Kingdom and be positioned to strike the Soviet Union within three days of the start of war. Once there, one group of 112 bombers would attack Soviet targets from the north over Scandinavia, while a second force of 89 bombers would come up from the Mediterranean and into the Ukraine. Ten B-36s would attack Moscow directly from the United States.

According to LeMay, the bombers would hit the Soviet Union in mass, flying in to thirty-two target areas where they would drop between sixty and ninety bombs on a precise timeline that called for the first targets to be destroyed at 7:05 P.M. "Within approximately four hours after borders are crossed all targets will have been bombed," said SAC.

Offtackle in fact had 123 targets but SAC had target folders for only 60. The remaining 63 would be found, photographed, and placed into new folders as the air atomic attacked continued. The second round would commence in three days and it would all be over in thirty days.

BECAUSE IT WAS stated policy that the United States would not attack first, Strategic Air Command would have to absorb a blow while still retaining the capability to deliver a counterattack. LeMay had his doubts. "I don't see how I can absorb, on my bases, an atomic attack and then get off the floor and carry out my mission," he said. "Our projected air defense system will provide only a very limited protection to the striking force . . . Our only other defense is to know when [the attack] is coming, so at best, you won't be there when it hits you."

LeMay paused and then began what by any measure was a manifesto for the prosecution of the Cold War: "I believe our national leaders must be impressed with the need for taking the following specific steps. First, provide an overriding priority for the establishment of an intelligence system which will tell us the where and when of the enemy's atomic force. Second, place the Air Force on a war footing without further delay. Third, provide funds in such quantities as may be needed to [e]nsure that the striking force will be operational as a long-range intercontinental force not later than July of 1952, and fourth, reexamine present policies which imply that we must absorb the first blow."

While the first three policies would become the foundation of the modern Strategic Air Command, it was LeMay's fourth platform that would color his career for the rest of his life. LeMay saw no reason why America shouldn't strike first, if the situation called for it.

A SOVIET DEFECTOR named Colonel G. A. Tokayev was something of a prize in the intelligence community. Tokayev was, among other things, a member of the prestigious Zhukovsky Air Force Engineering Academy and was privy to information on Soviet strategic capabilities. Tokayev confirmed the creation of the Soviet Long-Range Air Force and the increased production of the Tu-4 Bull bomber. He revealed fascinating details about which much could be conjectured, including the addition of a thermostatically heated bomb bay in the Tu-4, a new sling system to hold the atomic bomb, and new biological suits for the crew.

Tokayev also confirmed intelligence reports that the Soviets were attempting to develop a guided missile with range sufficient to reach the United States.

More important, Tokayev pointed out specific atomic- and missile-test sites, the location of aircraft factories, the location of factories that built critical components such as gyros, all of which, no doubt, were added to SAC's target folders.

ON JUNE 5, just minutes before midnight, SAC initiated an exercise that would simulate the war plan in Offtackle down to the minute. Every aircraft in the command would execute the plan exactly as they would in real life. From a standing start, the crews would pack their bombers, pick up bombs from the stockpile sites, and then fly a long-distance mission within the United States to simulate the flight to an overseas base. They would land, refuel, and wait until all the bombers were assembled for the attack. The exercise would conclude as the bombers hit their radar-bomb-scoring sites on a bomb range in the panhandle of Florida.

Exactly as presented, by the third day, 314 of the 395 bombers were flying their long-range missions and on E+6 they took off en masse to attack their assigned radar scoring sites as if they were Mother Russia herself. Sixty aircraft were the designated A-bomb carriers, 104 bombers were decoys or jammers, 19 reconnaissance planes swept prospective target areas, and 22 tankers provided support. Of the 60 bombers that dropped bombs, 58 struck their targets as tasked.

The exercise, which was code-named Becalm, was as solid a performance as any by a command that less than two years earlier could scarcely find Dayton. Nearly to the minute, SAC had completed a dress rehearsal for war. In the next seven years, SAC would repeat this exercise time and again, honing its skills and tactics and timing until six days would be compressed into fifteen minutes and sixty bombers would grow to more than one thousand.

RHYS M. SALE, president of Ford Motor Company of Canada, spoke about communism versus capitalism: "I want to see the people of Canada wide awake to the fact [that] we are living in a tinder-dry world in which a gigantic fire is raging and dangerously near to being out of control . . . In the arsenals of every land behind the Iron Curtain, the sweating slaves of Communism are beating out the weapons for world conquest . . . World War III is here. It is going on right now."

Added Senator James Duff of Pennsylvania: "In my opinion, it is impossible to overestimate the danger this country is in . . . We must measure up to the Revolutionary heroes who served in America's last great crisis."

To test the effectiveness of the ever-increasing number of radar stations, SAC launched mock attacks against Seattle and the well-guarded Hanford atomic plant. That the radar stations performed poorly was hard to hide. According to one after-action report: "Seattle citizens would not have had time to seek shelter." The Hanford plant, one of the most important nuclear assets in America and cocooned by air-defense radar stations and nimble fighter-interceptors, would have had no better than "an even chance of being forewarned."

Hoping for better, a second test was conducted in November, but it, too, went poorly. Four SAC bombers flew against the far more developed Alaskan radar fence but leaped over it as if it were mere twine.

The sinister beams were as yet falling well short of their mark.

General Kenney wrote a letter to General Vandenberg lending support to LeMay's manifesto and in particular the idea of absorbing the first blow. "I believe that we have got to do something about the conception that we must wait until Russia hits us before we can start shooting," said Kenney. "By all previous definitions, we are now in a state of war with Russia. The only way that we can be certain of winning is to take the offensive as soon as possible and hit Russia hard enough to at least prevent her from taking over Europe."

The strategy Kenney proposed would become known as "preemptive strikes." It was akin to taking a swing when someone was taking a swing at you. You didn't have to wait until the punch landed.

The first actual transfer of atomic bombs to the custody of the military occurred in 1950. In March of that year the Atomic Energy Commission recommended to President Truman that he transfer ninety of the twenty kiloton, MK-4 atomic bombs to the military for training. Truman approved the recommendation and the transfer of bombs was well under way when on June 25, 1950, the North Korean army invaded South Korea, setting into motion what would become known as the Korean War. Knowing that Congress would provide military assistance to the South Koreans, Truman smartly worried that the Soviets would think that America was dropping its guard in Europe and see that as an opportunity to make a land grab. Truman agreed with a recommendation made by the Joint Chiefs to send two groups of B-29s to Europe both as a show of force and as a quick reaction capability should it become necessary. When advised of the decision, General LeMay suggested that those bombers be atomic capable and that they be deployed with atomic bombs, less capsules. The Joint Chiefs concurred, as did British prime minister Clement Attlee, who approved the plan with the proviso that "no official statements link the bomber deployment to the war in Korea." It was decided that ninety bombs would be sent with the B-29s.

Although it has been widely believed that Truman authorized an additional ninety bombs for the B-29s, recent documents tell us otherwise. Truman in fact retrieved the ninety bombs sent to the military for training and sent those weapons to England. This deployment began in July. Truman then decided to reinforce those bombs by sending at least eleven more bombs to the Goose Bay Air Base in Labrador, where Strategic Air Command bombers refueled en route to Great Britain, and between eleven and fifteen more bombs to the aircraft carrier the USS *Coral Sea*, which was headed to the Mediterranean.

In truth, however, not all ninety bombs made it to England. A B-50 bomber from Biggs AFB, in Texas, spiraled into the ground not far from Cincinnati, Ohio, killing the crew of sixteen and destroying the bomber and its bomb. That this bomb was part of Truman's hedge against the outbreak of a second front in Europe is evidenced in several new documents. Robert Ogden, a member of the unit from which the bomber was based, said: "At the outbreak of the Korean War on 3 July 1950 the three squadrons of the 97th Bomb Wing (340th, 341st, 342nd) were deployed to England, leaving Biggs about 10th–13th of July. The purpose of this deployment was to prevent the Russians from entering the war. I recall upon arrival at RAF Station Sculthorpe, hearing of the plane crashing." Thus it is that official histories correctly report that Truman in fact sent eighty-nine bombs to England, not the ninety that he authorized.

Moreover, long recorded as the loss of an aircraft during a training mission, the fact that this bomber and its bomb were actually part of the historic deployment of atomic weapons to England in support of Truman's hedge adds a small footnote to the history of the Cold War.*

As THE SITUATION deteriorated in Korea, General Douglas MacArthur urgently requested the assistance of B-29s for conventional bombing in Korea, and that ten atomic bombers with ten atomic bombs be put on standby in Guam.

---

* That the bomber was being deployed was further evidenced by the remains of its flyaway kit scattered among the wreckage.

Somewhat surprisingly, Truman approved both requests, but he agreed with LeMay's position that the atomic bombers should remain under the control of SAC and not of MacArthur, the theater commander. On August 5, 1950, ten B-29s took to the runway at Fairfield-Suisun Air Force Base near San Francisco, each with an MK-4 atomic bomb. One would not make it.

The first nine departures for Guam were uneventful, but as the last B-29 accelerated down the runway two propellers ran away as the bomber lifted off, forcing the pilot to shut down two engines. In what would later be described as heroic flying, the pilot somehow pulled the fuel-laden, bomb-laden bomber into the air and managed to turn back toward the runway, but as he did, he lost altitude and the bomber simply went into the ground. "The crash was not hard," reported an aide to General LeMay, but twelve men were dead and eight were trapped in the burning wreckage, which came to rest at the edge of a trailer park that housed military families.

What ensued was an explosion as tragic as the crash. Said the Pentagon: "The weapons 5,000 pounds of high explosive detonated; the blast was felt for 30 miles and the fire was visible for 65 miles. Seven firefighting and rescue personnel were killed; 181 other civilian personnel received major or minor injuries."

Despite the magnitude of the disaster, a cover story was required to mask the atomic bomb. The B-29 had been on a "long range training mission," said the air force, and had crashed, causing "ten to twelve 500 pound bombs" to explode.

That an atomic bomb had been on board would remain classified for forty-four years. When the event was declassified, it was stated that the bomber had been bound for Hawaii, or, in another account, on a training mission. That this bomb was part of the deployment in support of MacArthur in Korea explains why the history books correctly say that Truman sent nine bombs to Guam, and not ten.

BOMBS SEEMED TO be falling like rain. Over the lower part of the St. Lawrence River, approximately one hundred miles upstream from Quebec, near the hamlet of St. Alexandre-de-Kamouraska, in an area that was surrounded by rugged terrain, an MK-4 detonated with a thunderous explosion, a sharp *boom!* that was heard twenty-five miles away.

The Pentagon issued a dismissive press release that attributed the explosion to "three 500 pound conventional bombs," but in truth, an SAC bomber had developed engine trouble and another atomic bomb had to be jettisoned and was set to self-destruct.

It was November 10, 1950.

Five atomic bombs had been lost in accidents.

AERIAL REFUELING ENTERED the training syllabus of Strategic Air Command. Pilots practiced looping the hoses with their grapnels, reeling in the lines, and then doing it all over again, but it was awkward and even to the untrained eye it looked unnatural. More practical were two new systems then in trials, one of which was called the flying boom and the other the probe-and-drogue. In tests, the probe-and-drogue was quickly the most popular of the two. Rather than trail a hose, the tanker unreeled a badminton-shaped cone or "basket" that a receiver aircraft would fly into or "plug," using a three-foot probe fitted to the aircraft's nose.

While popular, the probe-and-drogue was ill-suited for a two-hundred-thousand-pound bomber. Not only did gas flow slowly, but bombers had none of the agility of a fighter plane, so the second system, the flying boom, was chosen by Strategic Air Command. A forty-foot telescoping aluminum boom was attached to the rear of a tanker. The bomber would fly up to the tanker and a boom operator would maneuver the boom into a receptacle. Before approving the system, however, SAC tested where that receptacle should be placed and determined that it didn't matter where it was except that it be well outside a pilot's field of vision. Formation flying was hard enough without suffering the temptation to watch the nozzle as it plugged into the receptacle.*

LEMAY READ ALOUD a portion of a Joint Chiefs study titled "Implications of Soviet Possession of Atomic Weapons": ". . . the time is approaching when both the United States and Soviets will possess capabilities for inflicting devastating atomic attacks on each other. Were war to break out when this period is reached, a tremendous military advantage would be gained by the power that struck first and succeeded in carrying through an effective surprise attack. Such an attack might very well be decisive by reducing the atomic offensive capability, possibly to a critical degree . . ."

IN 1777, MOROCCO became the first country to recognize the independence of America and John Adams and Thomas Jefferson signed one of America's

---

* There are exceptions, most notably the B-47, which had the receptacle on the nose directly in front of the pilot, and the A-10. To this day, the navy and the marines continue with the probe-and-drogue system.

first treaties, the Moroccan-American Treaty of Friendship, which George Washington affirmed in a letter dated 1787.

On December 22, 1950, while under French Colonial rule, the Moroccans signed a new agreement with the United States allowing the construction of American bomber bases in Sidi Slimane, Nouasseur, and Ben Guerir. Work on the airfields began promptly. On July 14, 1951, a flight of B-50s and KB-29s landed at Nouasseur while fighter jets landed at Sidi Slimane. Although the arrival of aircraft was largely symbolic—the bases were hardly ready for occupation—in a matter of years, Morocco would become one of the most active forward bases for Strategic Air Command bombers. Entire wings of nuclear bombers would rotate in and out of Morocco for ninety-day deployments, a practice that no doubt further affirmed the Kremlin's position that forces from the West surrounded their borders.

Hostile encirclement, as it were.

ATOMIC COCKTAILS

ON JANUARY 27, 1951, a one-kiloton bomb burst in the sky like a sparkler over the Las Vegas Bombing and Gunnery Range, thus inaugurating its change in name and status to the Nevada Test Site. A bull's-eye large enough to be seen by a bombardier tens of thousands of feet in the sky had been painted on the floor of the valley that was called Frenchman Flat. Over the next eight days, SAC B-50s would bomb this bull's-eye five times. The crews made so many practice runs that they could fly the entire route with their eyes closed, which was fortunate considering that a few thousand feet off the mark meant something entirely different in the math of atomic bombs.

The first four bombs were small and yielded between one and eight kilotons. The fifth bomb, however, produced a twenty-two-kiloton blast at 1,435 feet, generating a clap of noise that was heard from Los Angeles to Salt Lake City. This noise marked the birth of the second postwar atomic-bomb design, the eighty-five-hundred-pound MK-6. The MK-6 was a bulbous, squat-looking atomic bomb that was of no particular note except that it could be produced with near assembly-line precision and near assembly-line quality. It was the first offspring of the nation's continental atomic-bomb proving ground, a pedigree it passed down to the countless other atomic bombs that would enter the stockpiles only after a final blast at the Nevada Test Site.

BRIGADIER GEN. HERBERT Loper, of the Military Liaison Committee of the Atomic Energy Commission, argued that there were large areas of the Soviet Union about which the Central Intelligence Agency possessed no information at all and where significant Soviet atomic-bomb infrastructure might already exist. Loper feared that the bounty of secrets handed over to the Soviets by British scientist and atomic spy Klaus Fuchs might well have accelerated the development not only of atomic bombs but of the more powerful thermonuclear bombs, which, in either case, might very well be hidden from view. While the CIA argued that it would be many more years before the Soviets had the atomic bomb, Loper thought otherwise and used these unmapped areas of the Soviet Union as proof that no one could possibly know enough to say, either way.

Loper's thinking, however unpopular, would prove remarkably prescient.

AN AMERICAN KNOWN only as Harry arrived at the Vorkuta forced-labor camp. It was 1951. Said a survivor of that camp: "He was in an air crash. He was brought from Berlin. He was approximately twenty-eight years old and had dark blue eyes, and very thin blond hair." His face was paralyzed on one side with scars that exposed the orbit of his eye socket. They said he was good with his fists.

Vorkuta held three thousand or so political prisoners and other dissidents. These prisoners were living under sentences that ran twenty-five years or more. They worked in coal mine 29. They were subject to almost constant propaganda. Said that same survivor: "A loudspeaker was installed in each barrack in the camp. Except for about a half hour a day it was running continuously day and night." He remembered one recording: "The U.S. were warmongers and that the heavy industry of the USA exploited the little man. They also reported of rapes of German and Austrian women by the Americans."

The propaganda was seen for what it was. Far worse was the truth. Prisoners in Vorkuta were routinely beaten or killed and far too many guards took sadistic pleasure from the cries of those tortured. On one occasion, a group of prisoners was simply machine-gunned down by the guards in the towers. On another occasion, fighter planes mowed down a cluster of more than one hundred as if it were target practice. The camp commander used "crowbars or shovels" to beat prisoners; escapees were hunted from helicopters and planes and shot like deer.

America, to those in the gulags, seemed the place to be, warmongers or not.

Gulags, on the other hand, seemed to reinforce an American image of a brutal, totalitarian breeding ground that spawned the faceless Russian soldiers that might attack American hometowns and slaughter families in the dark of night.

SAC, many Americans believed, was their one and only shield.

A STRATEGIC AIR Command historian said of the urgency one could now feel on an SAC base: "All combat units . . . were maintained on a most rigid training schedule. The aircraft flew test bombing missions constantly, regardless of weather and time of day or night. From altitudes of 10 miles or higher, the bombers attacked (simulated) American cities whose layout and surrounding geographical patterns made them a counterpart of some Soviet or other enemy target. The training missions were conducted as nearly as possible like SAC plans for actual combat operations. The targets within the cities were specific buildings or corners of buildings, for even with atomic and hydrogen bombs there was still a need for precision. Under this concept, the change for peacetime operations to global war would involve only . . . the loading of nuclear weapons. Each squadron had its own war plans which it could carry out as ordered; and each combat crew in these units knew its targets and alternates."

Said LeMay: "We practiced in SAC. We ran our war plan time and again. The crews spent hours and hours and made hundreds of bomb runs on their targets."

General David Burchinal, an SAC officer, added: "You flew a profile of your combat mission. You would do a radar-bombing attack, perhaps from Tucson, on a target in France. Then you would land in England, and you would come on back. You never did pack a bag. You had the bag packed, stored in operations."

According to LeMay: "People were down there in their beds, and they didn't know what was going on upstairs."

But they did in Washington. And in Moscow. LeMay liked his bombers to be visible.

IN APRIL 1951, the Soviets moved more than two hundred bombers to air bases in Manchuria and as many as seventy submarines to sub pens in Vladivostok, and with it sent a warning that if American forces moved north of the North Korean border, Soviet bombers would join the war and bomb Korea, Japan, and, with all their energy, American positions in South Korea.

The Joint Chiefs needed no more. They promptly drew up extensive contingency plans to bomb the Soviet air and submarine bases with atomic bombs if the attacks were carried out. They asked President Truman to release nine plutonium capsules for the nine bomb assemblies already on Guam. On April 6, 1951, President Truman approved the request and released the capsules, but in a nod to the restrictive language of the Atomic Energy Act, Truman released the bombs personally to air force chief of staff General Hoyt Vandenberg, who was formally designated a "personal representative of the President."*

---

* Truman previously held that only a president could make decisions about the use of bombs. Perhaps to be consistent he felt compelled to put the robe of presidential authority around Vandenberg's shoulders.

Truman completed this transfer by writing a brief letter to the Atomic Energy Commission: "The recent transfer to Gen. Vandenberg of custody of certain nuclear and non-nuclear components marks the end of [the] Commission's civilian responsibility over a portion of our war reserve of atomic weapons."

Thus it was that for the first time since World War II, war-ready atomic bombs with their plutonium capsules were deployed to a forward base and were ready to strike.

They simply needed the word *go*.

THE PLANS TO bomb 20 Soviet cities with 30 A-bombs evolved into plans to bomb 70 cities with 133 bombs and then 104 Soviet cities with 292 bombs. The RAND Corporation's Carl Builder gave some thought to what this meant. He said: "Just what it takes to destroy a society is uncertain but it could be the destruction of as few as a dozen and as many as a hundred of its largest cities. Strategic bombardment in World War II reached a pace where it could destroy, at most, one city each night. That meant that the cities not attacked could come to the aid of the one that was. The destruction of hundreds of cities in the space of hours is possible with only a small fraction of the nuclear arsenals of the two superpowers. A society may be able to continue to function after the loss of ten or a hundred cities over a period of months or years, but not overnight. We simply do not have any human experience with the loss of ten or a hundred major cities in one night."

"NUCLEAR WAR PRESENTED Air Force officers with stark options that had to be executed with little or no deliberation," wrote one air force historian. "Operational commanders had to determine in a matter of minutes whether the appearance of unknown aircraft or missiles on a warning system device constituted a nuclear strike or rather were phenomena related to atmospheric conditions or technical problems in the warning system itself. Based on that assessment, commanders then had a minute or two in which to order a nuclear counterstrike with bombers and later with missiles. A mistake either way—launching a strike erroneously or failing to launch the counterstrike quickly in case of an actual attack—would lead to the destruction of the United States."

The solution was to marry radar stations to emerging machines called computers. By accelerating the flow of data, more time could be applied to the understanding of those data, to analysis. "Although commanders in no way wanted machines to replace their decision functions, they were perfectly happy to have computers and radar replace people elsewhere in the chain of command . . . Radar extended the senses of the military, and computers promised to speed their reactions."

Extend the senses of the military and speed the reactions. Fewer words could as thoroughly underscore the need for technology as the margin of time between warning and war grew ever tighter—and the consequences of mistakes ever more deadly.

AT THE ONSET of World War II, hundreds if not thousands of bombers, tankers, reconnaissance aircraft, fighters, cargo planes, and troop transports would start moving across the United States to their forward bases, where they would refuel and begin the trip across the Atlantic. Harmon Air Base, in Newfoundland, and Goose Bay Air Base, in Labrador, would refuel aircraft using the northern crossing to England while Kindley Air Base, in Bermuda, and Lajes Air Base, in the Portuguese Azores, would refuel aircraft on the mid-Atlantic route to Morocco.

And therein lay the problem. No matter how well timed the crossings might be, the staging bases would be impossibly saturated with aircraft. Timetables would no doubt be thrown off by mechanical delays or equipment problems or unexpected headwinds or any number of other contingencies. All the more certain, each small variation would domino into a degree of congestion that would find taxiways crowded, the refueling pits slowed, the ground mechanics stretched to their capacity, and the skies congested as planes waited for landing slots. No doubt on Execute-day, the endless crawl of bombers from refueling pits to taxiways to runways would from a distance look like ants around a hill.

LeMay raised this issue at a meeting of air force commanders. The congestion caused by the concurrent use of these bases by all the commands was a recipe for disaster, LeMay argued. Aircraft arrivals needed to be staggered, and as far as LeMay was concerned, no one should be anywhere near them until his bombers and tankers had completed their transatlantic push.*

Remarkably, there was almost immediate agreement. SAC would have priority during the trans-attack movement of aircraft, behind which would fol-

---

*   LeMay's concerns were justified. During the forward deployment of aircraft in support of the Lebanese Crisis in 1958, the staging bases were so crowded that even tents could not accommodate all the aircrews. Kindley Air Base, in Bermuda, landed three hundred planes on a single day.

low the aircraft of the other air commands. LeMay's bombers and tankers would refuel and take off before there were other arrivals.

Less agreeable, of course, were the Soviets. While LeMay easily won the consensus of his peers, his plan would quickly be trumped by Soviet plans to bomb those bases back to the Stone Age. Preferably when they were bogged down by the very aircraft that intended to bomb their own cities.

SAC DISLIKED OTHERS speaking on its behalf and wanted its information unfiltered and firsthand. In years to come it would install television cameras inside Air Defense Command's situation rooms so that it could access and evaluate the radar returns on its own, but the immediate issue was the type of bombs America should be building, and on that point SAC felt its opinions should be heard. Nuclear tests had demonstrated that atomic bombs could be made using less fissile material than previously calculated. This opened the door to a discussion on the desired military characteristics of new bombs and in what sizes they should be built.

The first round of discussions seemed to lean toward more but smaller-yielding bombs, but this discussion had not involved SAC, which infuriated LeMay. In a letter to the air force chief of staff LeMay wrote: "[SAC] is concerned that, in the evaluation of the relative worth of the wide variety of weapons which could now be made available, insufficient consideration may be given to other factors which influence the strategic offensive. For example, since this command will be affected by the availability of bases, by restrictions on aircraft and engine operating time, by possible enemy action, etc., it does not necessarily follow that an increase in the number of bombs at the expense of unit striking power would represent a real increase in national potential."

LeMay's point was that the size of bombs should be based not on what was scientifically possible but on military variables such as the distance a given bomber could fly with a bomb of a certain weight, or the need for higher-yielding bombs to destroy hardened targets, or to account for the simple reality that bombers would be shot down en route to their targets, making it all the more important that the bombers that did get through had the largest bombs possible.

Said LeMay: "It is therefore suggested that [SAC] be represented at any discussions or conferences that may be convened on this subject prior to the establishment of an air force position with respect to the future composition of the atomic stockpile."

It was, of course, hardly a suggestion.

* * *

THE AMBITIOUS FLIGHT simulator started by the navy in 1944 used a computer developed by IBM called Whirlwind, but the project had spiraled out of control and in 1951 the air force joined it with the expectation that Whirlwind could become the heart of a new air-defense control system called SAGE. The SAGE system—a contraction for the spectacularly misnamed Semi-automatic Ground Environment network—would tie together the radar stations now dotting the perimeter of the United States into a single, real-time air-control display that would continuously show the presence and movement of all aircraft over or near North America.

In truth, however, SAGE needed a much better and much faster computer than Whirlwind. Four hours of maintenance were needed to nurse Whirlwind through a single day, downtime that was unimportant in a flight simulator but entirely unacceptable in the fast-paced environment of air defense. For SAGE to become an air-defense radar computer downtime had to approach zero, and the radar displays had to be updated in real time. That required enormous processing power—fast processing power. Unfortunately, Whirlwind could process data only as fast as the data could move across its electrostatic memory. With radar stations pulsing beams in the milliseconds, a computer needed to process data at speeds ten times that. As one historian would put it ever so casually, it did little good if the calculation of an aircraft's position took several hours to complete.

In what would be an ambitious undertaking IBM, the air force, and academia would join to overhaul Whirlwind and produce Whirlwind II, the world's first true mainframe computer. In perhaps one of the most important inventions to date, MIT discovered the magnetic core memory, a technology that would influence computing for decades. Using ferrite material for the core, they discovered that binary impulses could move to and from the electrostatic storage tubes into a memory core and be processed in parallel calculations that would take just nine microseconds—nine-*millionths* of a second. Almost 110,000 calculations could be conducted in a second, a thousandfold increase over the electrostatic core.

Maintenance time dropped from several hours a day to a few hours a week. Although the "computer" was a 275-ton affair with fifty-eight thousand vacuum tubes housed in a four-story windowless building, inputs from the ships, planes, and the early-warning stations were now digitally displayed and portrayed as dynamic data on a round radarscope. A phosphorescent blip appeared each time a radar station painted a target. The blip flared brightly, then slowly winked out, a neat trick one software programmer proudly developed. In another, data came in automatically over phone lines using something that would be called a modem. With unwavering regularity, the entire screen refreshed itself every eleven seconds, and the blips merged to trace ghostly tracks across the screens. In yet another clever idea, the simple touch of a penlight gun to the screen prompted a box to appear that displayed data such as the aircraft's speed, altitude, heading, and classification. The software could be calibrated to filter out friendly aircraft or to highlight "unknown" tracks, and "fakers," a term given to SAC bombers during training exercises.

Twenty-five SAGE control centers were built. In a marvel of redundancy, any one of the centers could take over the entire nation should the enemy destroy any one of the others.

SAGE, as one historian enthusiastically commented, combined "the talents of man with the best aptitudes of machines." More important, it turned Churchill's sinister beams into living displays that could pinpoint a Piper Cub as easily as a Soviet Tu-4 bomber.

THE ATOMIC TESTS added a degree of excitement to a city that made excitement its stock-in-trade. Las Vegas hotels advertised "atomic" room specials, sold "atomic cocktails" at their bars, and offered picnic baskets as part of packages and weekend deals that included field trips to nearby Mount Charleston and Angel's Peak to view the atomic blasts. There were precautions for sure but they seemed trivial. Said a gently worded press release from the Nevada Test Organization: "Observers on mountain peaks may have a direct line-of-sight to the fireball on almost all shots, so, we routinely caution them to look the other way at shot time."

Another press release warned that a bomb might catch the unprepared by surprise. "The most serious hazard to motorists is probably the startling effect of the intense light which suddenly blazes into a driver's eyes while the vehicle is in motion."

In another day and in another time atomic bomb bursts and sunglasses might have sparked protests, but in 1951 it inspired cocktails and field trips with boxed lunches for the entire family.

ROGUE WAVES

THE BREAKTHROUGH MOMENT for Leon DeLong caught the attention of the media. DeLong, known for his piers, was about to put his name on a new type of Gulf of Mexico oil rig. Said *Time* magazine: "Colonel Leon De-Long got wind of a new kind of jack, more powerful than any before, snapped up the patent rights and brainstormed the idea of a mobile drilling platform for oilmen."

DeLong, who knew the extraordinary expense of constructing oil-drilling platforms in the Gulf, saw jacks as a way to build a rig that could be mobile. Legs would be dropped to the ocean floor to which industrial jacks strong enough to lift a steel platform were attached. Once on site, a well would be drilled and then the platform would be moved to start another hole. As with his piers, the jack inched up a platform using heavy rubber boots to grip the legs.

To prove his point, DeLong went into his own pocket to build the prototype. He floated the assembly out to a drilling site using the platform as the hull. Once on site, he lowered the legs and drove them into the sea bottom. Ever so slowly the jacks lifted the platform up the legs until it was well above the sea.

It worked like a charm. DeLong's new mobile rig would become known as a "jack-up" and within a matter of years DeLong would have dozens of them operating in the Gulf and around the world. Jack-ups could be towed into position and jacked up and drilling could be performed, and if the hole was dry, the entire assembly could be floated off to a new site. His business would grow to more than eighty million dollars in rigs built, rented, or sold to drilling companies, maritime operators, the military, and soon a radar station in the Atlantic called a Texas Tower. "The lot of a pioneer is a rough one," DeLong testified before a Senate Committee investigating the collapse of one of the few jack-up rigs he had not built.

That rig would support the platform for a radar station the air force would build in the Atlantic. On it twenty-eight men would die.

* * *

IN JANUARY 1949, Texas A&M University combined its expertise in geology, atmospheric phenomena, and hydraulics into a new Department of Oceanography, which in short order received funding by Humble Oil, Shell, and Chevron to study wave forces on vertical cylinders—legs, as it were; off-shore oil rigs. Professors Charles L. Bretschneider and Robert O. Reid developed analytical models and practical experiments to determine the influence of wind, the topography of the seabed, the depth of the ocean, the size of the ocean fetches, thermoclines, and the length of sustained weather on the size of a wave, their frequency, and the likelihood of the far more powerful waves called cresting waves. From their work, they developed some of the first mathematical formulas for hindcasting waves, wave damage, and storm tracks.

The Bretschneider/Reid team was soon considered the leading authority on wave forces on oil rigs. They directed Texas A&M Research Foundation Project 38—Wave Forces on Pilings. They authored peer-reviewed texts used throughout the industry—"The Generation and Decay on Wind Waves in Deep Water," "Wave Action," "The Statistical Distribution of the Heights of Sea Waves," and, certainly the most germane of them all to those who would think about building radar stations in the Atlantic, "Surface Waves and Off-Shore Structures."

NO MATTER HOW impressive the credentials of the weather forecasters were, the men who labored on the platforms saw things that experts thought impossible. The winds that swept the Gulf were unspeakably hard. Sledgehammer gusts would shake an entire platform so hard that men would be thrown off their feet. The rains sounded like ball hammers pounding on the steel hulls. The waves would shake the pilings in every manner possible, some cresting against the wood or steel, others acting like the bow of the devil's own fiddle running across the man-made strings.

More troubling were rogue waves, freak waves, impossibly large and unexpected waves that would appear out of nowhere and sweep across decks 50 feet high. Seamen who had had the misfortune of riding out a North Atlantic storm spoke of walls of water 100 feet high preceded by "holes in the sea" that would swallow a small freighter. In 1903, the cruise ship RMS *Etruria* was just four hours out of New York when it was struck by a wave 50 feet high. One passenger was killed. A 112-foot wave was encountered by the navy ship USS *Rambo* in the Pacific in 1933. A lookout happened to glance back. All he saw was a wall of water with thin ripples etched down its dark face. The steamship

Glamorgan was swept by a rogue wave from stem to stern. She was 320 feet long. On an otherwise ordinary transatlantic crossing in 1942, the *Queen Mary* was broadsided by a rogue wave that nearly rolled her over. She listed fifty-two degrees before righting herself. The wheelhouse, normally 90 feet above sea level, was flooded.

Scientists dismissed these stories as hysteria, the understandable result of a harrowing situation. Waves could not gather to such heights, they said in the calm of their lecture halls. And then came the Draupner event.

On January 1, 1995, a low-pressure system developed over the Norwegian sector of the North Sea, producing near-hurricane-strength winds over an open stretch of ocean between Norway and Scotland. Ships caught in the maw of this storm pitched through twenty- and thirty-foot waves. It was from this sea state that a rogue wave was spawned, one that was measured and recorded on scientific lasers specifically calibrated to measure ocean activity. These precise lasers had been fixed to the sides of an oil-distribution platform in the North Sea called the Draupner S.

A clean spike printed out on the recording chart, forever speaking the truth. A nearly vertical wave ninety feet tall struck the platform head-on.

Rogue waves were no longer lore of the sea.

ASPHYXIATED

THE NEW B-47 bomber flowed onto SAC bases at an astonishing rate. In 1952 there were just 62 on hand but by 1954 there would be 795.

Also arriving on base was a reconnaissance version, the RB-47 bomber. The RB-47 at first carried cameras but later models carried a pod in their bomb bay that held electronic intelligence-gathering machines that "ferreted out" frequencies of the radar beams used by the Soviets. According to Colonel Sam Pizzo, a radar navigator on an RB-47H that flew reconnaissance missions off the coast of Russia near Murmansk, just east of Finland: "We flew from Thule, Greenland, along the coast of Russia, no more than 12 miles offshore. We were mapping radar sites. We carried three men in a pod in our bomb bay, the Ravens as we called them. They were our Electronic Warfare Officers. They did all the work; we just flew the plane."

The RB-47 ferret flights worked in some of the most hostile environments known to man. The bombers routinely transited the polar regions and their missions often required hours over the Barents Sea, almost always at night, radio silent, and alone. More than any aircraft SAC flew, the RB-47s required near flawless aerial support from the refueling tankers that met it. Said Pizzo: "Five or six KC-97s would take off a couple of hours ahead of us and wait for us to give us our gas. We'd be cruising at 35,000 feet and the tankers would be at 15,000 feet. Most of our missions were at night so when we started our descent we couldn't see them. We'd get down where they would be and we'd be behind them and they'd be lined up five or six abreast in front of us. You'd take as much gas as a tanker could give you then slide over to the next tanker and then slide over to the next and so on."

SAC tanker pilot Colonel Bill Ernst remembered: "We'd head to our air refueling point which was called our ARCP—Air Refueling Control Point—and wait for the hook-up. We had four primaries and one air spare, as we called him, all spread out in a formation, way up there in the dark 15,000 feet above the Barents Sea and some other places you really didn't want to think about. We'd echelon to the right, stacked up at 500-foot intervals and one mile lateral separation. The RB would come in behind #1 and take approximately 12,000 lbs, drop off, slide over behind #2 and climb up to the contact position and take on 12,000 from #2 drop off and go to #3 and then #4 repeating the process."

However impossible it sounded, in years to come SAC would fly as many as one thousand such missions a year, and out of this combination of tanker and reconnaissance bomber would come a list of more than six thousand Soviet air-defense batteries and radars.

True, too, the words *ferrets* and *ravens* entered the language of the Cold War.

A NEW WORD was used to characterize the size of bombs: *nominal*. A bomb's yield—its explosive force—would invariably be called "nominal" or "half of nominal," and so on. In truth, *nominal* was defined as twenty kilotons, a yield slightly larger than that of Hiroshima.

The word, however, served its purpose; *nominal* made the detonation of an atomic bomb seem harmless, routine, and certainly business as usual.

As was intended.

THE SUGGESTION BY a team of scientists to allocate defense funds to the construction of a new line of radar stations north of the arctic circle met with stiff opposition from the very air force generals most likely to benefit from it. In 1952, MIT hosted a Pentagon-sponsored study group to examine every facet of air defense with an eye toward identifying new benefits that might be derived from advances in electronics, computing, communication, data processing, and more. The Summer Group, as it would be known, grew to more than four hundred scientists, engineers, and physicists who spent the better part of the summer of 1952 in pursuit of such answers.

The group's primary conclusion was that every aspect of defense could be strengthened by building a belt of "distant early warning" radar stations north of the arctic circle in a line stretching from Alaska to Greenland. With these stations, Strategic Air Command, Air Defense Command, and civil defense would have at least six hours' warning before any enemy aircraft reached the United States. Moreover, identification, tracking, communication, control of interceptors, coordination among the commands—all this could be solved as one by applying advances in computers and digital technologies. The Summer Group even had a price tag—$370 million.

The air force balked at the idea with what seemed a priggish, not-invented-here attitude. Offensive air power would not be watered down by anything as insignificant as a radarscope, said the air force. "The shield is neither the strongest defense against aggression nor its surest guarantee against defeat," sniffed one air force general. "It is not the defense the aggressor fears the most; it is the realization that he may receive a harder blow in return that he fears the most."

President Truman disagreed. He promptly authorized twenty million dollars for a test and issued a National Security Directive identifying early warning and air defense as two national imperatives. Included in the recommendations were a cluster of ocean-based radar stations called Texas Towers. The Texas Towers would be strategically positioned off the East Coast to provide early warning of low flying aircraft coming in from the Atlantic. Years later the press would marvel at the Distant Early Warning line of radar stations (the DEW line). The Texas Towers would be dubbed an "inglorious failure."

AN AIR FORCE aircrew member who flew aboard a B-36 bomber during an atomic-bomb drop at the Nevada Test Site remembered: "You'd line up on a bomber run like you would line up on a target. We were one of ten B-36s. Ten B-36s in two groups of five, in what we refer to as a bomber stream, five airplanes in a row on each side, 500 feet above each other. I was in the left rear position at 43,500 feet. The B-50 came up from Kirtland. He had the atom bomb on board. He came up between us. We made a dummy run and came around, all eleven of us, and then made a final run. He dropped the bomb on that run. The pilot identified himself as the Playboy. That was his code name. To tell us he was going to drop the bomb, he identified himself as the Playboy and said, 'This is Playboy. I'm on the graveyard run.'"

IN JANUARY 1952, the president approved the movement of a still-classified number of atomic bombs, minus capsules, to the Sidi Slimane Air Base, Morocco.

The local authorities were not to be informed.

THE RADIO SPOT was a public-service announcement intended to recruit volunteers to work for civil defense. "Who will strike the first blow in the next war, if and when it comes? America? Not very likely. No, the enemy will strike first. And they can do it, too—right now the Kremlin has about a thousand planes within striking distance of your home."

Said another radio spot: "It may not be a cheerful thought but the Reds right now have about a thousand bombers that are quite capable of destroying about 89 cities in one raid. . . . Won't you help protect your country, your town, your children? Call your local Civil Defense office and join the Ground Observer Corps today."

More than three hundred thousand people did just that.

A WARM SUMMER night with confusing weather patterns and a steadily dropping barometer spawned a tornado that churned across Carswell Air Force Base, Texas, just as surely as a Soviet atomic attack. In a matter of minutes, buildings were reduced to "piles of rubble and maintenance sheds became piles of twisted steel." The fuel farm with its millions of pounds of jet fuel was breeched and under the bombers flowed a "lake of water and gasoline."

In less than one hour, seventy-two of the B-36s were out of commission, twenty-four of which were categorized as seriously damaged. One was destroyed. LeMay promptly removed Carswell's Nineteenth Air Division from the Emergency War Plan.

"Every aircraft on the base suffered some damage," wrote a unit historian. "The giant planes were lifted like toys and hurled into each other." Tail sections were bent or snapped off. Aluminum skin peeled off wings, tails, and engine nacelles as if they were cloth. Maintenance bays gouged holes in the planes that hours before they were protecting from the sun. Engines hung off wings by the threads of their fuel lines.

Later, when the concept of dispersing bombers to minimize the effect that the loss of any single air base would have on SAC's war plans started to gain momentum, Carswell would be proof enough that crowded air bases were targets too inviting to ignore.

IT WAS A persuasive comment on the need to remove a potentially contrary voice from the military chain of command. It was the argument for unity of command. It was also an argument to move bombs into the custody of the military.

"There must be a clear chain of authority originating with a single individual, the Commander-in-Chief . . . This chain should run straight and clean from the Commander-in-Chief to the basic units which will be called upon to fight. Wherever a division occurs or wherever a single function is to be controlled by two masters, there is room for failure to act on an essential matter— not necessarily from irresponsibility nor from willful neglect but from confusion or lack of full understanding as to what must be done and by whom.

"Unity of command must necessarily include control over materiel—the implements without which a fighting force cannot be effective . . . the user must know what the weapons look like, how to handle them, their state of readiness and the extent to which minor alterations or repairs may be made without impairing their effectiveness. And he must have the confidence which comes only from complete familiarity with both components and test equipment so that he can be completely certain that they will operate effectively."

AT ISSUE WAS Solomon's dilemma, albeit in reverse. The military was the user of the bomb but the Atomic Energy Commission was the custodian. Can two mothers claim one child?

Surprisingly, the divide remained unresolved for years.

WING ROTATIONS WERE designed to familiarize SAC crews with the air bases that they would operate from in accordance with their Emergency War Plan and to maintain a visible American military presence overseas. Said one historian of this training: "Under the rotation program, units deployed to the United Kingdom, North Africa, and Guam, usually for a 90-day period. Each wing rotation entailed the movement of 45 aircraft, about 1,600 people, and approximately 190 tons of cargo." Once in place, the wing trained as they did in the United States—bombing, navigation, air refueling—and, as weapons were moved to overseas storage, they would train with real bombs. To rotate a wing of forty-five B-47s was estimated to cost more than $42 million.

Said LeMay, with no small measure of satisfaction: "Moving an entire combat wing is comparable to picking up one of our major domestic airlines, moving it across an ocean, and putting it back in operation all within a matter of hours. This is now accomplished as a routine training deployment."

No doubt it was routine, but it was also a reminder to the Soviets that Strategic Air Command was run by the very same general who had pioneered the air strategies used by America to bomb Germany as well as the bombing strategies that systematically shut down Japan and led to its surrender without a land invasion. From an international perspective, the wing rotations were more than just training. They were LeMay's bombers, and no one questioned his resolve to use them if so ordered.

ON SEPTEMBER 2, 1952, more than eleven thousand soldiers, sailors, airmen, and scientists deployed to the South Pacific as part of Operation Ivy. On October 31, they successfully exploded the first hydrogen-fueled bomb, code-named Mike. The 10.4-megaton blast was nearly seven hundred times the power of Hiroshima and was felt through the earth's mantle as far away as Los Alamos, New Mexico. The flash of light was seen four hundred miles away. The fireball was three miles wide and it entrained eighty million tons of vaporized sand, coral, salt water, steel, and fish. The pull on the ocean was so pronounced that the coral bottoms on neighboring lagoons were exposed by the receding waters. The mushroom cloud rose more than one hundred thousand feet and splashed against the stratosphere. Hues of pink and red bristled and flashed as radionuclides collided and swirled inside the cloud. Below, the navy ships looked like bathtub toys. Elugelab, the island on which Mike was built, was now a hole in the Pacific two miles wide.

Within months of its roll-up, staff headquarters for Operation Ivy, under the command of army major general P. W. Clarkson, had the filmmakers at the Hollywood labs on Lookout Mountain, California, make a documentary film highlighting the Pacific endeavor. It ran one hour and seven minutes. Clarkson said to the cameras: "This is one of the most momentous events in the history of science."

IT WAS ALSO one of the most provocative events in the history of science. In less than a year, the Soviet Union responded by exploding a partial hydrogen bomb of their own.

The word *proliferation* began to appear in the press. So, too, did *H-bomb, doomsday, nuclear winter,* and *arms race.*

LIEUTENANT COLONEL HARRY Pike, a faculty member of the Air Command and Staff College, published in 1949 what in hindsight set into motion a debate about percentages. Wrote Pike: "If our enemies send out great numbers of aircraft carrying enough atomic bomb-type weapons . . . and if our air defense is capable of destroying about ten percent of their planes and probably a lesser percentage of their missiles, is the expenditure of an enormous sum of money—probably billions of dollars—for air defense feasible and acceptable?"

It wasn't really a question, but it stirred the embers of a simmering debate. Was air defense oxymoronic?

The air force turned to one of its preeminent consultants to study Pike's estimates, Dr. George Valley of the Massachusetts Institute of Technology. Valley conferred with his associates and in early 1950 concluded that with updates to the current air-defense systems, the kill ratio could be improved from 10 percent to 30 percent.

Valley recommended to the air force that MIT establish an air-defense laboratory that would focus chiefly on a better radar fence.

The air force concurred with Valley's recommendations, and his "thirty percent" seemed to stick. Speaking publicly on the matter, U.S. Air Force chief of staff Hoyt Vandenberg said that the American public should expect their air-defense system to destroy no more than thirty percent of an enemy's bombers before they reached their targets. "A predictable 70 percent of the enemy's planes," said Vandenberg, "would penetrate our defenses."

Not that anyone fully understood this.

At about the same time as Vandenberg's pronouncement, a consortium of Ivy League universities had gathered under the umbrella of Project East River to examine air defense from a civil-defense standpoint. How could the nation be better prepared for atomic war and, more subtly, how could hysteria be prevented in a time of attack, "emotion management," as they called it?

In their interim report, the study group introduced a concept called "leakage." To effectively mobilize the civilian population to safety, civil-defense leaders would need at least one hour's notification of an impending attack, and then only under the assumption that active air defenses would perform "so effectively that civil defense would only need to deal with limited leakage through the defensive net."

"Unrealistic," said then secretary of defense Robert Lovett. "Naïve."

Lovett freshened the conversation by suggesting that instead of limited leakage, the group work on the assumption that the enemy would mount attacks that would, in his words, be "crippling." Thirty percent, as it were.

How that group reacted is not known but how the media reacted is. Joseph and Stewart Alsop, the popular columnists based in Washington, D.C., and syndicated to more than three hundred American newspapers, began a series of attacks aimed at the air force and its leaky air-defense system. The Alsops called the current state of defense "terrifyingly feeble." They argued that it was entirely possible to build an air-defense system so impermeable that even a suicide mission could not get through.

Leakproof, as they called it.

IT WAS A watershed event in the control of atomic bombs. After years of enforcing civilian control of the bomb, Truman finally relented and agreed to allow the military to store war-ready bombs—bombs and their plutonium capsules—on the bases where the ships and planes that would carry them were located. A report titled "Agreed Concepts Regarding Atomic Weapons" was prepared by the National Security Council's Special Committee for Atomic Energy at President Truman's behest. The report, presented in September 1952, summarized a new set of agreements regarding a permanent change in custody for complete weapons. In addition to the nine bombs with capsules sent to Guam for MacArthur in Korea, the bombs that were currently stored in Britain, Morocco, and Labrador, and on aircraft carriers would be immediately supplied with capsules, thus making them instantly available for use against the Soviets. In a broadly worded grant of permissions approved by the president, the agreement allowed the release of capsules equal in number to the bombs already in the custody of the military and that the military be given further bombs and capsules for all the bases that had atomic missions, even those within the United States, "as might be required to assure operational flexibility and military readiness."

Owing largely to the delays near the end of his presidency, the plan was carried over to the new administration. President Dwight D. Eisenhower was sworn into office in January 1953. The new president concurred with the proposal and agreed to the transfer of capsules, the movement of which began in May 1953. Eisenhower also approved the release of additional bomb assemblies for storage in Hawaii and Alaska, and other locations that today remain classified.

Far from the rigid and centralized control of bombs at the National Stockpile Sites, the nation's military stockpile of atomic bombs was inching its way across the face of the globe. Proliferation would now take on a geographic connotation.

IN THE AFTERMATH of Operation Ivy, RAND issued a report titled "Implications of Large Yield Nuclear Weapons." RAND said that the new megaton-size bombs were "fantastically destructive," with effects that were "terrifying." Even fallout shelters would do little good. "There is serious doubt whether conventional shelters will be adequate. People in such shelters may be asphyxiated or roasted. Those who try to leave the shelters will be killed in the firestorm."

RAND ended their analysis with a comment on the utter void one would find after thermonuclear war: there would not be a "large, industrially powerful nation left outside the areas of devastation to offer help to those afflicted."

It was reasoning that made serious the oft-heard comment that nations with hydrogen bombs could bomb each other back into the Stone Age.

WHILE ONE MIGHT think a bomb was a bomb and that was that, in fact atomic bombs were unfinished works of art that underwent a constant process of evolution even after arriving in the stockpiles. Atomic bombs were upgraded, modified, retrofitted, converted, field modified, and, in some cases, had interchangeable parts with other bombs. Taken together, it took an expert with a slide rule and a furrowed brow to know what casing contained what core with what parachute and what sets of fuses and for what yield. For the MK-6, the nation's second postwar atomic-bomb design, the choices were staggering, a virtual dial-a-yield bomb, as it was called. There were 8-, 26-, 80-, 154-, and 160-kiloton yield variations available inside the same outer casing. Between 1952 and 1953, the forthcoming MK-7 was modified nine times and there were at least two versions of the MK-15 hydrogen bomb, including an interim field modification, not that one looked different from the other.

Little wonder that, in matters of the bomb, accurate records were an imperative, no room for guesses, no hedging bets with last-minute notes or scribbling or marking out a set of numbers to insert another.

But then again, that was precisely what would happen in 1958.

Or so some would claim.

THE SWORD AND THE SHIELD

IN 1953, THE nation's television networks gathered in Las Vegas to broadcast a live atomic detonation from the Nevada Test Site. A tall radio tower elevated the bomb many hundreds of feet in the air. Around the base of the tower were various objects. Human mannequins were attached to poles five miles from ground zero. Cars were scattered about the desert floor like seed. Homes were built around ground zero as if on Main Street. The exercise came with the rather obvious name of Operation Doorstep, the implication being that the Soviets could be on America's doorstep at any moment.

The blast occurred before dawn and the atomic flash light lit up the sky. The houses heated up and exploded. Mannequins melted, and cars flipped over and spontaneously burst into flame. A soldier who was in a foxhole two miles from ground zero remembered: "I looked around and there were some sheep but their wool was on fire. And there were some pigs running around squealing. On my right a pig just fell over dead."

Television gave America a front-row seat but when the shock wave swept the desert floor, the TV camera vibrated and the signal blinked off the air. Viewers at home suddenly faced a TV screen reduced to black-and-white static, perhaps not unlike what one might see in the aftermath of a real Soviet attack.

It lasted three seconds.

EACH SOVIET GROUND zero that America would attack was assigned a VN—a Vulnerability Number—that indicated its vulnerability to certain types of atomic weapons and the amount of destruction those weapons would achieve. The Vulnerability Number was based in part on the physical characteristics of a target—the size of buildings, the density of buildings, the terrain, the shielding that one structure afforded another—and in part on the weapons yield, burst height, thermal pulse, blast effects, and the like.

Oddly, despite the evidence from Hiroshima, not included in the calculation of damage was the effect of residual fires, and on this point there was considerable disagreement among the war planners. On one hand, fire itself was an indeterminate variable and thus could not be reliably included. On the other hand, because damage probabilities determined the number of bombs applied to a target, some said that without calculating the effect of fire, SAC planners were underestimating the damage a bomb could do and thus were overbombing targets. "Both blast and fire will damage targets [industrial sites] and nontargets [apartments]," said the authors of "Fire Damage and Strategic Targeting," "but fire will generally go farther and cause more complete damage to both."

Rather than ignore fire, the authors of "Fire Damage" advocated a new index they called the FVI—the Fire Vulnerability Index. Their argument was sound if not strikingly cold. "If 'moderate damage' to 'steel frame' buildings is the appropriate guide for destroying a city of a million or so inhabitants, then fire can only complete the job more effectively."

THE KOREAN WAR ended in 1953 and to military war planners it had been something much more than a regional conflict. Because the Russians and the Chinese were backing North Korea, the conflict was widely viewed as a clear indication of Russia's willingness to "employ war as an instrument of national policy."

No doubt Moscow viewed America's support of the South Koreans in much the same way.

All the more reason, some argued, to view it as what it was. Said army general Omar N. Bradley, Korea was "the wrong war in the wrong place."

WROTE *TIME* ON October 5, 1953: "Punctually to the second one morning last week, the wail of the air-raid sirens rose over New York City. Waved down by cops and white-helmeted wardens, the stream of auto traffic, from Staten Island to The Bronx, froze at the curbs; drivers and passengers scurried to shelter. In the schools, children left the classrooms, and huddled together along inside corridors. Shoppers vanished from Fifth Avenue; the subway stations filled up. Television went off the air, and radio switched to the emergency network. Within minutes, the city was silent, the streets deserted.

"Fifteen minutes later, the all-clear sounded, the city came to life again, and the biggest public-participant practice drill in history was a resounding success."

* * *

THE AIR FORCE had been charged with "striking from enemy hands the weapon most dangerous to this nation," as one historian wrote with a measure of drama, but how to do that was the subject of much debate. Until the early 1950s, the Emergency War Plans assumed that strikes against Soviet industry would eliminate its ability to continue hostilities on the ground. But as atomic parity seemed ever more likely, this approach, variously called "countercities" or "countervalue," seemed dated. A move was afoot to target Soviet military bases.

Said former secretary of the air force Thomas K. Finletter in a 1954 book titled *Power and Policy,* "[The] old counter-industry concept for Strategic Air Command should be given up. . . . The first emphasis would be on the enemy's atomic air, on the fields, installations, planes and missiles from which his atomic attack on us would come."

This new thinking became known as "counterforce." "By counterforce," wrote one air force general, "the Air Force means the ability to selectively and decisively destroy enemy military forces that could otherwise destroy us."

By 1953, Curtis LeMay, a countercities advocate, conceded the need to target Soviet war-making capabilities instead of Soviet industry: "We have to go back to the rule books and the principals of war . . . we must as quickly as possible destroy their capability of doing damage to us." Said air force secretary Nathan F. Twining in a speech delivered in 1954: "We can now aim directly to disarm an enemy rather than to destroy him as was often necessary in wars of the past."

Surprisingly, counterforce moved in fits and starts. Despite the considerable credentials of those who supported it, there remained an unyielding faction of planners who argued with ever louder voices that counterforce would mean simply that American forces would be attacking empty airfields and empty silos from which a Soviet first strike had already been launched.

The debate between countercities and counterforces would continue for another decade until a new term gained currency: *assured destruction*. Assured destruction more or less called for destroying everything.

IT WAS, TO use a phrase contained in a report prepared by the Pentagon, an era of "nuclear plenty." The development of levitated composite cores had greatly increased the power obtained from a unit of plutonium, while the successful test of hydrogen as a nuclear fuel freed weapons developers to think smaller. This opened the door to seemingly unlimited possibilities. Instead of the five-ton behemoths such as the MK-4, an atomic bomb might be made into a device as small as an artillery shell or a depth charge or an air-to-air missile. In time there would be nuclear howitzers, and even backpack bombs.

Such was the era of plenty.

IN JULY 1953, Strategic Air Command and Air Defense Command were pitted against each other in a mock war game. According to a terse, two-sentence summary of this event: "On July 11, 1953, SAC flew 99 bomber sorties against U.S. cities launching in a coordinated 'attack' using aircraft surreptitiously flown out of the country just before the commencement of the designated 48-hour drill period and arriving within the first 30 minutes of the exercise. The Air Defense Command achieved only two 'kills' of bombers before the simulated bomb release points and four 'kills' after bomb release."

Some later described the radar stations as being in a state of "pandemonium," a word that gave Curtis LeMay no pleasure to hear. In LeMay's mind, the most useful thing that the air-defense radar could do was to provide SAC with the warning it needed to launch its bombers. And *pandemonium* was most certainly not a word used in the disciplined ranks of Strategic Air Command.

SOME OF STRATEGIC Air Command's most sacred cows were being sacrificed by the logic of the think tank RAND. In 1953, RAND analyzed the vulnerability of Strategic Air Command bases to a surprise Soviet attack and concluded that SAC would be all but decapitated. According to RAND, the attack would begin on a Sunday morning when hundreds of Tu-4 Bull bombers swarmed into American airspace at two thousand feet and continued high-speed flights to some fifty targets, where they would pop up and release one-hundred-kiloton bombs from twenty thousand feet.

Said RAND: "As the enemy approaches the defense network, they are detected by radar, identified as hostile, and attacked by area defenses . . . upon receipt of warning at SAC bases, evacuation is ordered by the base commander."

But evacuation was a cumbersome affair and as a result RAND estimated that 73 percent of SAC's U.S. bases would be caught with their bombers on the ground, and even more overseas. "On the overseas bases the picture is considerably worse. It is estimated that all areas except the U.K. will get virtually no warning. It can therefore be concluded that *all wings on rotation overseas will be caught on the ground.*"

RAND prepared two alternate scenarios but they ended with similar results. They then presented a fourth scenario, which was a trap. In that scenario, the Soviets would draw out SAC's forces by bombing just a few industrial centers in the United States and then withdrawing their forces to the Soviet Union. Strategic Air Command would rush to mobilize and bombers would begin to stream to the overseas bases. Once the bombers landed at the staging bases for refueling, they would be savagely attacked on the runways.

In this scenario, America's retaliatory capability would be extinguished.

PERHAPS OWING TO the RAND report, the language of nuclear deterrence escalated. Wrote an air force historian, deterrence depended on the "maintenance of a massive retaliatory capability that could not be neutralized by a Soviet surprise attack." Further, it required "the clear communication of the U.S. intentions to the Soviet Union." Those intentions included a clear picture of the "violence of the counterattack" if the U.S. should strike.

"Power," said John Foster Dulles, secretary of state under Eisenhower, "never achieves its maximum possibility as a deterrent of crime unless those of criminal instinct have reason to fear [that it] will actually be used against them."

It was in all other respects the language of war.

A NEW STRATEGY evolved that would be known as the "sword and the shield." The idea was to use a one-two punch to halt a Soviet invasion of Europe, a countercities-and-counterforce combination, as it were. To blunt the advance of the Red Army, air force fighter jets would attack the Soviet army and attempt to pin them down with small atomic bombs while SAC bombers would strike the Soviet industrial base. The fighter jets, wrote an air force historian, formed the "shield that defended Europe," while Strategic Air Command would "thrust a sword into the vitals of the Soviet Union."

Said Bernard Brodie, a nuclear strategist with RAND and former Yale University professor, of such plans: "A people saved by us through the free use of nuclear weapons over their territories would probably be the last to ever ask for our help again."

A FORMER SENIOR Soviet official during the Cold War made a candid admission: "In practice, the General Staff did not have any real working definition of victory in a nuclear war and the operation simply was not discussed in those terms. It was well understood on the General Staff that the Soviet Union would not come out of such a war in anywhere near the same state in which it began the war. The general hope was that some undestroyed pocket of civilization would survive, perhaps in Siberia, that might form the basis for rebuilding the state."

STRATEGIC AIR COMMAND developed a communications strategy that even the air force disagreed with. In SAC's view, any sudden increase in their communications traffic would be detected by the Soviets and interpreted as preparations for hostilities. To eliminate that possibility, SAC would saturate its communications pipelines with traffic twenty-four hours a day. White noise would bridge the gaps between real messages. The concept, which was in many ways nothing short of brilliant, allowed white noise and messages to flow on a continuous basis so that at all times the level of traffic was constant.

It would be called their "full pipeline philosophy," and, air force agreement or not, that was how SAC ran its networks.

As an SAC historian later wrote, if you weren't in SAC you simply didn't have the same high sense of urgency and could not keep up.

IT WAS OCTOBER 1953. According to a magazine reporter: "Across the land, there was a chilling awareness that America and the world might be moving toward a climax of the atomic age." They quoted a speech given by retired AEC chairman Gordon Dean to a convention of textile workers: "Can we as a nation permit the Soviet Union to reach the position where, if it chooses, it can completely annihilate this country?" asked Dean. "Aggressions cannot be crushed without the employment of the most crushing weapons . . . Russia has the capability today to hurt us badly, and . . . within two years she will have the capability to virtually destroy us if she moves first."

IN OCTOBER 1953, President Dwight D. Eisenhower endorsed National Security Council 162/2, which would become known as the New Look. New Look called for "retaliation" against Soviet hostilities when and where America chose. No longer would American forces try to "contain" the Soviets by meeting aggression where it occurred; rather, New Look called for retaliation at a time and place most suitable to America.

Eisenhower's secretary of state, John Foster Dulles, later explained New Look in a speech: "The way to deter aggression is for the free community to be willing and able to respond vigorously at places and with means of its own choosing." The means, he said, would include "massive retaliatory power."

Dulles's choice of words would quickly morph into a phrase that would join the lexicon of the Cold War: *massive retaliation.*

* * *

THE SECOND SACRED cow to be slaughtered by RAND was LeMay's much-loved wing rotations and the overseas network of air bases in Puerto Rico, England, and Morocco, which now numbered eleven. RAND's Albert Wohlstetter equated the tornado that struck Carswell Air Force Base to a forty-kiloton bomb and came up with the sobering calculation that a surprise attack with just 120 such bombs would "destroy 85 percent of SAC European-based bombers." The overseas bases were rich targets of opportunities and an all-too-obvious weak link in SAC's war plans, thought Wohlstetter, so he took his highly classified calculations to the air force and immediately recommended canceling overseas wing rotations, returning bombers to the U.S. bases, and enclosing U.S. bombers in hardened shelters.

"Piss on shelters," said LeMay. And, he might have added, on Wohlstetter, too. But Wohlstetter's arguments were impossible to dismiss.

It was Colonel Ed Jones who came up with the saving grace. Using aerial tankers, fully loaded B-47s in their Emergency War Plan configuration could launch from the United States, refuel over Iceland, bomb their targets, and then *recover* at the overseas bases. Overseas bases were far from useless, Jones said, they just needed to be used differently. Moreover, by leapfrogging over the forward bases, SAC could reach its target faster, thus slashing the time it would take to strike back.

The idea immediately appealed to LeMay, and in October 1953 he put it into motion. A series of tests called "Quick Strike" were developed. A certain number of SAC bombers would be set aside in a state of readiness that would allow them to take off upon receipt of an execution order. Those bombers would rendezvous with one another, refuel, and proceed to their targets in the Soviet Union.

Using routes within the United States to simulate the strike, the results were near perfect. Bombers could launch from the United States, refuel, bomb Russia, and then with their remaining fuel recover at a base in the United Kingdom or Morocco.

In fact, what Wohlstetter had set in motion was not so much the end of the time-consuming overseas wing rotations but the beginning of an agile, fast-reacting bomber force, a force that General Spaatz had spoken of in 1945, a global force that could within minutes of warning strike anywhere in the world from bases in the United States. "Indeed," wrote an SAC historian, "it was probably one of the most important developments in the ten-year history of the command. It was a harbinger of a new era."

That era would be an era when everything was measured in minutes.

* * *

SAID EISENHOWER: "WHERE these things can be used on strictly military targets and for strictly military purposes, I see no reason why they shouldn't be used exactly as you would use a bullet or anything else."

Eisenhower's "things" were nuclear bombs.

"ALTHOUGH IT WAS often admired, respected, cursed, or even feared," wrote former Strategic Air Command chief of staff Major General Earl G. Peck of the B-47, "it was almost never loved."

To include more takeoffs and landings during a training flight, SAC used a risky maneuver called a "touch-and-go." A touch-and-go required a pilot to land a bomber but rather than come to a stop the pilot would apply full power and promptly take off. The brief contact with the runway would be the moment to transition from one mode of flight to the next, from the landing to the takeoff. To accumulate the required number of monthly takeoffs and landings, it was common for a pilot to end a training mission by flying three or more consecutive touch-and-goes, despite the size of the impressive bomber.

Common, too, were crashes. In 1953, the first year for such statistics, more than half of all the crashes of the new B-47 involved touch-and-goes. One plane dragged a wingtip and exploded, killing the entire crew. Another crashed during takeoff, and a third cartwheeled down the runway in a ball of flames.

Some say Strategic Air Command ushered in the jet age and worked out the bugs of modern jet travel. That may be so. But if they did, they did it the hard way.

ON DECEMBER 8, 1953, President Eisenhower appeared before the General Assembly of the United Nations to talk about the thermonuclear bomb. He said that the hydrogen bomb was so powerful that both the Soviets and the Americans could inflict "hideous damage" on the other even against the best air defenses in the world. Armed with the H-bomb, the two superpowers could "eye each other indefinitely across a trembling world" with weapons that would "annihilate" mankind and condemn it "to begin all over again the age-old struggle upward from savagery toward decency, justice and right."

"No expenditure can guarantee the absolute safety for the cities and citizens of any nation," said Eisenhower, and with only a few of these terrific bombs, "an aggressor's land would be laid waste."

No doubt his words echoed through a chamber silenced to a shocked whisper.

TOWER FOUR

A SOVIET BOMBER force could theoretically loiter out of radar range in the Atlantic Ocean before turning inward to strike Washington, D.C., or New York City. This gap was compounded by radar's perplexing line-of-sight limitation, which bedeviled the scientists. Radar stations on the East Coast could detect aircraft flying at high altitudes an hour or more before they penetrated the defenses but were largely blind to low-flying aircraft until minutes before they appeared.

In the summer of 1952, the United States Air Force commissioned the Lincoln Radiation Laboratories at the Massachusetts Institute of Technology to study this gap. Their report, titled "Preliminary Report on the Substitution of Off-Shore Towers for Picket Vessels in the Continental Air Defense System," concluded that a necklacelike chain of stations positioned in the Atlantic Ocean would provide as much as thirty minutes' extra warning and that placing stations there was not only feasible but practical and desirable.

MIT called these radar stations the Seaward Extension of the Contiguous Continental Radar Coverage network. The Seaward Extension would use oil rig–like structures as platforms, on top of which would be placed fully equipped radar stations. They would be called Texas Towers. Each tower would be located eighty to one hundred miles offshore. Two of the platforms would stand in waters that were between 60 and 90 feet deep; one would be at a depth of 185 feet.

On January 11, 1954, the United States Air Force formally approved the plan and appropriated funding in the amount of $30 million. The United States Navy Civil Engineering Corps, First Naval District, Boston, was selected to build it. Because nothing like it had ever been built in the Atlantic, the first $150,000 was earmarked for a design study.

The air force was curious, as was the navy, as to exactly what sort of tower might survive in the waters of the Atlantic.

*   *   *

THEODORE KUSS HAD a remarkable understanding of hydraulics. Kuss had been an engineer for the Pacific Bridge Company, which stood at the edge of San Francisco Bay and, against impossible odds, built the Golden Gate Bridge. In 1949, Kuss joined with Ralph Denton Russell of Oakland, California, to place in the Office of Patents and Trademarks patent application number 2,586,966, titled "Deep Water Oil Well Drilling System." This system employed a method of constructing an oil rig on its side, towing it out to sea, then upending it on site, using a complicated system of chambers and valves to flood the legs with water. Hydraulics.

In Kuss's vision, oil rigs would in time go out into ever deeper waters and that would be problematic. Because it was industry practice to erect a rig in the upright position and tow it out to sea, and because most shipyards were in ports that had drafts of fifty feet or less, deep-water rigs would have to be constructed differently. Kuss's solution was to build the rig on its side, then, at sea, tip it over. The tip-over method of erection, as it would be called, was at the heart of his patent.

The Kuss patent was issued on February 26, 1952.

There were no immediate takers.

ON MARCH 23, 1954, the navy's First Naval District in Boston began meetings with heavy-construction outfits to discuss the Texas Towers. The navy had been appointed to oversea the design and construction and one of the first calls they made was to the engineering firm of the Anderson-Nichols Company of Boston. Anderson-Nichols promptly contacted the foremost firm for foundations, Moran, Proctor, Mueser & Rutledge of New York. They met the following day and agreed to team up for the work. Moran, Proctor would design the foundation. Anderson-Nichols would design the legs and the platform.

On March 29, 1954, they met with navy captain John J. Albers.

CAPTAIN JOHN J. Albers of the United States Navy's Civil Engineering Corps and the officer in charge of construction for the Texas Towers was a 1933 graduate of Vanderbilt University and a well-regarded civil engineer. Albers's career spanned more than twenty years, during which he had built piers, dry docks, breakwaters, quay walls, and other marine projects.

A rigid, serious person, Albers had a penchant for sweeping generalizations and an air of superiority that sometimes grated on those around him. When answering questions before a Senate investigating committee, Albers sat ramrod straight and in the tone of a schoolmarm addressing her children told the senators what they should think of the Tower Four disaster. "These towers were the first structures ever built in the open ocean anywhere and very little reliable data existed at that time on wave heights and wave forces to be expected at sea," said Albers. "I trust we can establish to the satisfaction of all concerned that the tragic loss of Texas Tower Number Four was more an act of God than of man."

It was not the kind of remark that made friends on an investigating committee that convened largely under the preassumption that the tragedy had not been an act of God.

CAPTAIN ALBERS CONTRACTED with the Woods Hole Oceanographic Institution of Woods Hole, Massachusetts, to project the maximum wave heights and winds that the Texas Towers would face at their respective positions in the Atlantic Ocean. More important, they were asked the question that bedeviled the offshore-oil industry—how high should the platform be elevated above the sea to provide for safe passage of the largest wave?

Woods Hole hindcast a peak wind velocity of 128 miles per hour, this occurring during the hurricane of 1938, and a peak wave height of sixty-six feet, which occurred during a nor'easter in 1945. Woods Hole then calculated that one wave in a thousand would be larger than the peak hindcast wave by a factor of 150 percent. In other words, in a train of one thousand waves sixty-six feet high, one wave would build to a height of ninety-nine feet—the extreme wave. Because height is measured from the crest of the wave to the trough, and because 40 percent of a wave is below sea level and 60 percent is above sea level, the twenty-year wave event for Tower Four would be a ninety-nine-foot wave, just over sixty feet of which would be above sea level.

Concluded Woods Hole, adding in a few feet for the tides: "If the bottom of the platform is at an elevation of 67 feet, a 6.5 foot clearance of such a wave is provided."

ON JANUARY 24, 1955, the navy forwarded to Bretschneider/Reid a copy of their nearly completed "Feasibility Report on Texas Towers."

Professors Charles Bretschneider and Robert Reid manipulated the Woods Hole data and came up with an entirely different set of predictions, which they presented to Captain Albers. "We feel the design wave heights are somewhat low for the possible storm conditions which may be encountered off the East Coast. Mr. Bretschneider has made some comparison computations of heights using the same storm data given in [your report] . . . It shows that one wave out of the whole train of waves will attain a height of 133 feet." Bretschneider/Reid concluded that the base of Tower Four's platform had to be elevated not sixty-seven feet above the waterline but seventy-two to eighty-one feet above the waterline.

But that wasn't all. Bretschneider and Reid were concerned about the slope of the ocean bottom and the possibility of a shoaling wave. Farther out to sea, the ocean plunged into the 5,000-foot-deep Hatteras Trench. A sine wave that formed over the trench would encounter the shallow waters along Unnamed Shoal, Tower Four's location on the Continental Slope. As the bottom of that wave started to drag on the shoal, the top of it would push forward, causing the surface waters to back up. As surface waters backed up, a wave would begin to rise. The ideal conditions for a large shoaling wave were the exact features of the Tower Four site—a gradual rise in the seabed and an ocean depth of between 170 and 190 feet.

To eliminate the possibility of a shoaling wave, the Texas professors recommended that the navy move the tower back to shallower waters. Tower Four, they said, should be confined to "depths much less than 170 feet" to avoid "extremely large waves."

A less-receptive audience could scarcely be imagined. Albers rejected the Bretschneider/Reid recommendations out of hand. "Previous experience with offshore oil drilling platforms in the Gulf of Mexico was of limited value, due to the much more severe wave conditions expected in the Atlantic," sniffed Albers.

And that was that.

MORAN, PROCTOR, MUESER & Rutledge was founded in 1910 by Daniel Moran, a turn-of-the-century Columbia University graduate who was fascinated by the problems of building the foundations for bridges and buildings in "unsuitable soils," as he termed it. Observing that most great cities were built along waterways, which were, in general, unsuitable soils, Moran devised more than twenty patented approaches to laying foundations in almost any geologic condition. Indeed, Moran's firm engineered the foundations of many of the landmark buildings in New York City—"the man who made the skyline of New York City," as one accolade gushed—and his company grew in stature and in revenue.

KUSS READ ABOUT the Texas Towers and the impossible depth of 185 feet for Tower Four. Associated with the project was a navy officer he knew from years earlier, Captain Albers.

Kuss and Albers visited in Albers's office.

A few days later, Kuss was hired by the architecture-engineering firm of Moran, Proctor, Mueser & Rutledge.

ON JUNE 18, 1954, Albers selected the architecture-engineering firm Moran, Proctor, Mueser & Rutledge of New York and Anderson-Nichols Company of Boston to conduct a feasibility study in matters related to the building of the Texas Towers. Moran, Proctor would examine the caissons—the underwater foundations for the legs—while Anderson-Nichols would focus on the legs and the platform itself. That plan changed on July 22, 1954, when Albers called the two firms into his office and notified them that he wished Anderson-Nichols to focus on the platform while Moran, Proctor would examine not just the foundation, for which they had specific expertise, but the entire underwater structure, for which they had none.

What they did have was Kuss. And a patent.

THE FIRST REQUIREMENT for the Texas Towers was that they be equipped more or less as any radar station would be—with one long-range radar antenna and two height-finding radar antennas enclosed by round weather domes 55 feet in diameter called radomes. The three radomes would be on a straight line, which meant that the platforms had to have a lengthwise dimension of at least 165 feet. Because for any given surface area a triangle has the longest sides, this favored a three-legged platform in the shape of an equilateral triangle.

The three-legged idea, however, met with resistance. When presented with the plans, the air force objected and asked for extra legs as a measure of safety. Moran, Proctor seemed to agree. The auxiliary legs would enhance safety, albeit at an overall increase in the cost of the project, and for that reason it was rejected. According to notes from a meeting in 1954: "The degree of increase of safety which is provided by a system of four supports . . . is not considered to be worth the additional cost to provide it."

The Texas Tower radar stations would be three-legged structures; Tower Four would require legs longer than any yet used in the offshore-oil industry, and so it would be built on its side and towed out to sea, where it would be tipped over, using Kuss's patent.

The one limiting factor to Kuss's patent, however, was that to tip a tower over, that tower had to have *precisely* three legs.

WEATHER ISLAND

THE BOW OF the USS *Curtis* sliced through the water as she made her way across San Francisco Bay and passed beneath the Golden Gate Bridge. The first wispy tendrils of fog reached in from the west; the afternoon air was redolent of salt water.

On either side of the *Curtis* were 68-foot cutters from the United States Coast Guard, each with a single five-inch gun mounted on the foc'sle manned by an enlisted man wearing a combat helmet and a flak vest. Although the *Curtis* was a navy ship and capable of defending herself, this was not an ordinary voyage, nor were her magazines filled with ordinary munitions. Two days earlier, three motor convoys bristling with machine gun–clad guards had arrived at the docks at Port Chicago U.S. Naval Magazine, California, from Los Alamos, New Mexico, and unloaded crates stenciled TOP SECRET.

In those crates were the components for seven thermonuclear bombs, including one that if tested correctly would become the first air-transportable hydrogen bomb for Strategic Air Command.

Two miles offshore, the ships came abeam the harbor light and the cutters turned back. As they did, navy destroyers slipped into their places. With signal lights stuttering instructions from one ship to the other, they fanned out into a defensive formation called a bent-line antisubmarine screen, and got under way. They steamed south for two hours as a diversionary measure, then turned west, setting a course for Oahu, Hawaii. Their orders were to run silent and, at night, blacked out.

It was January 10, 1954.

So began the movement of nuclear weapons to the Pacific for a series of nuclear explosions that would be known as Operation Castle.

TINKER AIR FORCE Base, Oklahoma, was home to an elite corps of mobile weathermen known as Weather Reporting Element (Provisional) 236, or WREP-236. WREP-236 was trained to build and operate weather stations from scratch anywhere in the world. When they deployed, they were entirely self-sufficient. They carried every nail, every plank of wood, every piece of wire and cable, every balloon, every refrigerator, and every knife, fork, and spoon necessary to build a station from raw dirt, and man it twenty-four hours a day.

The commanding officer of 236 was Warrant Officer Junior Grade John Kapral. A tall, quiet, unassuming man, Kapral graduated from the air corps' weather training program in the late 1930s and immediately deployed to build weather stations in New Guinea and then in Curaçao before joining the war effort in England, where he built and staffed a half-dozen more. When World War II ended, Kapral returned to Oklahoma to command a section of air force weather stations that operated in Oklahoma and Texas. His crews consistently received the highest marks and Kapral was soon moved to the mobile detachment.

In October 1953, Kapral's squadron was assigned to Operation Castle and given the responsibility to build a weather station on the Pacific island of Rongerik. "We knew we were going somewhere important," remembered Kapral. "We got the best equipment the Air Force had."

On Christmas Day 1953, Kapral led his men across the rain-slick tarmac at Tinker Air Force Base, Oklahoma, to three fully packed C-54 cargo planes. As the last cigarette was flicked off into the darkness, the men, many of them little more than twenty years old, climbed into the transport and flopped into mesh rigging that would be their home for the next three days.

CORPORAL ROBERT BALL, a twenty-five-year-old from West Hartford, Connecticut, was called back to duty from the air force reserves to serve with the military police. He reported to McGuire Air Force Base, New Jersey, where he was told to take command of an eight-man police detail in Hawaii. When he arrived at Hickham AFB, he found that his orders had been changed. He and his command were going instead to the island of Enyu, located at the end of the deep-water channel markers inside Bikini lagoon. Ball had been assigned to Operation Castle.

"I was tasked with the job of taking Drs. Teller and von Braun around when they would come to the islands, as well as General Groves, which was quite interesting," Ball said, referring to Edwin Teller, the father of the hydrogen bomb, Wernher von Braun, the rocket scientist, and General Leslie Groves, the man who had headed the Manhattan Project. One day Ball was escorting his scientists around the other island of Namu, where the first bomb, Bravo, would be exploded. Teller landed at the site and walked across the sand to where Ball was sitting. "He laughed and said to me, 'Do you know what you are sitting on?'"

"I said, 'no.'"

"He said it was the nuclear bomb."

JOHN C. CLARK, PhD, a scientist from the nuclear labs in Los Alamos, New Mexico, was a specialist in detonation phenomena. Having been hand-picked to join the Manhattan Project in 1943, Clark had led the firing party for almost every atomic bomb detonated since the end of World War II. It was a job he did with remarkable ease. In the dark of night, he climbed steel towers to disarm bombs that hadn't exploded, no doubt an unnerving thing to do, not that Clark thought anything about it. Not only did he understand the physics of these weapons, he knew how they exploded and what made them work and what made them fizzle. He was comfortable around bombs and it was something you could see in his walk and in his posture. A photographer captured this aspect of him in a 1950s publicity still, a rarity in the secret world of nuclear testing. He is dressed in a short-sleeved white shirt, open at the neck, with an undershirt on. He has his glasses on, black frames, and in his left hand he is holding the wand of a Geiger counter. Yielding perhaps to a bit of theatrics, his brow is deeply furrowed as he "listens" to the chirps coming through the headphones clasped over his ears. The sense of this photograph is unmistakable—that America need not worry; that knowledgable, intelligent men like Clark were standing on the ramparts of the nuclear age, men who had subdued the atomic beast, scientists who had tamed the bomb.

Not to say that this was unjustified. Quite the contrary. None of the cataclysmic predictions made by the Franck committee had come home to roost—*"with no other invention of mankind have the consequences of misuse been so dire!"* (emphasis mine). There had been no accidents, no unexpected explosions; the fear of nuclear weapons had given way to a feeling of comfort and familiarity. In 1953, the ridge along Frenchman Flat had been lined shoulder-to-shoulder with camera crews and reporters and grip trucks and tall dishes on spindly legs for a live broadcast of a test bomb. *Boom!* The fireball ripped through the dark sky and sprung off the desert floor, and in less than twenty seconds the hot-white burst of color drained from the sky and the unmistakable icon of the atomic age emerged—the mushroom cloud—and it was instantly beamed into millions of homes. Mothers and fathers and sons and daughters marveled at this thing on their television sets.

Even Walter Cronkite fumbled for superlatives. Scientists had such *control.*

* * *

MAJOR GENERAL PERCY W. Clarkson, United States Army, commander of Operation Ivy, was named the commanding general of Operation Castle. General Clarkson sent Strategic Air Command commander in chief General Curtis LeMay an invitation to observe the blasts. "SAC has a special interest in our operations and thus warrants any courtesies we are able to extend . . ." wrote Clarkson, referring to SAC's air atomic mission. "If you do come to see us, be sure to bring your skeet gun. I can't guarantee to shoot up to your high standard, but I am sure you would enjoy trying out our ranges at Enewetak."

LeMay, ever on a war footing, declined.

AS 1953 BECAME 1954, almost ten thousand people began moving to the Pacific Proving Grounds for Operation Castle. Soldiers, sailors, airmen, and marines would come from nearly every state in the union and with every rank represented from private to general, from seaman to admiral. The navy sailed thirty-four ships to the Pacific, including the *Curtis* and aircraft carrier the USS *Bairoko*. The air force flew out seventy-two airplanes, including bombers that would photograph the explosions, fighter jets that would collect cloud samples, converted B-29s that would track the movement of the mushroom clouds, and specially instrumented bombers that would be subjected to the blast and heat of a bomb to determine the distance necessary to prevent the blast of one bomb from destroying the aircraft behind it.

Inside the test site, security was high and breeches were not tolerated. Kapral and WREP-236 disembarked from their cargo plane and were promptly escorted to a briefing room next to the runway. WHAT YOU HEAR HERE, STAYS HERE, said a sign on the wall. As the humidity soaked their shirts with sweat, a guard began talking. "He told us about security and not taking pictures or even writing about anything in our personal journals, or be court-martialed," remembered one airman. "We were plenty put in our places." Their duffel bags were emptied and inspected top to bottom. The heels of their shoes were inspected, their carry-on kits and toilet kits were opened and spread out—even the toothpaste was pressed to see if it was real.

Everyone wore an official badge and movement within the test site was impossible without one. A group of replacements from the navy arrived to catch their ship but they had no badges. "They were placed under restraint, interrogated, and finally escorted to the boat landing for further transfer to their ships," said the incident report.

Three fighter pilots attached to the *Bairoko* made an impromptu landing on Bikini Atoll. It made no difference that each wore a flight suit with a squadron patch on the breast and an American flag on the shoulder. "When these aircraft landed on Bikini, the pilots were immediately challenged by the sentries and held until identified. They were finally permitted to proceed by boat to the *Bairoko,* but at the same time they were told not to return to the airstrip [for their planes] until they were properly badged."

Such an undertaking would produce tens of thousands of pages of documents, yet no matter which group issued the report—army, navy, or air force—and no matter how unrelated the topic might be, all reports would have one theme in common.

Contamination. And a hairy-chested attitude toward it.

BLUNT FORCE

THE HYDROGEN BOMB seemed to be on everyone's mind. Lewis L. Strauss, chairman of the U.S. Atomic Energy Commission, answered questions from reporters.

> **REPORTER:** Many people in Congress, I think many elsewhere, have been reaching out and grasping for some information as to what happens when the H-bomb goes off . . .
>
> **STRAUSS:** Well, the nature of an H-bomb is that, in effect, it can be made to be as large as you wish, as large as the military requirement demands, that is to say, an H-bomb can be made as—large enough to take out a city.
>
> **CHORUS:** What?
>
> **STRAUSS:** To take out a city, to destroy a city.
>
> **A REPORTER:** How big a city?
>
> **STRAUSS:** Any city.
>
> **REPORTER:** Any city? New York?
>
> **STRAUSS:** The metropolitan area, yes [i.e., the heart of Manhattan, as he later elaborated].

BY 1954, AVIATSIYA Delnevo Deyst-viya, better known to American fighter pilots as the Soviet Union Strategic Air Command, or, SUSAC, but formally known as the Soviet Long-Range Aviation Force, was thought to have more than twelve hundred bombers at air bases around the rim of the Soviet Union. SUSAC pilots were well trained in air-to-air refueling, global navigation, instrument flying, and precision bombing. Moreover, they were training in airspace that was uncomfortably close to our own. Said a Strategic Air Command historian: "Observations of Soviet maneuvers both in the Arctic and elsewhere revealed that by an extension of their maneuver pattern their attack capability could be expanded to the point where the United States could be dealt a fatal blow."

It was the sort of language that kept SAC on their toes.

ON FEBRUARY 24, 1954, President Eisenhower approved the construction of the Distant Early Warning line of radar stations, a chain of sixty-three radar stations impossibly clawed out of the frozen tundra two hundred miles north of the arctic circle in a line thirty-two hundred miles long, beginning at Point Barrows, Alaska, and ending at Baffin Island, Greenland. The main contractor for the DEW line would be the Western Electric division of Bell Labs. Under Western Electric's supervision, more than forty-six hundred companies would be employed to build the roads, foundations, stanchions, buildings, water service, heating plants, roads, and airfields. Each station would be a self-sustaining city complete with its own power plants, water supplies, food and fuels stores, and even libations for the men.

Said Air Defense Command, in words that were no doubt music to LeMay's ears: ". . . we believe that our primary mission in the Air Defense Command is to defend the bases from which Strategic Air Command is going to operate."

A NUCLEAR-WEAPONS SPECIALIST at a nuclear weapons storage site remembers: "The security during the movement of the weapons to and from SAC was very high, as you can imagine. Every vehicle carrying or pulling a weapon had a driver and an armed guard. There were armed guards lining the convoy route as well, and on both sides of the road. The SAC Air Police were not allowed near our convoy until it reached a certain point. At that point, our Air Police stood back and SAC took over.

"Our police waited there for the empty vehicles to return and they would then accompany them back to Stony Brook. They were given instructions that no one other than Stony Brook vehicles, personnel and Air Police were allowed beyond a certain point on the route back to our gates—not one of the SAC personnel was allowed near Stony Brook, unless accompanied by our people."

One of the bomb carriers was a four-legged mechanical crawler built for the lumber industry called a "straddle carrier." This carrier straddled a ten-thousand-pound bomb and lifted it up as if it were a mere feather.

Stony Brook Air Force Station was located inside SAC's Westover Air Force

Base, in Massachusetts, but they were worlds apart. Some might say that the men on the two bases treated one another like wary strangers walking down a dark street on the wrong side of town.

IN ELEMENTARY SCHOOLS and in high schools, teachers conducted "duck-and-cover" drills and admonished their students not to look at the flash. Office buildings were surveyed, and those with deep basements were designated public fallout shelters; yellow-and-black signs were affixed to their sides. The Civil Defense Administration distributed air-raid sirens and the wail of a test became commonplace at noon. In countless cities, exhibits were erected in town squares displaying various types of home fallout shelters, most with build-it-yourself instructions printed on pamphlets that were passed around freely by men and women wearing armbands and hardhats that said "CD."

IN 1954, IT became official SAC policy that no more than forty-five B-47 bombers or fifteen B-52 bombers could be permanently positioned at any one base. The concept of dispersal as a passive means of protecting SAC's bombers was now in effect. Said an air force historian: "Dispersing the deterrent force throughout the United States [would] create more targets than the Soviets had the means to destroy." Another explained it this way: "[Dispersal] would also force the enemy's aircraft, during an attack, to fan out, thereby making them more vulnerable to defending fighter aircraft."

But there was more to it than complicating the enemy's efforts. "Widespread dispersal of SAC must be considered in the light of two considerations," said a memorandum for the secretary of defense. "Dispersal as a passive measure, and dispersal as a measure to get a larger number of aircraft in the air within a shorter period of time."

Said differently, more runways meant more takeoffs, which meant more bombers in the air faster.

And "faster" had become SAC's mantra.

WHILE IT WAS widely held that the United States would never launch a first strike, the circumstances behind a decision to launch a retaliatory strike might arguably include misreading an enemy's actions—a mistake, as it were. That such a thing might happen was hardly imaginable, but in those time-compressed moments when decisions had to be made, such mistakes have happened, notably during World War II. "Although Germany bombed London before Britain bombed Berlin, Germany stumbled its way into the bombing of

London," wrote RAND analyst Carl Builder. It happened on the night of August 24, 1940. Flying through the fog and clouds over England, two German bombers were separated from their radar-equipped pathfinder guiding them toward a target in the Midlands north of London. Unable to regroup, they meandered through the sky until they attracted antiaircraft fire from the ground. Knowing that they were hopelessly lost, they jettisoned their bombs and turned for home.

As things happened, the pilots were over London and the bombs did incredible damage. One bomb hit a national monument, one exploded on a church, another killed civilians coming out of a late-night movie, and more.

Retaliation was nearly instant.

Wrote Leonard Mosley in *The Battle of Britain*: "Churchill ordered Bomber Command to attack Berlin as a reprisal, which in turn provoked Hitler to order that London should now become his air force's main target."

By accident.

BOMBS CONTINUED TO move onto military bases. Said a formerly classified Strategic Air Command history: "SAC did not attain the bombs-on-base for all of its bomber force until late 1956," but the first bombs began to arrive in 1954. To qualify for bombs-on-base, Strategic Air Command had to demonstrate that its men were trained, that the bases had hardened storage facilities, that there were weapons-maintenance facilities, weapons load-and-unload-training protocols, and the attendant equipment necessary to store and maintain atomic bombs.

The first bases to receive additional weapons were overseas. In April 1954, President Eisenhower authorized the dispersal of 183 nuclear and nonnuclear components to air bases in the United Kingdom, Germany, and Morocco. In May, the president authorized the release of nuclear capsules for the atomic warheads on the Regulus guided missiles carried by four navy cruisers and two navy submarines.

In June, Eisenhower approved a memo recommending that Strategic Air Command be allowed to maneuver with complete bombs, meaning bombs with capsules, on all SAC bombers. In December, he approved bombs-on-base storage of complete weapons at twenty-two more air bases and stated that he expected to authorize more capsules for submarine fleets and air-defense installations.

Eisenhower then made a far-reaching decision and added the twenty-thousand-pound thermonuclear hydrogen bombs to his approvals and notified the Joint Chiefs of that on December 6. On December 16, the secretary of defense was provided a summary of the locations of thermonuclear bombs with respect to SAC bases, suggesting that by at least this date some of the early hydrogen bombs were already under military control.

ATOMIC WEAPONS REQUIRED regular cleaning, which forced technicians to literally reach inside a nuclear bomb. One technician remembered: "Inspection and cleaning of the pit areas of the weapons were done in the Mechanical Bay using latex gloves, a flashlight, a mirror, Kimwipes and trichlor [trichloroethylene]. A visual inspection was conducted first with the flashlight and mirror by looking through the IFI [In-Flight Insertion] tube. The pit was then wiped down with Kimwipes and trichlor. The most difficult part of this process was trying to reach the back part of the pit. With the MK-6 the entire arm of the specialist was inside the pit, and the specialist's head was pressed again the High Explosive [HE] sphere and a detonator."

An entire arm.

SAID *THE NEW York Times*: "Europe's reaction to the United States' decision to go ahead with production of the hydrogen bomb was a mingling of hope that the existence of the terrible weapon would frighten the world into peace and fear that it would lead to the destruction of civilization."

THE ARTICLE'S AUTHOR wrote with near-breathless enthusiasm, such was the sheer *size* of SAC: "The Strategic Air Command represented a direct fixed capital investment upwards of an estimated 8.5 billion dollars, and this sum considered only the cost of its aircraft and installations. The largest industrial corporation in the United States was Standard Oil of New Jersey which represented a 4.5 billion dollar fixed capital investment. The Strategic Air Command's 185,000 personnel . . . compared favorably with Standard Oil of New Jersey's 119,000 personnel . . ."

While in another era such comparisons might be used to buttress a cry to bring military spending to a halt, this was 1954 and such comparisons were greeted with relief.

IT WAS ONE thing to be a pilot and quite another to be a Strategic Air Command pilot. SAC pilots wore silk ascots and white dickeys and lived by rules different from those of the rest of the air force. SAC trained more, subjected their men to more tests, busted rank and spot promoted, but also had their own lines for meals and their own checkout lanes in the base exchange. In a word,

SAC had *swagger*. Strategic Air Command was the service young boys dreamed of when they dreamed of silver birds in the sky. SAC was loved by the media, was exceptionally well funded by Congress, and had the best facilities with the latest aircraft and did things *right*.

Basking in the glow of this celebrity was Strategic Air Command's MacDill Air Force Base, in Tampa, Florida. In 1954, so the records show, social visits were paid on MacDill by Charles A. Lindbergh, the Duke of Windsor, and the air marshal for Turkey. The base even participated in the filming of the movie *Strategic Air Command* by Paramount Pictures, starring Jimmy Stewart. In one scene, a bomber boldly banks away from the camera and sun glints off the white underbelly to the sound of music so stirring that viewers would most certainly find a small tear in their eye. The movie was nominated for an Oscar and the stars proudly walked the red carpet dressed in their finest.

Such was Strategic Air Command.

RADAR DATA MOVED about Air Defense Command and SAC to an almost endless number of end users. In the Regional Direction Centers, large Plexiglas plotting boards were used to update the air-traffic situation. So as to not stand in anyone's way, women worked from the back on ladders and with grease pens. New aircraft and new positions were marked with precision. Women were particularly talented at this, as one report indicated: they were proficient at writing backward.

SAID FORMER AIR force general David A. Burchinal, a veteran of Strategic Air Command: ". . . military force is a pretty damn blunt instrument. You use it for maximum shock effect—hard, fast, and continuous—and get the job done."

Blunt.

THE QUICK STRIKE concept was tested throughout the year with ever improving results. Tests concluded that bombers from all of SAC's U.S. bases could take off, refuel in the air, and fly a mission that represented the distance they would have to fly to bomb their Soviet target and reach their designated recovery base in England or Morocco.

The airmen were enthusiastic and suggestions poured in. A quick-strike bomber could be airborne in less than six hours, but half that time was spent loading the bomb, one person noted. The suggestion was made to preload the bombers with bombs and place the bombers in special "ready" hangars guarded by armed soldiers. These "ready" bombers, as they would be called, could be airborne in just an hour.

Ever faster ticked the beat of the metronome that set SAC's battle rhythm, faster and faster and faster.

WROTE *TIME* MAGAZINE: "Air Defense Command is ready every minute of the day and night. Its radar and interceptors could make the difference between life and sudden death for millions of Americans and perhaps for itself."

It was December 1954.

"MY PARENTS BUILT a fallout shelter," remembered a woman who grew up during the Cold War. "That's where I picked up the fear."

Said another: "My mother put shoes and socks at the edge of my bed so we'd be prepared to run somewhere fast."

A CLASSIFIED 1954 briefing by Strategic Air Command laid out the latest version of the war plan. The new plan called for 750 bombs to be dropped on 118 Soviet cities and 409 airfields with exact targets selected from a target data inventory of seventeen hundred potential ground zeros.

The attack was described by an attendee: "It was estimated that SAC could lay down an attack under these conditions of 600–750 bombs by approaching Russia from many directions so as to hit their early warning system simultaneously. It would be about two hours from this moment until bombs had been dropped by using a bomb-as-you-go system in which . . . targets would be hit as they reached them. This part of the briefing was skillfully done by showing successive charts of Europe using one-half-hour intervals after SAC bombers first hit the Russian early warning screen. Many heavy lines, one representing each wing, were shown progressively converging on the heart of Russia with pretty stars to indicate the many bombs dropped on DGZs. The final impression was that virtually all of Russia would be nothing but a smoking, radiating ruin at the end of two hours."

Of course, the United States would attack only after being attacked first, which meant, as author Jonathan Schell put it, that the United States was itself "on its way to becoming a radioactive desert," with the vast majority of its population dead or dying, its cities disfigured and unrecognizable. Thus, it would inevitably be the case that the weapons delivered according to SAC's plan would be ordered by "leaders of nobody, living in underground shelters or in 'doomsday' planes that could not land . . . with no nation to defend."

EVEN THE CANADIANS expected to use atomic weapons, at least in air defense to destroy Soviet bombers, or so said an internal memorandum from the Canadian undersecretary of state, External Affairs. "The only way of obtaining a sufficiently high attrition rate at a cost which would be within the bounds of reason is for our continental defence forces to use atomic weapons against enemy aircraft. The primary weapons would be air-to-air missiles armed with atomic warheads. They would be carried by our long-range interceptors and fired at the enemy while he was over the uninhabited parts of the continent [i.e., Canada] and over the ocean approaches. The development of these weapons is already in hand and will be pressed forward as rapidly as possible. It is expected that they will come into service in the autumn of 1956."

General Herbert B. Thatcher of Air Defense Command was more succinct: "We seek an enemy kill as far from our shores as possible."

AS 1954 CAME to a close, Strategic Air Command had 1,765 bombers and tankers on thirty air bases in the United States and eleven overseas.

The nuclear weapons' stockpiles brimmed with 2,063 bombs, of which 167 were under the control of the military. The Soviets had 150 atomic bombs.

A new term appeared this year and it, too, related to the bomb, a term that described a phenomenon that the scientists at Los Alamos certainly hoped to avoid. It was a bomb that underwent an unexpected chain reaction and over-exploded, a "runaway bomb" as it was called. Nineteen fifty-four would be the year of the runaway.

THE ROCK

THE PERMANENT HEADQUARTERS for Operation Castle was a cluster of buildings on the island of Enewetak in Enewetak Atoll, which was some 180 miles west of Bikini Atoll, 300 miles northwest of Kwajalein and more than 1,000 miles into the western Pacific from Hawaii. Enewetak a thin, teardrop-shaped island of just 2.4 square miles, sat at the southern entrance to the Pacific atoll, cleaving a neat divide between the ocean and the lagoon. On one side giant combers crashed headlong into the exposed coral and gnarled roots of the rugged shoreline, while on the other side, the lagoon side, the waters were calm, the navy ships were at anchor, and the light sparkled as it reflected off the ocean.

Airman Paul Sulky remembered his first trip to Enewetak: "I thought of swinging palm trees and maidens with swaying hips. When I got to Enewetak, gee whiz, it looked like a regular air force base." The southern half of Enewetak was given over to a 140-foot-wide runway 7,000 feet long that ran from the seawall to the middle of the island. Around it were the control tower, the navy pier, maintenance sheds and hangars, and the tie-down ramps for as many as sixty airplanes, including those as large as SAC's B-36. On the opposite end of the island were living and working quarters, including forty-foot-long command buildings, depots, and a web of power lines and phone wires running in nearly every direction. The coast guard marked the entrance to their small headquarters with an anchor flanked by two large conch shells. The army placed a pair of 105-millimeter guns in the sand that was their front yard. The Radiation Safety offices built a clever sign with the symbol of the atom swirling beneath the words RADIATION SAFETY COMMAND.

Those who went to the Marshall Islands remembered the stifling heat and the constant winds. "The dust was always kicked up by the trade winds," remembered Harold Wainstock, a weatherman during the test. "Salt spray settled on everything and collected the dust making a thin scum on everything." Said Seaman Jack Seaman, twenty: "During our morning wake call they would say 'the temp is 90 something and the humidity is 90 something.' Most all of us suffered from heat rash and nothing would heal with all the humidity."

While rain and humidity were a near constant, the recreational facilities were plentiful and the food was almost universally loved. According to one airman: "There were all-you-could-eat bacon, eggs, toast and hash browns at midnight chow." An air force MP agreed: "There was steak night three times a week, with lines for rare, medium, and well done—as many steaks as you wanted; six or seven different styles of potatoes, the same for fresh vegetables, and a dessert line that would knock your eyes out! At the bars, any beer from around the world was ten-cents a bottle, while any of the rarer whiskeys were 25-cents a shot!"

There was a hobby shop, a skeet range, an officers' club on the south beach, three baseball fields (one called Pershing Field, after the famous army commander General John "Black Jack" Pershing), a chapel, a movie hall with no roof—aptly called the Starlight Theatre—a bakery, an NCO club, and, the most popular spot of them all, Dutch's Tavern. Said an airman who was barracked on Enewetak during the tests: "Dutch's endeared itself to us all with two for one nights, half price drink nights so you couldn't afford not to pass an evening or two with your peers. The outdoor movie again was a very economical event, since it was free. I spent many a night sitting watching a movie in the rain and drying my body at Dutch's after the show."

But there was more to it than Dutch's and the Starlight and good meals for soldiers so far from home. "It was a different time," said Bernie Wynn, an airman. "Young airmen didn't question anything, we griped about things, but we did what we had to do. I guess you can say that we were very trusting of our superiors in 1954."

And then they would experience Bravo.

And in a blink of light, a poorly calculated risk their superiors would take would change their world.

UNITED STATES NAVY ship LST 551 rocked against her cleated lines alongside the Enewetak pier. Sailors in shorts and sweat-stained shirts drove forklifts up and down the ramps of 551, loading her holds with crates, lumber, radio gear, prefabricated building parts, tarps, tents, desalinization gear, refrigerators, generators, one bulldozer, one forklift, and one portable radio. Lieutenant Don Kanzenbach, 551's captain, watched with an appraising eye. Kanzenbach had sailed 551 from Norfolk, Virginia, a voyage that crossed the Gulf of Mexico, then passed through the Panama Canal and headed out in to the Pacific Ocean. He docked briefly at Pearl Harbor for some repairs.

On January 9, 1954, Warrant Officer Kapral and his men boarded Kanzenbach's landing ship for the final leg of their journey, a voyage of more than four hundred miles in length almost due east across the open ocean to the uninhabited island of Rongerik. There they would land and for two days the crew would unload their freight.

After a rough start, Kapral had an operating weather station sending data to the command post on Enewetak. Four times a day his men would release weather balloons that would soar seventy thousand feet or more into the atmosphere. Four times a day a radio tethered to the instruments would broadcast back data that Kapral's men would reduce to generate charts that showed the direction and speed of the winds aloft. Four times a day they sent those data, and at the end of each day they would gather for food in the mess hall, play cards, or, as the day turned into an ink-black night, watch a movie.

AS MORNING DAWNED on February 28, Bikini lagoon was a swirl of activity. Ships cut across the wind-whipped waves, their bows frothy with explosions of white water as they made their way to and from the islands to pick up groups of men and bring them alongside the ships. Above them, helicopters beat through the sky, moving one group here, checking one experiment there. It was noisy and boisterous, the skies were brilliant, the ocean was royal blue, and there was electricity in the air, a sense of moment. In mere hours the Bravo bomb would be exploded and now some fourteen hundred men were being evacuated. Shouts rang out, radios crackled to life, and lines formed on beaches as D-day minus 1 got under way. Three hundred men boarded the aircraft carrier USS *Bairoko,* another 175 were taken on the USS *Belle Grove*; 235 men were assigned to the seaplane tender USS *Curtis,* while another 450 boarded the USS *Ainsworth,* which, said the navy, had the "best large scale living facilities of any ship in the task group."

The USS *Curtis* was the first to weigh anchor, slipping through Bikini channel at 1:30 P.M. The *Belle Grove* was next, taking on her last boat and easing through the channel at 2:30 P.M. Both ships rounded the mouth of the atoll and made their way south into the Pacific, where some thirty miles from ground zero they joined the navy destroyer USS *Estes,* which was the command ship. There, this cluster of navy ships would watch the predawn detonation and, so the plans said, return to the lagoon later in the day.

Bravo would be exploded the next morning, March 1, 1954.

* * *

"MOST OF THE work in an atomic test can be done by automation," said John Clark, head of the Bravo firing party, "but for all the experimental bomb tests so far we have done the arming by hand." Burrowed into the coral on the lee side of Enyu, a small island twenty-two miles across Bikini lagoon from the Bravo bomb, was Building 70, a large, hardened bunker that would be used by Clark's firing party. Inside the bunker, eight men worked in a maze of rooms, including a radio room, rooms for experiments, and in the front, a room with devices that monitored classified instruments that would be used to fire the Bravo bomb. The bunker was built with steel-reinforced concrete walls three feet thick and covered with ten feet of dirt and sand to retard the inroads of radiation. It was anchored into the island for stability and was surrounded by a moat to absorb the surge of a tidal wave. The door was, in fact, a submarine hatch.

As Clark boarded a helicopter flown by the marine Helicopter Squadron HMR-362 of Santa Ana, California, and started back to the Bravo bomb. The helicopter hugged the curve of Bikini Atoll as it island-hopped west, the pilot following the necklacelike chain of sandbars and reefs and small islands along the perimeter until they reached the island of Namu. Here the jungle vegetation gave way to a clearing. Surrounded by banks of portable electrical lights were a dozen twelve-foot columns arrayed in a semicircle around three concrete towers and a black building three stories high, out of which came two-inch steel pipes that ran seven thousand feet across the water to a small spit of sand. On that sand was a steel building. In that building was Bravo, a 23,500-pound nuclear bomb.

The chopper descended and settled onto a pad near the platform. It was nearing dusk. Said Clark: "We are pretty darn sure the bomb couldn't accidentally go off but with the complex circuitry involved, there is always that one chance in a million that something might go wrong. The operational plans called for the ships to be safely out to sea before we armed the gadget."

Clark radioed the USS *Estes*: "Permission to arm the bomb?"

JOHN KAPRAL TOOK a late swim, changed into a fresh shirt, and had dinner in the mess hall. After dinner, he checked the duty roster. Airman Joe La Magna, age twenty-one, had the night security patrol and Tech Sergeant Joe Williams, age forty-four, had the midnight weather readings. Williams would be assisted by Airman Curtis Ogle, age twenty-two, and Airman Bill Williams, age twenty. The balloon run used for the midnight weather readings would take several hours.

Satisfied that all was in order, Kapral went to the mess hall and played dominos for an hour. At 10:00 P.M. he headed over to the communications shack to check for messages. There was a telex. "We presumed the test would be canceled," said Kapral. Four times a day they launched their weather balloons and four times a day the readings said the same thing—winds from the east. "The winds were so consistent that we could copy a report from the day before and fill it in without taking a new reading." The winds they felt in their faces were blowing straight down from ground zero.

But the telex said otherwise.

The telex said the test was on.

AFTER ARMING THE bomb, Clark returned to the bunker and released the chopper, which returned to the *Bairoko*. It was late; the sky was black. Clark entered the bunker and noticed a new arrival. "I refused to stay ashore," said Airman Gerald Scarpino. "I was convinced to go on the premise that I would set up my radio, check it for operation and then evacuate aboard ship to the sea."

In fact, the new man in Clark's bunker, had already been evacuated aboard the carrier *Bairoko* when a call came in requesting a backup radio operator for Clark's bunker. Scarpino was the only sailor with the proper qualifications and went back to help only after extracting a promise that he could do his work and then return to the carrier. Clark, however, was not informed. "They said they didn't know I was supposed to go back with the copters, and so I was 'volunteered' to stay twenty miles from ground zero with an experimental nuclear device. But I was told not to panic because the ships were close by and we would be evacuated if need be."

Little did anyone know.

BANKS OF FLOODLIGHTS threw pools of light onto the ramps and tarmacs as aviation mechanics and airplane maintainers hurried about. There were wing walkers to help pilots navigate the maze of parked aircraft, fire guards to stand by engines as they started, escorts to walk dignitaries and other observers unfamiliar with aviation out to their planes. At midnight on March 1, 1954, the control tower on Enewetak came up on the radio and advised the situation room on the *Estes* that they were ready to commence air operations. Four hundred miles away, Naval Air Station Kwajalein followed suit. There was a light breeze, the temperature was some eighty degrees, and the smell of salt water perfumed the air. Around the edges of the floodlights the flicker of electric light gave way to a coal-black night out of which came the sounds of waves thumping against rocks that were no more than a few feet away.

A Strategic Air Command B-36 began to move, its fifty-foot propellers turning in big flat arcs. The bomber moved slowly, like a cat, low on its haunches, inching its way around the taxiway and into position for takeoff. At 1:44 A.M., the pilot advanced the throttles and the B-36 lumbered down the runway until the nose rose up and it lifted off and was swallowed into the night sky. Behind it, another plane taxied into position.

Again and again the cycle repeated itself, a steady drumbeat of engines bursting to life and planes taking off, the red and green lights winking off as each plane turned away toward Bikini, camera planes, cloud trackers, cloud samplers, search-and-rescue aircraft, fighter jets, and transports packed with dignitaries, congressmen, and military brass.

Each would bear witness to a hydrogen bomb of unprecedented and unexpected power. And no doubt each person would in some way be forever changed by what he was about to experience.

RUNAWAY BOMB

"THEY MISSED IT entirely," said Harold Agnew, a Los Alamos scientist and eventual successor to Norris Bradbury as chief of the lab. In calculating the yield of the Bravo bomb, Los Alamos had broken down the experimental fuel, lithium deuteride, into its two components, lithium-6 and lithium-7. They thought lithium-7 would be largely inert.

But lithium-7 was not inert. "That's why it went gangbusters," said Agnew. "We were wrong." Bravo, expected to yield between eight and ten megatons, was a runaway bomb. The chain reaction produced a fifteen-megaton explosion, a blast that quickly overwhelmed the margin of error and made irrelevant the precautions taken by the task force.

At 6:45 A.M. local time, Bravo split the Pacific sky with a burst of light that turned night into day. Everything and everyone was absorbed into the white-hot radiance of the blast; all color washed out, all contrast was gone; it was as if the ships and the men were within the flash itself. "We lay portside to the blast," recounted Seaman Bob Mouse, who was aboard the destroyer the USS *Estes* when the bomb exploded. "At the moment of detonation pre-dawn turned into high noon; one had the feeling of being bathed in light."

On Enewetak the burst of light was so bright that it was impossible to look toward Bikini without grimacing in pain. Closer in, rabbits with their eyes surgically opened for medical tests were permanently blinded. Out to sea on the ships, those facing the bomb flinched at the brilliance, uncertain if their goggles had been enough to protect their eyes. About them, stanchions and divots stood out in stark relief, as if searchlights had been trained on them at point-blank range. The smallest cracks, the tiniest seams in door seals—anything that admitted light into the ships—burst forth with shafts of utter brilliance.

THE FIREBALL ROSE and grew to four miles in diameter. It ascended into the sky at the astonishing rate of one thousand feet per second. The inward suction entrained millions of tons of coral and sand—all of it pulled into the boiling mushroom cloud that now crowned the stem. The fireball splashed against the atmosphere and spread across the sky. It flickered and sparkled with flashes of light as radionuclides churned inside. Said Sergeant Ball, the MP on Enyu: "It was the cloud. In the time it takes for me to say this, it was over our heads. I'm thinking to myself, what the hell was happening here?"

As the fireball ascended, three condensation rings radiated outward around the toroidal shape towering over the ships on a scale that made them look like toys. "We all stood with our jaws hanging open," said Airman Ray Durden, who saw it from the aircraft carrier *Bairoko.*

In mere seconds the sailors sensed that something unspeakably wrong was occurring. Said Yeoman Seaman: "We soon found ourselves under a large, black and orange cloud that seemed to be dropping bright red balls of fire all over the ocean around us. I think many of us expected we were witnessing the end of the world."

Battle-hardened men who had served in World War II went to their knees and prayed. "It was a religious experience, a personal view of the apocalypse or transfiguration," said Bob Fitton, who was on the destroyer *Philip.* "An almost reverent silence fell over the normally boisterous group as we watched the boiling atomic cloud reach for the heavens." Said Lloyd Kosted, who was on that ship: "I and anyone else who were in on that Operation Castle would hope and pray to God to never see one again."

THE HEAT PULSE from Bravo radiated across the Pacific and made distance seem irrelevant. "It was like a blowtorch going across the back of my neck," said a sailor who was at sea more than thirty miles away. Said Airman Robert L. McIntyre, a twenty-three-year-old plane handler on the carrier *Bairoko*: "I remember feeling the heat going through my entire body, it was like you stepped into a blast furnace."

The pilot of the B-36 bomber reported a bright orange glow around the edges of his flash shields, then being slammed by two sharp blows. The crew called on the intercom: the rubber seals around the bottom of the observation blisters were smoldering. The copilot reported that the exhaust temperatures on the four jet engines were spiking into the overtemp region. One probe on the skin was already reading 341 degrees, nearly enough to burst the bomber into flames. When it landed, it was discovered that sheet metal had been pushed inward between the ribs of the airframe. Dozens of burn marks pocked the underside of the fuselage. The bomber had been nearly eight miles away and thirty thousand feet in the sky. Had this been war, the crew no doubt wondered how any SAC aircrew might survive their own bombs.

THE BRAVO SHOCK wave raced across the lagoon and in less than two seconds peeled off the ground vegetation on the islands in the western curve of the atoll. Palm trees snapped and fronds flew through the air like missiles; hills and outcroppings were flattened to nothing. "Practically all prominent features ashore were blown away," said one navy admiral. The landmarks used to navigate the tricky channels were gone.

The military encampment on the island of Eninman, fifteen miles from ground zero, was flattened as if swatted down by an invisible hand. Tractor-trailers were tossed about like toys. Tents littered the camp. The one-ton steel mats that made up the runway were scattered like poker chips. Electrical connections short-circuited, fires broke out, and columns of black smoke dotted the horizon. "Whole palm trees were blasted apart," said Kosted, one of the first to survey the island three days later. "There were dead fish everywhere and debris everywhere. It was a tremendous sight to all of us."

The shock wave passed over the western curve of Bikini and raced out into the ocean. Behind it, a speckling of dots appeared as fish floated to the surface, their bellies ruptured by the concussion. In front, hundreds more jumped from the ocean, their sensory systems triggering synapses that in every way said something terrible was coming their way.

Many of the sailors described an apparition, a cellophanelike wall racing toward them, rising as it approached, growing larger and larger until it slammed into the ships. "It was terrifying," said Seaman George Cowan, a twenty-six-year-old boilermate first class on the *Estes*. "It looked like a wavy cloud." Seaman McIntyre said of the moment when it hit: "I was looking out the battened down portholes and saw something coming across the water. It appeared to be a wall about ten to fifteen feet high above the water. When it hit the ship it blew the porthole covers off." Steel bulkheads flexed inward; antennae bent like straw. The porthole covers had been affixed with half-inch steel hinges.

BACK IN THE bunker, the men across the lagoon experienced Bravo. John Clark had been in earthquakes before, "but never anything like this. The entire building started slowly rocking in an indescribable way. I grabbed the side of the control panel for support. Some of the men just sat down on the floor."

One man asked: "Is this building moving or am I getting dizzy?"

One of the men became nauseated. It was as if the bunker were "resting on a bowl of jelly." Quipped a third scientist: "This was the subject we had joked about for years, that one of these days an explosion would be strong enough to shear the top off the atoll and send [the bunker] plunging down into the depths of the Pacific Ocean."

And perhaps it had. In another room, the toilet erupted in a geyser of water. Water flowed out of conduits that should have been dry.

"We were all shook up considerably and scared stiff," said Scarpino.

But more was to come.

KAPRAL SAW IT from the bathhouse. "The western sky was brilliantly illuminated, almost requiring me to shade my eyes. When it returned to normal you could see the top of the mushroom cloud."

"It was a terrific bright light," said Technical Sergeant Sam Seville, the medic on Rongerik. "It was an orange, rust-colored glow spreading over the horizon."

Said another: "At our distance, the fireball was below our horizon, but the sky color instantly changed to an intense yellow white. Then gradually the sky color changed to orange, then red, and finally dull red. It made the sky look too hot to touch."

The sound arrived several minutes later. "I noticed the Gooney birds leaving the trees and a small breeze began. In quick succession, we were hit with the double boom of the pressure wave and everything was rumbling."

As the light faded, Kapral dried off, put on his T-shirt, shorts, cap, socks, and boots, and left the bathhouse.

The wind was coming from ground zero.

BRAVO TERRIFIED THE Marshallese living on Rongelap, an island between Rongerik and Bikini. "We were in the middle of the reef that connected two islands when the whole of the western skies lit up so brilliantly that it seemed as if it were noon instead of five o'clock in the morning," remembered a woman who at the time was just a girl. "We cowered among the large boulders on the reef too frightened to decide whether to flee back to the islet or dash across the reef to the main island. It was one of the boys that finally galvanized us to make a mad rush towards the main island. Just as we reached the last sand bar the air around us was split by a most horrendous noise. We could actually feel wave after wave of vibration. We made the last hundred or so yards to the main island in total pandemonium."

"We woke up in great terror not understanding what was happening," remembered another. "A short while after, the skies lit up and an indescribable sound shook the island. Some concluded that maybe the 'Big War' between the United States and Russia had come to pass."

THERE WAS AN uneasy silence. The task force ships remained in position and prepared to execute their postshot tasks. The men on Rongerik turned away from the ocean and walked back to the mess hall. In the bunker, the scientists gathered themselves and prepared to open the door. On Rongelap, the village was wrapped in a hush of shock interrupted only by the sound of waves breaking on the ocean side. The first streaks of light were washing the morning sky.

Unknown to anyone, an invisible plume of radiation had begun to drift downwind in a shape that would grow to more than one thousand miles in length. If it had been visible, it would have looked like the tail of a fox. But it was not.

And it was headed in a direction nowhere near the airborne cloud trackers who had been positioned to find it and track it.

Thus began March 1, 1954, the day of Bravo.

MATERIAL CONDITION ABLE

AT 7:15 A.M., one of the scientists in the bunker looked through the hatch and saw dry land, thus dispelling any notion that the bunker might have been submerged. He opened the door and stepped outside. Across the lagoon, a thick, smoky shaft two thousand feet wide, twisted in gnarled, angry knots, reached up and touched a brilliantly white mushroom cloud that towered over him.

The bunker emptied and the men walked forward, mesmerized. "The shot cloud had spread out and it was pure white," remembered John Clark. "It was an awesome sight."

A light mist began to fall, then a heavier mixture of water and sand, sloppy stuff with no real consistency. John Clark gathered his Geiger counter and looked down. The needle was twitching. "We could hardly believe it," Clark said. "The wind was supposed to take the fallout in almost an opposite direction."

Clark turned a knob to change the scale.

The needle leaped.

THE *BAIROKO* LAUNCHED a helicopter at 7:25 A.M. to take six airstrip operators back to Bikini to reopen the facilities on Eninman Island. They were as yet unaware of the contamination moving their way, nor did they know that Bravo had torn apart their steel mats and scattered their airstrip about as if they were parts of a toy.

CLARK AND HIS men retreated into the bunker. They closed the door and Clark took a reading by the hatch and was again puzzled. He called the *Estes* and talked to Dr. Alvin C. Graves, scientific director for the test. "The radiation is building up pretty fast, Al," Clark reported. His comment was met by a puzzled silence.

"We really didn't know what to expect," said Clark. "The pointer kept climbing."

ARMY CAPTAIN WILLIAM Hume and Major John Servis, both of the Health and Safety Division of Los Alamos, were standing on the captain's bridge on the USS *Bairoko*. It was 7:55 A.M. Hume held a Geiger counter in his right hand. He leaned over and whispered to Major Servis: "Sir, we are in fallout."

AT PRECISELY 8:00 A.M., visible material began to drift through the air and radiation devices flickered to life on the destroyer USS *Philip* and the aircraft carrier *Bairoko*. In mere minutes, the air was streaked with particles of all sizes, some as small as pinpoints, some much larger. Airman Second Class Donald Summers was among the hundreds of men seated on the flight deck of the *Bairoko*. "Fallout from the blast covered the ship," he said. "There was sand, coral, and seaweed all over the flight deck, catwalks, gun tubs and every other exposed area."

Ray Durden, the helmsman on the *Bairoko*, remembered: "No ship could outrun this, even if we had started to leave before the explosion. Ash fell two to four inches thick on the deck before most men were ordered below."

THE FLIGHT-DECK CREWS on the *Bairoko* prepared to land their helicopter but as they waited the men could see that their arms, eyes, and faces were dotted with radioactive particles.

Minutes after 8:00 A.M., the navy ships received an expedited order to withdraw immediately from the area to a position more than fifty miles from Bikini. All men were to go below decks, vents were to be secured, and each ship was to activate its washdown equipment. As if in a ballet of one, the bows of the ships curved across the face of the ocean as they turned away from ground zero and made their best speed. All except one.

"As we prepared to land our helicopter, we could not turn on our sprinkler system," Jack Seaman, who was on the *Bairoko*, remembered. He said: "We watched as every other ship in our sight turned around and ran for it. It was a lonely and scary old sight to us as we headed into the black cloud which seemed to have balls of fire in it."

BERNIE O'KEEFE, A contractor for the Atomic Energy Commission, swept the corridors and interior rooms with his Geiger counter. The lowest readings came from the data room, a fifteen-by-twenty-foot room covered on the outside with an extra margin of dirt to protect its sensitive instruments from potential fallout. It was large enough to hold all nine men.

Said Clark: "It was now about H plus one hour and I was most concerned about what was happening to the radiation levels outside. I took the radiation meter, opened the door and gingerly placed it outside at arm's length for a quick reading. It read forty roentgens. I quickly closed the door."

"The fallout had started an hour ago," said O'Keefe, "which meant that any bird or animal that had survived the tremendous blast would already be sick from radiation."

What O'Keefe might have added was that radiation was now tracking through their own bodies.

ACCORDING TO THE ship's log, *Bairoko* captain Emmet O'Beirne ordered his ship to Material Condition Able at 8:30 A.M., a state of alert describing the onset of nuclear contamination at sea. Men scrambled down the ladders and battened down the hatches. The ventilation equipment and the heat exchangers were turned off. O'Beirne ordered a new heading and the *Bairoko* raced to escape the fallout.

The *Bairoko* and the *Estes* turned on their washdown equipment. With a clanking of pipes and a wheezing of water pumps, thousands of pounds of salt water surged toward spray heads mounted on stanchions all over the ship. In minutes, plumes of water erupted from scores of nozzles, throwing an impressive, drenching spray of water into the air. The water flushed the decks and the superstructures of the deadly fallout. Particulates of microsize coral bursting with alpha, beta, and gamma radiation raced along the edges of the hull and leaped out of the scuppers like molten steel into the sea.

BURNED OUT

ONE OF THE most controversial subjects in nuclear circles is precisely how much radiation a human can be exposed to without suffering harm. Radiation is a process of decay, the emissions of excited electrons from a particle until there are no more electrons and it extinguishes itself and it is no longer fallout. If you could see these electrons, you'd see a sky dazzling with spears of light as the fallout came down. The larger particles would burst forth with brilliant explosions of rays not unlike a phosphorescent shell, exploding and exploding and exploding all the way down until the fallout settled and began to coat the ground or the deck of a ship. Once settled, the surface would become a porcupinelike carpet of photons firing upward, sending ionizing radiation into human flesh and traveling two thousand feet into the sky until they lost their energy and expired.

The alpha and beta rays are weak and are blocked by shirts and pants or a sheet of paper or, for beta, a thin sheet of aluminum. Gamma rays, on the other hand, slice through steel and concrete and clothing and human flesh like a hot knife through butter. All three of these particles are called "ionizing radiation" because they affect the electrons in human tissue on a molecular level, which in turn can cause radiation sickness, tumors, genetic defects, cancer, and death. Each electron travels on a "track" and just one unlucky track might be enough. In intense fallout, the body can simply be overwhelmed by tracks of particles going through the tissue and cellular damage is done. A defective cell divides and then divides again and then again and again until millions of defective cells are coursing through one's body, which becomes a human vessel with a biological time bomb inside. *Tick! Tick! Tick!*

The body burns out.

The perplexing question was, how many tracks, how much exposure was too much? No one knew, in 1954; nonetheless, the military settled on the industrial standard, which was 3.4 rads of exposure, the equivalent of three full chest X-rays. Any soldier accumulating 3.4 rads was considered burned out and would be restricted to safe areas.

But that's not how it worked out.

WITH THEIR HATCHES closed and the engines turning to generate speed, the temperatures inside the ships began to rise. Robert Ball, the army MP based on Enyu and now on the *Bairoko,* remembered the heat: "They put two hundred of us in a twenty by forty foot steel-walled room," he said. "It was so crowded, some guys fainted but they couldn't even fall down."

On the *Philip,* the men in the engine compartment were dizzy and felt faint. The captain had no choice but to open the vents and power the blowers. Feeling wisps of fresh air ripple through their compartment, the men crowded the ventilation screens. Cool air blew into their faces. They rotated positions, each getting a minute or two, then moving back, waiting their turn, twenty-six men all striped bare to their waists.

Three days later, these same twenty-six men would report to sick bay with painful radiation burns on their faces and necks and shoulders and around their waistlines, where radioactive sweat had soaked into the hems of their trousers.

Because they exceeded the maximum exposure permitted during the test, the radiation-safety offices saw fit to issue these men waivers, although it is unclear if any sought the waivers on their own.

THE WITHDRAWAL OF the ships to the south farther from ground zero was unwelcome news inside the bunker. "While contemplating a decision for evacuation," remembered Scarpino, "the ships started getting fallout so they decided to go out to sea so as not to endanger the ships and the people on them. At 9:00 A.M. no more ship radio contact."

ON THE ISLAND of Kwajalein, a P2V-6 Neptune patrol aircraft prepared to take off. It was 7:30 A.M. The pilot's mission was to search an area of the Pacific Ocean called the Green Quadrant for ships that might accidentally have steamed into it. Green Quadrant was a 450,000-square-mile area that extended from Bikini Atoll in a large rectangle to the southeast. The patrol was largely precautionary.

Spotting ships at sea is at best a tricky business. More than one pilot has chased a ship only to discover that it was the shadow of a cloud rippling across the face of the ocean. The Neptune had radar that swept a fifty-mile V ahead of it, but even then mistakes could be made.

The pilot, of course, never saw it coming. At 10:00 A.M., the Neptune flew head-on into a radioactive air mass of considerable intensity. The radiation meter swung hard to the right and immediately read one thousand millirads. The pilot banked the plane but the meter didn't budge. Knowing full well that his aircraft and crew were now thoroughly contaminated, he had little choice but to make an immediate 180-degree turn and return to base. When he landed, he filed a report with the radiation-safety offices on Enewetak, saying that a radioactive air mass was on a bearing that would bring it directly over Rongerik.

The report would be lost for five days. The unnamed pilot was promptly granted an increase in his maximum permissible exposure limit: a waiver.

A TWENTY-FOUR-YEAR-OLD SEAMAN in the communications center on the *Estes* noticed that the radios were not working properly. The heavy streams of water caused by the washdown equipment were blasting the antennas, which, as one navy historian wrote, "raised havoc with voice and radio-teletype circuits to the ship."

Not that anyone had a plan for havoc.

Said a sailor in the radar section on the *Estes*: "The radar failed as a result of salt water being sprayed on the antenna during ship decontamination periods. During these periods, VHF and HF communication difficulties were experienced for the same reason."

THE AIR OUTSIDE the bunker was so heavily contaminated that the men inside could do little more than wait. They manned the radios, but while the ships were out of range there was nothing to be heard.

And then the generator that powered the bunker inexplicably failed.

The lights dimmed, then winked out.

"Someone yelled 'Don't anybody move,'" remembered Gaylord Felt, one of the firing team. "We were worried that someone might hit a switch or do something that would give us more trouble when the lights came back on."

But they didn't come back on. Said Scarpino: "No lights. No communication with the ships. No air. Radiation levels unknown because all of the meters went to peg on the high end of the scale. We were desperate."

HELICOPTER FLIGHTS INTO the radiation zones were called "hot hops" and extra precautions had to be taken. To prevent contamination from sticking to the exterior of the choppers, the skin of each helicopter was washed and waxed and then waxed again. Door seals and window seals were taped closed, and paper mats lined the floors. All the hot-hop choppers had rescue winches and flew in pairs, so that if one helicopter went down in the radioactive water the other could rescue the men. The pilots wore radiation suits, gloves, respirators, and cloth caps.

At ten-thirty, the *Bairoko* launched two helicopters to fly into Bikini and take radiation readings around the rim of the atoll.

The flight took two hours.

AT 1:48 P.M. the needle on Rongerik twitched, but there was no one there to see it. It wasn't until 2:50 P.M. that Master Sergeant Ron Pletsch noticed that the needle was pegged.

A few minutes later, fallout began streaking the air. "It looked like snow," said Airman D. L. Baker. "Particles the size of grains of sand, but they floated down." Baker was dressed in a short-sleeved shirt and shorts.

Corporal Don Sieber put some of the material on a cathode ray tube in the electronics shop. It glowed in the dark. Private First Class G. R. LaMagna saw it. It *glowed*.

Airman L. L. Azbill noticed the cloud. He described it as an X-shaped cirrus cloud that later formed into the shape of a funnel. He thought the material in the air looked like ash.

Private First Class W. Thornton was in the woods, reading a book under a tree. He noticed particles in the hair on his forearms. He likened it to pollen.

Although they couldn't see such things, out of these bits of pollen and ash-like flakes burst particles of ionizing radiation, each tracing a microscopic track through the air like a point of light from a sparkler, each track that same potentially deadly microscopic bullet that could alter cellular material and trigger mutations in the human body.

IT WAS "EERIE" in the bunker, said O'Keefe, a feeling of "what-can-happen-next pervaded the building as we sat around waiting word from headquarters." A plan, however, was in place. The bunker had a portable walkie-talkie that could reach the ships if it was taken out to the front room. Because the forward area of the bunker was highly contaminated, exposure was dangerous and contact would be attempted for just five minutes. Every thirty minutes someone new would go out and try to raise the ships. "We drew straws to see who would go," said Scarpino. "I was number five."

*   *   *

THE MARSHALL ISLANDERS on Rongelap didn't know what to make of the flakes. They fell into pots and changed the color of drinking water but no one knew what that meant, so they drank the water anyway and washed with it as they had before. One woman discovered dots of a powder-white substance in her hair. She tasted it.

A young boy seemed amused by the powder and played with it. He scooped it up and filled empty bottles and it became a game. Said his sister: "When he tired of filling bottles, he poured some water into one of the filled bottles and was quite perplexed when the mixture began to foam and give off smoke. He stirred the mixture with his fingers."

A BELL CHIMED in the army communications center on Enewetak. It was 3:00 P.M., Bravo day. A message was logged in: "Attention Mr. Breslin, Info Commander, Weather Reporting Element, Provisional. GR 12 MIKE over 100 Charlie—Over 100."

The message was from John Kapral and the message said that their radiation device was off the scale. The message was forwarded to the radiation-safety offices for Operation Castle but they dismissed it. "The off-scale reading was not viewed with much concern since task force ships were experiencing readings of more than 100mr/hr," explained an after-action report. "The weather detachment was advised of this assumption and that the suspected conditions constituted no significant health hazard to personnel."

In fact, there was no way to quantify the amount of radiation on Rongerik. With each breath, each step, every movement the men took, the invisible particles were tracing deadly tracks through their bodies, any or all of which could ping the wrong electrons and mutate their cellular material. The radiation-safety offices of Operation Castle advised Kapral to have his men change into long-sleeved shirts and pants, but to resume their normal activity.

And, more or less, that was that for Kapral's men. Except of course it wasn't. Every minute in radiation counted.

KAPRAL WROTE IN his diary: "Particles could almost be seen falling. Visibility had decreased to 3 or 4 miles."

There had been no further word from Enewetak.

It was 4:00 P.M.

RESCUE

BACK IN THE bunker, one by one the men left the data room and tried to raise the ships. One by one they returned and shook their heads.

ON RONGERIK, THE message to change into long-sleeved shirts and pants seemed to trivialize their situation, and that caused tempers to flare, but when they subsided a sergeant distributed extra clothing to those who needed them. Still, many ignored the flakes. One of the cooks split his time between cooking and washing pans outside, in the fallout. He wore shorts but no shirt; however, he did change into pants and long-sleeves at 4:30 P.M. Another sergeant worked in the radio shack while yet another worked on records in the supply building; both were assisted by an airman and all three were indoors. However, an airman named R. L. Roper operated his water distillation unit outside until dinnertime and then went inside.

A sergeant and an airman had KP that afternoon and cleaned pots and pans. Neither wore shirts. They both were outdoors. Near them was the medic, who was repairing the outdoor movie screen. He told them to cover up and then he himself changed into coveralls, had dinner, and went back to the dispensary before going to bed.

INSIDE THE BUNKER, the radios unexpectedly crackled to life. The ships were on the way. While it was impossible to know how much radiation their bodies had absorbed, they most certainly knew that mere minutes on the outside could be every bit as deadly as the hours they had spent inside. Clark opened the hatch and took a reading and with relief told the men that the radiation levels had dropped. Clark believed that they could get down to the helicopter pad and be off the island with no more than a few minutes in the heavily contaminated air. Two choppers would come in from the *Bairoko*, buzz the bunker, then hover above the pad until the men were sighted. One chopper would land, load the nine men, and be off without delay. The second chopper was the hot-hop spare.

The pickup was set for 4:30 P.M.

BECAUSE EVERY LAYER of clothing added protection against the piercing radiation, the men stripped the cots, found scissors and tape, and began to mummy wrap one another. "To keep the 'hot' dust off us, we wrapped ourselves completely in bedsheets," said Clark.

Scarpino remembered: "We used two sheets each and left only eye holes to see and small ones at that."

Mummies.

AT 4:30 P.M. the helicopters buzzed the bunker, then disappeared over the crest of the island and settled into hovers on either side of the landing pad. Clark opened the door and the men flinched against the sudden brightness, then leaned a shoulder and hurried to the jeeps next to the bunker. Had radiation been visible, it would have looked like the ground was emitting spears of light particles, and through this they would have to run. The next few minutes would expose them to some of the most intense radiation yet. "We all got in the abandoned two vehicles to drive down to the landing pad, about two miles," Scarpino remembered. They drove as fast as they could, but they were cautious. "We couldn't afford a breakdown," said Scarpino.

"Every minute counted against us," said Clark. "The chopper guys couldn't just wait, what with the radioactivity."

THE SOUND OF the rotor blades thumping above them seemed distant and surreal; the mummy-wrapped men stared out the windows, saying little, absorbed in their own thoughts. The helicopters beat through the sky and the ocean slipped beneath them and in time the ships began to appear on the horizon. The pilots radioed the *Bairoko* and requested a "dirty signal," meaning that they would be landing in a "bathtub" erected on the aft end of the ship, where they would discharge their passengers and where the ground crews would begin to decontaminate the choppers.

The men from the bunker would be hosed down on the flight deck before being allowed inside the ship.

"I WAS THE last to shower," said Scarpino. "We were told to walk over an open grated companionway that stretched over open sea and we were salt water showered nude and checked with a Geiger counter until we read '0' gamma. I had no other clothes and was offered none so I redressed in my old clothes."

Scarpino made his way down to the hangar deck. It was hot and stuffy and crowded with men who were restless and annoyed that the evacuation had carried on so long with as yet no end in sight. Scarpino gathered up some blankets. He looked about; every inch seemed occupied. "I slept on the first hangar deck with the wheel of a helicopter for a pillow that night."

TWO DAYS LATER, Scarpino woke up in excruciating pain. It turned out that the hoses that had washed him down had scarcely whisked any of the contamination from his face and head. "I had a severe headache, a tight forehead with loss and blurry vision. [I] was feverish and very nauseous." He went to the decontamination station. His head read 35R, a number ten times greater than the permissible exposure level.

He was promptly sent to the showers. "I go and wash and also lose fistfuls of hair. I came out, get checked and I am still hot, about 12R. I return to the shower with a brush and scrub my head until I am sore. I now read about 75R. Again I go to the shower and stand under it for a long time letting the water hit my head because it is so sore from scrubbing."

Three weeks later, Gerald Scarpino's commanding officer ordered him back to the radioactive bunker to retrieve the tools that he had left behind.

He did as he was told.

BRAVO'S FALLOUT CONTINUED to take its toll. By the end of the day, many of the men of marine Helicopter Squadron 362—the crews that rescued the nine men in the bunker and flew the hot hops back to Bikini— were burned out. To keep Operation Castle on track, their exposure limits were promptly increased from a total of 3.4R to 7.8R, although, again, there is no evidence that anyone personally made the request.

WHILE THERE IS little doubt that the men in the bunker were heavily contaminated, available records make no mention of an airman named Gerald Scarpino.

That he had been in that bunker would remain unknown until many years later, when Scarpino appeared at a VA hospital in Houston, Texas.

MOST OF THE men on Rongerik spent the evening in the mess hall. Some remained disgruntled and were agitated, some were resigned, and some were simply oblivious to the fallout. Most watched the movie or played cards. One airman wrote home, another played dominos. John Kapral's tent was on the windward side of the island but before he went to bed he walked down to the radio shack and composed one more message about the fallout.

He sent it to the command center on Enewetak. It was 0000 hours, March 2, 1954, Bravo+1.

KAPRAL'S MESSAGE WAS handed to Major Fellie Robinson, Kapral's immediate superior, who, upon reading it, decided to wake up his own commander, Colonel Mahlon B. "Max" Hammond. Kapral's midnight message included two important details that had not been included in his first message. The first detail was that he had a radiation device called an "auto monitor." The second detail was that the "pen" on the auto monitor had been off the chart since 2:50 P.M.

Hammond rustled awake three of his own radiation-safety officers. They promptly identified the device and expressed surprise that it had been off the chart for so many hours. That the pen hadn't come down meant that Hammond's weathermen were in true fallout, not merely a dusting by a transient cloud.

Hammond had his executive officer dispatch a message to Kapral ordering the weathermen to remain indoors until further notice. Hammond then assembled five of his officers in his quarters to discuss their options.

It was nearing 2:00 A.M. A C-54 cargo transport of the Military Air Transport Service was scheduled to depart Enewetak at 4:00 A.M. for the three-hour flight to Kwajalein Island. The plane would arrive in time to meet a navy seaplane scheduled to depart Kwajalein for Rongerik on a regular resupply flight that would leave at 8:00 A.M. "We decided that we should take advantage of a scheduled MATS flight to Kwajalein and meet the regular weather service flight departing at 8:30 A.M.," said one of the officers present at the meeting. It was also decided not to advise the rad/safe offices of Joint Task Force Seven. "It was determined that the Air Force group should take steps to determine themselves what the true radiological situation was at Rongerik and not wait for JTF Seven notification."

Air force captain Louis B. Chrestensen volunteered to make the trip. He gathered a handful of radiation-film badges.

THE NAVY PBM seaplane took off from Kwajalein at 8:30 A.M., March 2, Bravo+1. Lieutenant Joseph McDaniel, the air force supply officer for the weather islands, was aboard, as was Chrestensen. Both men would later write notes to themselves to document the actions they took, and why. These notes were declassified some forty years later.

After a flight of nearly three hours, Rongerik appeared on the horizon. Chrestensen asked the pilot to fly the length of the island at 250 feet while he took a reading. The meter recorded 340 millirads, an astonishingly high number so far above land. He needed to report the contamination. "We climbed to five thousand feet in an attempt to establish contact with [Enewetak] or the *Estes*," said Chrestensen, in his notes. "Neither attempt was successful so further messages were relayed through . . . Kwajalein. After about 30 minutes of intermittent and frequently garbled messages, I requested the pilot to return to Rongerik and prepare to evacuate as many as possible in our aircraft realizing that if other planes were not available, the Navy PBM would have to make two trips. Since it was already approaching noon, this entailed getting the first trip over with as quickly as possible in order to avoid an after dark takeoff from the lagoon with the last load of evacuees."

Chrestensen, however, did not have that authority.

THE RADIATION-SAFETY OFFICES for Joint Task Force 7—Operation Castle—was headed by United States Air Force lieutenant colonel Richard House. Among the rather substantial list of responsibilities given to House and his group was the weighty task of monitoring the radiation-exposure levels for the thousands of men in the task force. An individual's exposure to radiation came down to a policy that House called "military need." Said House: "It was assumed that a policy of strict adherence to the radiological standards prescribed for routine laboratory or industrial use was not realistic. The intent of the Castle plan was to strive for a reasonable and safe compromise considering conservation of personnel exposures, the international import of the tests, and the cost aspects of delays chargeable to excessive radiological precautions."

In practice, this system seemed to allow soldiers to absorb contamination in direct proportion to the importance of their jobs. The more important you were to keeping the tests on schedule, the more exposure you were allowed to receive. According to the after-action report written by Colonel House, "real" exposure wasn't a number set in stone. "The standards were interpreted in terms of 'real safety' versus 'rule safety'. At no times, however, were recommendations made involving tongue-in-cheek approaches to real bodily safety of personnel." House explained to his safety officers that any subordinate officer denying a man's need to increase his maximum permissible exposure levels should take into consideration "the need for completion of the Castle mission."

In what was fast becoming the largest radiological disaster in nuclear testing, some eight hundred men required waivers and some eight hundred men were given waivers.

HOUSE PICKED UP fragments of Chrestensen's first messages but he called the fragments "puzzling" and took no action. Chrestensen's second message, however, was not garbled and it came through clearly—"Should Rongerik be evacuated at once? Request immediate answer." The communications control room again sought out House, and asked him what to do. Said House, writing in the third person as he often did: "At approximately 12:00 noon, 2 March, Radsafe of the task force was advised of the [air force's] monitors intentions to evacuate Rongerik. In the absence of intensity readings it was mutually agreed not to authorize evacuation and to request radiation intensity readings."

THE ORDER NOT to evacuate was received by the seaplane and it created a dilemma. There was no doubt in Chrestensen's mind that an evacuation was imperative but as they descended toward the island he also knew that he had an order. As a junior officer, to continue the descent and to evacuate the men could mean a court-martial, while not to do so could do Kapral's men harm. No doubt Chrestensen looked appraisingly at the island below him and at the blue ocean and the beautiful sky that surrounded their seaplane.

Chrestensen, fully aware of the risk he was taking, told the pilot to land.

As the seaplane descended and the ocean swelled in their windshield, the radio burst to life with an urgent call. The command center wanted an additional reading. Chrestensen told the pilot to say, "340 at 250 feet."

There was a moment's silence and then the radio crackled to life with a new message. "Disregard the message not to evacuate," said the communications center. "Disregard and evacuate. Hammond sends."

Chrestensen no doubt breathed a sigh of relief.

CHRESTENSEN DROPPED THE wand of the Geiger counter to the sand. It was 2.4 rads hot at one inch. He walked up to one of the tents. He went inside, bent over, and pushed the Geiger counter under the bed. It was hot—3.2

rads hot. He took five more readings. They were all the same—too high, too hot. He found some film badges. Eight were stored inside a refrigerator. They were reading 38 rads. He took one that had been rigged to a tent pole inside a tent. It was reading 98 rads. One man, La Magna, had a badge. His, too, read 98.

Chrestensen gathered his thoughts and explained what had happened with the Bravo bomb, how the winds had shifted and the fallout had spread across the navy fleet. "I briefed the men on what I knew of the situation and what I knew was being done," wrote Chrestensen. "There was no panic, no apparent dismay, and all of the men were willing to do whatever was necessary to secure the island before evacuation . . ."

Kapral came up to him. "How many can you take?" he asked.

"Eight," Chrestensen answered.

"We'll send them alphabetically," Kapral answered.

"Does that get you off, Chief?" asked Chrestensen.

"No, sir," answered Kapral. "I'd be nine."*

T H E N A V Y P B M seaplane cleared Rongerik lagoon and flew back to Kwajalein but the news was scarcely good—airplanes were in short supply and no seaplane was available for the return trip to Rongerik. "We heard on the way to Kwajalein that additional planes were not available, which meant that the 20 people remaining on Rongerik would not be moved as soon as I had given them to believe," wrote Chrestensen.

With a flying time of nearly three hours, unless they found a seaplane soon, the sun would go down, which would make an ocean landing out of the question. If they didn't get back soon, the twenty men remaining would be forced to remain overnight. With the fallout, that was akin to a death sentence. Remarkably, there was a volunteer. Wrote Chrestensen: "The pilot of the aircraft stated that he would return and airlift the remaining 20 after he had time to get a brief lunch."

The pilot did ask for some help, as it were. With twenty passengers, the seaplane would be at its maximum takeoff weight, if not a hundred pounds overweight, not that that unnerved him in the least. Instead, he asked to have his PBM emptied and Jet Assisted Take Off bottles affixed to the tail.

Chrestensen no doubt smiled.

---

* It's unclear why only eight were able to get off on the first flight. Some versions say the PBM departed Kwajalein with "dignitaries" or "observers" on board while other accounts suggest that it carried supplies for the scheduled stops on other islands.

* * *

THE SEAPLANE RETURNED to Rongerik and water-taxied to the beach. The twenty remaining men ferried themselves out on a small boat and one-by-one they climbed into the seaplane. So crowded was it that some were forced to lie on the floor.

Using every inch of throttle he had, and what seemed like an eternity bouncing across the waves, the pilot lifted the seaplane to the surface of the water and when the hull was hydroplaning he ignited the JATO bottles and with a *whoosh* they were airborne.

He landed at Kwajalein as the last fingers of daylight drained from the sky.

THE EVACUATION OF Rongelap began not by seaplane but by a ship steaming at twenty knots, which took yet another day to arrive. As the destroyer inched into the lee side of the island, there was a palpable sense of apprehension in the wheelhouse. The effects of radiation were visible. Said a Rongelapese remembering when the ship arrived: "Nearly all the people on Rongelap became violently ill. Most had excruciating headaches and extreme nausea and diarrhea. By the time of our evacuation all the parts of my body that had been exposed that morning were blistered and my hair began to fall out in large clumps."

CLUMPS OF HAIR aside, on March 11, 1954, the Atomic Energy Commission issued a press release about what had occurred out in the Pacific: "During the course of routine atomic tests in the Marshall Islands 28 U.S. personnel and 236 residents were transported from neighboring atolls to Kwajalein Island according to a plan as a precautionary measure. These individuals were unexpectedly exposed to some radioactivity. There were no burns. All were reported well. After the completion of the tests, they will be returned to their homes."

ONE BOMB APART

CURTIS LEMAY SPOKE to an audience in Quantico, Virginia, about the progress made under the quick-strike concept. It was July 1955. Strategic Air Command, LeMay said, could now launch an attack of 180 atomic bombers within twelve hours of notice. If given forty-eight hours, that force could be more than quadrupled to 880 aircraft. If given three or four days, his command would launch a strike of 1,000 aircraft in a "simultaneous strike against Soviet objectives."

No doubt someone in the Soviet Long-Range Aviation would make a similar speech to a similar audience somewhere in his own country.

ON SEPTEMBER 12, 1955, *Time* profiled a simulated combat mission. A B-47 departed from March Air Force Base, California, to bomb the Campbell Soup plant in Sacramento and then up to Spokane, Washington, to bomb the Centennial Flour Mills plant. From Spokane, the crew then flew 890 miles to the Hoover Dam as a navigational training exercise and then turned back to Los Angeles and bombed the Jorgensen Steel Company offices.

Out of a possible 1,000 points scored for accuracy, the crew earned 853, becoming, as the magazine reported, "the world's deadliest bomber crew."

THE ONLY ACCEPTABLE outcome of a war between the United States and the Soviet Union would be victory, said President Eisenhower, speaking to the National Security Council. Said one of the attendees: "The President concluded by admitting that his point of view might seem brutal, but in view of the fact that we would never enter the war except in retaliation against a heavy Soviet atomic attack, he simply could not conceive of any other course of action than the course of action which would hit the Russians where and how it would hurt most."

Eisenhower then continued with a sobering observation about nuclear war.

If the United States was attacked and fifteen of our cities were destroyed, troops would be mobilized but, unlike prior mobilizations, they would not go overseas. Instead, Eisenhower said, they would be needed at home. Hiroshima, much of its population incinerated by the fireball, lethally irradiated, crushed by the blast wave, killed by flying debris, half naked and burned, and doomed to die of their open wounds; such a Hiroshima would be repeated across America fifteen times over.*

In the aftermath of a nuclear exchange, everyone would be needed at home.

OWING TO A puzzling lack of accurate charts and coupled with an underlying suspicion that the Soviets were increasing their military presence in Vladivostok, Curtis LeMay was asked to gather reconnaissance of that area. To do that, LeMay brazenly sent as many planes as he could. "We picked a clear day and all of our electronic reconnaissance planes crisscrossed the area. They practically mapped the place. Two of our planes saw some Migs but there were no interceptions. And as far as I know the Russians never said anything about it," he said.

GERMAN ROCKET SCIENTISTS captured by the Soviets in the aftermath of World War II began returning home in the early 1950s and reported "intense" Soviet interest in missile technologies, with hints of a Soviet project to send a ten-thousand-pound warhead over "intercontinental" distances.

Pentagon think tanks were alarmed and urged a speed-up in the development of America's missiles. Initial work had begun on an intercontinental ballistic missile (ICBM) called Atlas as well as a two-stage missile called Titan, although the pace was slow and unhurried.

President Eisenhower agreed and in 1955 approved the development of not only Atlas and Titan but also an intermediate range ballistic missile called Thor. As if to underscore the sense of urgency, the contract to build Thor was let to the Douglas Aircraft Company on December 27, 1955.

In what would perhaps have been unthinkable if not impossible in the business of developing new intercontinental bombers, America now had three major systems in development for missiles.

STRATEGIC AIR COMMAND considered evolving quick strike into a more doctrinal approach to reaction, which in short order became what would

---

* Jonathan Schell (*The Fate of the Earth*) describes the many ways a person would die in a city hit by the bomb.

become known as "ground alert" bombers. German scientists aside, it was widely believed among military planners that the Soviet Union would have ICBMs that by 1961 would be able to hit the United States in a surprise attack against which "advance warning might not exceed 15 minutes." SAC readily acknowledged that a single multimegaton bomb detonated above an SAC airbase would almost certainly destroy the bombers based there but, if the bombers were ready to go and could take off before the missiles arrived, at least some of the retaliatory force would survive.

Trading off the enormous financial and physical expense of such an intense operational concept against the need to have a surviving retaliatory capability large enough to inflict devastating punishment to the enemy, SAC believed that the survival of one-third of its projected forces in 1961—approximately 550 bombers and 350 tankers—would create a force too powerful to gamble against.

The next question was time. Given that a B-47 wing consisted of forty-five bombers and thirty tankers, the one-third concept would mean that fifteen bombers and ten tankers per base would have to be prepositioned at all times for immediate takeoff. If the first bomber got off the ground in fifteen minutes, the entire force could be airborne in under an hour. Better still, with the dispersed and smaller wings of B-52s, an alert force would consist of five bombers and four tankers per base. If the first aircraft could take off in seven minutes, all these planes could escape within fifteen minutes.

Ground alert was approved in principal on December 14, 1955. Strategic Air Command was ordered to develop the skills necessary to have 33 percent of its bombs and tankers on fifteen-minute alert by 1960.

Exactly how this would be accomplished was unimportant for now. What was of enormous consequence was that Strategic Air Command was now moving headlong into its new era. The buildup of bombers and bombs that marked SAC's first ten years, the development of bombing skills and aerial refueling— all this would now yield in importance to a new measure of air power, a measure that would shape every single SAC practice for the next forty-seven years.

Speed.

Speed of reaction.

15 minutes.

TOWER FOUR

THE MEDIA WERE fascinated by the Texas Towers. They were futuristic, military, mysterious. They had been created on "top secret drawing boards," as one news account put it. Said another, they were "man-made islands," and another, "radar islands," but always a marvel of technology and extra defense against a Soviet attack. "They will tower far above the sea but be rooted to the bottom, and an important gap in the nation's radar defenses will be closed," wrote *The New York Times*.

That Nature might flick any of these towers into the hereafter, however, was never mentioned.

DESPITE THE HUBRIS, the Texas Towers were indeed important. Captain John Albers obtained an emergency allocation of steel for Bethlehem Steel of Quincy, Massachusetts, to fabricate the Texas Towers. Tower Two would be built first, constructed with the three legs attached to the platform, then towed to sea using the platform for flotation. On site, the three legs would be dropped to the ocean floor and pile-driven fifty feet into the seabed. The platform would then be raised above the Atlantic using Colonel Leon DeLong's jacks, which would elevate the radar station as if it were a mere car being jacked up to replace a tire.

Texas Tower Two would be the first radar station in the seaward extension and thus the first fixed military structure in the Atlantic Ocean. Texas Tower Three would follow; Texas Tower One was canceled, making Tower Four next.

THE BIDDING FOR Tower Four revealed deep divides regarding design concepts. Theodore Kuss's design specified a three-legged structure with legs that would travel through 185 feet of water and elevate the platform 67 feet in the air. Because of the depth of water, Kuss specified three sets of underwater "K" braces to provide added stability.

Explained Colonel DeLong to the Senate investigating committee: "When you're building in deeper than one hundred feet of water, the freestanding column, or legs, is inadequate. Deeper than one hundred feet the column becomes so large it's impractical. The K-brace is the best known method of construction."

On that all the designers agreed. On Tower Four, each set of K braces would consist of a twenty-ton horizontal beam running between the legs, joined in the center by two diagonals rods of two tons each—much like the trusses under the span of a bridge. The braces would be constructed like the letter "K" with the "K" facing toward the bottom of the ocean. The braces would be stacked one on top of the other at 25, 75, and 125 feet below the waterline.

Because there were no ports with drafts deep enough for legs the length of Tower Four's, the legs could not be preattached to the platform and floated out to the erection site, as was the general practice in offshore rigs. Rather, Tower Four would be built on its side, towed out to sea on its side, and tipped over. Once upright, the top tier of bracing would be folded down and the platform would be floated between the legs, attached to jacks, and jacked up. The bracing would be reattached, the thirty-inch-thick, eight-hundred-pound bolts would be driven back into place, and a rigid, upright tower would be erected in 185 feet of water.

It was deceptively simple, but on this there was great disagreement.

"WE JUST STATED positively that we did not want any part of it, any part of it," said Leon DeLong, referring to the bolts Kuss planned to use on Tower Four. Why? "For the following reason," said DeLong. "You have a pin in here. You must have some slack to insert the pin. . . . We did not want any possibility of a pin connection and having a clearance where it would move." However small the opening, DeLong knew that the motion of the sea would work on the bolts—or, as he called them, the pins—inevitably causing them to bang in their crevices until they were loose or fell out. As the bolts loosened, the tower would weave and move with the currents, causing other parts to weaken, and so on. "The sea works on it at all times. . . . There is one thing you can be sure of, the ocean is not going to get tired. You will get tired or metal or anything else will tire before the ocean will get tired."

DeLong further objected to towing the structure on its side and tilting it in the ocean, stating that it was impossible to calculate the forces the structure would have to take as it undulated over the ocean waves—and just as impossible to calculate the forces as it was tilted over. Instead, DeLong proposed an entirely welded structure built in two pieces. The first piece would be an undersea "base" one hundred feet tall affixed to the ocean floor by driving the legs fifty feet into the seabed. On top of that base would be attached the upper section, complete with the platform. No tipping. No bolts. An entirely rigid base welded throughout, on which the rigid platform would also be welded.

DeLong presented this to Albers as "Scheme B."

Albers promptly told him no.

DAVID ABBOTT, a forty-eight-year-old welder, went to work dressed in a flannel shirt and khaki work pants with a dozen salted capelin stuffed into his back pockets. Abbott was the son of an immigrant family who in 1925 arrived from Newfoundland and settled in Somerville, Massachusetts. When he was old enough to work, Abbott's uncle steered him to Local 56, the Brotherhood of Carpenters and Joiners, Welders, Divers, Pile Drivers, Wharf & Bridge Builders, in Boston. Abbott signed on as a general laborer and chewed his capelin and a little tobacco all day.

At the West End Iron Works, where he apprenticed to become a welder, Abbott met Vinnie Brown, also a Newfoundlander and, like Abbott, a man with a sense of humor. "Who knows brown?" Abbott liked to ask. "Brown nose Brown," he answered.

Vinnie played a mandolin that he kept in his locker at the iron works and broke out during the breaks. As Vinnie played, Abbott danced a jig, scuffing the dirt with his feet until blossoms of dust billowed up around his shoulders.

David Abbott grew up, married, started a family, and settled into a life that suited him well. By day he was a welder and by night a father of five, a homeowner, a landlord with rental units, and a man well respected in his community. When he walked down to the hardware store he'd tip his hat to the ladies and say hello to the men, and when he bought his supplies his credit was such that he simply signed for his goods with his name.

Welding was not a job without risks, however, and in 1954 Abbott had a brush with death. It was a Saturday morning at the Fore River Ship Yard. Long catwalks of steel staging stretched over the cavernous hold of the freighter *Collier Maiden*. As Abbott made his way across it, the staging snapped, sending him falling forty-eight feet down into the ship's hold. That he survived was a near miracle. He was hospitalized with a fractured skull and the hearing in his left ear was gone.

While recuperating, a representative of Local 56 came by and told him he had been awarded a slot on the new Texas Towers. Vinnie, too, he was told; it was the least they could do.

With extra money in every paycheck, and no small measure of prestige to be working on a project of national urgency, Abbott was no doubt pleased by this unexpected turn of events.

THE TWO-MAN RULE

SAID COLONEL BRUCE Hinton of Nellis Air Force Base, Nevada: "That is the thing to remember. Today's pilot is a professional. Like other professionals, he has a set of ethics. What are they? To press on to a target. He's not like a rifleman going over the top where, if the social stimulus of the other men doesn't push him over, someone will carry him over. No, our pilots go into targets alone. It's a matter of ethics whether they press through the attack. I don't think many would poop out in what you journalists call the moment of truth."

THE ENORMITY OF surprise in the era of nuclear war was periodically evaluated, and with each evaluation new and more sobering statistics would emerge. By 1956, the National Security Council's nonpartisan Net Evaluation Subcommittee believed that the onset of a general war would begin with the explosion of two ten-megaton H-bombs, one from inside the walls of the Soviet embassy in Washington, D.C., and the other from within the Soviet offices near the United Nations. Behind these two blasts would come some seventeen hundred Soviet bombers with sixty-six megatons of bombs. The attack would be coordinated, simultaneous, and deadly, said their report titled "Actions and Results Under Conditions of 'Strategic Surprise.'" But it would not go uncontested.

According to Net, Air Defense Command's network of surface-to-air missiles and fighter jets would attack, and 1,300 of the Soviet bombers would be shot down or would simply exhaust their fuel and crash. The SAC quick-strike forces would receive warning sufficient to launch their bombers, the first of which would escape their base in five to seven minutes. In the trans-attack period of some several hours after the initial warning, a total of 642 quick-strike bombers would be able to take off, with a second wave of 740 bombers not far behind.

Still, the results were nothing short of near annihilation. The United States government would be "virtually wiped out," and all of SAC's air bases and other military installations would be destroyed, with casualties in excess of 65 percent. Of the 642 SAC bombers launched in the first wave, 610 would not make it home.

Of interest was a truth largely lost to all but the most careful reader. On one hand, Air Defense Command would stop more than 1,300 of the incoming Soviet bombers. On the other hand, the Soviet air defenses would stop an equally large percentage of the incoming American bombers. Strategic Air Command registered no disagreement with either number. Both forces would largely be destroyed, just as would the countries they were tasked to defend. Nuclear war, it was increasingly apparent, was all but unsurvivable.

BOMBS OF ENORMOUS power were also moving out to the bases. Per Eisenhower's instructions, the "emergency capability" H-bombs—produced in limited quantities—were now under military control. The 21-ton 15-megaton MK-17/24 was mated with the B-36 and was now on SAC bases. The lighter but nevertheless potent 5-megaton Mark-21, a result of Castle, was now on base. So, too, was the 1.6-megaton 7,500-pound MK-15, another bomb developed out of Castle, as well as the nearly ubiquitous 40-kiloton general-purpose MK-6 atomic bombs.

Strategic Air Command was fast becoming the deadliest bombing force in the world.

And it was just the beginning.

"NUCLEAR WEAPONS AND nuclear weapons systems require special consideration because of their political and military importance, their destructive power, and the potential consequences of an accident or an unauthorized act," wrote an analyst for Sandia Labs. One consideration was the two-man rule, which stated that whenever nuclear weapons were handled, two men had to be present. Said the Atomic Energy Commission: "A minimum of two authorized persons, each capable of detecting incorrect procedures with respect to the tasks to be performed and familiar with safety and security requirements, will be present during any operations requiring access to the weapon." The concept was designed not only to prevent a technical slip such as the wrong sling attached to the wrong bomb but to prevent sabotage, say in the instance where one member has become psychotic or is otherwise mentally unstable.

The two-man rule led to the creation of two-man-rule boundaries around weapons-storage areas and painted or roped boundaries around parked aircraft with bombs on board. Signs were posted to remind crews that the two-man rule was in effect. To this rule SAC added passwords to be sure that the two men were who they said they were. SAC guards were trained to assume that even a flight crew in SAC flight suits were imposters until they gave the correct response to a password or number code. Remembered one pilot: "If we were running out to the aircraft [we] wouldn't cross the red line unless we knew the number. There was an armed guard around the plane. We had a number we had to know to get past him. If the number was 'five' the guard would hold up two fingers and we'd hold up three and he'd let us through. Then we'd start engines, copy the message and see what we had to do."

"My ID badge gave me access to the SAC flight line and alert aircraft (those loaded with nukes)," said Clarke Ketter, a former nuclear-weapons specialist. "I went to the alert aircraft a couple of times to check the nitrogen pressure in the weapons on board. The weapons were pressurized with nitrogen to reduce the possible impact of sparking at higher altitudes. It was a little nerve wracking to approach those aircraft that were being guarded by Air Police with 'shoot to kill' orders. They had a rope or barrier around the bombers about a foot high and four or five armed SAC air police. It was always startling to us to see an SAC policeman put a round in his chamber and point his gun at us. They'd tell us to put our equipment in front of us on the ground and our IDs and step back. They'd look at our IDs all the while the gun was pointed at us. Then they'd tell us to step forward and proceed."

To each Strategic Air Command air wing was added the special-ized Air Base Groups (later to be renamed Aviation Depot Squadron). The Air Base Groups were to be responsible for issuing the necessary paperwork upon receipt of a bomb, placing a bomb into a storage igloo, removing that bomb from the igloo, and performing ready-strike maintenance on it before it was sent to the flight line, where it was their job to upload it into the bomb bay of a bomber in two hours or less. If during an inspection the bomb was judged to be a dud on target, a measure resulting from some misstep in the ready-strike preparations, the unit would receive an unsatisfactory rating, followed by reas-signments out of the squadron by the officers responsible, including, in some cases, reassignment out of SAC entirely.

Naturally, as with any new procedural process, there were growing pains.

One air wing most familiar with atomic bombs knew little or nothing about the MK-15 hydrogen bomb and flunked their first inspection. Had it been a real mission, the bomb they loaded would have been "unsafe." In another inspection, the technicians didn't know the difference between the bomb-bay configurations for an MK-15 or the far more powerful MK-21. They flunked. One group was monitored as they loaded and unloaded no fewer than six different bombs on a B-47. They flunked because of errors in assembly. One upload took four hours thirty minutes. They flunked. Another unit was proficient at loading MK-6 and MK-21 bombs into B-36s, but failed when they bungled the load of an MK-15 in a B-47. They, too, flunked.

Many of the officers who were reassigned bristled at their treatment. Perhaps they had a point. But to SAC, atomic war was as black-or-white as it got, and atomic war lacked those comfortable shades of gray that harbored the also-ran.

And Strategic Air Command did not harbor the also-ran.

A SAILOR REMEMBERED a nuclear test in the Pacific: "A few hours after the Cherokee shot, we were playing softball and drinking beer on the island of Bikini which was about 20 to 25 miles from ground zero. The mushroom cloud had spread out for hundreds of miles. Someone noticed a change in the color of the film badge of a shipmate. We checked ours and saw the same thing.

"About this time the ship's whistle and fog horn began to sound. This was to alert us to return to the ship immediately.

"The ship was closed completely. All doors, hatches, and ventilation systems were closed. The ship was steaming out from underneath the fallout from the mushroom cloud."

The lessons of radiation safety piled one on top of the other. Not that anyone was paying attention.

"NUCLEAR WEAPONS WERE designed with multiple objectives, including safety, security and reliability," said a Sandia report. Reliability, they wrote, was "the probability of achieving the specified yield, at the target, across the Stockpile-to-Target Sequence of environments, throughout the weapon's lifetime, assuming proper inputs."

Of particular interest was the term *at the target*. To the exacting weapons planners at Sandia, "at the target" included the safe release of the weapon from the carrier, the safe freefall of the bomb through the sky, the safe deployment of a parachute to retard the fall of the bomb, and an explosion in a "window in space, encompassing both distance from the target, Circular Error Probable (CEP) and Height of Burst (HOB). The weapon must detonate within this window of space to achieve the desired damage."

To determine the ability of a bomb to survive across the entire Stockpile-to-Target Sequence, a war-ready bomb was withdrawn from storage and used in what would be called an Operational Suitability Test. An Operational Suitability Test simulated the entire mission, including the weapons' release and the explosion of the bomb inside the all-so-critical "window in space." A bomb carried for an Operational Suitability Test was in all measures the same as a bomb used in war except that the plutonium capsule was replaced by a dummy capsule.

Operational Suitability Tests, as later documents would reveal, took months to plan and were flown as if they were real bombing missions against Moscow. They would also account for at least one lost bomb.

"THE CONCLUSION THAT 'the presently planned radar network is not adequate to meet a high elevation attack of the B-52 type bombers even in advance of countermeasures' is not entirely meaningful . . ." wrote the air force to rebuke an MIT report critical of air-defense radars. "Surely anything short of 100 percent detection, tracking and kill is not adequate in the atomic age."

One hundred percent kill. It was a welcome voice of reason.

IN THE LOGIC of war, the detonation of a nuclear weapon anywhere over enemy territory was far better than no detonation of that bomb at all. To that end, Strategic Air Command created the Special Weapons Emergency Separation System, called SWESS. Said a formerly classified Atomic Energy Commission document prepared for the Pentagon: "This system provides a means for an automatic release over enemy territory in the event that the aircraft and/or crew are incapacitated during a combat mission. When the SWESS is armed the bomb will be automatically released if the aircraft falls below a preset altitude."

Some pilots called this system the dead-man fuse or a dead-man switch.

The first bomber to receive it, and apparently the only bomber, was the B-52. Lest the crew inadvertently self-destruct, the switch was to be activated only when the B-52 was at altitude.

IN 1956, SOVIET premier Nikita Khrushchev fired off an intemperate barrage. "You say we want war, but you have now got yourselves into a position

I would call idiotic," he said, referring to America's forces in Europe. "If you withdraw your troops from Germany, France and Britain—I'm speaking of American troops—we will not stay one day in Poland, Hungary and Rumania."

Said Nikita: "If you don't like us, don't accept our invitations, and don't invite us to come to see you. Whether you like it or not, history is on our side. We will bury you!"

In hindsight, some historians would say that this outburst was not so much a threat of war but rather the frustrations of a leader who had no desire for war whatsoever.

Others would quote Khrushchev as if World War III were imminent.

Both seemed to be correct.

ON MAY 20, 1956, a B-52 bomber released a thermonuclear bomb over Bikini Atoll fused to burst at four thousand feet. This would be the first air drop of a live hydrogen bomb and was part of a weapons-testing program named Operation Redwing.

The bomb exploded at the designated altitude with an enormous 3.8-megaton blast, roughly the equivalent of two thousand bombs the size of the Hiroshima bomb.

It was, however, four miles off target.

In the business of the Cold War, there was always another hill to climb.

IN A BRIEFING given to Congress, the Department of Defense made casual mention of a "breakthrough" that had accelerated the development of intercontinental ballistic missiles and intermediate-range missiles. Light elements of hydrogen in a dry state used to fuel fusion bombs had led to the design of a lightweight, high-yield warhead that would reduce the size of the booster rocket required to launch it. The new hydrogen fuels would drop the weight of a warhead from 3,000 pounds to 1,500 pounds while still delivering a .5-megaton yield. In turn, this reduced the booster requirement from 440,000 pounds of thrust to 240,000 pounds of thrust. Moreover, a yield of .5 megatons—500 kilotons—"eases the guidance problem by lowering considerably the requirement for accuracy," or so said the report.

The success of Operation Castle, largely seen by historians as a precursor to a deliverable hydrogen bomb for SAC, in fact greatly benefited the emerging missile program. In a word, Operation Castle sliced off more than a year in the development of ICBMs not because of any breakthrough in boosters or guidance systems but because of bigger blasts that compensated for both.

* * *

UNTIL STRATEGIC AIR Command developed its operational requirements to implement the 15-minute ground-alert concept, quick-strike remained its only formal plan for quick takeoffs. In 1956 an interim goal of six hours from warning to take off was established. Wrote a Strategic Air Command historian: "In the summer of 1956, with the world situation becoming more critical, SAC believed it needed a capability to launch its forces with only tactical warning; therefore in addition to the strategic warning plan, a tactical warning plan . . . was adopted. This gave SAC a total of 592 bombers that could be launched from receipt of execution to twelve hours later with the first increment of bombers taking off at E+6 hours."

The goal to launch 592 bombers in twelve hours, with the first wave of them in six hours, was based on "generation rates" for those bombers. Every bomb and every bomber had a specific generation rate—that is, the time it took to prepare it for a strike and get the plane airborne. This included the time required to assemble the crew, ready the bomber, pull a bomb from storage, prepare it for strike, fuel the bomber, load the weapon, and take off.

While 15 minutes was well into the future, SAC now had a specific reaction time. SAC was now on six-hour ground alert.

IN NORTH DAKOTA, a missile range with 150 silos was planned. The range would be spread over eighty-five hundred square miles "in an arc from the base to within a mile or two of the Canadian border." In Montana, 200 missile silos were planned on a range that would occupy twenty-three thousand square miles. That such a scale was necessary had to do with the requirement that silos be planted in the ground "at least one bomb apart."

One A-bomb, of course.

WHILE THE MISSION requirements for a particular weapon remain largely classified, how a weapon was to perform was specified in what was known as the Military Characteristics document. This document established parameters such as a particular weapon's explosive yield, weight, fusing options, blast characteristics, method of delivery—such as missile, artillery, bomber, and so on—and the method of employment, that is, against hardened structures, softer targets like refineries, and under water such as against enemy submarines and the like.

The Military Characteristics document also included specific safety features for maneuvers with that bomb in normal operations, such as on a bomber or in "abnormal operations," a somewhat formal term for what would otherwise be known as a crash. Whether on a B-36 en route to Moscow or engulfed in flames, the bomb had to be capable of operating in both normal and abnormal operations without detonation.

As more people brought their specialized knowledge to the matter of nuclear war, new consequences emerged, some darker than others, some more complicated than others. Such was the case of Major General Richard C. Lindsay, United States Air Force director of plans. Lindsay was responsible for monitoring American industry, meeting with corporate CEOs, touring plants, and estimating industrial capacity to meet the war-making requirements of the air force. In peacetime, his was a relatively easy job complicated only by labor strikes, shortages of steel, and the like. In the aftermath of a nuclear exchange, however, it was a far more ponderous task.

Said Lindsay: "While the exact pattern of destruction to U.S. forces and production facilities during the first days of general war cannot be foreseen, such destruction must be presumed to be extensive."

Lindsay warned that the air force should not expect replacement bombers to be immediately forthcoming from American factories and that under no circumstance would there be any hope of building new plants or converting other plants, such as auto factories, to aircraft manufacturing.

Said Lindsay: "The peacetime level of aircraft production would be the greatest production capability which we can expect."

The recuperative powers of American industry were no match for the destructive powers of the atomic bomb.

The merging of talents from academia, industry, and the military gave rise to breakthroughs in computing, electromagnetic radiation, jet engines, guidance systems, and rocketry. But it was precisely this combination that concerned the president. Said Eisenhower: "The government contract becomes virtually a substitute for intellectual curiosity." Eisenhower called this a "technocratic state" where research and intellectual creativity were driven by military requirements and military purchasing instead of the natural processes of research and development. This combining of resources no doubt led to great breakthroughs but was tagged by Eisenhower with the rather derisive name "military-industrial complex."

And thus a new word entered the language of the Cold War.

* * *

SAID AN SAC historian: "To test . . . the capability of the units to execute their EWP, the SAC Inspector General began performing 'No-Notice' inspections in mid-1956. He would arrive on an SAC base unannounced and give to the Division/Wing Commander an execution order for a simulated EWP mission." The wing, remembered one SAC pilot, was to drop everything just as if the klaxons had rung and the Soviets were over the horizon. (No-notice inspections were later called Operational Readiness Inspections, or ORIs.)

An SAC pilot explained what happened next: "The first event was to evaluate the response of the bomber and tanker alert force [or the ICBM force] to a simulated emergency war order . . . The crews who happened to be on alert when the ORI was initiated were evaluated first. The entire wing was then required to generate the remainder of the bombers, tankers, or missiles up to full combat-ready status, with nuclear weapons loaded as if prepared to go to war."

THERE WERE DIFFERENT truths.

Senator Stuart Symington, a vocal critic of the Eisenhower administration, chaired a subcommittee that held hearings in 1956 on the adequacy of the air force's overall readiness. Symington, who would later run for the Democratic nomination for the 1960 presidential elections, released much of the testimony to the public, including the testimony of General Curtis LeMay.

Said the cover page: "The attached 44 questions were asked by Senator Symington's Subcommittee on Armed Forces and were answered as indicated by General Curtis E. LeMay in open hearings on 30 April 1956."

In truth, there were sixty-four questions, seventeen of which were omitted for security reasons, three of which had answers written by someone other than LeMay, and forty-four of which were edited by either the Symington Committee or the secretary of the air force, Donald A. Quarles. The point Symington wanted to make, no matter how LeMay answered, was that SAC was not as ready as it could be, owing only to the stingy budgets of the Eisenhower administration. LeMay did not entirely agree.

Asked the Symington Committee: "Why has the provision of bases generally lagged behind the provision of aircraft?"

According to the transcript released to the public, LeMay said this: "As a general rule it is easier to obtain money for airplanes and equipment than it is to get public works funds for bases, including housing."

In fact, LeMay answered that there were adequate provisions for the construction of bases but that bases were subject to delays in the receipt of construction materials, nagging labor problems and strikes, and time spent negotiating for overseas-base rights.

This portion was never released.

Asked the Symington Committee: "How would you describe the situation that will exist under present programs as to the ratio between jet tankers and jet bombers by 1958–1960?"

LeMay's actual answer was that at the current ratio of tankers to bombers, nothing would change.

LeMay's edited answer, much of it inserted by Quarles, was quite the opposite, that the ratio had reduced SAC's capability: "That ratio of tankers to bombers . . . is the best compromise we could come up with at the time . . . we could increase our international strike capability considerably . . . if we had more tankers . . ."

Asked the Symington Committee: "If the present plans were changed to accomplish an adequate ratio between jet tankers and B-52s would this require the acquisition of substantially more jet tankers than is now planned?"

"No," said LeMay under oath. Then he went on to explain that the ratio of tankers to bombers was based on the offload of gas in each air refueling. A tanker only partly filled a bomber's tanks—22 percent was the norm—which in most cases meant that one tanker refueled two or more bombers. The ratio, said LeMay, was fine.

But in the transcript released to the public, LeMay's answer was changed to a simple "yes," meaning that he agreed with Symington's inference that the ratio was inadequate and that the air force needed more tankers.

And so it went. Truths. But different truths. Truths that no doubt helped make Symington's case that the current administration wasn't spending enough on defense.

Differences that no doubt contributed to a prompt supplemental congressional authorization for an extra $900 million for additional bombers and fighters.

ON APRIL 1, 1956, the 307th Bombardment Wing, based at Lincoln Air Force Base, Nebraska, flew their last B-29s to the air force boneyard in Arizona and were declared combat ready in the B-47. Far from what would otherwise have been cause for celebration, the acceptance of the B-47s began a year that saw one tragedy after another cast a shadow over the entire wing. Forty-three B-47s were initially placed on the flight line in Lincoln, Nebraska, but within a week a B-47 broke up in flight, killing all four on board.

There were now forty-two.

The unit participated in a wing rotation and for ninety days they were in England. They flew simulated bombing missions using radars and cameras, including a mission against the Tower of London and Windsor Castle, but while practicing touch-and-goes they lost a second B-47 when a wingtip caught the ground and the bomber cartwheeled across the field in a ball of flames until it slammed into a storage igloo with three MK-6 atomic bombs inside. Three more men were dead.

During the rotation back to the United States, one of the air transports flying the maintenance and ground crews disappeared over the Atlantic Ocean and fifty more died.

So it was for the 307th. Two bombers destroyed. Fifty-seven men dead.

Adjusted for different dates and different circumstances, almost any air wing in Strategic Air Command could tell a similar story.

WITH A LIMITED number of quick-strike bombers on six-hour alert, the first in a series of fifteen-minute ground-alert tests began and was assigned to the Thirty-eighth Air Division, at Hunter Air Force Base, near Savannah, Georgia. The operation was fittingly given the code name Try Out. The objective of the test was rather basic—to see if an air division could simply maintain one-third of its aircraft on alert for five months. Because the Thirty-eighth had two wings of bombers and tankers, this amounted to thirty B-47 bombers and fourteen KC-97 tankers in "full Emergency War Plan configuration," which meant that they were to be "operationally ready, weapons loaded, and pre-take-off checks complete."

Takeoff times were not set and none was specified for this test, but metrics were generated as various tasks were performed. The depot squadrons and ground maintainers were timed against a stopwatch as they loaded bombs, attached JATO bottles to the backs of bombers, and put ammunition belts onto the planes. On 621 occasions an atomic bomb was loaded and unloaded and each time the process was timed.

On four occasions the forty-four-plane alert force was launched while the clock counted down. To determine how fast an air division could launch everything it had when one-third of its planes were on alert, on three occasions the air division launched eighty of its ninety B-47s and thirty-four of its forty-five KC-97s. This, too, was timed.

What soon became evident was that the workload of ground alert was staggering. Maintainers and weaponeers were exhausted by the schedules. Accidents happened and some were tragic. In his haste, one airman pulled the chocks from the wheels of a tanker during a night exercise and promptly walked into the spinning propeller. On another night, a crewman forgot to set the brakes on his plane and it rolled forward into another plane.

Still, the test ended in March 1957 with some promising numbers. Foremost among them, one-third ground alert was indeed possible, but equally encouraging were the metrics from the test takeoffs. "Tests showed that . . . the first aircraft could be safely launched 15 minutes after the alert sounded and the remainder of the force could be launched in one minute intervals."

SAC promptly scheduled a second series of tests.

ALTHOUGH ORIs CONTRIBUTED significantly to SAC's readiness and proficiency, there were consequences that now involved bombs. On November 30, 1956, a B-47 took off as part of a no-notice Operational Readiness Inspection. Well into its lengthy flight plan, something went wrong and the bomber spun into the ground, killing all three crew members.

The crash was near the Canadian border but the incident does not appear in any of the official records declassified through 2010 covering accidents involving nuclear bombs. It was, however, SAC's practice during an ORI to launch the alert bomber with the weapon on board.*

AN OPERATIONAL SUITABILITY Test was scheduled for an MK-21 nuclear bomb, the details of which appeared in recently declassified documents. The test would be a comprehensive stockpile-to-target test that began with C-124 transports arriving at an undisclosed storage site to collect and ferry four MK-21s to March Air Force Base, California. The MK-21 bombs would be loaded onto four B-47s. The flight plan called for the B-47s to take off from California and fly an eight-hour flight plan including one air refueling. As they neared Eglin Air Force Base, Florida, the pilots would drop down and fly a low-altitude penetration leg ending with a pop-up maneuver to release the bomb. Wrote an SAC historian: "One aircraft would fly a 300 nautical mile low-level navigation leg at 500 feet altitude prior to its arrival at the initial point. Climbing then to bombing altitude, the aircraft would release the weapon at 20,000 feet at a speed of .81 Mach. After the MK-21 had been released a breakaway maneuver would be carried out in accordance with SAC Tactical Doctrine. The three other B-47s would release their weapons at 37,000 feet."

---

* SAC received permission to maneuver freely with atomic bombs in June 1954.

The description of this test includes one of the earliest indications of the growing concerns within SAC about the increasingly sophisticated Soviet air-defense radars and the increasingly lethal Soviet surface-to-air missiles. The three-hundred-nautical-mile low-level leg at five hundred feet would have been below some of the Soviet early-warning radars and well below most of the aim points for surface-to-air missiles. But a low-level leg of three hundred nautical miles would have been challenging particularly at a time when low-level penetration tactics were not fully developed. And while the climb to altitude was common in the 1950s, it would soon be considered too risky and would be replaced by low-level bomb releases using new fuses and new types of parachutes that would allow the bomber to drop a bomb and escape. The breakaway maneuver was a blast-avoidance maneuver.

The MK-21 was a "dirty" bomb and in all four tests the four bombs were fused for a near-surface burst. According to the test summary, the bomb released at 20,000 feet detonated 59 feet above the ground, with an impressive circular error of just 490 feet. The three bombs released from 37,000 feet burst 10 feet above the ground, 50 feet above the ground, and 140 feet above the ground, with errors of 2,250 feet, 950 feet, and 1,360 feet, respectively. All four bombs were rated favorably and the suitability test confirmed that the Mark-21 performed as expected.

True, too, this test was yet another indication of the growing nuclearization of SAC. While it is often taken for granted that SAC was always a nuclear force, it neither began that way nor ended that way but rather evolved into an all-nuclear force and remained all-nuclear for several years. The expanding bombs-on-base capability and the requirement to certify the stockpile-to-target reliability of a new H-bomb like the MK-21 were indicative of a pressing shift in weaponry from conventional bombs to nuclear. Indeed, within a few short years, so complete was SAC's makeover that one SAC historian would note that on most of SAC's bases, the last of the old-fashion explosive bombs were now gone.

AIR FORCE CHIEF of staff General Nathan Twining made headlines when he announced the results of a recently completed Strategic Air Command exercise called Operation Powerhouse. In a two-week period more than one thousand Strategic Air Command bombers had flown nonstop combat training missions averaging eight thousand miles each over North America and the Arctic. Sixteen million gallons of fuel had been used. "This is the first time that the nation's Strategic Air Force has tested the operational capability of its strike force in such large numbers during such a short period of time," said Twining.

According to *Time* magazine: "It was news heard all the way to Moscow."

ARMY CHIEF OF staff General Maxwell Taylor pressed his point. Limited wars were far more likely to occur than a general nuclear war, thus the United States needed to be able to fight and win a limited war with conventional weapons. Taylor believed that the Joint Chiefs, of which he was one, were placing too much emphasis on the ability to win an all-out nuclear exchange when in fact such a war was unlikely. Maxwell argued that a general atomic war would happen only if America's very survival was at stake. If America's survival was at stake, that in turn could mean only that a war had begun that "threaten[ed] the continued existence of all nations." If such a war had begun, Taylor argued, SAC would already have absorbed a first strike, which, in Taylor's view, would already have turned Strategic Air Command, and the billions invested in atomic bombs, intercontinental bombers, and bases, into "sterile assets." The point was that if SAC was ever used as presently planned—if SAC went to war—a devastating first blow had already landed and much of SAC was already gone.

Taylor's arguments had merit but the argument could go both ways, that a powerful nuclear force was the only thing that kept a general war from erupting out of a limited war. However one took the point, this was nonetheless one of the earliest hints of a subtle shift in military sentiment away from retaliation in one massive strike toward a military posture that would in some years hence be known as "flexible response," which would at some point involve more than ten thousand retaliation options.

ACCIDENTS WITH BOMBS continued to plague SAC. A B-47 en route to Ben Guerir Air Base, Morocco, disappeared over the Atlantic Ocean with two plutonium capsules. The B-47 was maneuvering into position for a scheduled air refueling off the coast of Algeria, but after entering a cloud it was never seen again. Search teams had no luck—no trace of it was ever found.

In October, the Atomic Energy Commission issued two replacement capsules to the Department of Defense.

Like the bomber they flew, the crew of four was never seen again.

STRATEGIC COMMAND'S PUSH for more bombs and more bombers continued. As 1956 came to a close, SAC's cup brimmed with 2,474 tankers and bombers on thirty-six air bases in the United States and nineteen overseas. The military had direct custody of 1,358 nuclear weapons, the vast majority of which were on SAC bases. The National Stockpile numbered 4,618 nuclear weapons.

GRAPE BABIES

HOLLY BARKER, OF the embassy of the Republic of the Marshall Islands, in Washington, D.C., went to the Marshall Islands to record the stories of those who had lived through the Bravo bomb of Operation Castle. Said one woman, ". . . it was only a matter of two or three years before women on the island started to give birth to things less than human."

One woman described what she had seen: "After the testing, she got pregnant. When the baby was born, it had two heads. One was on top of the other. Here [touches the top of his head] it came out of—it was small."

Said another: "It's [sic] head was open. There was a head coming out [of the opening]."

"My second son, born in 1960, was delivered live but missing the whole back of his skull—as if it had been sawed off," added another woman. "So the back part of his brain and spinal cord were exposed. After a week, the spinal cord became detached and he too developed a high fever and died the following morning."

"Some [woman on Rongelap] gave birth to things that resembled bunches of grapes," remembered another. "I had an older sister that gave birth to a grape baby. Unfortunately she died during the delivery along with her baby."

One child could scarcely walk: "I know of a young boy, actually a young man now, whose head is so large that his body is unable to support it and his only means of getting around is crawling backwards dragging his head along. Like the movements of a coconut or a hermit crab."

One woman had twins. One died. "I think he died in my stomach days before I gave birth to him. When he arrived, he was all spongy and smelly. When you squeezed his head or body, water would gush out. His eyes popped out. His body was decomposed."

But then one interviewee said this, and his words seemed to sum up Bravo from the perspective of the Marshall Islanders: "I was mad. I told them, why didn't they do their experiments in their own country? In America there are deserts, there is so much unused public land. Instead, they chose some small islands to poison and kill the people."

AIRMAN GERALD SCARPINO left the military and married. In November 1974 he traveled to the VA hospital on Holcombe Boulevard in Houston, stood before a VA medical examiner, and dictated his story.

Felix J. Pircher, MD, chief of Nuclear Medicine Service, knew of the servicemen on Rongerik but not of the men in the bunker, so he was skeptical. "Scarpino claims he was 20 miles from ground zero while in fact Rongerik is listed as 105 miles from zero," Pircher wrote to the head of Medical Research at the Brookhaven Lab in New York, suggesting in effect that Scarpino was wrong and had been on Rongerik. "This appears to be a discrepancy unless there was a second group of American servicemen somewhere else than Rongerik." Which, of course, there was.

It is unclear what treatment Scarpino received, but the lack of awareness of the men trapped in the bunker illustrates the importance of transparency in matters of proper health care. "Of course," said Pircher, "I do realize that almost all of Gerald Scarpino's problems are not related to the incident, at least physically. Yet I do want to be fair and correct in my judgment."

A redacted copy of his admission papers was placed in the archives of the Atomic Energy Commission. That document was the Rosetta Stone that helped decipher several thousand pages of declassified documents on Operation Castle.

OPERATION CASTLE WOULD be remembered for its contrasts—both as a radiological disaster yes, but militarily, as one of the most important series of nuclear tests yet. All but one of the seven experimental bombs were proof tests of weapons or elements of weapons that when confirmed would be manufactured and placed into the stockpiles. For Strategic Air Command, Castle was nothing short of a transformation from small atomic bombs to powerful hydrogen bombs. The first thermonuclear bombs to be stockpiled by the military—the "emergency capability" thermonuclear bombs code-named the EC-14, EC-17, and EC-24—were tested at Castle and would become the MK-14, MK-17, and MK-24, the latter two bombs some of the most powerful ones ever built, yielding between 15 and 20 megatons. The 1.69-megaton MK-15 was proof tested at Castle and some twelve hundred would flow into SAC stockpiles. One of the seven bombs was an unexpected fizzle. Two, Bravo included, were runaways.

Bravo was the first of the bombs to be tested in the Castle series but John Clark would not return to the bunker. The bunker remained too contaminated; he decided to fire the remaining six bombs from afloat.

MOST OF THE men on Rongerik received eighty times today's maximum permissible radiation exposure. Thirteen of the twenty-eight men are now dead. Kapral lived symptom-free in Oak Ridge, Tennessee, until he died in 2004.

The sixteen men on the *Bairoko* and the twenty-one men on the *Philip* who stood around the ventilation vent and came down with radiation burns sufficient to require medical attention have never been identified, nor are their fates known.

COCKED BOMBERS

YET ANOTHER GROWING pain that confronted Strategic Air Command had to do with its inability to communicate with its bombers once they were airborne. In the past, this would have been unimportant; in combat missions during World War II, bombers and fighters were routinely out of radio range, but with nuclear weapons inside, communication with bombers deployed around the globe was essential to convey orders.

Curtis LeMay, who was an amateur radio hobbyist, went to the base shop and experimented with a kit radio. His deputy, Lieutenant General Francis Griswold, also an amateur radio operator, knew something about the unlimited range of a new technology called "single sideband" (SSB). SSB was a powerful radio wave that maintained its strength by eliminating much of the "overhead" that clogged the bandwidth. One writer likened the technology to the stream of air going through a pipe organ modulated by the keys to produce notes of music. By eliminating the air and sending only the instructions generated by the pipe organ's keys, the receiving end would reconstitute the music by manipulating its keys in accordance with the instruction and add its own bursts of air to hear the music. This turned the single-sideband radio wave into a radio wave with almost unlimited range.

Griswold suggested that they experiment with single sideband, so LeMay put a SSB transceiver on a bomber and told Griswold to fly around. Griswold took that to mean anywhere, so he promptly headed to the Far East, chatting to LeMay from Okinawa as if over a backyard fence.

The air force was entirely unimpressed. They sent LeMay their director of Communications and Electronics, whom LeMay promptly sent on another lengthy flight. From Thule, Greenland, the signal was heard as far away as the South Pole.

"So, I take operation funds and buy a dozen ham radio stations," remembered LeMay. "Put one in SAC headquarters, put one in Goose Bay, the Azores, Morocco, England . . . and we put twenty-four-hour crews on them . . . and the fact that we could talk to our airplanes anywhere in the world, this finally convinced people."

In meetings of the Joint Chiefs of Staff, the army and the navy criticized the need for large numbers of "high yield nuclear weapons." They used the terms *overbombing* and *over-destruction* to describe the absence of any real military value to the enormous stockpile being built for Strategic Air Command.

It was March 1957.

Two more tests of fifteen-minute ground alert were conducted during 1957, both having as their principal requirement that the first bomber begin its takeoff roll within thirty minutes of the alarm. Ten B-47s and five KC-97s formed the basic alert package. On each occasion they met the standard to have the first bomber airborne in thirty minutes.

The results were so encouraging that in July 1957, twenty B-47s loaded with MK-21, MK-15, and MK-6 bombs, with capsules, were sent to Morocco to start one-hour ground alerts. In truth, this was a test within a test called Reflex. Reflex was a much-slimmed-down version of the ninety-day wing rotations involving overseas deployment of some fifteen or so bombers, plus tankers, on short, twenty-one-day trips. Bombers on Reflex would immediately assume ground alert upon arrival at their foreign bases. Surprisingly, the Moroccan results were even better than the excellent results in the United States. At the forward air bases, the klaxons rang, the bombers were airborne, and time seemed scarcely to matter.

"This is the type of operation for which Jet Bombardment has been striving," said one wing commander of the Reflex operation, and that seemed to be the sentiment echoed by pilots up and down the flight line.

Ground alert was tested in one air wing after another and the reaction time dropped in gulping increments. By October 1957, eighty-seven aircraft were on two-hour ground alert in the United States, with another forty-three bombers on ground alert overseas. In addition to Morocco, aircraft stationed at Brize Norton Air Base, in the United Kingdom, Andersen AFB, in Guam, and Elmdorf AFB, in Alaska, were now on one-hour alerts.

In December 1957 the order was given for all alert aircraft to be prepared to go on thirty-minute alert by January 1958, but in truth by December 1957 there were already 134 aircraft on thirty-minute alert, fueled and loaded with bombs.

INTERESTINGLY, FIFTEEN-MINUTE GROUND alert was to apply to the new missile force as well. The specifications for the new ICBMs called for the "capability to launch 10 missiles within 15 minutes after warning, another 10 within two hours."

LARGELY OWING TO budgets and technology, the first missile-launch sites would not use hardened launch silos but rather "soft" launch sites—that is, sites unprotected from the blast of an enemy bomb. Oddly, when these unprotected sites were discovered by the Soviets they caused considerable concerns.

John Hines, who in 1990 interviewed several senior Soviet officials, wrote that the Soviets assumed Americans "were not stupid" and that they certainly knew how vulnerable their soft launchers were. Said Hines: "On the basis of satellite photography, Soviet planners observed that U.S. missiles were not very well protected by overhead cover and were grouped relatively close to each other as well as to the launch control center. These observations convinced the General Staff that U.S. land-based ICBMs were not intended to ride out an attack but instead were first-strike weapons and were routinely referred to as such by Soviet military planners in all subsequent discussions and internal writings."

"SAC HAS IDENTIFIED a list of targets which we call the 'Air Power Battle Target System,'" said General LeMay in one of his last speeches as commander in chief of SAC, a speech recently declassified. "This system includes the Soviet long range air forces . . . their bases, their supporting POL and material resources, governmental and military control centers with their allied communication networks, and nuclear weapons stockpile and production facilities. Destruction of this Air Power Target System is currently based on 1,530 desired ground zeros, of which 954 require immediate attack in order to minimize the enemy's capability for initial strike."

Nine hundred fifty-four immediate targets. And to think that less than ten years earlier it had been but a handful.

BOMBS-ON-BASE SEEMED TO be powered by some unseen accelerant. By 1957, Strategic Air Command was able to report that every bomber in its command now had at least one bomb assigned to it. Each of the 127 B-36s, the 243 B-52s, and the 1,285 B-47s were now paired with an MK-15, MK-21, MK-17, or the MK-6—a total of 1,655 bombs, many in the megaton range. SAC could say with confidence that it had more bombs on its air bases than did the Department of Defense—some three-quarters of the 2,250 bombs in military custody.

THE ALL-JET KC-135 tanker entered SAC service in 1957. The KC-135 flew at the same altitude as the B-47, at the same airspeed, lifted four to five times the fuel as a KC-97, and, in what had to be one of the most comforting sights, could fly *with* the bombers. Said one pilot, describing an RB-47H reconnaissance flight that departed RAF Brize Norton, near Oxford, England, and was refueled by KC-135s at night above the Barents Sea near a Norwegian Island called Bear Island: "The KC-135s departed with us, flew on our wing for about 3½ hours going north, after which we slid over and we took 20,000 to 25,000 pounds [of gas]. That KC went back to Brize to stand strip alert. The second KC stayed with us until around the Bear Island area when we would take on 55,000 pounds and start our mission. He would orbit in the area for the several hours before we came back out of the sensitive area. We would flash our lights as we came out and he would form on us and follow us back to Brize."

Buddy refueling.

GROUND ALERT CONTINUED to be refined and with each refinement a few more seconds were carved off the time it took to get a bomber airborne. One innovation was to build concrete parking stubs at forty-five-degree angles to the main runway. In the rush to get a heavily loaded bomber airborne, the forty-five-degree angles would allow the bomber to turn onto the runway without having to slow down. From the air, the alert stubs had a herringbone pattern, while to some they looked like a Christmas tree, and both nicknames stuck.

There were other time-saving innovations, some of them remarkably obvious but revealed only against the urgency of a ticking clock. Because it took so long to taxi a bomber from one end of a runway to the other, alert bombers would be positioned at both ends of a runway, thus preserving 15 minutes in the face of the fickle shifts in the winds.

WHY THE SOVIETS rarely protested the overflights by CIA U-2s has been the subject of speculation among historians, but in fact it may have been a gentleman's agreement of sorts. Khrushchev's relatively mild letter to

Kennedy about airspace intrusions during the Cuban missile crisis was one indication of such a thing; the CIA's own contention that their "denied access" flights were observed and monitored by the Soviets—but not attacked—was another. Said the CIA: "At the time, the Soviet Union and its satellites denied normal access to its territory, the need for a method to collect all kinds of intelligence became readily apparent and the requirement was of the highest priority." The U-2 was that method and the flights were frequent. Diplomatic protests were lodged by the Soviets in 1956 and again in 1958, but between 1956 and 1958 the CIA flew twenty denied-access flights without diplomatic consequence, many with the knowledge of the Soviets. Said the CIA: "Violated countries were, in most instances, aware at the very least that a prohibited flight was being made."

But why take no action? It may well have been due to the easy access the Soviets had to the type of intelligence the U-2s struggled to generate. Said the CIA in a report on the state of intelligence gathering in 1957: "When one considers how much time, effort, and money the US spends to locate fragmentary geodetic data about the USSR it is frustrating to think that they can so readily obtain in the US, for example, any number of large-scale maps and charts from which to position principal US targets for Soviet missile weapons systems." In short, a good map found at a gas station would do what a U-2 could scarcely hope to accomplish in a dozen missions—something the Soviets may have taken into account.

The Soviets may also have been swayed by the tacit American acceptance of Soviet "base watchers." Base watchers were not the saboteurs that LeMay vigorously trained his military-base forces to detect and deter—"SAC bases are alive with armed guards, or dog handlers walking their fierce trained dogs at night," LeMay once said—rather, they were agents sent to America to monitor activities at American military bases. At little expense to Soviet treasury or energy, base watchers could position themselves where they could count the number of aircraft departures, map radar sites and frequencies, note increased or decreased activity, and acquire a feel for the everyday tempo of ordinary air operations. Equally, they could be an early-warning radar network of sorts. If SAC started launching B-52s, the base watchers could alert their superiors. During the Cuban missile crisis, SAC asked its air wings to take "covert action" as they increased the number of bombers and tankers on ground alert. The extra bombers were to be generated "quietly," said one declassified document—quietly because of base watchers.

While maps and base watchers hardly compared to the complicated, risky, cutting-edge technologies and dark-of-night stealth of the U-2 overflights and RB-47H ferrets, that they provided the Soviets with reams of data for what amounted to a handful of quarters was perhaps amusing to Khrushchev and thus part of the bargain. Of course, when a U-2 was eventually shot down, Khrushchev was irate, but against the value of the intelligence that traveled to the Soviet Union, ignoring a lone airplane tracing a thin line across the vast emptiness of Soviet airspace was perhaps the perfect trade-off to maintain the sort of hands-off access the Soviets had in the United States.

A gentleman's agreement.

INTERVIEWS WITH FORMER Soviet officials reveal surprising contrasts. While LeMay felt that war demanded an all-out opening salvo, the Soviets came to a dramatically different conclusion. Nations, the Soviets concluded, would cease hostilities before even a small fraction of their stockpiles was delivered. Said one former Soviet officer: "The analysis was begun at 20 percent of the arsenals available to both sides and the exercise was halted when the modelers had exercised strikes comprised of 2 percent of the arsenal. The losses, even at an exchange of 2 percent, were so great that all operations and movement ceased for 2 days while surviving commanders and staff assessed the potential for regrouping and resuming operations. Even then, resumption of Front operations was problematical . . ."

"Problematical" was perhaps the most rational assessment of the bomb yet. The thought of any military functioning in the aftermath of a nuclear fireball that left radiated soldiers walking with burnt arms held in front of them like lobster claws could most certainly be considered "problematical." The recognition that even a limited nuclear exchange would do much to exhaust a large portion of human life within the borders of two nations was as honest as any report yet written.

WILLIAM E. MONTAGUE, a behavioral specialist with the United States Navy whose published papers touched on such complex topics as human cognition, aptitude, learning methodologies, and behavioral processes, attended an atomic-bomb explosion in Nevada as an official observer. Montague, it seems, wanted to be his own guinea pig. This countdown started at 2:55 A.M.

Wrote Montague: "The floodlights illuminated the grotesque little Joshua trees and the low clumps of brush for about fifty yards beyond the wire down the slope to our front. Beyond the light, the vast expanse of the valley was inky black, pinpointed here and there by the many-mile distant lights of a road marker, a tower, or a vehicle traveling on some late, pre-shot business."

The night, said Montague, was "cool." An observer near him was cold. The shot was code-named Shasta. It was 1957.

"The time tones were coming every minute," wrote Montague, "and with each one the tension went up a notch. At H minus eight minutes I stopped taking notes. I didn't want to clutter up the subjectivity of the experience. At H minus five minutes we turned around on the benches without waiting for the order to do so and covered our eyes. I removed my glasses and held them firmly by the temple pieces in my right fist. I buried my eyes in my left elbow and pressed my left arm against my face with my right fist. It was dark and lonely in there. I began to tremble. My stomach muscles knotted up. Then the tenseness spread to my chest muscles. I became irritated at myself and made a definite effort to relax, which relieved the muscle strain but did little to reduce my mind's tension. I imagined running away, then thought how trivial would be the increase in distance that I could add by running for the short remaining time, since a twelve mile distance already separated me from the device.

"H minus one minute.

"I pressed my arm tighter against my face.

"H minus thirty seconds.

"The awful, marching inexorability of the thing came over me. Zero time was speeding toward me like a car you cannot dodge. In the darkness I heard Boyd say, 'It's going to be too late to postpone it!' I thought rapidly of something witty to say, such as yelling 'Shasta is postponed for another twenty-four hours' but gave it up.

"H minus twenty seconds . . . H minus ten seconds . . . five, four, three (I scrunched my eyes shut and pulled my arm in on them) . . . two, one, zero.

". . . [W]e turned and I saw this thing that had been created. Far out across the miles of wasteland below us there was now dimly visible in the first morning light the golden fireball boiled and churned like a genie from a bottle, cooled to orange splotched with a deep dirty brown, cooled to heavy violet and as it cooled its shimmering blue corona contracted and glowed around it. The fireball rises . . ."

PREDELEGATION WAS A concept that in its most dangerous iteration suggested that a junior officer might someday be in a position to order the use of atomic bombs, and in its best iteration might enable the nation to execute a defensive or retaliatory plan if the nation's leaders were cut off or killed. Somewhere in the middle, however, was a way for a military commander to fend off an attack that might otherwise get through if an advantageous moment was lost while the commander in chief was tracked down to get approval.

In what was perhaps the best-kept secret of the Cold War, President Eisenhower gave a specific number of air-defense military commanders authority to use nuclear weapons without further consultation with him. He granted these powers by defining the circumstances under which this authority could be exercised—circumstances largely having in common the ability of a commander to engage hostile forces far from American shores. Eisenhower's "Policy Statement on Interception and Engagement of Hostile Aircraft" approved the use of atomic weapons against enemy ships at sea, enemy aircraft engaged over the oceans, or enemy aircraft engaged at high altitudes. This authority was affirmed in a document titled "Authorization for the Expenditure of Atomic Weapons in Air Defense," which was approved by the president.

Predelegation, however, went well beyond air defense alone. The soldier in Eisenhower knew that there would be other circumstances that might require an unhesitant response, windows of opportunities that could close if the president had to be found to approve the use of nukes. Recognizing this, Eisenhower predelegated additional authority to use nuclear weapons without further approval from him in a 1957 document titled "Instructions for the Expenditure of Nuclear Weapons in Accordance with the Presidential Authorization Dated May 22, 1957." Said Eisenhower: "When the urgency of time and circumstances clearly does not permit a specific decision by the President, or other person empowered to act in his stead, the Armed Forces of the United States are authorized by the President to expend nuclear weapons in the following circumstances in conformity with these instructions." The circumstances included the defense of the United States or its territories against an attack by air or sea, the defense of U.S. forces based in foreign countries, and to retaliate in the event of a direct attack against the United States.

The instructions cautioned that the expenditure of nuclear weapons should be "limited to circumstances of grave necessity," and that the predelegated authority was "an emergency measure necessitated by the recognition of the fact that communications may be disrupted by the attack."

As to who could issue these orders, Eisenhower created a class of officers known as "Authorizing Commanders." Authorizing Commander, empowered to use atomic weapons in air defense, included all commanding officers authorized to "declare aircraft hostile," a surprisingly broad definition that would include, as but one example, a senior officer in an air combat command center.* Much narrower was the pool of Authorizing Commanders approved to launch a retaliatory strike after a direct attack on the United States, a list limited to five commanders in chief including CINCSAC. "In the event that a nuclear attack has in fact occurred, as authenticated through prescribed procedures as approved by the president, on the United States and it is impossible to communicate with the secretary of defense and the Joint Chiefs of Staff, expenditure of nuclear weapons for retaliatory purposes may be ordered by an Authorizing Commander."

Reflecting no doubt the sensitive nature of predelegation, Eisenhower insisted that predelegation be kept secret from all but a handful of people. Wrote John S. D. Eisenhower in notes from a meeting with the president: "[The president] agreed that it is most important that word of any delegation from the President be withheld from our allies. It is in the U.S. interest to maintain the atmosphere that all authority stays with the President without predelegation."

Said the document: "The existence of these instructions and the provisions thereof are TOP SECRET classified information. In addition, the fact of the existence of these instructions will be limited to a highly restricted group of people."

As late as 1998, government historians with the highest security clearances would not find these documents, commenting that if they existed they would be some of the governments "best kept secrets."†

IN 1957, SAC flew three B-52s nonstop around the world. It was a breathtaking display of intercontinental air power and was news the world over. Lesser known, however, was that it took seventy-eight KC-97 tankers to refuel them. One could scarcely replace the old piston-engine tankers fast enough.

---

* The chain of command for the execution of military orders differs from the civilian chain of command for continuity of government.

† The secrecy surrounding predelegation was so high that even the Institute for Defense Analysis, a highly regarded Washington nonprofit organization that works solely for the U.S. government, was unable to uncover any evidence that it existed. In 1974, under a Defense Department contract, IDA spent six months reviewing Cold War documents. The study was conducted with the assistance of the chief historian in the office of the secretary of defense. They found no evidence of predelegation. Said the IDA: "It was always possible for a President to quietly instruct the Secretary of Defense, the JCS, and operational commanders as to the actions he would wish them to take if they were unable to obtain command direction from him in certain nuclear attack situations, but if that was done it was one of the best-kept secrets in government." The National Security Archive published the first official documents in 1998 confirming predelegation. In 2001, the archive released a second set of documents.

More than 600 B-17s and B-24s can be seen in this aerial photo of a post-WWII storage and reclamation area. This is roughly equal to the number of bombers that would strike a single target over Germany or Japan but it pales to the force of one Hiroshima bomb. More than 3,000 WWII bombers would be required to equal a single A-bomb. *(National Archives)*

Like all good propaganda material, pictures like these not only helped shape public opinion but reflected public opinion, too. Subliminal themes in this photograph suggest that knowing, responsible mothers and fathers stand shoulder-to-shoulder with our rugged, always-ready American fighter pilots, something that was not too far from the truth in 1955. *(National Archives)*

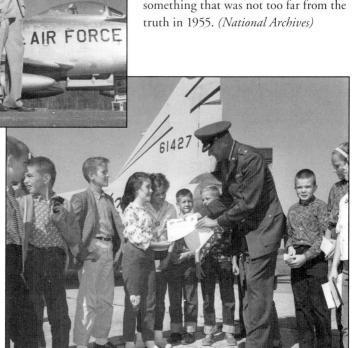

A pilot hands out honorary pilot certificates to the boys and girls visiting an air base in Missouri during an event cosponsored by the Air Force and the local Kiwanis Club. Steve Canyon and Sky King were still heroes of the comic strips and TV serials. *(National Archives)*

A rarely seen photograph of Curtis LeMay. LeMay, an avid amateur radio operator, shares his radio gear with the son of one of his neighbors in the Washington, D.C., area. The two are listening to a signal broadcast by a ham radio transmitter aboard an orbiting Air Force payload. LeMay placed amateur radio sets on his bombers to maintain contact with them during their lengthy missions. *(National Archives)*

The crew of a B-36 bomber makes final preparations for what no doubt will be a mission of twenty hours in length or more. The B-36 was so long that a small tunnel connected the forward and aft crew cabins. *(National Archives)*

A scanner sits next to an observation blister inside a B-36 bomber. The cockpit on a B-36 was so far forward that a pilot could not see his wings, engines, or landing gear. When called upon, the scanners would excuse themselves from their normal crew activities to scan these areas for problems. *(National Archives)*

This B-47 is demonstrating a Jet Assisted Takeoff, also called an Assisted Takeoff (ATO). The ATO was a contingency maneuver that would be used to take off on runways cratered or damaged by Soviet bombs. Rocket bottles attached to the tail provided the extra boost to get the bomber airborne without the ordinary takeoff roll. *(National Archives)*

A B-52 bomber inches in toward the refueling boom trailing a KC-135 tanker. On at least two occasions B-52s collided with their tankers, spilling nuclear bombs. Note the thermal reflective white coating applied to the lower surfaces. This paint provided a degree of protection from the heat of an atomic bomb blast. *(National Archives)*

The base surge phenomena is seen in this high altitude shot of the underwater Baker explosion during Operation Crossroads at Bikini Atoll. The blurred, small black shapes in the foreground, right and left, are actually military warships. The enormous wall of radioactive mist and water is rolling over them as if they were toys. In almost all of the secret American war scenarios, underwater detonations of Soviet bombs placed clandestinely in the harbors of New York, Boston, and San Francisco would mark the start of a general war. *(National Archives)*

Troops prepare to maneuver in the aftermath of an atomic blast. Atomic indoctrination exercises with troops were held at the Nevada test Site under the name Operation Desert Rock. As was seen at the tests in the Pacific, there was a "hairy-chested" attitude toward radiation exposure. *(National Archives)*

This is the Bravo fireball as seen from the destroyer USS *Estes* more than thirty miles from ground zero. This photograph was taken less than sixty seconds after the bomb exploded. Sailors on the *Estes* said the fireball felt like a blowtorch going over the backs of their necks. *(National Archives)*

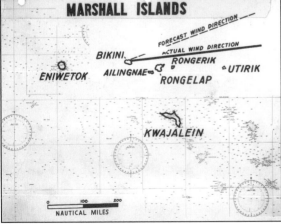

This original map shows the expected and actual wind directions during the Bravo explosion. One official later remarked that everyone and everything at the Pacific test site was to some degree contaminated. *(National Archives)*

This is the radio room inside the concrete-and-steel firing bunker on Bikini Atoll that sheltered—or trapped—nine men in heavy fallout. The men in the bunker mummy-wrapped themselves in bedsheets to keep radiation off their bodies as they escaped. *(National Archives)*

CWO John Kapral, USAF, leader of the twenty-eight men trapped on the Pacific island of Rongerik. It was Kapral's last-ditch midnight message that led to their evacuation the next day and may very well have saved these men from permanent radiation injury. *(Courtesy the John Kapral family)*

Because of the radiation they would encounter after a test explosion, helicopter flights back to ground zero were called "hot hops." After a hot hop, a helicopter would land in a "bath tub." Here a plane handler on an aircraft carrier checks the wheel of a helicopter for contamination. A decontamination wash down would follow. *(National Archives)*

An Air Defense Command radar operator demonstrates the light gun. When placed on the face of a radarscope, light guns triggered a pop-up display next to a target with flight information. Radar operators were affectionately called "scope dopes." *(National Archives)*

In the early years of Air Defense Command, large Plexiglas panels were used to display situation reports and air traffic targets from radar stations. So as not to interfere with the viewing, the updates were written from behind. Women were selected for this job because they were better than men at writing backwards, or so claimed ADC. *(National Archives)*

A fighter pilot makes last-minute adjustments to his flight gear before taking off with Genie air-to-air atomic missiles under his wing. The use of atomic weapons in air defense was called "the nuclear shield." *(National Archives)*

A B-52 refuels with two Hound Dog missiles under its wings. The B-52s would use their Hound Dogs to blast open penetration corridors or to attack heavily defended targets. The Hound Dog had an atomic warhead. *(National Archives)*

This is the distinctive case that held a nuclear bomb's plutonium capsule. The length of the cylinder reflects the length of the insertion handle used to push the capsule down into a bomb's pit. Strategic Air Command crews were given these birdcages before a mission. The birdcage would be opened only inside the bomber's bomb bay. *(Courtesy Clarke Ketter)*

Nuclear weapons were maintained and moved by Air Force Aviation Depot Squadrons. In this rare photograph, new squadron members are trained to service an MK-15 nuclear bomb. Howard Richardson ejected a bomb like this over the Savannah River. It was never found. *(Courtesy Clarke Ketter)*

The cavernous bomb bay of a B-36. For scale, note the three airmen in this photo. After takeoff, and before landing, a crewman would go down into this bomb bay and insert a ball of plutonium, or a simulated ball of plutonium, into the atomic bomb. The size of this bomb bay is a good indicator of the enormous girth of the early atomic bombs. 1949. *(National Archives)*

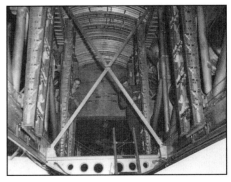

To save precious seconds during takeoffs, SAC designed these gently curving ramps and parking stubs so a pilot wouldn't have to slow down en route to the runway. These configurations were called "Christmas trees" or "herringbones." Seen here with KC-135 tankers. *(National Archives)*

A Strategic Air Command crew makes its way to the crew facilities. SAC alert crews moved together, usually tethered to their station wagon. The shape of the exit tunnels led to calling the alert bunker "moleholes." A KC-135 tanker is in the immediate background, behind which are several B-52s. 1960. *(National Archives)*

This is an impressive view of the tarmac as a ground-alert crew scrambles to their KC-135 tanker. Although less publicized, tanker crews sat 15-minute ground alerts just as the bomber crews did. Considering that this is one of ten tankers on alert, one gets a sense of how large a SAC air base had to be. *(National Archives)*

Inside an air wing's operations center during an Operational Readiness Inspection. Strategic Air Command routinely subjected its wings to these no-notice inspections. The entire air wing was expected to react just as they would in times of an actual attack. The gravity of the inspection is evident on the faces of these men; air wings rarely failed twice. *(National Archives)*

A bomber crew races to the cockpit of a B-47. *(National Archives)*

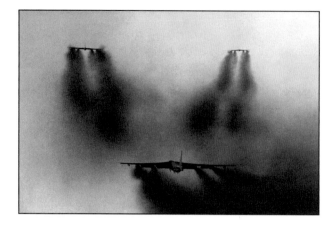

The Minimum Interval Take-off (MITO). During MITOs the swirl of black exhaust would often reduce visibility over a runway to little more than instrument flight rules. During MITOs the spacing was a scant twelve to fifteen seconds between bombers. These are B-52s. *(U.S. Air Force)*

Curtis LeMay strongly believed that public displays such as this flight of fifteen B-47s sent an important message to the Soviets. Unlike the single bomber that struck Hiroshima, or the formations of 600 to 900 bombers that bombed German targets during World War II, the Cold War nuclear strike mission used a very different tactic. Soviet targets would be hit by a small cluster of as many as ten bombers. Through the late 1950s, an air atomic strike would begin with something that looked like this. Photographed at the 1955 National Air Show in Philadelphia, Pennsylvania. *(National Archives)*

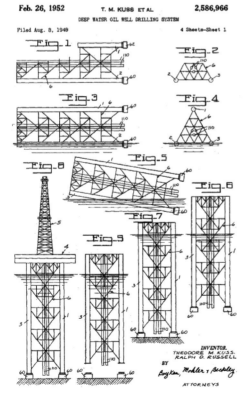

22 APR 1966

NND 903025
HR-M/RSC   1-28-94

Honorable Chet Holifield
Chairman
Joint Committee on Atomic Energy
Congress of the United States
Washington, D. C.

Dear Mr. Chairman:

During my testimony of April 19th I was asked to furnish for the record
a list of accidents in which nuclear weapons have been lost and never
recovered.   SANITIZED COPY   O.S.D.E.O. 12356, Sec. 3(C)(1)(C)(7)
SENSITIVE INFORMATION DELETED
There have been two such incidents involving complete weapons:

   1. On 8 February 1958 near Savannah, Georgia, a B-47 carry-
      ing a ▮▮▮▮▮ weapon collided with an F-86. The
      weapon was jettisoned in 100 feet of water in the Savannah
      River. The weapon was never recovered. This accident,
      including the weapon loss, was released to the press.

   2. On 5 December 1965 in the western Pacific an A4 aircraft
      with a ▮▮▮▮▮ weapon on board was lost over the side of the
      aircraft carrier USS TICONDEROGA in 2700 fathoms of
      water. The aircraft, pilot and weapon were not recovered.
      No public announcement of this incident has been made, nor
      is any intended. This subject is considered sensitive be-
      cause of its potential impact upon visits of the TICONDEROGA
      and other warships to foreign ports.

There have been two additional incidents resulting in the loss of weapons
less capsules:

   1. On 29 July 1957 at sea off the New Jersey coast a C-124
      lost power on two engines and was forced to jettison two
      ▮▮▮▮▮ without capsules into the Atlantic Ocean. This
      accident was not released to the press.

This is the 1966 letter written by one of the senior-most Pentagon officials in matters of atomic energy, W. J. Howard. Howard states, for the record, that the MK-15 bomb that Howard Richardson ejected over Savannah was a complete weapon. Richardson strenuously disagreed. Almost forty years later, Mr. Howard would be convinced that this letter was wrong. *(National Archives)*

Far from the user-friendly, ultra-simplified glass cockpits of today, this panel of switches, knobs, and a bombscope was the panel used by a radar navigator to line up a target and release a nuclear bomb. Photographed inside a B-52 bomber during a training mission against a Radar Bomb Scoring site. 1958. *(National Archives)*

An illustration from the Kuss Deep Water "tip-up" patent application. The Kuss design was used to build Texas Tower Four but was a sharp departure from the proven construction practices of the offshore oil industry. One experienced builder of offshore oil rigs wanted nothing to do with this design. *(Office of Patents and Trademarks)*

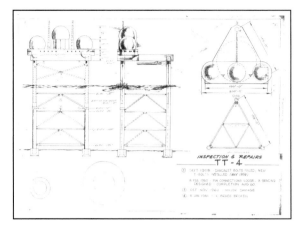

These three views of Texas Tower Four were included in exhibits submitted during the Tower Four testimony. The side view shows the flying bridge suspended below the platform that was destroyed by waves during Hurricane Donna. The top section of the underwater K-bracing had to be folded down, which led to the use of bolts connectors instead of welds—a fatal flaw, some said. (National Archives)

This is Texas Tower Four after the installation of the above-water X-bracing. The X-bracing increased the tower's resistance to the free passage of waves, another fatal error, according to some experts. (National Archives)

This is a wave sketch made during the testimony of witnesses appearing in the aftermath of Tower Four's collapse. While exceedingly basic it nonetheless clearly illustrates one of the key issues related to Tower Four. A Texas team of oceanographers thoroughly experienced with offshore oil rigs recommended raising Tower Four's deck to 72 feet above mean sea level. The design team hired by the navy disagreed and recommended a deck height of just 66.5 feet, which was the final decision. This diagram indicates that the clearance for a 97.5 foot wave, a wave possible for that area of the ocean, was essentially zero. This sketch also illustrates how wave height is calculated, that is, from crest to trough. (National Archives)

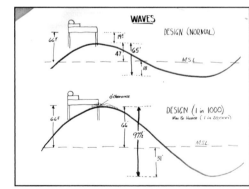

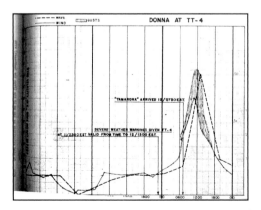

A page from a set of air force briefing documents on Tower Four. This chart shows how waves quickly built to fifty feet in height during Hurricane Donna. During that storm at least one wave struck Tower Four, which if graphed on this chart would have gone off the top. (National Archives)

The helicopter pads on the Texas Towers were some 85 feet above mean sea level. As impossible as it might seem, waves hit Tower Four so hard that they bent steel on the side of the platform just a few feet below the helicopter pad, seen here. For a sense of how large that wave was note the horizon to the left of the radome. *(National Archives)*

An aerial view of Texas Tower Two. Tower Two was the much photographed, first offshore radar station in a line of three radar stations placed in the Atlantic Ocean. Texas Towers provided an extra thirty minutes' warning to Strategic Air Command and filled in an important low-altitude coverage gap off the East Coast. 1959. *(National Archives)*

A minimum of two men was required to be present when working around a nuclear weapon. This was based on the belief that one man would keep the other in check should one of the two secretly contemplate sabotage. The two-man rule was effective even when a bomb was on board a bomber, as seen here. *(National Archives)*

A nuclear weapons carrier with a four-bomb, clip-in rack for a B-52. *(National Archives)*

This is the Ballistic Missile Early Warning Station at Thule, Greenland. The radar antennas, foreground, rose more than 160 feet and provided SAC with a 15-minute warning of an incoming missile strike. Because it was possible that a simple power outage would be confused with the first wave of a Soviet strike, SAC kept an armed B-52 orbiting this station day and night. The crash of the Thule Monitor B-52 on the frozen bay seen in the background, the second crash of an armed bomber on foreign soil, contributed to the end of airborne alerts. *(National Archives)*

These three B-52s demonstrate the high-speed, low-level penetration profile that would be used to sneak in under Soviet air defense radar coverage. Bombers would remain low all the way to their targets and would release their bombs at these altitudes using parachute systems that slowed the bombs' descent and allowed the bombers time to escape. By the late 1950s the low-level strike formation had largely replaced the cluster of ten bombers as the primary nuclear bombing tactic. Photographed during the World Congress of Flight in Las Vegas, 1959. *(National Archives)*

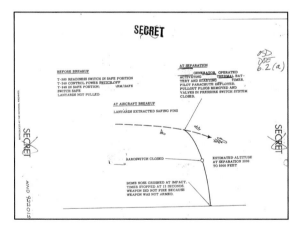

A diagram showing the break-up of a B-52 air-alert bomber and the sequence of events inside one of the bombs that fell free during the crash. In this case, several of the bomb's fail-safe gates were tricked by the forces of the airplane's disintegration and "believed" that the bomb was actually being dropped, thereby progressively arming the bomb as it fell. A portion of this bomb remains buried in a farm field near Goldsboro, North Carolina. *(National Archives)*

An Atlas missile explodes as its engines ignite. Strategic Air Command favored manned bombers over guided missiles and such early launch failures merely hardened SAC's resolve during the often heated missiles-versus-bomber debate. *(National Archives)*

One can only imagine driving down a country road and seeing missiles coming up from behind the next hill. This was a salvo launch of two Minuteman missiles from Vandenberg Air Force Base, California. *(National Archives)*

President John F. Kennedy meets General Curtis LeMay and General Thomas Power. At the time this photo was taken LeMay was the new Air Force Chief of Staff; Power, on the right, was SAC's Commander in Chief. 1961. *(National Archives)*

This is an aerial view of a typical underground Minuteman silo. Because of the absence of distinguishing surface features, bomber crews called this a no-show target. A no-show target was bombed by using a clearly identifiable land feature as an initial aiming point, then flying an offset course from that point on the bombing run. *(National Archives)*

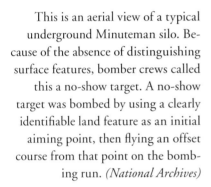

By the 1960s the distinctive thermal reflective white paint on the lower surfaces of the B-52s had been replaced by black. Black paint helped the bomber blend in with the sky over Vietnam. *(U.S. Air Force)*

* * *

PERHAPS THE MOST important refinement of ground alert was called "cocking the bomber." Cocking entailed pulling a bomber out of a hangar, positioning it on the alert ramp, presetting switches in the cockpit, selecting departure frequencies, opening navigational charts, and laying the departure checklist on the seats. The bomber was fueled, a war-ready nuclear bomb in strike configuration was in the bomb bay, auxiliary power was connected to the jet, and the generator was readied. Finally, the hatch was opened, the ladder was pulled down, the crew's headsets were plugged in and placed on the seats, and a sign was placed next to the jet that said "COCKED."

At the sound of the klaxon, the crew would scramble out of their alert bunkers and up the ladder, and the pilot would place his Smith & Wesson .357 Magnum behind his seat and check in with the tower.

Ground-alert bombers would henceforth be called "cocked bombers."

THE EFFECT OF airborne jamming on air-defense radarscopes was described by a radar operator: "[The] scopes would begin to light up with the jamming, beginning with multiple, long lines of . . . 'chaf' sometimes extending for 60 or 80 miles each across the scopes. Later would come electronic jamming, causing the scopes to pulsate with indecipherable strobes of light. In this electronic mess, our scope dopes [radar operators] would have to find the bombers . . ."

QUITE APART FROM the "sword and the shield" was the "nuclear shield." To penetrate American airspace, a Soviet bomber would have to fly through a gauntlet of nuclear air-to-air missiles, nuclear surface-to-air-missiles, and long-range nuclear guided missiles, each having a kill box of unprecedented size and lethality. The 1.5-kiloton Genie air-to-air missile carried by a jet interceptor, for instance, had a kill box the size of three football fields. The 40-kiloton Nike Hercules surface-to-air missile would deliver a warhead twice as powerful as the bomb dropped on Hiroshima with a kill box many times that of Genie. In both cases, close enough was close enough. The blast effects of these warheads could take down as many jets as were close enough to the burst points.

At its peak, the nuclear shield consisted of some 1,600 Nike launchers, 224 long-range antiaircraft guided missiles, and, at any given hour, some three hundred or more fighters on strip alert. More than 10,900 atomic warheads were earmarked for air defense.

* * *

THE COMBINATION OF Reflex and ground alert went so well that in July 1957 the test ended and Reflex became a standard SAC air operation. Every twenty-one days, a fresh crew would "Reflex" overseas and take over ground alert from a previous crew. The arriving bombers were serviced, fueled, and loaded with the all-new eleven-foot-long, six-thousand-pound four-megaton MK-39 thermonuclear bombs.*

"Without exception, Reflex is the most effective, practical, best planned and coordinated Emergency War Plan," said the crewman of one bomber squadron. Said an SAC historian, "[T]his was the type of readiness the American people had been led to expect of SAC."

A B-47 BOMBER in Texas crashed on takeoff in July 1957, killing the crew members on board. According to the crash report, the bomber had been generated to its Emergency War Plan load.

As of this writing, no 1957 bomber crash in Texas is included in any official document disclosing accidents involving nuclear weapons.

IN JULY 1957, the Distant Early Warning line of radar stations was completed and handed over to the air force. Sixty-three new radar stations spaced fifty miles apart now covered the arctic approaches to North America with interlacing beams of radar so sensitive that they could give SAC six hours of warning against a Soviet attack over the northern approaches where before there had been none.

Surprisingly, not everyone was entirely happy. Said a disgruntled member of the Canadian House of Commons, the DEW line wasn't there to destroy enemy bombers but to give the retaliation force of friendly bombers warning enough to "get in the air so they will not be destroyed on the ground." That thought was hardly reassuring to the member: ". . . it does not hold out much comfort for the rest of us because we are going to be burnt to a crisp anyway."

Which was the paradox of deterrence. The moment a fireball appeared, both nations would be burnt to a crisp.

ON JULY 1, 1957, after a historic nine years as the head of Strategic Air Command, General Thomas Power replaced Curtis LeMay as commander in

---

* The formerly classified section of new documents clearly states that the B-47s were loaded with MK-39s, although this bomb is generally associated with the B-52 or B-58.

chief of Strategic Air Command. In no way, however, did LeMay's presence shrink. General Power was of the LeMay mold. SAC would not just continue the disciplines put into place by LeMay; under Power those disciplines would be hardened, the standards would be raised, and the emerging concept of ground alert would be extended to the air. Power believed, as did LeMay, that SAC was at war.

And LeMay? LeMay was on his way to the highest office in the United States Air Force. He would begin that journey as vice chief of staff of the United States Air Force.

A C-124 CARGO plane with the Strategic Support Squadron was bound for Sidi Slimane air base, in Morocco, to deliver three atomic bombs when it ran into engine trouble over the Atlantic off the coast between Rehoboth Beach, Delaware, and Cape May, New Jersey. To lighten the plane, the pilot ejected two of the three atomic bombs and diverted to an air base in New Jersey, where he landed safely.

The air force asked the navy to search for the bombs but no debris was spotted and no bombs were found and the search was abandoned. The ocean in that area varied but in many places it was as shallow as 150 feet.

To this day, the two ten-foot-long, three-thousand-pound MK-5 atomic bombs, each packed with uranium and high explosives but no capsule, have never been found.*

ON AUGUST 26, 1957, the Kremlin announced that they had successfully tested a "super long range intercontinental multi-stage ballistic missile." It would be called the SS-6 Sapwood. Sapwood could travel the impossible distance of six thousand miles.

Khrushchev spoke of this new missile and its warhead. The Sapwood could turn Europe into "a veritable cemetery," he said, and the United States was "just as vulnerable."

IN A REMARKABLE feat of problem solving, RAND's Albert Wohlstetter visualized what he would call "fail-safe." Wohlstetter knew that Strategic Air Command would launch its bombers within minutes of any warning, but what puzzled him was how those bombers might be recalled if the warning

---

* These MK-5s were likely intended for the air force's Quick Reaction Alert fighters in Europe and not SAC's Reflex bombers.

turned out to be false. Wohlstetter had no issue with launching the bombers but he saw numerous situations that could confuse aircrews and lead to potentially catastrophic consequences. Against endless combinations of methods to recall the bombers, he found fault with each until he saw the one way that would recall the bombers with absolute certainty, and it had nothing to do with Emergency Action Messages or "go" codes or double authentication of codes. "Initial response," wrote Albert Wohlstetter, "does not include launching of a retaliatory force without the possibility of recall . . . initial decisions are preparatory in nature . . . by a fail-safe procedure we mean one in which the bombers will return to base after reaching a predesignated point en route— unless they receive an order to continue." *Unless they receive an order* being the operative words.

Fail-safe was not the *receipt* and confirmation of the go code, as has become popularized. Rather, it was the absence of a go code. Said one historian: "Bombers, flushed by some serious yet not unambiguous warning, [would] return to base unless they are specifically directed to continue forward." If a message to proceed was *not* received, that itself was a message to turn around. No order was order enough to break off an attack. To Wohlstetter, the quiet of a silent radio would ensure that a bomber turned back.

And that silent radio would be impervious to indecision, stand free of debate or discussion, eliminate crew confusion in the tense moments of prewar, make technical problems or communication problems unimportant, and render void countless other subjective measures. Fail-safe was fail-safe and that solved the final problem of 15 minutes. Strategic Air Command could launch its bombers.

And now it could stop them.

IN SEPTEMBER 1957, the United States Air Force successfully launched and controlled for three minutes the Atlas ICBM. That a malfunction necessitated its midflight destruction was of little concern; that it launched and flew and was controlled from the ground made success just a matter of time.

A NAVY CAPTAIN with extensive nuclear experience critiqued the Emergency War Plan planning process. "Two major handicaps restrict military atomic planning," he wrote in a note to the chairman of the Atomic Energy Commission. "First and most important is the inferiority complex still common to most senior officers. They tend to consider atomic weapons to be beyond their understanding without extensive study for which they have neither interest nor time. Atomic planning is therefore delegated to juniors who have completed various 'effects' courses. They frequently lack the maturity and judgment normally provided by guidance from their seniors. When these junior planners confront their seniors with effects terminology and apparently complex calculations, the seniors are unable to exert normal guidance. Instead, they are prone to endorse the computations without close questioning and without understanding procedures or implications—and in spite of personal misgivings." It became prudent, the author averred, to add a bomb here or a bomb there to be certain that a Russian air base was destroyed and a runway properly cratered or that a city like Moscow had been effectively decapitated. But the real problem was as old as the military itself. The author was speaking not just of the complexities of atomic planning but of the timeless problem of adapting to change.

And in matters of nuclear weapons, change was as complicated and daunting as change can be.

A NEWSREEL FLICKERED to life in movie theaters across the nation. The clip lasted less than two minutes but on everyone's lips were the seven words that headlined the story. "A new moon is in the sky," intoned the announcer.

That moon was a Soviet satellite named Sputnik.

It was October 7, 1957.

ONE MONTH AFTER the launch of Sputnik, the air force hurriedly approved the basing of nine squadrons of Atlas and Titan ICBMs at Vandenberg Air Force Base, California.

Missile production, too, was placed on a fast track.

At the same time, the design for a more reliable, solid-rocket ICBM named Minuteman received the go-ahead.

IN NOVEMBER 1957, General Power held a press conference and revealed to the American public the existence of ground-alert bombers. He stated that he had 11 percent of his forces on some form of alert and that some of those alert forces were in bombers that sat "at the end of runways, bombs loaded and crews nearby ready to take off in 15 minutes."

But then Power added a new wrinkle. These new alert forces were not just "a taut spring of bombers waiting to leap from the ground. Day and night I have a certain percentage of my command in the air. These planes," he said, "are bombed up and they don't carry bows and arrows."

Power had unexpectedly pulled back the curtain on what would become known as "airborne alert."

WHILE FAIL-SAFE WAS a communications system that worked in the absence of radio contact with its bombers, SAC also needed a communications system that would with absolute reliability make contact with its bombers. SAC needed a fail-safe way to issue the go code. SAC wanted a system to tell its pilots to "go," not just Wohlstetter's foolproof "turn around" system.

In November 1957, such a system was in place and was ready to be tested. Twelve global air routes were created over which sixty-five bombers would fly a mock combat mission. The go code or Emergency Action Message would be relayed through low- and high-frequency radios positioned along the routes including the new single-side-band radios. The results were encouraging. The go code was successfully transmitted and properly handled by fifty of the sixty-five bombers. The failures of the fifteen other bombers were the result of minor crew issues that were resolved with training, and some jumbled transmissions for which fixes were easily identified.

Over the next ten years SAC would improve its communications networks. These improvements would include radio repeaters strategically placed along almost every attack route to the Soviet Union and China, including routes that went down the coast of South America and across to Africa, from California to Guam, over the North Pole, and in time would include missiles that would broadcast the codes on trajectories that covered one-third of the globe.

THE REALITY OF 15 minutes was quite different from what most thought it meant. It wasn't to start takeoffs in 15 minutes but rather to *complete* takeoffs in 15 minutes. To accomplish this, the first bomber had to be airborne in just seven minutes. Said a 1957 SAC report: "Assuming that one SAC B-52/KC-135 base would launch five bombers and four tanker aircraft, and that a one minute takeoff interval between each aircraft could be established, the first aircraft would have to be launched within seven minutes after a warning to [e]nsure that all nine aircraft would be airborne within 15 minutes."

Busting out the alert force, as it was called, was to be finished in 15 minutes.

AS 1957 CAME to a close there were 6,444 nuclear bombs in the national stockpile, of which 2,250 were under military control. Strategic Air Command had 2,421 bombers and tankers on thirty-eight bases in the United States and, with the recent addition of bases in Spain, SAC had another thirty overseas bases. There were 134 B-47 bombers now on alert plus an unknown number of tankers and B-36s.

Two new weapons were approved for development in 1957, an air-to-ground nuclear-tipped missile called the Hound Dog, designed to strike heavily defended targets or air-defense sites, which would be carried by the B-52, and the Quail missile, a decoy missile also designed for the B-52 but intended to confuse enemy radars by appearing as another inbound bomber.

AN ENGINEERING NIGHTMARE

THE COLD WAR press called Tower Four a "marvel of engineering." Not only would it provide earlier warning of a Soviet surprise attack, but it was an object unlike anything seen before. Rifle-shot straight lines depicted a tower of architectural beauty standing on three powerful legs that rose through the ocean and stood sixty-five feet high, on top of which was perched a steel platform that bristled with antennas and microwave disks that would send and receive telemetry and bounce radio signals off the atmosphere. Storm winds might claw waves out of the Atlantic that would grow into mountains of water sixty-feet high, but they'd pass unobstructed between the broad legs as if nothing were in the sea. Winds as powerful as 125 miles per hour would be shrugged off as if mere gusts.

There was a helicopter pad as large as any on a naval ship and a twenty-three-ton tracked crane that ran the length of the platform. Three radomes crowned the platform, rising another fifty-five feet high. Red and green lights winked through the night and spotlights illuminated her weather deck.

Architectural renderings appeared in newspapers the nation over. Across the legs was drawn a water level as smooth as a millpond.

But the North Atlantic was rarely as smooth as a millpond. And Tower Four was rarely immune to the vicissitudes of the Atlantic. Indeed, on a calm day with a bright sun, to lean against the railing, perched above a sea that stretched as far as the naked eye could see—on such days the ocean glimmered with sparkles of reflected light and the air was pleasingly perfumed with the smell of salt water and there were few places on Earth more beautiful to be. There would be barbecues on the weather deck with rows of chairs brought out so the men could read or nap in the sun. In the evenings, a long, lazy sunset spilled a shimmering red across the sky in a postcard-worthy display of colors unlike anything the men had seen before. On a clear night, one could reach up and grab a clump of stars;

Doldrums would leave the surface of the Atlantic so still that a whisper could be heard a dozen miles away.

But when the winds stiffened over the open fetches and the waves made up, the towers became living things. Life on a Texas Tower required "fortitude," said an air force brochure handed out to new arrivals. "If you have it, fine; if you do not, you will have an opportunity to learn something of it on the tower." In heavy seas, the legs flexed and the tower tilted and shuddered and rocked. Wind would thump against the exposed platform with sledgehammerlike blows. Against a cresting wave, the towers lurched, not unlike the way a train lurches in its tracks.

Seasickness was common. "I was sitting in the dining hall watching a movie and I thought I was sick because I was getting dizzy," said a noncommissioned officer. "It was the movement on the tower that I was feeling. In our little NCO room, I saw the water in the tropical aquarium sloshing from side to side." Said another: "In high winds, you would be walking down the corridor which was approximately two hundred feet long, and you would sway from one side to the other."

Said a master sergeant who worked on Tower Two: "I arrived at the Tower before the Air Force took it over. I had no doubt in my mind that none of us would ever leave this three-legged monster alive. No one could sleep due to the noise, constant shaking, swaying and shuddering of the entire tower." The sergeant was on the tower when the Swedish cruise liner *Stockholm* rammed the Italian liner *Andrea Doria*. The *Andrea Doria* sank. The collision took place just miles north of Tower Two. "Deck chairs and suitcases and so on of that ship came floating by the tower. I would say that my duty on the Texas Tower Two was the worst duty I ever pulled in the twenty years of my career, and I was in Vietnam."

None of that, however, would match the experiences of those who served on Tower Four. Tower Four would take more than fortitude. Tower Four's legs traveled through waters three times deeper than those under Towers Two or Three. Tower Four's platform weaved above the seas in ways no man would forget.

Tower Four broke men's minds.

JUNE 26, 1957, Texas Tower Four was launched in front of an admiring audience at the South Portland Shipyard and floated into the bay on its side. Wrote *The New York Times*: "A huge steel tripod floating feet first on two of its three legs was towed into deep water on the night high tide. A cottony fog diffused the glare of floodlights adding to the eeriness of the scene."

For most of the next eight days, oceangoing tugboats pulled Tower Four through the ocean. On calm days the legs slid across the surface of the sea like a sled on ice. When the waves rolled ever so slightly, the long, spindly structure undulated gently over the rolling seas. On a day of no particular note, the tower undulated a little too high or perhaps a little too low and a two-ton brace snapped off as if it were a toothpick.

On July 4, the flotilla arrived at the tower's intended position, one hundred miles off the coast of New Jersey, and as they did, the winds whipped the ocean with unexpected gusts and clawed waves out of the sea. The flotilla pointed up and spent the night in a brief Atlantic storm.

In the morning, it was discovered that three steel bolts, each weighing eight hundred pounds, had snapped, and another brace was gone.

THE MEN HUDDLED on the boats, looking at the wounded tower lying on its side, rolling gently on the surface of the Atlantic Ocean. If the tower was to be towed back to the yard, weeks would be lost. On the other hand, repairs could be made at sea, but not without some modifications that would involve underwater hard-hat diving. Said Eugene Rau, vice president of the J. Rich Steers Company, which handled the actual construction: "There were only two ways of doing the work. One was taking it back to Portland, putting it back into dry dock, and actually putting the braces back exactly as they had been when we left the yard a week before. The other was to have a design made by the architect-engineer to install braces under water. It was pointed out that if we did go back to Portland, we would not be able to implant the tower in 1957 but it would have to be held over until 1958. It was then that the decision was made that we would go ahead with the upending and get a design for the installation of permanent braces under water."

In the aftermath of the tower's collapse, the investigating committee asked: "Do you feel that was the right decision?"

Answered Rau: "Well, sir, being out there knowing the urgency of getting the job done so that it would be put into the chain of the nation's defense. I think we felt it was the right decision, yes sir."

ON JULY 7, 1957, Tower Four, damaged as she was, was tipped over. During the tip-over, another diagonal brace tore free and sank to the bottom. As the four-thousand-ton platform was floated into position it rocked in the swells and banged against the legs and smashed dents ten inches wide and two feet long. Kuss, the architect-engineer, designed a collar of steel to be wrapped around the legs and bolted into place just below the waterline.

Said an air force historian of Tower Four's broken bolts and missing braces and the proposed steel collar: "It had become an engineering nightmare."

Leon DeLong could only sigh.

THE CONTROVERSIAL MATTER of wave heights was settled before the tower had become a radar station—not that anyone thought much about it at the time. While the tower was being fitted out, a storm blew up and a construction worker on a night shift happened to look out to sea. The horizon was gone. "I saw what I thought was something black," he remembered. "I couldn't see a crest on the wave and I said to myself what is that . . . where the hell is that thing coming from? I watched it grow and grow and the next thing, it hit. The water from the top of that wave splashed water on the deck at 87 feet. All the men down below came running up. They were hollering at me . . . why I didn't wake them up, and I say, just hang on boys, there's another one. There were three that hit us. They actually pushed the tower back. You could hear it screeching and groaning."

1958

HOT CARGO

MAJOR HOWARD RICHARDSON of Strategic Air Command's Nine-teenth Bombardment Wing, based at Homestead Air Force Base, Florida, and pilot of Ivory Two—the call sign for his B-47—walked around the nose of his bomber and approached the airman from the depot squadron. The airman snapped a crisp salute and handed Richardson a clipboard. It was February 4, 1958. It was an unusually cold night for Florida.

Richardson scanned the short form. Across the top read the words "Tem-porary Custodian Receipt [for maneuvers]." A 7,600-pound 1.6-megaton MK-15 nuclear bomb was in his bomb bay. It was now his.

"I signed for the bomb," said Richardson. "I really only noticed that it said it was unarmed."

Thus began what should have been, by almost any measure, a near-flawless combat training mission that instead inexplicably turned into one of the most puzzling nuclear accidents in the history of the United States Air Force. At the peak of the exercise, five aircraft participated in a simulated combat mission with a radar-bombing run that would pit two attacking nuclear bombers, Ivory One and Ivory Two, against three defending fighter-interceptors, Gold One, Gold Two, and Gold Three.

One jet would never come home.

And when Howard Richardson landed, his bomb bay would be empty.

FIRST LIEUTENANT CLARENCE Stewart flew the Republic F-86L, a cutting-edge fighter-interceptor equipped with airborne radar. Along with two other pilots on alert, Stewart would scramble his jet to intercept the B-47s as part of the training exercise that was called Southern Belle. His call sign was Gold Two.

THE TWO B-47s left Homestead Air Force Base and flew across the Gulf of Mexico to Louisiana, where they turned north toward Minnesota. Over

Minnesota, they turned again and on a diagonal track flew across the United States to the eastern seaboard, where they turned south to bomb a radar site near the small town of Radford, Virginia. Their mission included one aerial refueling and dispensing chaff, which they evidently did without incident. Richardson, in Ivory Two, trailed Ivory One.

Fewer nights were as beautiful as the night of Southern Belle. A high-pressure system had settled over the Southeast, leaving a crystal-clear sky with a beautiful full moon. The wind rushing down the sides of their fuselage as they flew thirty-five thousand feet above the earth, Richardson and copilot Bob Lagerstrom sat above their B-47, the canopy wrapped around their shoulders and the ink black of the heavens just outside. The stars appeared as bright pinpoints of light; the hum of the engines and the hiss of oxygen were the only sounds they heard.

Richardson looked at his watch and put his B-47 into shallow S-turns to allow Ivory One to pull ahead. Several minutes passed.

Then they released their bombs electronically.

THE FIGHTER JETS arced into the sky, streaking up through the night with no more than the blue flickers of their tailpipes marking their progress. Ivory One first reported the fighters.

Controllers vectored Stewart into position more than ten miles behind Ivory Two. Stewart leaned forward and watched the pip on his radar indicating that the bomber was several miles in front of him. Inexplicably, he felt a slight thump. "I thought it was jet wash and so I looked up," said Stewart. "There was airplane everywhere." Stewart yanked his jet into an evasive maneuver but broadsided Richardson's bomber. A flash of flames exploded around him; Stewart pulled his ejection handles, and *whoosh!* was blasted into the night sky. At the top of his arc, Stewart no doubt saw his burning F-86 drop beneath his feet and the lights of the B-47 slip away into the night.

And then he was alone.

He felt a yank as his chute caught air.

ROBERT LAGERSTROM, COPILOT of the B-47, remembered the mid-air collision: "We had completed the main part of our mission. I was taking a fuel reading and scanning the gauges that are over on the right side of the instrument panel. I'm left handed so I was bent over toward the right to write. I saw a ball of fire out the right side. I knew immediately that we had been hit by something. The Aircraft Commander alerted us to get ready for a bailout."

Said Richardson: "We had been on one of those SIMCOM [simulated combat missions] and we were supposed to be in friendly territory when it happened. I noticed some fighter guys go underneath me, but I didn't pay it much attention. Next thing I knew, there was a flash of light on my right wing—I knew it must have been one of the fighters."

Stewart.

"I looked over and saw number six hanging and the tank missing," said Richardson. The number-six engine was dangling nose-up and was useless. "I punched off the left tank to keep it balanced." The bomber held steady.

"We made radio contact with SAC; we had to tell SAC headquarters what we were going to do, but no one was there, just the night crew," said Richardson. "I never really got concurrence until I was on the way to the field, but we diverted to Hunter." Hunter Air Force Base, east of Savannah, Georgia, was an SAC bomber base.

"I let down to twenty thousand feet and put the gear down and some flaps and lowered the speed to see what would happen when I approached a stall," said Richardson, talking about the landing configuration for the bomber. "It wasn't wobbly or shaking—there was good controllability. We got down to 220 knots okay, so I figured it was safe for a long runway."

Richardson began a gradual descent. Lagerstrom switched the radio to Hunter's tower frequency and declared an emergency. The tower advised the crew that Hunter's runway was under construction; it was usable, but there was a dangerous one-foot lip on either end. They could land, but the lip was a problem. "If we hit it," said Richardson, "that doggoned weapon would be just like a bullet going through a rifle barrel."

The pilots were on their radios, one talking to air traffic control at Hunter, the other to Strategic Air Command. "Howard was talking to ATC and I called SAC," said Lagerstrom. "We advised SAC that we had to jettison hot cargo. It got very quiet on the radio."

THE MK-15 THERMONUCLEAR bomb was one of the newest and most secret bombs in America's arsenal, but inside Howard Richardson's jet it was also one of the most dangerous. The thought of it snagging on that one-foot lip of concrete continued to bother Richardson. "Aircrews have tactical doctrine that they follow," said Richardson. "The number one priority was the safety of the crew. If we had a problem that bomb would have gone through the plane like a bullet going through a rifle barrel. That's why I didn't mind dropping that weapon."

Sandwiched between the sky and the ocean below, Richardson asked Woolard, his navigator, to tell him where they were. Viewing the terrain through his bomb scope, Woolard said he had water in sight. "We were almost on downwind and were heading out over water to make our left turns back to base," said copilot Lagerstrom. "That's when we jettisoned it."

As they descended through seven thousand feet, the bomb-bay doors snapped open and *click!* the bomb snapped free from the suspension sling and silently dropped through the sky until it splashed into Wassaw Sound, a body of water surrounded by creeks and marshes east of Savannah, Georgia.

Richardson and Woolard scribbled coordinates on their knee pads.

None of them matched.

THE MIDAIR COLLISION took place over Hampton County, South Carolina, more than one hundred miles from Hunter Air Force Base and Savannah, Georgia. Local residents said that they were awakened by two loud explosions, and within minutes the switchboard at the local police station was flooded with calls. The next morning, the air force issued a press release saying that the noises had been those of a minor collision between a bomber and an F-86.

The *Augusta Chronicle* tracked down Stewart and interviewed him in his hospital bed. Stewart, who had ejected at thirty thousand feet, had landed in a snake-infested swamp and been rescued by a raccoon hunter, but he'd been in the freezing air so long that he had frostbite.

ON FEBRUARY 6, 1958, a navy minisubmarine quietly slipped up the Wilmington River and tied off abeam the Savannah Sheraton Hotel. An air force recovery team had checked in to the hotel and was setting up operations. Offshore, just over the horizon, a navy destroyer arrived to serve as a command post and as a "defensive screen" against foreign intruders.

Along the riverbanks, divers clad in black wet suits climbed into and out of rubber boats. A United States Navy tender laid marker buoys across Wassaw Sound. Five miles to the north, another navy tender started dragging the muddy waters near Tybee Island. To the west, a navy blimp appeared over the marshes and occasionally dropped red marker ribbons, most of them around the edges of the Sound.

Puzzled by this activity, reporters from the *Savannah Morning News* called the public affairs office at Hunter Air Force Base. They learned nothing.

On February 12, the air force issued a press release: "A damaged B-47 made an emergency landing at Hunter Air Field and en route released a portion of a nuclear weapon, which the navy is now mounting efforts to recover." To the local media, this was startling news indeed. The accident had occurred well to the north of Savannah, so, locally, they knew nothing about it, nor of Clarence Stewart or his interview from his hospital bed. Moreover, they knew nothing of Howard Richardson's bomber and the emergency landing at their nearby air base.

The next day, the *Savannah Morning News* ran a banner headline on the front page: "JETTISONING OF NUCLEAR WEAPON HERE DISCLOSED." The story continued: "Yesterday's release gave no reason for the jettisoning nor did it give any details about the 'portion' of the weapon that was dropped. Officials refused to elaborate on the release and to answer any questions from newsmen." The newspaper went on to say that no one knew "whether the nuclear device landed in the sea or on land."

The questions, of course, persisted.

On February 15, the air force issued a second press release. This one said that the bomb had been carried "in a transportable condition," which they further defined as meaning in "a form carried for safety reasons." Those in Savannah made little sense of this wording, but they took it to mean that the weapon was perhaps disassembled or in crates or perhaps it shouldn't be considered a weapon at all. This second press release, however vague, nonetheless seemed to have had its intended effect: it was calming.

But then the navy announced that another ship, the USS *Bowers,* had arrived. The *Bowers* brought with it fourteen more divers and men from the Explosive Ordnance Disposal Unit in Cedar Keys, Florida.

The air force explained this stepped-up activity by saying that the ejected component was "a very expensive piece of equipment."

BOMBS-ON-BASE

IT WAS WINSTON Churchill speaking, this time commenting on the dilemma of deterrence. Said Churchill: "Safety will be the sturdy child of terror, and survival the twin brother of annihilation."

Churchill was saying that to be safe in this nuclear age, the prospect of retaliation must be so terrifying that no sane person would launch an attack. To survive, annihilation had to be the price the enemy would pay the moment the enemy attacked.

THE FIRST OFFICIAL test of General Power's airborne alert bombers began on January 13, 1958, when two B-36 bombers with their EWP bombs began flying round-robin legs to and from Ramey Air Force Base, Puerto Rico, and Nouasseur Air Base, Morocco. One aircraft departed Ramey daily; another departed Nouasseur daily. For 139 days, one B-36 was in the air at all times—bombers that could never be destroyed on the ground, bombers that would always be able to retaliate, which was the entire idea of air alert. The only shortcoming Strategic Air Command saw was that the bombers were not on routes that took them toward their targets. That aside, General Power promptly called for a permanent airborne alert program.

With bombs.

CIA DIRECTOR ALLEN Dulles spoke at Yale University about the unexpected flight of Sputnik and the effect it had on the American people. "A free people such as ours seem to require at periodic intervals dramatic developments to alert us to our perils."

Dulles spoke of an America "complacently accustomed to being first" in whatever field of endeavor we chose, but now "rudely eclipsed" by the Soviets in a field as important and as deadly as missiles and space. It was February 3, 1958.

Dulles had a point but failed to mention that American industry had never been shy about playing catch-up.

IN WHAT WOULD no doubt fill the skies with bombers and interceptors, Strategic Air Command prepared for Operation Faxir, a simulated attack by some 50 B-47 bombers against targets in Chicago, Gary, Indiana, and Milwaukee, Wisconsin. In the air to oppose them would be approximately 150 fighter-jet interceptors. "The . . . tests will consist of a series of seven scheduled missions by the Strategic Air Command forces and will simulate a realistic penetration of the NORAD System with simulated aiming points in the Chicago–Milwaukee area and further south," said a USAF Information Plan sent to the commands involved. "The first mission is scheduled between 0100–0400." For added realism, twenty-three ground-based Nike-Ajax surface-to-air missile units and one Nike-Hercules unit would activate their radars and sweep the skies. Eight more units would go live around Milwaukee. All air traffic would be suspended in the area, which SAC worried would "excite public curiosity."

"To prevent public speculation, anxiety, or unrest during the periods of the forthcoming tests, the bombing would be described as a Strategic Air Command bombing exercise. Because such SAC maneuvers are commonplace, and because the press release in question would be based on fact, the integrity of the deception should be [e]nsured."

The next morning, thin strips of aluminum were found on the streets below.

Chaff.

SO HIGHLY CLASSIFIED were the U-2 overflights that even within the United States military establishment, the mere knowledge of them required a special clearance that included a lengthy, somewhat unnerving security oath that had to be signed by all. This level of security was called the TALENT Security System, and the intelligence within it, largely photographic, was called TALENT photography. Strategic Air Command was quickly one of the largest customers of TALENT intelligence, and in short order Strategic Air Command's Intelligence Directorate had more than three hundred analysts holding TALENT clearances. "It is perhaps enough to say that the effect of TALENT photography on the SAC target list has been substantial," wrote a CIA planner who visited SAC's TALENT Center vault in 1958. At that time, no fewer than 236 new Soviet installations had recently been identified by photo analysts within the directorate, and of those 106 had been added to SAC's Radar Order of Battle.

Not only was the CIA planner pleased that TALENT was proving so useful, he was satisfied that SAC's method of processing and duplicating the photographs sanitized them enough to preclude any trace back to their source. "I am personally pleased that through this means a considerable amount of information is made available to users not in the system and, in my opinion, without jeopardy to the Project." In fact, SAC had developed a special process for converting TALENT photographs into radar images so that a navigator would have an image that matched what he could see through his radarscope. These converted photographs were called "radar recognition charts," also known as 100 Series charts. Radar recognition charts, according to the CIA, had been significantly improved by the high quality of the TALENT intelligence.

Within TALENT, an additional clearance was required to view the most sensitive images, possibly biological or chemical plants or the homes of elected officials. These images required a clearance that was called KEYHOLE. Thus, those with a TALENT and a KEYHOLE clearance were called TALENT-KEYHOLE, a term that has become lore among black-operations-history buffs.

Over the coming years TALENT would expand exponentially and would include images from satellites that would orbit Earth. True, too, TALENT photography would in the end have much to do with who would be bombed, and who would not.

It was February 12, 1958.

SENATOR CLINTON P. Anderson, a member of the Joint Committee on Atomic Energy, railed against the Department of Defense. An atomic bomb had been accidentally released by a Strategic Air Command B-47 flying over rural South Carolina. The high explosives detonated when the bomb hit the ground, destroying one house, damaging a church, and causing injuries to six people.

The incident made headlines. The Department of Defense explained that a locking mechanism had failed in the bomb bay, thus causing the bomb to drop. The bomb, said the Pentagon, had been unarmed.

Anderson went to the media not because of the failure of the sling but because the Pentagon had used the term *unarmed*. Said Anderson: "To say that a bomb was unarmed is just like saying a loaded double-barreled shotgun is unarmed just because the safety is on."

But Anderson went a step further. He accused the Pentagon of withholding information on other "A-bomb misadventures," a surprising point of view considering Strategic Air Command's elevated status on Capitol Hill.

Either way, Anderson's comment did usher in an era when, in the sense of a nuclear bomb at least, the terms *armed* or *unarmed* would be a continued source of debate.

"UNITED STATES PLANES carrying actual atomic weapons—complete or in component form—fly daily over many parts of the country, and overseas as part of our readiness alert and for operation training," reported *The New York Times*. "SAC's announced goal is an alert status for one-third of its bombers. This means that in another two years or so when more bases and alert facilities are ready considerably more than 700 B-47 and B-52 bombers—most of them armed with A-weapons—will be either flying in the air or poised at the end of runways ready to take off with fifteen minutes notice."

Those who read the story might well have noticed an ever-so-slight hint of yet another criticism of SAC. The headline was "Are We Safe from Our Own Bombs?"

It was March 16, 1958.

SAID AN SAC historian: "Although it was planned that CINCSAC would retain direct central control of SAC forces during wartime, it was almost certain that the enemy would give high priority to destruction of SAC Headquarters . . . As early as September 1958 SAC took steps to initiate a communications system which could be expected to survive even under conditions of surprise attack . . . [These systems would have] a minimum capability to alert and execute the force under attack conditions."

In fact, they created three such systems, each of which was a last-ditch option. One would use rockets to launch transmitters that would broadcast prerecorded messages with the go codes during the trajectory of their flight. Another was a low-frequency earth wave that would send the go code using a ground current that would flow through the earth. The third was an airborne command post jet with airborne jets acting as relay stations that together would form a communications network in the sky.

However futuristic each sounded, all three would prove to be practical, and in the end, all three would be built.

WITH A COLLAR of powerful rocket bottles ringing its aft section, a B-47 could take off even if a runway had been badly cratered or damaged by a Soviet strike. This was an important option to have, but it turned an ordinary takeoff into a spectacularly violent act of flight.

In 1958, a jet-assisted takeoff (commonly called a JATO or ATO takeoff) devolved into a spectacular flaming accident that destroyed one bomber and killed a crew chief. Said the accident summary: "Eyewitnesses stated that at the time of ATO firing, instead of the small individual balls of fire at each bottle nozzle, a large blob of fire appeared about two thirds of the way back on the left hand side of the ATO rack.

"The aircraft continued its takeoff and the fire moved forward to envelop the ATO rack in flames. As the aircraft approached the 4000 feet runway marker, [the] fire had moved forward to the rear of the aft wheel well and past the tail of the aircraft. The entire underside of the fuselage from the wheel well to the tail was in flames. This flame . . . trailed thirty to forty feet behind the aircraft into the slip stream, burning furiously. Objects identified as ATO bottles . . . flew off in several directions.

"The aircraft continued its takeoff roll and left the ground . . . still burning furiously. Bits and pieces of the aircraft were falling off . . . a major portion of the ATO rack and most of the remaining ATO bottles fell from the aircraft. The brake chute, ammunition cans, parts of the camera compartment and battery compartment doors, the gun safe fire switch, and parts of bulkhead 861, dropped from the aircraft between the 8000 foot runway marker and the end of the 13,500 foot runway.

"The co-pilot discovered the fire at an estimated altitude of 200 feet . . . and alerted the crew to the existing emergency. The aircraft commander made a conscious effort to reach an altitude of 500 feet . . . in order to allow the navigator enough altitude for downward ejection.

"Ejections of the primary crew members were successful and no injuries were sustained. The three primary crew members were recovered in an area to the right of the runway centerline extension and within 3000 [feet] of the end of the runway overrun. The bomber rolled over and crashed nose down killing the crew chief who was aboard but had no ejection seat."

The flight lasted less than two minutes.

THE FIFTEENTH AIR Force, a component of SAC, was almost completely nuclear. "The high explosive type bombs used throughout World War II were being removed from [our] inventories as surplus to the needs of this command. Aviation Depot Squadron Commanders received instructions to clear their dumps of almost all conventional weapons."

* * *

ACROSS SAC AIR bases there was an uptick in morale and energy that was palpable—and was directly attributed to the heightened sense of purpose that ground alert and Reflex gave the men. Said one historian: "The vast publicity given to the alert crews by the base and local newspapers as well as by the national press did much to build [esprit] de corps and to establish a high prestige for these dedicated men."

THE FAIL-SAFE CONCEPT captured the imagination of the press. Frank H. Bartholomew, president of the newspaper syndicate United Press, penned a piece on the brilliance of fail-safe and how it let SAC take the initiative without risking an inadvertent bomb release. Bartholomew let his readers imagine that they were in command of a B-52 that had received the fifteen-minute warning and was now streaking toward a designated target in the Soviet Union. ". . . [Y]ou were airborne in six minutes; you have been flying for eight minutes; enemy missiles which must have passed you in flight would be due to strike North America in one minute."

Fail-safe, explained Bartholomew, allowed the bomber to be launched without a clear picture of the threat. With the bombers safely away, false alarms could be confirmed during the several hours of flight before the B-52s hit their turnaround points.

"The next time you see a vapor trail high in the sky," Bartholomew urged his readers, "remember the bombs on board and join a silent prayer that the mission will come to naught, that it will turn around under the rules of fail-safe."

IN 1956, GREAT Britain, France, and Israel joined to prevent Egypt from nationalizing the Suez Canal, beginning what would be known as the Suez crisis and culminating in the Sinai War. The Suez crisis fanned the flames of pro-Arab movements across the Middle East and calls arose for nations to sever their ties with the West. The Sinai War ended in an uneasy truce but the resentment against the West grew stronger when, two years later, it erupted in Lebanon. The pro-Western government of Lebanon headed by President Camille Chamoun held fast to its alliance with Great Britain and France, triggering violent Muslim protest from within its own borders, protests that bordered on civil war.

The situation boiled over into a multinational crisis when the pro-Western regime of King Faisal of Iraq was brutally overthrown in a deadly coup d'état now called the July 14 Revolution of 1958, and the royal family was executed in cold blood.

Fearing the entire region would be swept with violence, President Chamoun quickly called on the United States for help in his country. Marines and army forces moved in to secure Beirut, and Strategic Air Command went on high alert. Within seventeen hours of notification, SAC had 961 bombers loaded with bombs. Days later, that number increased to 1,132 bombers loaded, and 405 bombers and 182 tankers were on fifteen-minute alert. At the peak of the crisis, SAC had 1,297 bombers loaded and 792 tankers fueled.

It was a magnificent display of power in motion, disappointing only General Power, who had wanted his bombers deployed overseas and, as a show of force, to be seen in the Middle East. Nonetheless, convinced that the crisis was over, SAC was ordered to stand down on July 30.

It was Strategic Air Command's first test.

THE DIFFERENCE BETWEEN air and space took on a new meaning when the term *aerospace* entered the language of the Cold War. The ability to fly air-breathing manned bombers through the air and ballistic missiles through the lower fringes of space were of equal importance to the air force, and this continuum was called aerospace. Said air force chief of staff General Thomas D. White in a speech before the National Press Club in the aftermath of Sputnik: "We airmen who have fought to assure that the United States has the capability to control the air are determined that the United States has the capability to control space. In speaking of the control of air and the control of space I want to stress that there is no division, per se, between air and space."

Putting the term into print for perhaps the first time, in 1958 Air University's Research Studies Institute published what they titled an "Interim Glossary of Aero-Space Terms." From that point on, the term was official and only the hyphen would be removed.

INFALLIBILITY BEING IMPOSSIBLE, the term *fail-safe* took on unwelcome connotations and subjected the air force to both sarcasm and criticism, and because of that, *fail-safe* was officially replaced by the term *positive control*. Said Strategic Air Command of this change: "It will be remembered that at this time representatives of the USSR were loudly voicing their fears that WW III might be inadvertently started due to an error on the part of a

SAC crew. The term 'Positive Control,' being more absolute in intonation than "Fail-safe," assisted in dampening the Soviet propaganda attempt to turn world opinion against SAC's realistic training program."

Perhaps. But fail-safe would be impossible to dislodge and in time would be the centerpiece of a movie called *Dr. Strangelove*.

HOWEVER EFFECTIVE THE continental radar system was, it would be useless against ballistic missiles traveling through the lower reaches of space at some ten thousand miles per hour. Instead, three new long-range radar stations, called Ballistic Missile Early Warning Stations or BMEWS, would be built. Radar antennas that dwarfed anything yet built would rise 160 feet into the sky and could track Soviet ballistic missiles as far away as three thousand miles from American borders. The first station would be built in Clear, Alaska, the second at Thule, Greenland, and the third at Fylingdales Moor, Yorkshire, England. The Fylingdales station would monitor the space between Eastern Europe and Thule, Thule's radar would sweep the skies from Greenland to Alaska, and the Alaskan site would monitor the skies across the Pacific to Kamchatka. Taken together, BMEWS could identify and track Soviet warheads traveling through the lower fringes of space, calculate where they would land and when, and provide that information to SAC at least 15 minutes before the expected impact.

A prototype began operation in Trinidad in 1958 to track American missiles shot down the Atlantic Missile Range. The first station in the Arctic went operational in 1960. All three were fully operational by 1963.

THE AIR FORCE had not been satisfied with the routes chosen for the first test of air alert and decided on a second test that would maintain four bombers in the air twenty-four hours a day on routes that went to and from Greenland. Every six hours a B-52 would take off and begin what amounted to a twenty-hour mission. The bombers would refuel once and conduct hourly tests of their ability to receive the go codes, and at all times three of the four bombers would be capable of executing their Emergency War Plans and striking the Soviet Union. There was, however, one detail the air force alone could not decide. There was a new design in nuclear weapons called the sealed-pit bomb. To fly with this bomb on SAC bombers, a meeting with the president was first required.

STRATEGIC AIR COMMAND'S willingness to participate in small wars with conventional bombs was questioned with some skepticism by the general staff of the air force and the Joint Chiefs. SAC deflected the nature of the question by saying that it believed the best bomb to use in any war was a nuclear bomb and that to SAC a nuclear bomb *was* in fact a conventional bomb. If the Joint Chiefs needed explosive bombs for a conflict, Tactical Air Command had the jets and light bombers to do the job. In a tone that perhaps reflected LeMay's repeated assertions that not only was SAC trained to drop atomic bombs but SAC's aircrews wouldn't hesitate to do so, SAC reiterated that its men were "ready, willing and able to participate on short notice in any atomic or thermonuclear bombing involved in such a crisis."

This bring-it-on-attitude was a bit too eager for the audience they addressed.

ACCORDING TO A Strategic Air Command document, there was a new procedure to improve the reliability of the go codes: "Under the new system aircraft commanders were issued envelopes on the outside of which was printed a code word, e.g., 'Bulldog.' If after contacting a ground radio station along the mission route the crew was to receive a message containing the words 'Bulldog Baker,' the word 'Bulldog' would mean to open the envelope. The word 'Baker' would be found on the inside of the envelope and serve as a double authentication. This message would authorize the aircrew to proceed past the 'Fail-safe' point to the previously assigned target."

THE SECOND TEST of airborne alert contained a new wrinkle, which was the sealed pit bomb. Because of significant advances in arming and safing mechanisms, nuclear bombs no longer needed to have removable capsules; rather, the capsules could be sealed inside the bomb without sacrificing safety. In-flight insertion and removal of capsules, heretofore solely a safety precaution, would be a thing of the past. Said the air force in agreement: "By the end of FY1959 the bulk of our strategic weapons will be sealed-pit."

But therein lay the rub. Strategic Air Command had presidential authority to maneuver atomic weapons using the in-flight insertion and removal concept but it didn't have specific approval to maneuver with the new sealed-pit bombs. Because the second test of airborne alert was scheduled to start in early September, a meeting with the president was required. Notes from this meeting have been declassified.

SAC opened the presentation by updating the president on the current status of ground and air alert. "As you know the Air Force goal is that of ⅓ of the entire SAC forces [will be] on continual ground alert by 1960 with fifteen minutes reaction time. Approximately 200 SAC bombers are already on such alert status."

No-notice launches of these alert bombers were required to "condition and train" the crews, SAC said. By having bombs on board, SAC was able to "inject realism" into that training. Moreover, with real bombs on board, bombers on test missions would be war ready, which would "prevent degradation in the Air Force capability [to retaliate] which would occur if the force were test-launched without war-ready weapons." SAC told the president that they would test launch ground-alert bombers 190 times in the forthcoming year. "Aircraft would fly their emergency war plan routes under previously approved 'positive control' procedures, returning to their home stations at or before a pre-determined point." (Underlines in original.) The ground-alert B-52s would carry two bombs each; the B-47s would carry one. They asked the president for authority to load these bombers with sealed-pit weapons, which would require 250 bombs.

Then came the air-alert forces. The airborne-alert forces, as the president was reminded, could not be destroyed on the ground and could react instantly to Soviet aggression but, said the briefing, a retaliatory strike "requires or is contingent upon flying with complete, war-ready bombs."

The air force estimated that in the forthcoming year 750 airborne-alert sorties would be flown, carrying 1,500 weapons. Each sortie would be twenty hours in length and each B-52 would carry two bombs. "For approximately 18 hours of the sortie, each aircraft would have the capability of destroying Russian targets." The president was told that the first airborne sortie would leave the SAC base in Loring, Maine, on September 15, 1958. More tests would continue into 1959.

But that wasn't all. "In addition to the actual airborne alert capability, 20 other B-52s will be maintained in fully combat configured condition, in support of this operation. By combat configured, we mean an aircraft with fuel, weapon, and penetration equipment already on board—only the crew would be needed for launch."

The president was given a number. The air force wanted approval to maneuver 1,750 bombs starting with the September test of airborne alert.

There was no immediate answer.

A FULLY FUELED and bomb-laden B-47 broke apart during a ground-alert takeoff, rupturing a fuel tank, which caught fire and consumed the plane and the bomb. The bomb was configured for a strike mission, meaning that the force of a crash could cause some of the safing mechanisms to close. Well aware of this, the fire was fought for ten minutes and then the air base was evacuated.

The wreckage burned for some seven hours. When the base was reopened and the flames were extinguished, high quantities of alpha and gamma radiation were detected in the wreckage and plutonium contamination was extensive. The area around the base was contaminated, too. Radioactive clouds of smoke had drifted downwind and fallout was detected on a naval base as far as forty miles away. Repairs were attempted on the heat-damaged runway but the runway was so radioactive that it had to be bulldozed into the ground.

Although alpha and gamma radiation are associated with nuclear yields, official documents deny that the accident resulted in any nuclear contribution.*

There was, of course, no way to check at the time. The air base was Sidi Slimane, Morocco.

ACCORDING TO THE formerly classified document, for several years SAC had been trying to convince the air force that it needed a sixty-megaton bomb, which was some forty times more powerful than the MK-15 bomb that it routinely carried. SAC was turned down time and again, but they persisted in their argument that the large bomb would be an effective deterrent. President Eisenhower finally halted the debate when he would not allow a test of a weapon that big during an earlier series of tests in the Pacific.

In 1958, the issue of a sixty-megaton bomb was once again raised, this time with an entirely different military justification. The sophisticated Soviet air defenses had made it increasingly difficult to say with confidence that aircraft in numbers sufficient to achieve a desired degree of damage to a high-priority target would actually penetrate Soviet defenses and release their bombs. However, with a Class A weapon, as a bomb this large was called, destruction would be assured if just one bomber got through. Said an SAC report: "One Class A weapon placed on Moscow would destroy the city and neutralize or disrupt all airfields and installations within 14 nautical miles of the city."

It was a tantalizing prospect, but the records remain silent as to whether such a bomb was ever built.

THE EVER-GROWING NUCLEAR shield was proving ever-more effective. In August 1958 a technician at a SAGE radar command and control center in New York pushed a button. "Moments later," wrote a historian, "a BOMARC

---

* Safety mechanisms are known to have failed. At the Nevada Test Site, partial yields have been produced in tests designed to make safety mechanisms fail.

surface-to-air missile rose from Cape Canaveral, Florida, to intercept a simulated enemy bomber over the Atlantic Ocean."

It was more than a good kill. That day, computers, radar systems, guidance systems, data links, and one unlucky drone met in the sky over the Atlantic Ocean.

THE UNEASY TRUCE of 1955 between the Republic of Chinese Nationalists on Taiwan, led by Chiang Kai-shek and the Communist Peoples' Republic of China, led by Mao Tse-tung, was shattered when in August 1958 artillery fire began to rain down on the Nationalists' islands of Quemoy and Matsu. Following a meeting between Mao and Khrushchev, Soviet-built MiG-17s began to appear on airfields on mainland China. America, pledged to support Nationalist China in a mutual defense pact signed in 1954, moved forces to Taiwan. A full-scale confrontation seemed imminent.

In cabinet meetings, President Eisenhower's advisers agreed that nuclear weapons would have to be used if the Communists used their aircraft and naval vessels to quarantine the islands. Air force general Nathan Twining, chairman of the Joint Chiefs of Staff, outlined a plan to drop between ten and fifteen multi-kiloton bombs on the airfields closest to the besieged islands, near the Chinese city of Amoy. If this failed to break such a blockade, Twining planned nuclear attacks on airfields as far away as Shanghai. According to newly declassified documents, Twining admitted that these attacks might "bring down nuclear vengeance on Okinawa as well as Taiwan," presumably by the Soviet Union.

The commander of the Pacific air forces, General Laurence S. Kuter, drew up a plan that called for air atomic strikes against airfields on mainland China. He asked the Joint Chiefs to place the fifteen Reflex B-47 bombers on Guam at his disposal. As was his right, General Power declined to release his aircraft to another command, but he assured the Joint Chiefs that if so ordered, his B-47s would attack those airfields, and would as well attack Chinese cities and industrial centers if the initial atomic strikes triggered an escalation. Accordingly, in mid-August, General Power placed five of his fifteen ground-alert Guam-based B-47 bombers on 15-minute combat alert and readied to conduct nuclear raids. He maintained the other ten bombers on regular ground alert. The bombers were loaded with the 40-kiloton MK-6 atomic bombs.

The shelling and strafing of Chiang Kai-shek's forces escalated in intensity. Dogfights against Soviet Migs and American-built F-86s dotted the skies. Missiles streaked to their targets. Migs were shot down. The shelling caused more than 2,000 casualties. Eisenhower responded by sending American warships to escort ships carrying supplies to the besieged islands while sending aircraft carriers, fighter jets, marines and antiaircraft guns to Taiwan. The president publicly insisted he would not back down in the face of armed aggression; however, he made it clear to his generals that nuclear bombs were to be used only with his direct approval, authority he withheld throughout the conflict, much to the consternation of some.

In the end, Eisenhower, the author of massive retaliation, used only conventional weapons, thus saving future American generations from the unknown consequences that would have resulted had American fireballs incinerated Chinese cities.

TAIWAN FANNED SMOLDERING flames among the generals. In its after-action report on Taiwan, SAC would tersely write that any aggressor "should be confronted with the best weapon available," which, at SAC, was a nuclear weapon. SAC continued and added that it would "relieve itself of any conventional weapons delivery requirement" hereon out and would instead use the nuclear weapon of a yield appropriate to a target.

Agreeing with Strategic Air Command's assessment of the crisis, General Kuter thought the Joint Chiefs had been too cautious and had misunderstood the importance of atomic weapons. In a speech made sometime after the crisis, Kuter said that the military would feel less restrained if civilians were better educated on the point that nuclear weapons had become conventional weapons and that weapons were just weapons no matter what made them explode.

THE REQUEST TO equip SAC bombers with sealed-pit bombs was still pending presidential approval when on September 15, 1958, a B-52 was launched from Loring Air Force Base, Maine, to start the second test of airborne alert using the new polar routes. Eisenhower was inclined to allow the air force to maneuver with the new bombs but he wanted to get a measure of the safety aspects first. For the next two weeks he received daily safety reports summarizing SAC's flights. By October 2, the president seemed to be satisfied with the safeguards and he granted SAC's request. Almost immediately, multi-megaton hydrogen bombs were loaded into SAC bombers and thermonuclear weapons with capsules sealed inside them began to fly across the United States on training missions, to test ground-alert launches and the new airborne-alert routes.

At least ninety megatons of nuclear bombs would be in the air twenty-four hours a day for most of the next ten years.

* * *

AN AIR DEFENSE Command historian spoke with drama and patriotism. The interception of an enemy aircraft was now accomplished with an impressive degree of sophistication and the very latest technology. "Gone were the days of the 'heads-up' fighter pilot with his few instruments to follow and the seat of his pants to fall back on when things went wrong. The jet all-weather pilot flew by the radar scope and the beam given him by his co-partner, the radar director on the ground. An error on the part of either member of the team and the enemy would slip away unharmed into the night or fog."

IRRETRIEVABLY LOST

FROM THE DISTANT repose of Washington, D.C., the ejection of a nuclear bomb over the marshes of Savannah, Georgia, was startling, but surely it could be found. This was a seven-thousand-pound object, not a lost wallet. Assistant Secretary of Defense (Atomic Energy) General Herbert B. Loper notified the Joint Committee.

Said Loper: "This letter is to notify you of an aircraft accident which involved a nuclear weapon. A B-47 aircraft with a [censored] nuclear weapon onboard was damaged in a collision with an F-86 aircraft near Sylvania, Georgia, on February 5, 1958. The B-47 aircraft attempted three times unsuccessfully to land with the weapon. The weapon was then jettisoned visually over water off the mouth of the Savannah River. No detonation was observed. The B-47 aircraft then was able to land safely at Hunter Air Force Base, Georgia. The Navy has been notified and a search of the area is in progress."

How Loper's letter was received is not known, but the sense of it was that the situation was under control, which was no doubt reassuring to the committee. However, the letter was not entirely accurate. By claiming that the pilot attempted three landings unsuccessfully, Loper introduced a degree of drama that appears to have been of his own making. Years later, pilots Howard Richardson and Robert Lagerstrom would read this letter. "Nonsense," said Lagerstrom. "We landed on the first attempt."

Which, on this point, the official crash report was in complete agreement.

AFTER LANDING AT Hunter Air Force Base there was a debriefing, which, in consideration of the hour, was short. Howard Richardson made notes to himself before he fell asleep; as he remembered it, the others did, too.

As dawn broke, Richardson, Lagerstrom, and navigator Woolard were awakened by the arrival of SAC commander in chief General Thomas Power. Richardson and Power met in private. "I told him exactly what happened," said

Richardson. "General Power thought we did a pretty good job and he just wanted to help get us back to our base." In fact, Power recommend Richardson for the Distinguished Flying Cross, which Richardson received. The B-47 was towed to an isolated corner of Hunter Air Force Base. "That plane didn't fly again," Richardson said.

FOR THE NEXT nine weeks, salvage experts, search teams, and explosive-ordnance-disposal teams scoured the area around Wassaw Sound, but the bomb was nowhere to be found. Four months later, on June 9, 1958, General Loper wrote the Joint Committee to tell them that the search for the bomb in Savannah had been called off. "The weapon is considered irretrievably lost," said Loper, and that was that.

The most dangerous lost object on the face of the earth was, simply, lost.

THE AIR FORCE undertook a lengthy investigation of the midair collision between the B-47 and the F-86. The piece of evidence used to support their ultimate finding was recovered by a state trooper ninety miles north of Savannah. It was Clarence Stewart's flight recorder.

Based on an analysis of the data on the recorder, it was clear that Stewart's radar had in some way failed and had been displaying inaccurate data. The air force absolved Stewart of complicity in the accident; bad equipment was determined to be the ultimate cause.

ON JUNE 16, 1958, the Joint Committee received a third letter, this one to notify them that the secretary of defense had requested a replacement bomb for the bomb lost near Savannah. The author was Lewis Strauss, chairman of the Atomic Energy Commission.

The letter itself was in many ways unremarkable and largely unnecessary, but once again there was a statement that was confusing. In prior correspondence, the writers implied that the bomb had been flown with its capsule, but in this letter Chairman Strauss claimed that the lost bomb was carried "without nuclear capsule." It was well known by the committee that SAC crews carried their capsules in the distinctive birdcages. If the bomb was "without capsule," it meant that the capsule was carried by the crew in a birdcage.

But the aircrew had no memory of the birdcage. "You could insert the capsule in-flight," said copilot Bob Lagerstrom, "but the cap wasn't there. I'm sure we didn't have the cap."

So, where was it?

* * *

On October 8, 1958, the Joint Committee on Atomic Energy was again in receipt of yet another letter and again the news was about the Savannah bomb. Although the search had covered hundreds of square miles of marshes, swamps, creeks, rivers, ocean bottom, beaches, and land, there had been no clue, no debris, no hint of where the bomb might be. Still, it was somewhere. Conceded the Atomic Energy Commission: "There exists the possibility of accidental discovery of the unrecovered weapon through dredging or construction in the probable impact area. Accordingly, the Department of Defense has been requested to monitor all dredging and construction in the probable impact area."

The official word in Savannah, however, remained as it had been—there was no lost bomb, just parts, and expensive ones at that.

LIKE A SHIP

A RADAR OPERATOR on the Texas Towers said that at night the lights on the many Russian trawlers sometimes made the horizon look like Coney Island at night. Said another of the Russian ferret flights: "The Russians seemed to fly out there nearly every day. It was the busiest sector I'd seen." Twenty-four hours a day, three shifts of radar operators manned radarscopes and tracked and identified the phosphorescent returns of Russian spy flights in the sky.

ALAN DAVID CROCKETT, a commercial diver, leaned against the railing and looked down at the water. The skies were overcast, the winds were steady at eight knots, and the waves were rolling across the Atlantic in ten-second intervals at three to five feet. Beneath his dive suit, which was unzipped to his stomach, he wore a knit wool cap, white long johns, and heavy cotton gloves. Crockett studied the face of the swells, then stepped onto the platform. He had his helmet bolted to his collar by his tender and was swung toward the ocean. He directed his descent until the bottom of the platform was just a few feet above the water. He timed a swell, then gave the command. Crockett's platform dropped below the surface and disappeared into the Atlantic Ocean.

At minus-twenty-five feet, Crockett pulled his basket over to the truss to examine a pin plate and a keeper plate. Long manes of marine growth and dirty-green algae trailed off into the current. He brushed away the algae and stirred up a blinding cloud of green. After the silt settled down he examined the pins. They were tight.

He descended to minus-seventy-five feet and again cleaned off the growth. This time he noticed something different. "The top and bottom edges of the collar shined to bright bare metal," he wrote. "The bright metal was caused by vertical motion in the collar." He put his knife next to a pin. He swung the mallet. The pin plate moved up an inch. He swung downward. The pin plate moved down an inch.

Tower Four's underwater bracing was dangerously loose.

AS THE SUN dipped below the horizon on September 9, 1959, the cargo ship USNS *AKL-17* departed the state pier in the port of New Bedford, Massachusetts, slipped past the lighthouse at Clarks Point, and eased into the mouth of Buzzard's Bay. Her destination was Texas Tower Four. The ship's master, Captain Sixto Mangual, turned south through the inside passage around Block Island, then made good speed down the East Coast past Boston toward New York City. He carefully threaded the shipping lanes that fed into New York harbor; then, abeam Barnegat Inlet, New Jersey, he turned east, out to sea, and homed in on the beacon of Tower Four. The *AKL-17,* a coastal freighter, displayed her running lights, green on the starboard side, red on the port.

As the morning light spread across the Atlantic, the faint outline of Texas Tower Four appeared on the horizon. Standing in the middle of the Atlantic Ocean more than one hundred miles from land, coming up out of the water, part Texas oil rig and part Cold War spy stuff; it looked ominous and sinister and entirely unnatural in the ocean—and yet there it was, defiant, confident, three steel legs as thick as redwood trees climbing through the shifting Atlantic waters before piercing the surface and rising another sixty-five feet, where a four-thousand-ton triangular iron platform was perched. From sea level to the top of her radomes, with red, green, and white lights winking in the morning haze, she stood an astonishing fourteen stories tall.

Mangual eased off the throttles and nosed the *AKL* under the platform and moored on the C leg. At 0800 hours, air force captain Gordon Phelan, age thirty-three, of the 4604th Support Squadron, Boston Air Defense Sector, Air Defense Command, was lifted aboard, and in a brief ceremony he accepted command as Texas Tower Four's new officer in charge.

"It will be like a ship," Phelan said to Elinor, his wife, before he left. "This won't be bad," he said. "This is going to be real fine."

Here he would die.

CAPTAIN PHELAN MET Sixto Mangual when Phelan first visited the Texas Towers. Phelan had joined the navy as a teenager and served in the Pacific during World War II on ships and submarines. After returning home, he went to Officer Candidate School in the air force and qualified in fighter jets.

A ruggedly handsome man with surprisingly gentle eyes, Phelan was sent to Air Defense Command and eventually to the Texas Towers.

Phelan, the former navy man, and the ship's master, Sixto Mangual—a man who had lived most of his life at sea—often talked as they stood in the wheelhouse. Phelan, with nine years at sea, impressed Mangual. "He was an exemplary officer well respected by his subordinates and superiors. He was no ordinary passenger."

Phelan was profoundly influenced by the remoteness of the Texas Towers. As rigid structures in the Atlantic, the towers were always in motion. Hit by waves and buffeted by winds, the towers moaned, leaned, vibrated, and clanked as their braces caught up in their crevices. In his first weeks on Tower Four, even Phelan felt the effects. "My husband had a phone beside his bunk," said his wife, Elinor Phelan, to the Air Force Board of Inquiry. "While I was talking to him he asked me to hold for a second and when he came back I asked, 'What was that for?' He said he had to switch around because he was actually getting seasick. My husband was in the navy nine years; he was never seasick a day in the navy but he was actually getting nauseated aboard that tower."

Surrounded by endless miles of the Atlantic, Phelan developed a discipline that placed a high value on work ethic but an equally high value on respecting those under his command. In a word, Phelan kept his men busy but he also kept them informed. "Captain Phelan, I don't believe, ever kept anything from the military personnel on the Tower," said Chief Warrant Officer William A. Rausch, who served under Phelan, in his testimony to the Board of Inquiry. "He felt that he should be honest with his troops and he kept them abreast of the repairs and anything that would allay any fears within his command. Captain Phelan was a tremendous leader. There wasn't, to my knowledge, a man out there who did not volunteer. There wasn't a man out there but what was willing and ready to go on the day for him to go."

A JUMPY, ALERT-HAPPY FORCE

WROTE AN AIR force historian: "Robert Oppenheimer once compared the United States and the Soviet Union to two scorpions in a bottle, either of which could kill the other but only at the risk of itself being killed."

Scorpions in a bottle.

It was 1959.

ONCE THE ALERT bombers took off and rushed into the sky, the next priority was to protect the cockpit crew from being blinded by the flash of a nuclear warhead that might detonate near them.

"We'd saturate the runway," said SAC colonel Jim Maker of that moment they began their takeoffs. "When we were busting out we'd have 12–15 second spacing between bombers. We'd get airborne, fan out, pull down our thermal curtains and button up the bomber."

Button up the bomber. Because in the world of 15 minutes, who knew when a Soviet fireball would appear.

THE CONCEPT OF exchanging nuclear weapons tit-for-tat surfaced in serious military circles when, in the March 1959 issue of the *U.S. Naval Institute Proceedings,* navy commander P. H. Backus explained "finite deterrence." Because of hardened silos and dispersed bases, and the great number of forces standing on fifteen-minute alert, a Soviet first strike would invariably be survived by a retaliatory force sufficient to mount a second "first strike." That being the case, any nuclear exchange would devolve into a general war that would serve only to vanquish the populations of the adversaries and poison the planet's atmosphere for the noncombatants.

On the other hand, accepting that it would be impossible to accomplish anything more than annihilation might very well lead to the idea of "finite deterrence." The concept of finite deterrence meant that a Soviet strike, under certain circumstances, would not necessarily result in massive retaliation. For instance, wrote Backus, should the Soviets accidentally initiate war, the Americans might strike back by "destroying two or three designated Soviet cities" but this "controlled response," as he termed it, would be followed by a period of negotiations "between strikes."

However idealistic it sounded, as a military strategy it was not without precedent. It was through progressive destruction of Japanese cities and not through instant annihilation that America compelled Japan to surrender.

On March 9, 1959, Eisenhower again authorized SAC to carry sealed-pit weapons, this time for a third test of airborne alert on a new route called Head Start. Head Start routes would take bombers loaded with either the MK-15 Mod 2 or the MK-39 Mod 1 thermonuclear megaton bombs directly over Greenland and across the far north of Canada. The test would initially have eight bombers in the air twenty-four-hours a day, leading up to twelve a day. Each bomber would be airborne for approximately twenty-four hours.

The Head Start test was carried off without a hitch. Over the course of some 29,400 flying hours there were more than twenty-one hundred aerial refuelings and no serious accidents. The lengths of the flights were tiring but the flight surgeon monitoring the crews was impressed because "few personnel felt the need for stimulants during the flight."

That American bomber crews were chewing Dexedrine was hardly surprising, although this was perhaps the first official acknowledgment that they were. That armed American bombers were now overflying foreign countries was far more problematical.

Major General Bernard A. Schriever, commander of the Ballistic Missiles Division of the air force, the branch that oversaw the development of the ICBM, spoke to the Senate Committee on Aeronautical and Space Sciences. It was April 1959. Schriever told the committee that with speeds of ten thousand miles per hour or more, "the advent of the ballistic missile has made a massive sneak attack more attractive to an aggressor."

Said Schriever: "The advantages of striking first are so great that not only national security but national survival might be at stake."*

It was the Franck committee all over again.

---

* Schriever's organization was better known by its previous name, the Western Development Division, a name that was dropped in 1957.

* * *

THE DOCUMENT WAS a recap of the previous day's testimony by General Nathan F. Twining, chairman of the Joint Chiefs of Staff, before a 1959 Military Posture review held by the House Committee on Armed Services. Against the current SAC practices, some of the answers were puzzling. Said the recap: "There was a discussion of SAC retaliatory capability. General Twining described that SAC was a very powerful deterrent and Congressman Stratton asked do we include our airborne alert aircraft in our retaliatory capability? General Twining's answer was that we have no airborne alert aircraft with armed weapons and never have had it. Later Mr. Guber asked, 'Could SAC aircraft on normal training missions proceed immediately to strike Soviet targets if the balloon were to go up at any given moment?' Generally Twining responded, 'Generally, yes.'"

Why Twining so testified has not been explained, but secrecy was a most serious thing, and this committee may not have been cleared to hear the facts. That said, in Twining's mind, his answer may well have been related to the definition of *armed* versus *unarmed,* which, again, remained elusive.

SAID A FORMERLY classified Strategic Air Command history: "Sophisticated air defense weapons in the hands of the Soviets have greatly increased SAC's problem of penetrating to the target, but these same weapons in the hands of U. S. forces could also be deadly to this command." It was a problem that Strategic Air Command called "safe passage." In the chaos of an attack on the United States, outbound SAC bombers might be misidentified and shot down by Air Defense Command using missiles intended for the Soviets. The first solution was to avoid the air-defense batteries by funneling aircraft through a small number of designated safe-passage corridors, but the compression of time and the heavy concentration of American air defenses in the Northeast, plus new concepts such as dispersal and alert, made it impossible to funnel bombers from so many bases through so few corridors without depleting their fuel reserves just to get there.

A meeting was held between SAC and ADC to work out a solution, but the meeting failed to come up with much except to recognize that safe passage would be a problem on *both* sides of the Atlantic. The new Nike Hercules air-defense missiles with their powerful forty-kiloton warheads would be in use both by American air-defense batteries and by the European batteries. Safe passage out, and safe passage in, would be difficult. Wrote an SAC historian: "The only real solution was for SAC to avoid any area where an air defense battle was in progress, and to avoid critical air defense areas particularly during penetration."

But that solution was far from foolproof. The long-term solution would be a new electronic signaling system that air-defense installations would use to query the transponders carried on SAC aircraft. These transponders would instantly respond to the query with a signal that included the bomber's unique aircraft identification number, which would indicate that it was a friendly. This system would in time be called Identification Friend or Foe, or IFF; however, while it was under development, SAC and ADC decided to increase the number of safe-passage corridors and to train aircrews with those routes immediately, and if war came, simply hope for the best.

Safe-passage corridors remain in effect to this day.

GENERAL POWER CONCLUDED that airborne alert should be a permanent program, not a test program. It was obvious that this was the only way that SAC would have a retaliatory force that could survive the most unexpected of attacks by the Soviets. Others disagreed and said that it was expensive, unnecessary, and impossible to maintain on a meaningful level. Said Power in his testimony before Congress: ". . . I feel strongly that we must get on with this airborne alert . . . We must impress Mr. Khrushchev that we have it, and that he cannot strike this country with impunity."

The air force turned him down but they bartered a compromise. SAC could continue the program as a full-time training program but not as a full-time operation. The compromise was called the Airborne Alert Indoctrination Program.

It was July 1959.

A LOG ENTRY from a Distant Early Warning radar station: "This sector was penetrated by a Russian Tu-104 on a track from Gander Newfoundland to New York. Intercept by F-102."

And another: "Request received for this unit to provide close surveillance of Cubana 476 airborne with destination Czechoslovakia. Carried as track number X651."

And on September 15, 1959: "One Tu-104 and one Russian Tu-114 with Khrushchev over flew this area on way to Washington."

IN 1959, ARMY chief of staff General Maxwell D. Taylor told the House of Representatives that "the nation had enough nuclear weapons in its strategic force to annihilate the enemy 10 times over." The air force disagreed, claiming that some of the bombs in Taylor's calculation "might be destroyed and or made inaccessible by a surprise Soviet attack."

Nonetheless, Taylor's comment would hold sway, and SAC's retaliatory megatonnage would henceforth be known as "overkill."

Thus it was that *overkill* entered the language of the Cold War.

BY 1959, A wholesale change in SAC penetration tactics was under way. In place of high-altitude attacks, bombers would now come in below Soviet radar coverage and stay low to the ground throughout the attack, using at most a slight pop-up maneuver to release the bomb. To accomplish this it was necessary to make modifications to the B-52, including the addition of low-altitude altimeters, terrain-clearance radar, enhanced electronic countermeasures, improvements in the bombing-navigation equipment, airframe reinforcements, and improvements to the aircraft's cooling systems.

Low-level military-training corridors were created for the aircrews and they stretched across remote areas of the United States more than 500 miles in length and as much as 20 miles in width. Pilots would drop their bombers down into these corridors and, at some 450 miles per hour and no more than a hundred feet above the ground, practice lengthy formation flights at treetop level. Because the engines of the B-52s often trailed plumes of black smoke, these routes were known as "oil burner routes." Oil burner routes were at once some of the most dangerous parcels of airspace in America and some of the most exhilarating. Filmed footage from the 1960s shows military observers standing on hills just a few hundred feet from B-52s streaking past them. One could not fail to get a sense of brute power as eight engines propelled such a large aircraft at such close proximity to the ground.

Equally, one could not fail to notice that the bombers were actually flying below the vantage point of the observers. "Bunny sucking," as one pilot called it.

TO CONFUSE THE Soviet radars and complicate Soviet air defense decision making, the air force received its first batch of decoy missiles—the aptly named Quail missiles. The Quail, which was in truth more like a drone, was loaded with electronics and reflectors that, taken together, painted a signature on Soviet radars that was nearly identical to that of the B-52 that carried it. As the B-52 approached the outer edges of Soviet radar coverage, it would release a Quail from the bomb bay, which would fly alongside it as if it were another bomber. With hundreds of B-52s expected to strike in the initial nuclear exchange, and with each firing one or more decoys as they penetrated the So-viet defenses, it was expected that Soviet radar screens would be overwhelmed by targets.

This tactic would be known as a "mass penetration."

LOW-LEVEL PENETRATION FLIGHTS would be followed by one of several maneuvers to release the bomb. If the target was a soft target, for in-stance an air base with bombers in the open, the fusing that would cause the most damage would be an air-burst bomb—that is, a bomb detonated hun-dreds of feet above the ground. If the target was a hard target, such as a buried missile silo or a reinforced communications center, the bomber would use ei-ther a laydown bomb or a bomb fused to burst on contact with the ground, thereby causing the most subterranean damage. The laydown bomb required a combination of shock-mitigating spikes or nose cones, and parachutes to re-tard the bomb's descent. One parachute would pull the bomb out of the bomber, a second was engineered to yank it upward, while a third would float it to the ground. Once on the ground, the timer would count down to the burst and, in a few seconds or a few hours, the bomb would explode.

TO SLICE SECONDS off the process of launching the alert forces, a mini-mum interval takeoff, or "MITO," was developed. No longer would one aircraft have to wait for another to clear the runway before it could start its own takeoff roll. Quite the contrary. Using only a handful of seconds for spacing, pilots would take off nearly nose-to-tail. On bases with runways that were at least three hun-dred feet wide, near-simultaneous takeoffs were possible using paired bombers rolling down the runway in echelon formations. During an MITO exercise, one bomber after another would take to the runways, leaving behind black clouds of jet exhaust.

"The bombers would go first," said a KC-97 tanker pilot remembering his MITO takeoffs. "If a tanker broke into the stream, we were to take off one min-ute behind the bomber and then the bomber behind us had to wait one minute for us to get clear so they didn't run in to us."

But then it was back to what can only be described as a frenetic scramble to get airplanes into the air.

THE CONCEPT OF strategic deterrence came under attack as the budgets were prepared for 1959 and 1960. Strategic Air Command maintained its official stance, which was that overpowering nuclear force was its primary responsibility and that to fund anything less than a retaliatory force capable of vast devastation was contrary to national policy. The army disagreed, arguing that conventional forces and conventional weapons were just as important.

Surprisingly, there was division in the tactical-versus-strategic debate within the halls of the air force, which resulted in some agreement with the army's point of view, all of which worked its way into the press. Some air force generals argued that the use of strategic air weapons was now all but untenable and that it would never happen except in the direst of circumstances, but smaller, kiloton-range weapons, delivered by fighters, would be more practicable in small-scale wars. Still, it was the army's voice that resonated with the public—conventional bombs were as important as nuclear bombs—and for the first time, SAC began to hear critics including, as some irritated commanders called them, "civilian commentators on military affairs."

The media, as it were.

THE NET REPORT for 1959 was prepared for the Joint Chiefs of Staff. "In a comparison of the 1955 and 1956 reports, it is concluded that in 1959 the U.S would be in a period characterized by either side having a capability to launch an attack that would result in mutual destruction." It was a concept known as nuclear parity.

The analysis also noted that it would be unlikely for the enemy to consider chemical warfare because nuclear offered a far more "profitable" outcome.

In fact, the mutual exchange would do little more than disarm the two countries at little gain to either save the general knowledge that both nations would be so devastated that neither would worry about another attack for perhaps generations to come.

PILOTS LIKE "AIR under their wings," as they call it—a cushion of altitude to solve problems, 20,000 or 30,000 feet of airspace to work through options, enough altitude to bail out with time for a parachute to fill and land safely on the ground.

But there was no air under anyone's wings in the low-level training corridors. Speeding across the ground at four hundred miles per hour and with just a few hundred feet of air left no room for error or for mechanical failure. Said one crash report of a B-47: "The aircraft was departing the Iron Horse low-level route when an outboard engine failed. All aboard were killed."

Said another: "The aircraft crashed near Hurley, Wisconsin, on a low-level route . . . spatial disorientation was deemed to have been the cause of the accident."

And another: "The aircraft crashed into a mountain in Idaho while flying a low-level route killing all three crewmen."

And another: "An aft engine support pin sheared letting the engine drop creating sudden drag and yaw. The aircraft was too close to the ground to eject safely."

And another: "The aircraft lost the rear end of [the] #4 engine and #6 was shut down due to icing while climbing out after flying the Oil Burner Hangover Low Level Training Route. The aircraft proceeded to Plattsburg AFB to make an emergency landing. Prior to descending, a rear mount pin on [the] #1 engine failed leaving the rear of the engine hanging. As the aircraft broke out of the weather on final, the #2 engine failed . . . The aircraft crashed into the trees short of the end of the runway. Three crewmen were killed."

IN SEPTEMBER 1959, Strategic Air Command completed the first launch of an Atlas missile from the Vandenberg Air Force Base. The missile traveled more than four thousand miles at ten thousand miles per hour. General Power formally declared the Atlas "operational."

THE CIA WAS exceedingly impressed with Strategic Air Command and unimpressed with the hue and cry over a perceived missile gap between the Soviets and the Americans. The United States had lost ground to the Soviets in missiles, so the argument went, and the resulting gap was dangerous if not possibly deadly. Having an edge in missiles, the Soviets could launch a surprise attack, and if they did so, they could destroy the SAC bomber fleet on the ground and much of America.

This, the CIA claimed, was foolish thinking because the Soviets could not possibly engineer a strike that would catch all of SAC's bombers on the ground, and if it didn't catch all the bombers on the ground, that would certainly mean American bombs would be bursting over Moscow. To achieve complete surprise, the CIA argued, the Soviets would have to launch their missiles at perfectly timed but staggered intervals so that they would arrive at targets spread out hundreds if not thousands of miles with near-perfect synchronicity. The math for that was too complex, as was the probability that every missile would perform as specified. And even if it was attempted, Strategic Air Command would long ago have been in the air. Said the CIA: "I believe there has never been a military force more difficult to surprise than SAC. SAC is a jumpy, alert-happy force. There is little if any exaggeration in saying that if small fires were to break out simultaneously in the paint lockers of three or four SAC bases in the world, the bombers of the SAC alert force (numbering in the hundreds), bombed up and fully fueled, would within approximately 15 minutes take off and head for their assigned targets."

Said the analyst: "I personally doubt that the Soviets would willingly accept just one 10-megaton detonation on Moscow."

Thus, said the CIA, as long as SAC had bombers on alert, it didn't entirely matter whether there was a missile gap or a bomber gap or any gap at all. SAC was just too "jumpy" to be caught with its pants down, and no leader would accept the inevitability of a few dozen Hiroshimas in his own country in retaliation for an attack.

IN AUGUST 1959, Chairman Twining worried about the degradation of communications that would be inevitable in war. Twining felt that critical information had to be "flashed" from command posts to commanders so nuclear orders could be quickly communicated, but that would be nearly impossible because those messages were reliant on channels of communication that "lag too far behind" the real world and would "undoubtedly be degraded" even more in combat.

Said Twining: "From our experience in this area to date we can derive at least one fundamental principle. This principle is that atomic operations must be pre-planned for automatic execution to the maximum extent possible and with minimum reliance on post-H-hour communication."

It was precisely this concept of automatic execution, however, that the average Joe on main street feared the most.

AS 1959 CAME to a close, Strategic Air Command was at its peak strength, with 2,921 bombers and tankers, from which it would now steadily decline as missiles flowed to the bases. There were forty domestic bases plus twenty-five overseas, with 412 bombers and tankers on alert, including 149 on alert bases overseas.

There were 15,468 nuclear bombs in the U.S. stockpile, of which 8,337 were under military control.

The Soviet stockpile now numbered 1,060 bombs.

HURRICANE DONNA

TOWER FOUR WAS something of a celebrity. Military helicopters came and went with a steady stream of visitors, dignitaries, and civilian contractors. Navy blimps used the tower as a navigational waypoint, circling the platform often for a day or more at a time. Some of the pilots dropped newspapers and magazines, others practiced airmanship, the delicate hovers, the turns around fixed points, and the like.

Cruise ships often diverted to give their passengers a look. Submarines, too. The American submarine commanders raised their periscopes as they passed by, doing four knots; the stationary scopes were the Russians.

PIZZA, OUTDOOR BARBECUES, a ration of beer, and the occasional movie helped ward off "tower fever." There was a recreation room with a ping-pong table and a television, a hobby shop with woodworking tools, and an electronics shop. Television reception was sometimes good, and when it was, the men spread out on the sofas, most of them in white T-shirts and khaki slacks. Countless hours were spent having a smoke, reading a book, or just thinking.

Decks, ceilings, hallways, and floors were mopped, painted, and then painted again. The linoleum floors were waxed to a sparkling shine; the windows were washed until the glass seemed to have disappeared. Bedcovers were tight, latrines were clean, the inventory was counted, and the paperwork was precise, down to the number of nuts and bolts in the cardboard bins.

IN MAY 1959, Alan David Crockett returned to Tower Four to inspect the work of divers from the J. Rich Steers Company. The Steers divers had returned to tighten the underwater connections and to install more bolts to halt some of the motion of the tower.

Crockett was satisfied with the work, as he testified to the Senate investigating committee. He reported that motion in the undersea braces was now "zero."

The repairs, however, would not last a year. New noises and new motion would prompt his return.

IN FEBRUARY 1960, Crockett returned to Tower Four to again inspect the legs and the trusses. He descended past the braces until he landed on the ocean floor. Using a thousand-watt light, Crockett surveyed the seabed through the green water. "[There was] a build up of sand around the footings approximately six-feet in height," said Crockett in a report admitted as an exhibit attached to his testimony before a Senate investigating committee. "The bottom area around the tower had considerable debris; namely fifty-gallon drums, construction steel, wire cable rope, blocks, hoses, etc. The C caisson had an abandoned diving platform against the footing but none of the debris was doing damage."

Crockett made his way around the footings. He saw no visible cracks, no dents, and no impaction from the sand around the caissons. Satisfied, he walked his line back to the platform and made his way up.

He inspected the braces near the bottom and found the connections tight. He moved up the middle section of braces at minus-seventy-five feet and there he spotted problems. He found the K bracing at minus-seventy-five feet to be loose. So, too, was the bracing at minus-twenty-five feet.

Said Crockett: "The noise factor heard on the tower in the vicinity of the caisson is resulting from motion of the tower . . . bringing two metal surfaces together . . . causing a metallic bang."

The undersea structure was wobbly. More repairs would begin.

ON MAY 24, 1960, the seas around Tower Four were calm and the skies sunny. Divers, welders, and riggers from J. Rich Steers had arrived on the *AKL* to begin the laborious process of tightening the countless pins, bolts, and connectors that held together the undersea supports for the offshore radar platform. They hoisted up their equipment to the weather deck and set about the assembly of the dive platforms.

The divers would descend into the Atlantic and work their way beneath the sea to each of the three sets of underwater braces. The collars, pin plates, bolts, and all connectors were tested for rigidity. Despite the incredible depth and poor visibility, they detected no fractures in any of the legs. They tightened fourteen bolts on one dive, two on another, but reported one leg was as they had left it in 1959.

Unfortunately, most of the bolts used on an earlier repair were of a type that could not be tightened. Thus, there was little to be done but to design a brace that would compensate for the slack. Informed of the problem with the undersea braces, Moran Proctor proposed adding heavy X-braces between the legs above the waterline. These braces would strengthen the legs but they would also add weight to the top-heavy structure. Worse, because the steel beams of this X would be exposed to the waves each time a wave hit the new braces, the tower would be pushed and tilted and the undersea supports would be stressed even more. Leon DeLong viewed this solution with more than mere skepticism, and said: "I would feel that it was pretty close to dooming the tower."

The X-braces were nonetheless approved and installed on Tower Four by August 1960.

MOVIEGOERS WERE ABLE to see the Texas Towers in operation. "The men who serve on radar stations draw overseas pay during their lonely vigil," intoned the narrator. Moreover, because these men were manning radarscopes night and day, an extra thirty minutes' warning in the event of an attack might now be provided. The tower and the men on it, concluded the narrator, were "a silent sentinel that might mean life or death to thousands of Americans."

They would be known as the "airmen of the sea."

ON THE MORNING of September 10, a force of 206 B-47s and 100 B-52s penetrated the North American Air Defense Intercept Zone in a simulated Soviet attack called Operation Sky Shield. The radar operators on Tower Four were among the first to pick up the Soviet fakers. Over the East Coast, 24 planes flew low-altitude runs against the radar stations accompanied by 10 jammers; another 28 penetrated on high-altitude routes. The first unidentified blip appeared on Tower Four's radars at 0146. The radar-intercept officer promptly tagged the blip and gave it a track. At 0247, Tower Four was penetrated again, and again the bombers were detected and intercepted. At 0334 and again at 0337, they were penetrated, and two intercepts were completed.

At 1100 hours, the exercise was officially closed.

Scarcely noted, however, was that a group of SAC B-47s from Florida had to be diverted. A hurricane in the Gulf of Mexico had made an unexpected turn.

* * *

ON SUNDAY, SEPTEMBER 11, 1960, the tower observed its weekend routine. The chefs laid out cold cuts, bread, cut onions, mustard, and mayonnaise. A skeleton crew manned the scopes.

To the south, the hurricane that reversed course in the Gulf of Mexico had regained its strength and was now moving up the eastern seaboard at the breathtaking speed of 45 miles per hour. Hurricane Donna, a category 3 storm with winds of 132 miles per hour, was now headed directly toward Tower Four.

ACCORDING TO LATER testimony, the *Tamarora* arrived to evacuate Tower Four on Monday at 7:30 A.M. but it was too late. The winds were a brisk forty-five knots. The seas had made up to twenty feet. Phelan talked to the logs on Tower Four: "Attempted to transfer personnel from doughnut to *Tamarora* longboat but seas of 20-25' and winds of 45 knots prevented the evacuation. Tower personnel will ride out storm on board . . ."

THAT TOWER FOUR survived Hurricane Donna was nothing short of a miracle. Rifle shots of rain pelted the platform like ball hammers beating against the steel. Waves hurled against the legs. The tower snapped and jerked as if it were a rag doll. The flying bridge beneath the platform was torn free by the waves and smashed into the B leg with a sound that reverberated throughout the platform. A communications dish was torn from the side of the platform. Stress cracks opened in the new X bracing in both the primary beams and the cross braces. Waves fractured a collar on the K brace at minus-25 feet, tore loose the pin plates that attached two diagonal braces at minus-75 feet, and tore loose a diagonal brace at minus-125 feet. That brace was floating free.

One man went down to the utility deck to see the ocean below. "I opened these covers to look at the sea down through these holes and the water came up through the holes," he testified. He said one wave slammed into the bottom of the platform some six stories above sea level. The water came though the holes and it wasn't just a splash. "It might have hit the ceiling if it hadn't hit me," he said. In later testimony he was asked if it compared to the stream of water that came from a garden hose. "I wouldn't compare it to a garden hose at all, sir," he answered. "I would compare it more with a bucket of water being thrown in my face."

Exhaust vents and other unreinforced empennages were carried away or damaged. Said Warrant Officer Edward Rausch in his testimony: "The bottom of the platform is 66 feet above sea level. We had damage to the ventilators on the second floor of that platform—they looked like someone had taken a big sledgehammer, and knocked it in, the whole side was pushed in. Captain Phelan and I felt sure that we had sustained water hitting the side of the Tower." The ventilators were eighty-eight feet above sea level.

The men held back their fear but openly prayed. At 1:00 P.M., Phelan talked to the tower's log: "Full force of hurricane pounding TT4. Winds 115 knots, seas at 65'. Several personnel outwardly expressing grave concerns."

"We just had to sit there and take it," remembered Rausch. "We had people praying and saying their Rosary, people running around in lifejackets. In fact we stationed people at the door to keep some of the ones we felt would panic—to keep them from going outside on the weather deck." One man had to be restrained until he could be airlifted ashore and taken to a psychiatric hospital.

Asked a congressman in the aftermath of the storm: "After Donna, this month of October was a pretty rough time—different than at any other time you'd been on the tower?"

"As far as movement, yes, sir, it was."

"And a strain on everybody on board?"

"Yes, sir."

THE DAMAGE TO Tower Four was extensive and both underwater and above-water repairs started almost immediately. The J. Rich Steers men arrived to repair the flying bridge and to weld the cracks to the above-water X bracing. Their divers worked on the loose pin plates, the dangling braces, and the other damage under water.

The men worked nearly nonstop for most of October.

AT 11:00 A.M. on Tuesday, November 15, 1960, air force helicopter 44001 appeared on the horizon and approached Texas Tower Four to land. The winds were light, the seas calm. It was fifty-eight degrees. On board the helicopter was Brigadier General William E. Elder, commander of the Boston Air Defense Sector, which included Tower Four. "You could feel the darn thing moving," Elder said in his testimony regarding his visit to the tower. "The winds were fresh, but not strong, and there were long swells across the ocean but nothing really big but even in these conditions, which I would not consider unusual or dangerous, the thing vibrated."

Elder had attended a meeting the day before during which the damage to

Tower Four had been discussed. Elder had not been able to get an answer to the one question he thought was paramount—how strong was the tower? Testified Elder: "They know that the tower had sustained underwater damage but no one had any information as to what other damage might be present. Mr. Kuss, having been in this business, was the most knowledgeable individual that I know to get information to enable us to make a decision as to whether we should or should not evacuate."

He came to the conclusion that Tower Four needed to be evacuated but he wanted to see it himself. Phelan and Elder talked. "How many men do you need to shut this tower down, pack up the classified gear and mothball the rest?" asked Elder. Phelan requested fourteen airmen, plus a repair crew to strengthen it for the winter weather.

"WE COULDN'T JUST abandon the tower," said one officer. "The Soviets might board it and claim it as their own what with international waters and all. Plus, we had to remove classified manuals and gear."

At 10:00 A.M., Phelan held a commander's call. Effective immediately, the radar station was to be shut down, he said; only a caretaker crew would remain behind to mothball the gear until it could be reopened in spring. He asked for fourteen volunteers, all of whom promptly came forward. He ordered the rest of the men to pack and prepare to depart on the *AKL* immediately. Seventy-two men left that day. The tower was swaying and rotating.

Phelan's final entry in the tower's log for that day was made at 3:40 P.M. "Electronic equipment off the air."

THE AIRMEN PACKED radio gear, disconnected cables, drained fluids, snaked wires out of pipes, removed devices, and crated the most sensitive of the classified surveillance gear. The *AKL* came and went, sending up men, construction equipment, mail, and food and taking back others who had finished their jobs.

Twelve men from the Steers company were now aboard the tower. They went under water on Friday, December 9, and worked on the braces at minus-seventy-five feet. They drilled holes for new clamps that they hoped would tighten the bracing. The winds were gusting at thirty knots. The tower was rocking.

However, work progressed and the diving was nearly continuous, and by the end of December Phelan would write that the tower seemed more stable and that the Steers men should be commended for their excellent progress. They had burned holes, worked clamps and sleeves over broken braces, tightened braces, and significantly reduced the tower's motion. He would note that the divers went down twice on Christmas Day.

The *AKL* arrived on December 28 and uploaded twenty-seven tons of material. There were six new arrivals and four that departed. There was, said Phelan, "a dead sea and winds of 0. All hands enjoyed a good nights rest."

Twenty-seven men were now on Tower Four, thirteen from the Steers Company and fourteen from the military. Most were from Local 56.

On New Year's Eve, the winds gusted to fifty knots, but Phelan was in good spirits: "Tower unmistakably stable no cause for concern."

FIRE IS GRAVY

SAID LIEUTENANT COLONEL Jim Taylor: "We couldn't just pull alert. We had to be *certified* for the mission. Typically we had four or five bombers on alert at the same time each with its own set of targets. We'd go to the wing's plans shop and study the mission and the procedures and the specifics of the sorties in our package; the timing and what we did at each point and the positive control messages and what they meant. The pilots had things they had to know like fuel consumption, speeds, routes; we'd study targets and defenses and things like that. It took about a week to prepare."

Indeed, the typical combat mission folder carried by an SAC bomber crew specified the Emergency War Plan target and contained navigational charts and target identification aids that were generated by SAC's Intelligence Directorate. This included a high-altitude navigation chart, low-altitude operational navigation chart, the air target chart, a map of radar significant power lines and locations, the basic target graphics, the seasonal target graphics, the hard target graphics, delivery tactics, Soviet air-defense installations and other threats on the penetration route, and the timeline of the attack (time-over-targets, bomb-release lines, etc.)

To deconflict the attackers, there was a computer-generated master timeline with all attacking forces on their EWP sortie. Sorties were numbered—Sortie 42 or Sortie 109 and so on—and each sortie had a strike timing sheet. The strike timing sheet contained all the sequences of events in the attack with precise timelines worked out so that no one bombed the other.

Because coded messages would be transmitted to the bombers, the certification process began with simulated transmissions that were played for the crews. "We had tape training and testing prior to the actual certification. They'd play Emergency Action Messages, EAMs, and we'd copy them down and decode them and explain the procedures that went with them. The staff or the wing commander would ask us questions about the messages and we would answer. If you missed one question, just one, you failed. If you failed the tape testing, you never made it to the certification until you passed it. Once you passed the tape training, you'd go in and sit before a group who would fire questions at you about the mission.

"Normally we had four targets on each sortie (because that was the number of weapons we could carry). Depending on the type of weapon, we would do a popup maneuver or a flyover at terrain-avoidance altitude to release."

Less precise were the final legs of the sortie. "We had recovery bases," said Taylor. "But basically, we were on our own."

THE PROOF TESTING of the SS-6 Sapwood missile in 1957 was followed by the construction of launchpads in northwestern Russia. The Soviet Ministry of Defense chose the village of Plesetsk, eight hundred miles north of St. Petersburg. The installation was named the Plesetsk Cosmodrome.

The existence of Plesetsk was revealed in 1960 when an American spy satellite called Corona successfully photographed new regions of the Soviet Union including the Plesetsk area. Intelligence analysts compared the photographs to World War II–era maps and photos and discovered a new railway line—the type that could transport a Sapwood booster.

Plesetsk would thus be added to routes flown by RB-47s, which would circle in the night offshore flying a path abeam the Cosmodrome. The Ravens ran the instruments from the pods in the bomb bays and gathered telemetry as various missiles were fired.

TO INJECT REALISM into their training, SAC approved a plan to place a number of radar bomb scoring sites on railroad trains so that they could be moved from one place to another, thus eliminating the degree of familiarity an aircrew would develop with permanent sites. The trains would be called the RBS Express.

THE ALTERNATE COMMUNICATIONS networks to deliver the go codes progressed. The low-frequency ground-wave system was well along the way. "Send" transmitters would be placed at the SAC and other national military command posts, while receivers would be located at the air wings and at missile-launch-control facilities. The messages would come across with agonizing slowness. Those who saw the receivers in action gave the low-data-rate system the nickname "thumper." *Thump . . . thump . . . thump* went the receiver as it banged out each letter of the EAM (Emergency Action Message).

* * *

IN 1949, A Strategic Air Command bombing competition was won by a crew that used what would soon be known as "offset radar bombing." According to an official publication, offset radar bombing "allows a pilot to destroy unseen targets using the known offset distances north–south and east–west from a landmark visible on the radar. When the crew enters the offsets and positions two cursors over the radar landmark, the onboard radar shows the invisible target's position, and how to reach it."

Offset bombing would become increasingly important due to the emergence of underground missile silos and buried command-and-control facilities. In the language of nuclear bombing, there were "show" and "no-show" targets. A ball-bearing plant two stories high was a "show" target, while an underground missile silo was a "no-show" target. A photograph of a Minuteman silo in Missouri, for instance, reveals little more than trees, a fence, and two poles. In Colorado, the location of a silo looks barren and windswept. In Nebraska, the silo is just prairie grass—no visible concrete, no gatehouse, no bunker—just a hardscrabble of land, a fence, and a few poles.

Said an SAC radar navigator: "Ninety-nine percent of our targets were no-show targets. If a target was radar significant, we could bomb it radar direct but most were radar offsets. You want at least one and hopefully two or three features to aim off."

Using a significant radar feature, the offset was plotted and a ground zero designated. Releasing the bomb was largely automated. "We'd use what we called a synchronize release. When the aircraft reached the calculated release point the system would open the doors automatically, the weapon would release, the door would close."

If all went well, there would be little to show for the bombing run save a crater in the ground in a place as barren as Wyoming.

STRATEGIC AIR COMMAND was now completing an in-flight refueling every 6.8 minutes.

IN EARLY FEBRUARY 1960, the roar of engines generating three hundred thousand pounds of thrust marked the launch of a Titan missile from Cape Canaveral, Florida. After the first stage expired, connecting bolts blew it away and the second stage ignited. The second stage pushed the nose cone farther into a trajectory, arcing it up through the atmosphere and 2,020 nautical miles downrange, where it impacted two miles past the target and one-tenth of a mile to the right.

In the math of megaton warheads, it was a bull's-eye. In time, ICBMs would be flung six thousand miles or more downrange, landing in the Ascension Island splash net with circular errors probable of one thousand feet or less.

Wrote a British reporter: "This, above all, I learned in a week of talking to America's top military and space people. They are over the hurdle. The rockets are going up almost daily without hitches . . . And the Earth satellites are running like trains."

SAID A FORMER pilot with Strategic Air Command: "After takeoff, we'd go get gas and then we'd fly to our first waypoint, our PCTAP—the Positive Control Turn Around Point. If we were executed, that is, if we were told to proceed, we'd go as far as the H-Hour Control Line. If we got the proper codes, at our Start Descent point, we'd push over the nose. At our Terrain Avoidance Point we'd be flying low level inbound to our target, maybe two hours out, as low to the ground as our sortie required. We were always low level. The Soviet fighters couldn't see us down low. When we got to our Initial Point, which was where we'd start the bomb run, we'd go another four, five minutes then pop the bomb bay doors at ten seconds, pull the nose up at five seconds, release our weapon, then push it over and get back down. We're going 390 knots with our hair on fire."

IN THE END, the effectiveness of a bomber came down to its crew being coordinated. "There are six of us in the bomber. The pilot, copilot, electronic warfare office to jam and punch out chaff and flares if need be; the gunner, the navigator and the radar navigator called the RN," said one pilot. "To me, the pilot, a target was just a triangle on a map. It had a name but I never cared what it was; my job was to keep us out of the rocks. The RN identified the target using radar, did a radar offset aim if there was no significant feature to see in or around the target, like, say a missile silo, and do the pre-arming. I only authorized the release of the bomb. Basically, we're all doing our jobs so the RN can do his. That's what the B-52 was built for: To get the radar navigator into position to release his weapons."

Countless pilots of Strategic Air Command could say the same thing.

ALMOST EVERY WAR scenario called for Soviet agents to implant bombs clandestinely within the United States and detonate them at the onset of war. Because such an attack would begin *inside* the early-warning-radar network, on the blind side of the radarscopes, nothing would appear in the radar stations to alert SAC that an attack was under way. Because they wanted to "squeeze every bit of useable reaction time from any warning situation," as they once put it, SAC wanted a system that would provide warning of any bomb burst irrespective of how it got into America.

Thus it was that a most unusual patent was filed on May 26, 1960, by the Western Union Telegraph Company for a "Nuclear Bomb Explosion Detecting Device." The Bomb Alarm System, as the full system would be called, was centered around a telephone-pole mounted device in the shape of an ordinary power transformer with a glass sensor on top shaped like an industrial lightbulb. Using an embedded "profile" of the signature of a thermal flash against which any observed phenomena could be compared, the detection devices could distinguish between an ordinary event—lightning, an explosion, and so on—and the real thing. Said the patent application: ". . . because of the tremendous burden of proof which rests on the device, it must be foolproof—to being selectively sensitive only to the occurrence of nuclear bomb explosions—never to sunlight, fire, lightening [sic], thunder, or other natural or artificial events."

According to the plan, three sensors would be placed around eighty-four military targets and thirteen major population centers. If a device sensed a legitimate flash, the system would simultaneously alert the Pentagon's National Military Command Center, Strategic Air Command headquarters, and North American Air Defense Command headquarters.

The Bomb Alarm System proved itself during the Cuban missile crisis when a radar station indicated that a missile had been launched from Cuba and was due to impact within minutes near Tampa. The time interval passed without a blast, so NORAD checked the Bomb Alarm System's display board.

There had been no flash. As it happened, a training tape had mistakenly been inserted into a console at the radar station that reported the missile.

UNTIL 1952, STRATEGIC Air Command was the only force capable of delivering an atomic bomb, but during 1952 secretary of the air force Thomas K. Finletter disclosed that "nearly all" the combat aircraft of the United States Air Force were being modified to carry the bomb, an announcement similar to the one made that year by the navy in regard to navy carrier aircraft. Because SAC, the air force, and the navy each had its own war plans, and thus its own targets, an "atomic coordination machinery" evolved, a series of groups and committees and annual meetings that between 1952 and 1960 attempted but largely failed to coordinate targets, timelines, and bombs. Indeed, computer tabulations in 1960 revealed that after eight years of meetings there were still more than two hundred conflicting time-over-targets, each one capable of destroying an American bomber by friendly fire or bombing an already destroyed target.

In 1960, Secretary of Defense Thomas Gates broke through what seemed to be a helpless gridlock and named the commander in chief of Strategic Air Command to the position of director of Strategic Target Planning and created a Joint Strategic Target Planning Staff under him that would prepare "integrated targeting plans for general war, embodying all the strategic forces of the United States." The Joint Chiefs would assist by providing guidance in the form of a National Strategic Targeting and Attack Policy, which would contain the objectives for the attack. The Strategic Target Planning Staff would use that guidance to create a National Strategic Target List, from which they would prioritize targets and draw up the plans for a coordinated attack.

That plan would be called the Single Integrated Operational Plan, or SIOP. The first SIOP plan was developed for fiscal year 1962 and was thus called SIOP-62.

SIOP-62 would become the ultimate instrument of nuclear war.

THE NEW GROUND-ALERT facilities were for all practical purposes plush, although no one would have dared call them that. They had a kitchen that served hot meals twenty-four hours a day, a game room, a TV room, a briefing room, and crew quarters divided into two-bed areas that included bedside lamps and personal dressers. They were, of course, under ground. When the klaxon rang, the pilots would use an upward-sloping tunnel to reach their aircraft. Because these tunnels had the appearance of mole runs, the bunkers were given the nickname "moleholes." At the sound of the klaxon, the aircrew would run through their moleholes and out to their aircraft and be airborne in minutes.

"IN SPITE OF what American officials say," said Nikita Khrushchev, "bombers are useless. Bombers are obsolete."

Khrushchev thus fanned the flames on a simmering American debate between missiles and bombers—a debate that with the appointment of a new secretary of defense in 1961 would erupt into a full-fledged fire, pitting the Department of Defense against Strategic Air Command. Of course, Khrushchev was using a bit of psychological propaganda. It was well-known that

America had more than fifteen hundred bombers but had only a handful of missiles. So far.

It was May 9, 1960.

SIOP WAS IN many ways the tip of the iceberg. At the height of the Cold War every jet, every bomber, every reconnaissance jet and refueling tanker; every ship in the navy, every aircraft carrier and submarine; every army squadron, every company and battalion of soldiers; every marine in the corps—all of the men and women of the armed forces had an Emergency War Plan mission. If the balloon went up, fighter pilots would race to their jets, flight crews would run to their bombers, and tankers would position themselves for the refuelings. At sea, submarines and aircraft carriers and their destroyers would swing their bows toward their targets and increase their propeller rotations as they made haste to sail to their stations. Every fighter jet had an offensive or defensive mission, every bomb on every bomber had a ground zero, every soldier was trained for a specific combat mission, and while SAC was perhaps the most visible arrow in this Cold War quiver, if it came to war, the emergency plan was coordinated, deconflicted, and trained by soldiers, sailors, airmen, and marines, time and time again.

THE RESULTS WERE disheartening. Of the sixteen attempts to launch the Atlas D missile, two missiles had to be destroyed after liftoff, two malfunctioned and fell between five hundred and one thousand miles short of the target area, and nine never even left the pad, leaving just three that performed as expected. Said General Thomas Power: "Missile reliability . . . still causes me deep concern. As a result of our experience at Vandenberg with Atlas, our probability of a successful launch . . . is almost zero."

Power urged accelerated production of more B-52s to stand in place of the flailing buildup of ICBMs. LeMay, now vice chief of staff, was surprisingly more forgiving of the Atlas. New bombers had to be broken in, too, said LeMay; missiles were no different.

THE QUESTION OF where to base the new ICBMs posed a unique set of circumstances. In the effort to install silos at Pease Air Force Base, in New Hamphire, some objected to putting Boston in the crosshairs of the Soviet attack forces, while others were more pragmatic and noted that Boston and New York would be "primary targets anyway."

* * *

THE JOINT CHIEFS of Staff and the secretary of defense recognized the need for a high-level independent study group that would impartially analyze proposed and existing weapons' systems and tactics. In 1948, they established the Weapons System Evaluation Group. In September 1960, the Weapons System Evaluation Group issued their analysis of the vulnerabilities to the nation's command and control in what would be known as Report 50. This report was a precisely worded criticism of a system that would fail: "On the basis of tactical warning, the time the president may confidently think he has for the response decision, prior to bomb impact, is between zero and 15 minutes. In using the upper extreme of 15 minutes he will be assuming that every procedural and physical element in the whole warning and strategic command and control structure works perfectly." But the Weapons System Evaluation Group was skeptical; they felt certain that the entire chain of command would be eliminated in a first strike.

According to Report 50: "In a deliberate attack on the national political and military command structure . . . only a few Soviet weapons . . . are needed to eliminate the U.S. capability to make or transmit a political or high-level military decision . . . nearly all of those on the succession list would be as likely to be incapacitated as the president and by the same event . . .

"Under present circumstances, the most that would likely to be launched against the Soviets would be a delayed, uncoordinated and ragged response of reduced size." Soviet bombers would be roaming the devastated American landscape on "search and kill missions," hitting surviving targets at will.

It was imagery as stark and perhaps as brutally realistic as any yet authored by the Pentagon.

THE "EMERGENCY WAR Plan" sounded ambiguous. Was it a "plan," and thus subject to review and revision, or was it an order? This question was raised and was quickly resolved in true military fashion.

The Emergency War Plan would now be called the Emergency War Order.

While the change might seem slight, an "order" was at the heart of the concept of command.

ON JULY 1, 1960, an RB-47H reconnaissance aircraft disappeared during a mission along the edges of the Soviet Union over the Barents Sea. There were three men in the flight crew and Ravens in the bomb-bay pod.

On July 11, the Soviet Union announced that they had shot down the aircraft and that two men had survived and were imprisoned and that one body would be returned to the United States for burial. Three were missing.

The United States said that the aircraft had been on a mapping mission; the Soviet Union claimed it had violated their airspace. In what seemed to be further evidence of a shift in public sentiment about things military, the press was skeptical of the air force's explanation.

THE MISSILES-VERSUS-BOMBERS debate continued but the center of gravity was tilting toward missiles and away from bombers, even when it came to anticipating the form of attack on the United States. Said the planning board of the National Security Council, speaking of the Soviet Union: "The period is drawing to an end when the primary element in the threat to the United States is manned bombers . . . the period of the early 1960s will represent a gradual transition from a largely bomber threat to one mainly composed of ICBMs . . . in a few years, the principal element of the threat to the United States will be ICBMs."

ONE OF SAC's three alternate communications networks began its testing phase in 1960. This was the Airborne National Command Post concept, a modified tanker brimming with electronic communications gear that would sit on fifteen-minute ground alert with the other ground-alert forces. If the klaxon rang, the command post would launch and take up station above SAC headquarters. If communications failed, it would take over. If SAC headquarters was hit by a Soviet bomb, on board the command post was an Airborne Emergency Action Officer (AEAO). This officer was an air force general officer given authority to issue the go codes if he actually saw a fireball rise above Omaha.

In July 1960, the first command post was placed on ground alert, and over the course of the next six months it received forty-two no-notice fifteen-minute launches. On average, the aircraft was airborne in less than twelve minutes. While airborne it successfully transferred messages from Washington to other bombers participating in the tests.

As it happened, one aircraft was not enough to create an effective communications network. In time, the airborne concept would expand to a fleet of twenty command posts and thirty-six airborne relay stations. It was a virtual network at thirty thousand feet, with each aircraft acting as a communications node.

It was redundancy built on top of redundancy.

* * *

BECAUSE FIRESTORMS WERE considered unpredictable and thus difficult to put into the math of vulnerability indexes, fires and firestorms triggered by atomic bombs continued to be excluded from the equations used to calculate the probability that a target would suffer severe damage during a nuclear attack. "To my mind," said the deputy director of the Joint Strategic Target Planning Staff, "fire is gravy. What ever you can get from fire just makes everything worse. And you don't need to measure it. It's just there."

Another bonus effect, as it were.

IN 1960, CBS, NBC, and ABC typically went off the air at 1:00 A.M. and, more or less, America went to bed. To end their broadcasts the networks often transmitted patriotic images including images of an American flag and the playing of the national anthem. On many occasions, they added pictures of SAC bombers streaking across the sky.

To a nation laced with the tensions of the Cold War, it had just the right touch.

IN A TIME of national emergency, Washington, D.C., was no doubt where the president of the United States would feel compelled to be, but in the event of a warning of an incoming Soviet nuclear strike it would be the last place the president should be. With that in mind, the topic of an alternate command post was raised, a post near enough to the White House for the president to escape to but far enough away to survive a thermonuclear burst.

The navy came forward with an idea they called the National Emergency Command Post Afloat. The navy would use a fast cruiser to motor on the Chesapeake Bay and through the adjacent coastal waters. When the warning was sounded, the president would reach the ship by car, helicopter, speedboat, or even a submarine, but once on board he would be sped out of the target area.

The air force pointed out that in a nuclear attack, the Chesapeake Bay and the nearby coastal waters would be blanketed by intense fallout, so they suggested a National Emergency Airborne Command Post (NEACP), pronounced "kneecap." This command post was based on a heavily modified KC-135 tanker with communications equipment and a supporting battle staff that when aloft could connect to governmental and military chains of command, including the Strategic Air Command alternate command post. The air force proposed that

NEACP KC-135s be positioned at nearby Andrews Air Force Base, where they would sit on fifteen-minute alert.*

Said a military think tank of this plan: "Either before or after tactical warning, the president and key officials would go to an airfield by helicopter and be airborne and out of the Washington area within 15 minutes (the time expected to be available from warning by BMEWS). The NEACP would orbit an area west of the city until initial strikes were over, then proceed to a surviving fixed site as quickly as possible. While in flight, it would contact ground stations and SAC's airborne command post."

The Joint Chiefs of Staff responded favorably to both proposals and funded both, although there were murmurs of the truth, and the truth was that there was little chance that anyone could react in 15 minutes. Still, NEACP became operational on February 19, 1962, and assumed fifteen-minute ground alert under a program that would be known ominously as "Night Watch."

DURING THE SHAKEDOWN period preceding its switch to full operational status, the Thule BMEWS site detected multiple incoming threats, causing the system to display the highest alarm level it was programmed to transmit. Oddly, no impact predictions followed and thus they declared a false alarm, but a subsequent analysis revealed a most unusual occurrence. Radar waves had bounced off the moon and, owing to the slight rotation of Earth, the moon appeared to be coming toward the station, which of course was interpreted as an attack. Those who knew radar were not surprised: radar routinely bounced off the moon. Slight adjustments were made to the equipment and the moon quickly reverted to being an object in the sky and nothing more.

---

* Although highly modified, the planes went by their tanker designation, KC-135s, until January 1, 1965, when airborne command posts were redesignated EC-135s.

ONE-POINT DETONATION

BETWEEN 1956 AND 1961, the Joint Committee on Atomic Energy received more than two dozen letters detailing accidents that had resulted in a lost or damaged atomic bomb. One A-bomb fell through the bomb-bay doors of an SAC bomber and exploded in New Mexico, a B-47 crashed and exploded in Florida, and then another near Abilene and another near Dossier City, Louisiana, all resulting in destroyed bombs.

A bomb was destroyed in a crash near Lake Charles, Louisiana, and three more bombs were destroyed in a crash near Shreveport; one bomb was ejected off the coast of Washington from a navy seaplane that caught fire, and another was lost when a plane accidentally dropped an Operational Suitability Test bomb off the island of Hawaii. Two bombs exploded during an SAC B-52 crash in Kentucky, four more were destroyed in a B-52 explosion over Utah, and another bomb was destroyed in a crash in the United Kingdom.

And then there is the SAC B-52 that broke apart in the air and the hydrogen bomb that remains buried in a farm field near Goldsboro, North Carolina.

A TANKER BASED at a North Carolina SAC base was refueling a B-52 on airborne alert. While giving it gas, the boom operator noticed a stream of fluids coming from the right side of the bomber. He radioed the B-52, and the bomber's captain promptly disengaged from the refueling boom. An inspection confirmed the leak, which according to the checklists of actions to take in emergencies meant the bomber should land immediately, but the B-52 had just taken on gas and it was too heavy to land so the pilot was sent out over the ocean to dump fuel. But the leak was worse than it seemed and, within minutes, the B-52 had lost an astonishing 37,000 pounds of gas. The pilot turned back toward the base and requested permission to land but the bomber was becoming increasingly difficult to control. As the B-52 neared Seymour-Johnson AFB near Goldsboro, North Carolina, a wing twisted against the fuselage and exploded. Flames filled the night sky as the wing tore away and fuel cells ignited. Five of the eight crew members safely ejected. The spinning bomber slammed into the ground and a second explosion sent burning wreckage careening across a rural road and into a farm field. In the wreckage were two multi-megaton MK-39 H-bombs.

On January 24, 1961, Brigadier General Loper wrote to inform the Joint Committee of the crash: "One weapon exploded from a one-point detonation; one weapon was apparently thrown free of the airplane when the aircraft exploded, and landed 1½ miles from the wreckage. This weapon was recovered intact."

The one-point detonation was more troubling than it sounded.

THE NEW GENERATION of sealed-pit bombs had to be "one-point safe," or "single-point safe"—that is, if there was an inadvertent detonation at any single point over the surface of the plutonium capsule, the resulting yield would be no more than the equivalent of four pounds of TNT. While seemingly harmless, the implication of a one-point detonation was rather profound. That a detonator would actually fire was in and of itself a sign that many interlocking safety mechanisms within the bomb had failed.

The Sandia Corporation was asked by the AEC to analyze the warheads recovered from the Goldsboro crash. The first MK-39 had been ejected more than eight thousand feet above the ground. Sandia reported that the extreme forces of the bombers' in-flight destruction had activated the arming system as if it had been dropped on purpose. The breakup forces "pulled" the safing pins out of the "Bisch" generator and the "pullout valves" operated by closing, which activated a low-voltage thermal battery that powered a timer that then ran down. A barometric gate "sensed" that the bomb was falling through the sky by "feeling" the changes in the surrounding atmospheric pressure and it correctly concluded that the bomb had been dropped. The barometric switch closed, thus bridging another gap in the energy pathway. The impact with the ground presumably caused the contact-fusing plates to close, thus triggering the high-voltage batteries to fire. Said the analyst, "[I]t can be assumed that it supplied a fire signal at impact." That the detonators failed to fire came down to the Armed/Safe switch, which had remained in the Safe position, holding back the final gate and thus blocking a nuclear explosion.

The second bomb was released at a lower altitude. It, too, was activated by the forces of the crashing bomber but impacted the ground twelve seconds before the timer ran down. This bomb appeared to have come even closer than the first. The Arm/Safe switch was in the Armed position when recovered. Said Dr. Ralph Lapp, who at the time of the Goldsboro crash was head of nuclear physics in the Office of Naval Research: "In this case, the warhead was equipped with six interlocking safety mechanisms, all of which had to be triggered in sequence to explode the bomb. Five of the six interlocks had been set off by the fall. Only a single switch prevented the 24-megaton bomb detonating and spreading fire and destruction over a wide area."

But then the game changed. Loper wrote the Committee a second letter and retracted his statement from his first. Evidently none of the detonators fired. "There is no positive evidence to support the earlier allegation of a one-point detonation," said General Loper. "No high explosives have been found in the crater. Salvage efforts are under way to recover the portion of the weapon at the base of the crater."

Explosive Ordnance Disposal teams streamed in to Goldsboro, and for months they searched for the missing component but the secondary of the second bomb was nowhere to be found. The crews dug into the ground but they hit groundwater and an ever-growing pit of mud stymied their efforts.

The hydrogen portion of the second bomb, the secondary, was never found.

ON MAY 17, 1961, General Loper again wrote the committee regarding the Goldsboro bomb and said, "All components of the weapons functioned normally before the crash up to the point of impact," which was a matter-of-fact way of saying that both bombs had almost exploded. "The warhead went through all of its arming sequences, including parachute deployment, actuation of internal timing mechanisms, development of high voltage, etc," remembered a physicist investigating the accident. His point was that nothing like that should have ever happened inside a sealed-pit bomb.

What caused the bombs to self-arm was the destruction of the bomber. What was important was to prevent the dynamic stresses of a crash from doing that to a bomb again. It is unknown exactly what the solution was but the cover letter on the Sandia report mentions that "modification kits" were being delivered to the air force on an expedited basis.

OF THE LOST hydrogen secondary, little more would be said. Groundwater filled the muddy pit as recovery teams tried to dig it out. In the end, the harder they worked, the deeper it sunk. Loper reported on May 23 that all reasonable effort had been expended to find the bomb but the recovery was being abandoned. The air force purchased an easement around the property that would at the very least alert those who intended to dig in the area that the property was controlled by them. A press release was issued to "dispel any rumors and assure the local population" that there wasn't any danger from the unrecovered component.

Later, tabloid magazines would make this bomb the subject of more than one front-page story about a nuclear fireball rising from a farm field, which served only to obscure the truth, which is that a highly classified nuclear portion of a thermonuclear bomb remains in a farm field twenty minutes from downtown Goldsboro, at the intersection of North Carolina State roads 117 and 70.

THE CLOBBER FACTOR

GENERAL WILLIAM CAMPBELL, one of the SAC bomber pilots who participated in the Sky Shield exercises, remembered while speaking to an air force historian: "We would fly out into the Atlantic about 500 miles with large numbers of bombers—in the range of 400 and 500 bombers—B-46s, B-36s, B-52s. We were given selected patterns and tactics to fly, dropping chaff, jamming, flying high, flying leap frog maneuvers where we would fly in for 10 minutes, make a 180, go back out for five [minutes], make a 180, go back in for 10, crisscrossing tracks, some day but mostly night . . . I was amazed at the high survivability of the bomber forces. I think we had a 95 percent plus rate on getting through whatever NORAD could muster."

Said Campbell: "[The Sky Shield exercises] gave me a sense of the belief that I could do my strategic mission, that I could fly the route I had briefed and certified and fly at 40,000 feet across the Soviet Union over Moscow, taking off from Greenham Commons across Riga, Moscow, turning south, exiting down the Black Sea and landing in Turkey. I had some confidence that we could really do that and make it."

STRATEGIC AIR COMMAND fully realized that it was a unique organization and that few outsiders could maintain its sense of readiness. SAC had developed its communications networks, intelligence directorates—indeed, its entire operational standards—to meet its own demands. Said SAC: "Experience has shown the extreme difficulty if not impossibility, of getting the same degree of motivation and dedication from organizations which must support but are not a part of SAC."

THE NATIONAL STRATEGIC Target List of SIOP-62 consisted of 3,729 targets, of which 2,220 were considered primary targets and 835 were active air-defense installations that had to be destroyed. Because some targets were clustered into target islands, several targets on the list could be destroyed by a single bomb, thus reducing the total number of aiming points or Desired Ground Zeros.

That said, the alert force would immediately strike 748 critical targets, which included 76 primary Soviet air bases, 56 nuclear storage sites, 199 urban-industrial complexes, and 85 government centers or control centers in the Soviet Union and China. This strike force would consist of 874 bombers, missiles, or fighter jets carrying 1,447 nuclear weapons, not counting weapons expended to blast open penetration corridors.

That death on an unprecedented scale would shatter the tempo of everyday life and unalterably change the Soviet Union forever was revealed in the expected destruction. Destroyed in this first wave would be 75 percent of the military capabilities of the Soviet Union and 90 percent of the industrial floor space targeted.

"SIOP-62 is, to put it mildly, an extremely blunt force instrument," said one analyst. "These are brute force tactics . . ."*

THE ENTIRE SIOP capability totaled 2,258 delivery vehicles with 3,423 atomic weapons, which included every bomber and every missile SAC owned plus seven types of navy planes and missiles and eight types of air force fighter jets and light bombers. It would take about six hours for the SAC bombers to reach their Positive Control Turn Around Points, but if this force was executed it would be all or nothing, the perfection of nation killing, the perfection of human extinction, as nuclear fireballs blistered the Soviet Union and China and burned tens upon tens of millions of people in a strike that once started could not be stopped.

THE RULES THAT enabled the launch of an ICBM were necessarily complex and appropriately filled with iron-clad procedures and safety measures, many of which have been characterized with reasonable accuracy in several movies. In the Launch Control Centers, the Emergency Action Message had to be authenticated and two men at opposite ends of the control center had to simultaneously insert and turn launch keys. There were many other rules and requirements, but a 1961 history of Strategic Air Command states that there

---

*   See Appendix I to the Memorandum for the President, Subject: Recommended Long Range Nuclear Delivery Forces 1963–1967, September 23, 1961, DoD FOIA Reading Room. At the end of 1961 there were 836 delivery vehicles with 1,651 megatons.

also was a dead-man option, too. To ensure that at the very least the sole survivors in the underground launch-control centers would be able to launch missiles even as missiles rained down on them, there were launch timers that could be set for delays of between one hour and six hours. Launch control officers, who in the face of their own all-but-certain deaths, could set timers for automatic launch. If they were not interrupted during the delay, the missiles they controlled would be fired.

In Russia there was a parallel system called the "dead-hand switch." The last surviving launch control officer before his own death could open a circuit that connected to a network of external sensors similar to our own bomb-alarm system that would launch missiles if they detected the light pulse or blast of an atomic bomb.

Taken together, there was more truth than fiction to the idea that machines might end the world. Indeed, after Washington and Moscow were long gone, after most of the urban areas in two of the largest countries in the world had been turned into ruins, each country could still launch one more volley.

Initiated by machines.

ON FEBRUARY 3, 1961, a converted KC-135 tanker took off from Offutt Air Force Base, Nebraska, in a flight that would remain airborne, uninterrupted, until July 24, 1990. As that KC-135 took off, so too did nine B-47s strategically positioned across the United States. This marked the end of the fifteen-minute ground-alert test of the SAC Airborne National Command Post and the beginning of the airborne-alert version of the same thing, which would eventually be called Looking Glass. Every eight hours on the hour, one airborne team took off and moved into the place of the other, in an airborne passing of the baton that maintained an SAC command post in the air, twenty-four hours a day for almost thirty years.

As before, if the Airborne Emergency Action Officer confirmed visually or by radar that a nuclear bomb had destroyed SAC headquarters, he would take over.

Said *The New York Times*: "The Looking Glass plane is the best-known part of the doomsday machinery for fighting a nuclear war. It belongs to the Strategic Air Command, and is called Looking Glass because it's designed to mirror SAC's underground command headquarters. If that were destroyed, the general aboard Looking Glass has the power, if authorized, to launch Minuteman missiles from their silos, to send strategic bombers on their missions . . ."

Looking Glass would grow to a fleet of more than fifty command posts and relay aircraft, including the impressively large B-47 jumbo jet.

* * *

SECRETARY OF DEFENSE Robert McNamara was briefed on SIOP-62 by a group of twelve officers from the staff of the Joint Chiefs. His questions were pointed.

"Have you applied your procedures to Hiroshima," asked McNamara.

Answered the staff: "Yes. Three DGZs at 80 KT each."

A no doubt startled McNamara was well aware that a single bomb of just under twenty kilotons had destroyed most of that city.

THE PENETRATION TACTICS Committee was asked to determine the expected attrition rates for SIOP bombers and fighters attacking the Soviet Union. By examining the penetration routes and the known Soviet air defenses, each sortie was assigned a probability factor of making it to their bomb-release line. There were, however, a great number of sorties that would be flown over uncharted territory. For these sorties the committee argued that a "clobber factor" had to be applied. High-speed bombers flying on low-level routes across unmapped terrain at night could fly head-on into an uncharted smokestack or a high power line or a radio tower or even a sudden rise in terrain for which there would be little warning.

That, then, was the clobber factor: a high-speed, low-level aircraft flying point-blank into an "unknown flight hazard."

Forty years later, the thought still gave pilots the chills.

IN MARCH 1961, President Kennedy spoke to a special session of Congress to recommend a significant increase in the SAC alert posture. "Strategic Air Command bombers standing by on ground alert of 15 minutes can also have a high degree of survivability provided adequate and timely warning is available. I therefore recommend that the proportion of our B-52 and B-47 forces on ground alert should be increased until about half of our total force is on alert."

Fifty percent ground alert began within weeks. By July 1961 there were 664 bombers carrying 1,423 weapons supported by 494 tankers armed, cocked, and ready on fifteen-minute alert.

More remarkable, in tests, SAC determined that it could launch all these thousand-plus bombers and tankers in just eleven minutes. At the peak moment of the breakout, two hundred aircraft would take off in a single minute.

ON MARCH 1, 1961, Strategic Air Command put into operation its first railroad-mounted radar-bomb scoring site, the RBS Express. SAC bombers would now hunt and kill railcars. Within a year, thousands of practice bombing runs would have been flown against three sets of trains located in three parts of the country. The attack profiles—high or low altitude—would vary, the flight crews would be graded, and 10 percent or so would fail each test.

IN MAY 1961, the new supersonic B-58 Hustler bomber flew from New York to Paris, setting a speed record of three hours and nineteen minutes. One week later, the entire flight crew was killed during a breathtaking aerial demonstration at the Paris Air Show that ended in a horrifying crash.

THE MAY DAY Parade of 1961 celebrated the launch of the first man into space. The parade was themed "Triumph in Space." Yuri Gagarin was the honored guest. Official footage from the Soviet news agency TASS panned a Red Square packed with tens of thousands of Russians who cheered as a plastic rocket floated into the air. The commentator described this crowd as the "face of a people whose leader would wipe out democracy."

The newsreel cut to footage of a similar parade in Cuba. Cuba's president Fidel Castro gave a speech that lasted three hours. In it he promised to "make New York another Hiroshima, if war ever came."

THE INITIAL AIRBORNE-ALERT flight paths were ladder-type routes over the Atlantic and Pacific that went to and from the Canadian Arctic. These routes could handle at best a few bombers, which was far too limiting at a time when SAC wanted to have more than seventy bombers in the air.

In early 1961, SAC planners devised a bomber-stream approach on routes that were called Chrome Dome routes. These routes were lengthy flight paths into which could be funneled one bomber after another with sufficient spacing for air refueling. The northern Chrome Dome circumnavigated North America in a counterclockwise rotation that included an overflight of the Canadian polar regions. The southern Chrome Dome route crossed the Atlantic Ocean and then flew over the southern tip of Spain and into the Mediterranean, where the bombers would turn around and return to the United States.

The president authorized SAC to fly twelve fully armed B-52s on these routes. To refuel them, tankers were positioned in Alaska, Spain, and in the northeastern part of the United States with enormous quantities of fuel. The tankers in the Northeast, for instance, were expected to deliver a minimum of

192,000 gallons to the B-52s every day. The Alaskan tankers would deliver 237,000 gallons of gas, and the tankers in Spain were required to deliver 205,000 gallons a day.

And that was for just twelve bombers. SAC wanted to have more than seventy in the air.

SAID GENERAL POWER before an appropriations hearing: "I like to tell the commander at Thule that he will probably be one of the first ones to go if we go to war, but that there is one thing I would like to know from him and that is when he went."

Amusing or not, the Ballistic Missile Early Warning radar station in Thule guarded the direct, Soviet polar route of attack on America. If there was war, Thule would no doubt be the first American installation to be attacked and the radar station would go dark. Unfortunately, owing to the harsh arctic climate, a radar station going dark wasn't necessarily proof that an enemy attack was under way.

To differentiate a Soviet attack from a power outage or a communications problem, SAC created a third airborne-alert route called the Thule Monitor. A B-52 would fly up to Greenland and orbit above the radar station twenty-four hours a day. If there was a power outage, the crew of the B-52 could confirm the situation. As with all alert bombers, the Thule bombers flew these missions loaded with their EWO loads, which were typically four H-bombs.

The Thule Monitor was approved and the flights began in August 1961. Within just months, a Thule B-52 successfully halted what otherwise might have been a full launch of the ground-alert bombers during an unexpected breakdown in SAC's communications networks. On the other hand, the Thule B-52s would also be the undoing of air alert. A Thule Monitor bomber would crash, with consequences not anticipated by Strategic Air Command.

THE TWO COLD War combatants had come to essentially the same conclusion with respect to targeting. Wrote John Hines of his interviews with Soviet leaders and their Cold War battle plans: "In the 1960s and 1970s, Vitaliy Tsygichko explained, the Soviet Union had a comprehensive plan for retaliation against nuclear attack. The plan, which was updated every 6 months, called for a Soviet launch under-attack using all Soviet silo-based systems. This annihilating retaliatory nuclear strike would be directed not against U.S. silos, which Soviet planners assumed would be empty, but rather against military targets (such as airfields, ports, and C3 facilities) and against the U.S. political and economic infrastructure (including transportation grids and fuel-supply lines). Soviet doctrine relied on the threat of a massive response as the best way to prevent nuclear use."

Thus it was that both countries relied on the prospect of nuclear annihilation for deterrence, bombers and missiles on hair-trigger alerts that would vanquish two nations.

A CONCEPT CALLED "constraints" was introduced in SIOP-62. *Constraint* was a term used to mean "limiting fallout on friendly, neutral, and satellite areas on the periphery of the Soviet Union and Communist China." If three or four or five warheads on a single target created an unacceptably intense fallout pattern over a friendly nation, SIOP planners would attempt to shuffle yields or fusing while still attaining the desired destruction. SIOP-62, however, was reasonably blasé about the whole thing. It calculated constraints based on the fallout from only the largest bomb on a target, not the total of all bombs on a target.

SIOP-63 partly rectified this and was more inclusive but was criticized because constraints failed to include the fallout from Soviet surface-to-air missiles bursting in the air, nor did it vary the direction of the fallout according to the seasonal changes in winds.

Then there was the navy. The dithering about how to calculate constraints missed the point entirely, or so they said. It was the "off-continent winds" that mattered. Said the navy: "Off-continent winds aloft may cause us to be more concerned about residual radiation damage resulting from our own weapons than those of the enemy."

One could only imagine the sense of helplessness of the navy ships operating in the Mediterranean enveloped in the fallout from bombs delivered by Strategic Air Command.

"AIR FORCE PLANNERS realized," wrote one historian, "that Soviet ICBMs could destroy all or part of the U.S. air defense radar system long before the first of their bombers crossed the arctic circle." The same historian quoted a NORAD commander who remarked that the aboveground NORAD command center in Colorado could be taken out by "a well aimed bazooka shot."

NORAD would promptly move underground. Carved out of Cheyenne Mountain, Colorado, would be a vast array of buildings with 170,000 square feet of space, against which a nuclear bomb would be a mere annoyance.

* * *

ICBMs MOVED FORWARD with astonishing speed. The new Minuteman was successfully test fired in 1961, Titan had logged thirteen consecutively successful launches since July 1961, and operational missiles were arriving at an air force base in Colorado.

Minuteman was scheduled to have 600 missiles in hardened silos by 1964, with 100 more added each year until the total of 1,000 was reached. Their silos would be three nautical miles apart, buried deep under ground, and hardened to 700 psi. In 1961, initial authorization for 150 missiles was approved.

ON SEPTEMBER 8, 1961, Nikita Khrushchev appeared on the cover of *Time*. His face is contorted in a ball of angry flesh. He stabs the air as if making a point. His head is silhouetted by the fireball of an atomic explosion. The message was easily understood.

SAID A PILOT who flew Chrome Dome alerts: "There was no qualm in my mind that when we flew the Chrome Dome missions we were fully prepared, mentally and technically. I was just as confident as can be that everybody else was the same way. Those were long sorties, over 24 hours, and you could come down pretty tired. But we flew those Chrome Domes, and I think having the weapons was an attention getter and a sense of purpose of what we were doing and always the possibility that you might be needed."

AS A SPECIFIED command in matters of operations, SAC reported not to the air force but to the Joint Chiefs and the secretary of defense, and it was comfortable with that but politically speaking it was on its own. SAC therefore created the rather Orwellian-sounding position of political adviser to CINCSAC, or POLAD. The POLAD helped SAC navigate the potentially complicated and often murky political waters of Washington, D.C. The first POLAD assumed his duties in September 1961.

"EVERYTHING WAS BASED on timing," remembered Colonel Taylor, a B-52 radar navigator during the Cold War. "When one B-52 went into a target we had to be sure it wouldn't be blown up by another missile or another bomb. That was true transiting over our own target areas as well as transiting over the target areas for other bombers. We didn't want to fly into a bomb that was exploding or blow up another jet with our own weapon. We had to be deconflicted."

The bombers would proceed with their flight plans from one designated ground zero (DGZ) to the next, flying their low-level routes, streaking through Soviet defenses at four hundred knots, dropping weapons like seed, parachutes trailing out of bomb bays, then snapping full as they caught air, then gently descending, a thermonuclear weapon landing on a silo or an air base or in an industrial plant waiting for a timer to close the last gate. Flashes of white would suffuse the target areas, some close, some distant—flashes that would not be seen by the crew because the entire mission would be flown with thermal shields down, no outside visibility, just a peephole for the pilot, if he chose to use it.

That was nuclear war. That's the way it would be. Shields down.

SAID THE AEC: "The H-Hour Control Line is an imaginary line encircling the enemy territory just outside the enemy early warning radar. This line is the departure point on which computations for timing over target are based. It also is a point at which crews perform final check lists pertaining to such things as fuel reserves, ECM, and weapons arming."

The safety rules specified that the seals and switches that needed to be broken or set could not be broken or set until the bomber crossed the control line. But this was "inappropriate," said the secretary of defense. Soviet air-defense fighters would surely engage bombers as far from their borders as possible. If a crew had to wait until they passed the H-Hour Control Line, it would mean that they would be breaking the seals on arming devices and going through the checklists as they were engaging the enemy.

The Department of Defense proposed a change that would allow crews to arm their weapons 15 minutes before they crossed the HHCL. The Atomic Energy Commission agreed: "The proposed changes will permit sufficient time for careful weapon preparation performance, completely and safely, prior to the intense operational activity which occurs at the HHCL or low-level penetration and thereafter."

Intense operational activity.

THE MEETING OF The Business Council was held at the Homestead in Hot Springs, West Virginia. Surrounded by immaculately tended grounds that included a golf course rated among the finest in the nation, the evening presentation was anything but pastoral; among the topics the speaker would touch on were the new Berlin crisis, the prospects of nuclear war, and the use of high-megatonnage weapons for the sake of terror, to name but a few. The guest of honor was Deputy Secretary of Defense Roswell Gilpatric. From the podium, Mr. Gilpatric recognized the assembled leaders as extraordinary people who at times had themselves served "the public welfare" and that without them and their companies "the defense of the United States could not be maintained." It was October 21, 1961.

After discussing the nuclear-striking capabilities of the Soviets and the United States he turned to a topic recently in the news. "It might be appropriate at this point to say a few words about the Soviet's announced intention to explode a 50 megaton thermonuclear device at the end of October," said Gilpatric. "Our own scientists and military leaders examined the utility of weapons of this and even larger yields several years ago and concluded that the military value was so questionable that it was not worth developing such weapons even though we have the know-how and capacity to do so. While there might be some military advantages from extremely large yields, there are also operational disadvantages. It is therefore quite clear that Russia's primary purpose is terror."

In little more than a week, a Soviet bomber flew over the nuclear-test range on the island of Novaya Zemlya in the Arctic Ocean and released a bomb that when detonated was estimated to have yielded been between fifty and fifty-seven megatons.

As was the case, Strategic Air Command had a reconnaissance aircraft orbiting the area for the precise purpose of monitoring that test.

The bomb was called Tsar.

GENERAL POWER WAS awakened in the predawn darkness with the sort of news that kept SAC on 15-minute alert. The BMEWS station in Thule had gone dark. More than that, the communication lines to NORAD were down and a dedicated SAC hotline was down, too. That so many communication routes could go dead at once seemed unlikely—during the design of the networks SAC had insisted that there be no single point of failure that could cause multiple circuits, or routes, to drop at the same time—but there it was, "an entire loss of BMEWS routes," as the logs would later say, and there were only two possible explanations: the network had suffered some sort of catastrophic failure or the United States would soon be under attack by the Soviets. Power had little choice but to assume the worst, so he triggered the alert force.

Across the United States klaxons rang and air bases sprang to life. Clouds of black smoke billowed behind countless engines as bombers and tankers spooled up their engines, pilots checked in with their towers, and, in what had to be the most riveting moment in many of their lives, they were told that it was not a test.

Officially, that's where the history of this event usually ends, but new documents tell us more. One by one, a total of 577 bombers and 393 tankers completed their engine starts and threaded their way down the ramps and to the taxiways to the hold-short lines or in their position-hold spots on the runways. This lethal alert force of bombers and tankers was now in the hyperkinetic phase of readiness called a Minimum Reaction Posture—engines turning, bombers holding at the edge or on the runway with all aircraft in their "proper position in the taxi order," atomic bombs cradled in their bomb bays, and not one word to say if this was it or not. It was no doubt as intense a moment as any the crews had experienced. Hundreds of bombers and tankers on SAC air bases lined up as one, nose to tail, the air reverberating with the high-pitched whine of jet engines on the edge of flight, red and yellow lights spinning and flashing in the predawn darkness, armed guards hunched low, gates secured, commanders waiting. No doubt the flight crews peered into the night with hearts pounding and crisp conversation in their headsets as they went through their final checklists.

It was November 24, 1961.

Every available asset SAC had, including the Thule Monitor B-52, was at that moment trying to determine if an attack was under way and, thankfully, within minutes, the radios crackled to life with the most welcome news that the distant radar station was asleep, but very much alive.

General Power ordered his command to stand down.

Because the blackout was traced to a fault on a microwave tower near Black Forest, Colorado, it has become known as the Black Forest incident. By moving bombers and tankers into their takeoff positions, SAC came as close to launching as it ever had.

THE SPEED OF the intercontinental ballistic missile would seem to be its primary asset and would seem to make it impervious to any method of defense, but in truth that was hardly the case. Although the nose cone of an American missile would reenter the atmosphere at speeds greater than ten thousand miles per hour, a ballistics trajectory would have been computed by the Soviets as soon as the missile was acquired by Soviet radar. With a trajectory plotted and an impact area determined, antiballistic-missile batteries would have calculated a solution and would engage the warhead with nuclear-tipped surface-to-air missiles. The likelihood of shooting down an incoming warhead, accordingly, was surprisingly good.

To defeat these Soviet antiballistic-missile defenses, ICBM warheads carried penetration aids. According to new documents, both the Atlas and the Titan were equipped with a penetration pod that had two types of decoys—one type that would be released in the vacuum of space to complicate the calculation of the missile's ballistics and "darts" that would be released after reentry. Both the darts and the vacuum "balloons" were designed to simulate the radar cross section of the reentry vehicle and thereby confuse the Soviet defenders and complicate their ability to calculate intercept solutions.

Surprisingly, the new Minuteman missile would at first have no decoys. Instead, it would rely on its low-profile radar cross section to mask its reentry, although decoys would be added later as the assessments of Soviet air defenses made ICBM penetrations without decoys seem increasingly unlikely.

SECRETARY OF DEFENSE Robert McNamara reported to Congress on the vulnerabilities of the DEW Line and other radar installations. According to the secretary, an enemy could very well feed radar stations false data, thus forcing the radars to display inaccurate tracks or tracks that might not be there at all—"spoofing," as it was called. Equally, a radar station could be "spooked" to exhaustion by enemy aircraft repeatedly flying an attack profile and penetrating the outer limits of the radar beams (thereby sending the crew of that station into a frenzy), only to turn away.

Curiously, "jamming" a radar station, a classic and relatively easy way to blind a radar scope using equipment carried by most enemy bombers, was of little concern. Said McNamara: "Jamming, in itself, would provide early warning."

It was November 1961.

SAID ROBERT MCNAMARA: "The introduction of the ballistic missile is already exerting a major impact on the size, composition, and deployment of the manned bomber force and this impact will become greater in the years ahead. As the number of ballistic missiles increases, requirements for strategic aircraft will be reduced."

SAC disagreed. Wrote a Strategic Air Command historian of the SAC point of view: "Although SAC's missiles increased in number and reliability during 1961, the most powerful military force in the free world remained SAC's manned aircraft fleet . . . The missile provided speed and penetration capability. The manned aircraft provided human judgment. In addition, the manned aircraft was in many cases the most economical means of target destruction. It could deliver a number of weapons. It was recoverable and reusable. It could select and observe. It could be in the air or on the ground maintaining an alert or performing a show of force."

McNamara responded with his own list of advantages of the missile over the bomber: ". . . most of the aiming points in the Soviet target system can be best attacked by missiles . . . a higher portion of the Minuteman force than of the B-52 force can be counted on to reach their targets in a retaliatory strike . . . surface-based missiles can reach their targets far more quickly, and this is of critical importance in attacking some types of targets . . . we can predict the results of a missile attack with greater confidence than those of a bomber attack." McNamara pushed for congressional funding that would diminish the nation's reliance on manned bombers.

This debate caused Senator Richard B. Russell, chairman of the Senate Armed Services Committee, to settle the matter if only for the moment: "I think it is still too early to abandon manned aircraft in favor of missiles," he said, and that was that.

But it was far from over.

DECLASSIFIED DOCUMENTS PROVIDE continued insights into the size of the nuclear forces ready to strike the Soviet Union or China. The actual number of SIOP alert forces on April 1, 1961, consisted of 836 delivery systems with 1,651 megatons of bombs. At the end of the year, SAC alone had in its fleet 881 bombers and tankers on ground alert, 12 bombers flying Chrome Dome, and 63 ICBMs consisting of 62 Atlas missiles and one Titan.

The Soviet stockpile numbered 2,471 bombs.

COLLAPSE

ON JANUARY 7, 1961, a new and troubling vibration was felt on Texas Tower Four and divers went down to look. "It never feels natural," said one, referring to diving under the sea beneath Tower Four. "It's this steel Goliath, really a very large structure underwater, and we try to get around it but we could get twisted up in it pretty good if we were not particularly careful."

One diver descended to the braces at minus-125 feet, then floated out on a horizontal truss across the 155-foot span between the legs. Back and forth he moved, inch by inch, hand over hand, careful at this life-threatening depth, and there it was. The bolts were missing along the main horizontal brace at minus-125 feet and a diagonal reinforcing rod had bent inward and was floating inside the legs.

All three underwater tiers of bracing beneath the radar station were now in some way weakened.

ASHORE, AIR FORCE engineers met in the New York offices of the J. Rich Steers Company to discuss contract issues related to Tower Four, but the conversation shifted to the news of the new broken brace and what it meant to the tower's remaining strength. Eugene Rau from J. Rich Steers scrapped the agenda and turned the focus of the meeting to the implications of this new information. There were cracks in the X bracing above the water, a broken brace at minus-25 feet, a second broken brace at minus-75 feet, and a third one at minus-125 feet.

Said one of the attendees: "Mr. Rau went on to state that it was a very grave problem and that corrective action would require favorable sea conditions with fifteen to twenty hard hat divers acting as a relay team and that, accordingly, a temporary suspension of repair work was in order until some time in late April or early May when favorable weather returned."

Said Rau: "Before any discussions could be started I felt that I had to suggest that the tower be evacuated, particularly in light of the bad storms that could be anticipated in the months of February and March."

If the others agreed, said Rau, the mothballing of the radar station would stop and it would become an operation to evacuate the tower. "Frankly, I was relieved," said air force warrant officer Hardy, who attended the meeting. "We had been sweating about having to evacuate the tower in bad weather and I know that once the weather is upon you, you don't get off."

THE REQUIREMENT TO evacuate Tower Four gained momentum but there were sticking points. "The representatives of the air force said it would be necessary to winterize the equipment on the tower as well as remove classified equipment and deflate the radomes," said Rau. "They said that this work would take two weeks. I pointed out that we had some materials on the tower that had to be removed to insure space for the helicopters. We agreed that this material, which in general was sand and gravel, would be placed down the legs. We thought that we could get our work done by January 21 and be off the tower."

But the weather failed to cooperate. The very next day, Tower Four was cocooned in a blizzard of heavy blowing snow.

ON FRIDAY, JANUARY, 13, 1961, a low-pressure system in the Gulf of Mexico began to move into the Atlantic Ocean. Phelan received a weather warning. The warning stated that a storm would hit the tower by noon on Saturday, January 14, with thirty-knot winds that would gust to fifty knots.

Phelan received a call and discussed his situation with his immediate superiors. He was told that the *AKL* was being diverted to Tower Four. Because the winds were calm, he was told, an evacuation seemed unnecessary at the moment, but then Phelan was told that a decision to evacuate might yet be made but that they were awaiting a decision by the commanding officer, Colonel William F. Banks.

A more paralyzing exchange of words could scarcely be imagined.

BY THE END of Friday, more than a third of the gravel on the helicopter pad had been poured down the B leg and a stabilizing clamp was in place on the horizontal brace under water at minus-125 feet. Surprisingly, Tower Four felt better. Better still, the weather remained calm.

LONGSHOREMEN IN NEW Bedford began to load the *AKL* for the trip to Tower Four. Said Sixto Mangual as the ship was ready to leave, "By 1430, twenty (20) measurement tons had been loaded and one (1) passenger had been embarked."

Airman Larry V. Woolford.

THE *AKL* STEAMED through the night and arrived at Tower Four just before 5:00 A.M., on Saturday, January 14, 1961. Mangual tied off to a leg and sent his only passenger up at 5:48 A.M. He then took on two hundred tons of crated electronics gear. The winds were fresh but the seas were calm, with rolling waves that built to no more than three feet. Mangual nonetheless saw to it that his cargo was securely lashed down. He expected rough seas later in the day.

AS MANGUAL CAST off, Phelan asked the master to keep his ship in the area in case he was ordered to evacuate the tower. Mangual asked why he didn't evacuate now. Phelan called the base. In an odd confluence of bad timing, three of his direct superiors, among them Colonel Banks, were unavailable or off duty. With no clear instructions to guide him, Phelan was left with his last orders, which were to stand by until the weather developed one way or the other. Because the seas were presently calm and because storms had a way of dissipating or changing course, Phelan's orders, as vague as they were, left him little choice but to remain on the radar station.

AS THE DAY drew to a close and night fell, the storm began to churn through the Atlantic with ever-increasing velocity. One hundred fifty miles to the southeast of Texas Tower Four, a convoy of seven navy ships conducting antisubmarine exercises steamed down the barrel of what would be known as the gale of 1961. Geysers of white water exploded off their bows as they plunged down yawning thirty-foot waves and punched through the bottoms. Aboard the destroyer USS *Lloyd Thomas* was Seaman Second Class Ralph Sutton, a radar operator. Said Sutton: "I was on the four-to-midnight shift and I was running the radarscope when we passed Texas Tower Four heading south. We were getting battered by the high waves."

Said a sailor who was at the helm of the aircraft carrier USS *Wasp*: "The seas were so rough that I had to use up to 30 degrees rudder both ways just to keep within 10 degrees of the course we were heading. The waves were breaking over the flight deck, which is 65 feet up from the water line. I'd never seen weather that bad."

Sutton agreed. "The waves were coming over the bow of the ship slamming into the five-foot gun mounts and washing up onto the windshield of the bridge." Sutton's ship was 390 feet long. The windshield of the bridge was forty feet above sea level.

THE MEN ON Tower Two made contact with Tower Four. "None of us slept that night," said a former surveillance technician on Tower Two. "Tower Four was in contact with us and they said they were deeply concerned about their safety."

SUNDAY MORNING DAWNED and there was no doubt a sense of relief to see the skies lighten, but the storm had only worsened. At 5:00 A.M., Staff Sergeant Wilbur L. Kovarick, who was manning the radios, reached the squadron and advised them that they were receiving winds gusting to nearly sixty knots. At 6:00 A.M., the *AKL-17* reported that she was "shipping water over her foredeck" in rough seas and "high heavy swells." By 8:00 A.M., the *AKL* was taking water over the main deck aft. Mangual ordered his men to check the cargo lashings, the deck gear, and the lifeboats hourly. Sprays of salt water raked off the cresting waves; from inside the wheelhouse, the seas appeared to be boiling.

THE FIRST INDICATION that Tower Four was breaking up was a loud *crack!* from below the platform that everyone heard at 10:30 A.M. The tower lurched and began to shake with a new motion. Phelan and Henry Schutz, a foreman with J. Rich Steers, found each other and descended through a hatch in the bottom of the platform to inspect the legs. What they saw was scarcely imaginable. Frothy sprays of white exploded off the steel and spit high into the air. Waves that should have been sixty-five feet below him were swirling directly under the platform. A new crack had opened in the X bracing but the loud sound was presumed to have come from the rupturing of the steel sleeve placed over the bracing at minus-75 feet.

BETWEEN 1:00 P.M. and 4:00 P.M., information flowed ashore, one call here, another there, important information delivered in pieces both within the squadron and out. Elinor heard from Phelan at 1:00 P.M. "I was baking cookies," she remembered. "He said the tower was gyrating, which was a different word for him. Our conversations always started with 'How are you?' 'I'm fine how are you?' and then I would say 'How's the tower,' and he would say 'Towerish.' But in this conversation, he said it was gyrating, which was a new word. He had said it was shaking or waving but he hadn't used that expression before. He said the tower was gyrating, which was a new word.

"I remember I talked to him about what would happen if the tower collapsed. . . . I asked him if he thought it would float and he said 'no,' it would not; I asked him if there were compartments that they might use because he was ex-submarine and he said 'absolutely not.'" Elinor then remembered another question. "I recall asking him if it would float for a short while to allow them time to use the boat and he said when it went in, it would go in real fast."

PHELAN CALLED THE *AKL* and told Mangual that they could not possibly evacuate in those seas. Mangual, who had before been steaming in circles, began steaming for the seas. He decided to stay near the tower.

AT 1:39, SCHUTZ contacted his supervisor at Steers. The supervisor remembers Schutz telling him that the tower was gyrating and that the men were unable to get on the deck but that they were "okay."

AT 3:00 P.M., Captain McKinney, the transportation officer for the 4604th, called to inquire about Phelan's plans for Sixto Mangual and the *AKL*. Phelan said that he had been outside on the maintenance bridge inspecting the braces and that the winds were between forty-five and sixty knots and the waves were at least thirty-five feet high. They had at least one gust of seventy-two knots, hurricane strength. Phelan told McKinney about the sharp cracking noise they all had heard at 10:30 A.M. "I haven't notified anyone in the squadron about it," Phelan said, but he thought it was time to plan for an evacuation in the next lull of the storm.

Phelan asked McKinney to survey the various weather forecasts and call him back.

TOWER FOUR WAS in fact being battered. Sharp, concussive gusts of wind were slamming into the platform at more than sixty knots. Waves engulfed the X braces and geysers of white exploded as high as the weather deck. The rain came down in spears mixed with ice and snow. The tower heaved and tilted sometimes two feet off vertical. On occasion there would be an eerie silence as the water level fell away into the trough of a rogue wave that would climb into a near vertical face and slam into the legs.

The storm was now spreading over the Grand Banks and was generating fifty-knot winds and twenty-five-foot waves. New York was being hit by near-horizontal shafts of rain and snow. Coastal advisories were posted from Maryland to Massachusetts. McKinney called the air force and the coast guard for weather reports while Phelan called the weather desk at Otis Air Force Base. All three sources were forecasting sustained winds until at least midnight on Sunday, with the possibility of a lull at about 1:00 A.M., but all three services were also forecasting a second low—a dangerous "double low." The second low was expected to come down from Cape Cod toward the tower and arrive just behind the gale.

McKINNEY AND PHELAN talked again. McKinney asked about the *AKL*. Phelan said the weather was too intense for the cargo ship to be of any use. He instructed McKinney to release it from the area. Phelan then said: "I want to evacuate before the next storm."

McKinney suddenly switched gears and did something that in the grand scheme of things was small but in retrospect was perhaps the most important action taken that day. McKinney placed a call to Major William J. Sheppard, of the 460th Support Squadron (Texas Towers), the senior officer in the squadron on duty and recently returned from deployment. The line was busy. He called a second time. The line was still busy. Sheppard thought it possible that the line was tied up by Major Sheppard's wife. "Believing it possible that two women were having a conversation on the telephone and it might be some time before I could contact Major Sheppard by telephone I drove over to Major Sheppard's quarters."

No doubt when he opened the door Sheppard knew in an instant that Tower Four was in trouble.

RAIN LASHED AT the windows of the 4604th's command building, and winds howled across the air base. The race to evacuate Tower Four was now in motion. Sheppard and McKinney manned the phones and contacted the navy, the coast guard, and the air force and requested immediate assistance. By 4:30 P.M. Sheppard had rescue helicopters on standby. Good news came from navy lieutenant commander Edward Tinny, the duty officer for the Eastern Sea Frontier, who had a task force of ships no more than two hours away from Tower Four's location. The command ship for the task force was the aircraft carrier USS *Wasp*, which had its own helicopters. Said Commander Tinny in his testimony: "We hoped to launch the choppers but the weather was bad and that might not be an option. So I talked to the XO on the *Wasp* and we discussed the possibility of bringing a ship alongside and using the bosun's chair for a rescue." Using a line strung from the tower to the aircraft carrier, men could be evacuated from the tower one at a time.

Navy admiral Allen Shinn, commander of the task force, ordered his ships to battle stations and told them to make their best speed, using their radar for safe navigation. The ships turned and pointed their bows into the towering sea. In a pitching motion of extraordinary violence they pushed over the top of one wave only to plunge into the trough of the next, each ship's bow exploding with bursts of white water as they labored through an ocean stirred angry by the sharp winds on a winter day that was fast growing dark.

PHELAN WAS APPRISED of the plans to divert the *Wasp* and attempt a rescue either by helicopters or bosun's chair. Despite the dangerous winds and near-icing conditions outside, Phelan promptly ordered all hands on the weather deck to clear the blocked helicopter pad. Everything possible was to go overboard.

HENRY SCHUTZ MADE a phone call to Rau at the J. Rich Steers offices. Said Rau: "I was told that the helicopters had been alerted for evacuation and, that all hands, including military personnel, were out on an emergency call tossing everything overboard so that the helicopters might land. I was also told that a twenty-inch crack had appeared in one of the vertical plates in the above-water bracing and that the tower seemed to be gyrating in excess of two feet."

AS RAIN AND sleet streaked the sky, the men lined the decks and passed bags of gravel and tossed them into the seas.

That anyone could keep his footing was nothing less than a miracle.

AT 5:55 P.M., Phelan went below and called Sheppard. "Phelan had issued orders to clear the helicopter landing area of the main deck by jettisoning overboard the sand, cement, and gravel which had been off-loaded and stored there," said Sheppard. "Phelan said that the men were making good progress."

At 6:00 P.M., Phelan called Elinor. "They are finally sending the *Wasp*," Phelan said to his wife. "I have all hands turned-to on deck. I'm clearing the way for the choppers. [W]e're being evacuated. The tower is breaking up." But she also heard encouraging news: "I will call you from New York."

At 6:15 P.M., the *Wasp* reported radar contact with the tower 18.5 nautical miles north by northwest.

Phelan's next call was to the base. He informed the duty officer that cracks were appearing "as fast as they could look."

Phelan returned to the weather deck to help clear the debris. He ordered Master Sergeant Roald Bakke below to man the communications room.

It was 6:45 P.M.

THE NAVY SHIPS struggled against towering seas and progress was slow. Said an officer who was on the *Wasp*: "I'd never seen the sea that angry. From sea level to the top of the flight deck it was about sixty feet and from there another fifty feet up to the bridge. Our deck was being washed by thirty-five foot high waves and when the bow of the ship went down we dropped one hundred feet. It was a terrifying scene."

Said a second seamen from the *Wasp*: "We were heading into forty and fifty foot corn rows of waves. The ocean was mostly white. We were taking green water on the bridge and burying the bow in the waves. The old *Wasp* wasn't riding well." Three rogue waves hit the *Wasp* but she labored onward. A crewman reported that the captain ordered a reduction of speed and the *Wasp* seemed to take the head seas better.

Searchlights swept the night but visibility was almost nil.

DESPITE THE BLOWING rain and the cloud cover, the communications lines remained open, and at 7:15 P.M. Henry Schutz called Dick Tower, his friend and one-time boss at Steers. Schutz told him that everyone was out on the weather deck, clearing room for the choppers. The storm was too intense for helicopters to take off from shore but the helicopters on the *Wasp* were a possibility. Schutz said he was worried that the motions were stressing the underwater braces and those that weren't already broken were flexing well past their design tolerance. Would it hold? he asked Tower. Tower, who had been on Tower Four and supervised repairs in 1958, thought it would.

"It's well braced for these winds," said Tower. "Just watch the wind."

THE MEN CONTINUED to labor at their task, tossing sand and gravel over the side, their muscles aching, the roar of the sea echoing in their ears, the disheartening clanking of steel ever present as the tower struggled to stay upright. They worked in water-streaked pools of light as ominous shadows sixty feet tall swept past them on both sides. The tower tilted and shuddered from the sledgehammer blows of the seas. From above, if one had been able to see such a thing, they no doubt looked frighteningly small—a tiny oasis of humanity laboring in a pool of light, impossibly surrounded by miles and miles and miles of angry, swelling seas.

One can scarcely imagine circumstances more dire.

ON THE *AKL*, Sixto Mangual kept one eye on the sea and the other on the radarscope. With each sweep of the arm, the blip that was Tower Four burst forth with a ping of phosphorescent green. He looked out from the wheelhouse into the exploding seas and then pressed his face to the hood of the radar. The arm swept his face. Tower Four had disappeared.

Mangual switched to the backup scope. Nothing.

He picked up his microphone and radioed the tower. *Tower Four! Tower Four!*

But he heard only static in return.

"WE WERE STUNNED," said Seaman First Class Wilbur Lee, who was on the bridge of the *Lloyd Thomas*.

"It seemed impossible," said an officer on the *Wasp*.

Ralph Sutton was an eyewitness. "I actually watched the tower, via the radar picture, slide into the waves of the ocean. In a total of three sweeps of the radar the image of the tower disappeared." Sutton said the tower shifted, then tilted, and then slid into the sea.

It was 7:20 P.M.

Tower Four was gone.

SLOWLY, TENTATIVELY, VOICES floated on the charged air. Could it float? Were there survivors? In the dark of night could the ships slam into the steel hulk and breach their own bottoms? Could the tip of a leg be just below the churning seas and put holes in their ships? What dangers lay beyond the next wave?

"Emergency conditions were set . . . and the deck department was called and put on lookout," said Mangual. The navy asked him to make his best speed to Tower Four's location. Mangual changed course to what he considered "the safest approach to the tower in case of the presence of wreckage." At 8:40 P.M., he began firing red flares in hopes that "any possible survivors in life rafts, in the water, or clinging to wreckage would understand that aid was forthcoming."

Said Admiral Shinn in his testimony: "There are always survivors. But we didn't think they'd last long in the seas. The temperature was nearly freezing and the winds were lifting so much water into the air that a man might drown floating on the waves. There was just so much water everywhere."

AT 9:40 P.M., Mangual spotted two white lights bearing off his starboard bow. Because this was in the general direction of the tower he was hopeful that these were survivors with emergency gear but twenty minutes later he made visual contact with the navy ships.

ON THE *LLOYD Thomas,* Commander Van Acker lined the weather decks with his seamen, positioned them in twos, each man bundled in a life vest, rain gear, and hailing ropes. "It was dark, cold, raining with high seas and saltwater spray coming over the bow," said one seaman. "As we got close to the area, extra lookouts were posted and all destroyers turned on their searchlights to comb the heavy seas."

What they saw haunted some for years. At the exact location where the tower once stood, at the exact point where iron had risen up from the sea and red, green, and yellow lights had blinked through the darkness, only hills of gray water rolled across the face of the ocean.

TAPPING

NOT ONLY WERE ham radio operators listening to the unfolding drama at sea; so, too, were the media. And when it was obvious that Tower Four was down, the press scrambled.

Elinor Phelan went to bed aware of the weather around Tower Four but hopeful. "I just knew he was safe aboard the *Wasp*," she said. But in the middle of the night her mother-in-law called from Los Angeles. "She said the tower had gone down and they couldn't find the men. She was literally screaming over the phone." Elinor hung up and promptly called the squadron at Otis Air Force Base. She reached the Orderly Room. When she identified herself, she was put on hold for perhaps one minute longer than normal. Captain Oliver Stafford then came on the line. "I knew something was wrong because I knew Captain Stafford wouldn't be hanging around the Orderly Room otherwise."

"We have lost radar contact with Tower Four," Stafford said.

DAVID ABBOTT'S WIFE got the call at two in the morning. Abbott had been gone for only a few days to help with the work on the tower. "I heard my mother grab the phone," recalled Don Abbott, her son. "She was talking to my Aunt Ethel. Aunt Ethel said something and my mom started to scream! I came out of my bedroom and I walked into her bedroom and she was screaming. She went from her bedroom down to the kitchen phone because she wasn't hearing things so well and continued to listen to my aunt. My aunt point blank said, 'Frieda, the tower is gone, Dave is dead.'"

ALAN DAVID CROCKETT also got a call but his came in at 4:00 A.M. Monday and it had nothing to do with the press. On the other end of the line was the United States Air Force. Crockett was asked to gather his divers and prepare for an immediate departure. An air force car would meet him and take him out to Otis Air Force Base.

Crockett knew without asking that Tower Four was down. He also knew why they wanted him.

HOWEVER AWKWARD THE phone calls, there was much to be done at sea. A rescue effort was in full swing. The *AKL, McCaffery, Lloyd,* and *Wasp* searched the ocean to the lee of Tower Four. The *AKL* moved as far as thirty miles down the current. One ship crested a wave and sailed into an oil slick—the diesel fuel stored in one of the tower's legs. In a shaft of light, a mattress, "the type issued by the air force," was lifted up by a rolling wave. The lookouts on the *Wasp* spotted a lifeboat, "her bottom holed and upside down with her davits still in," meaning that there had been no time to launch it before it was swept off the deck. A life jacket, two oil drums, an inflatable life belt, broken pieces of wood, and other debris were spotted.

And then they spotted the body of Master Sergeant Troy F. Williams.

And recovered it.

Master Sergeant Williams's body was placed in a body bag and, because there was little else they could do, stored in a refrigeration unit.

AS DAWN ARRIVED the skies were lighter and the seas were calmer and the *McCaffery,* an antisubmarine destroyer, was ordered to sweep the bottom with her sonar. "Sonar works like radar," said Commander Hollie Tiedmann Jr., who was the antisubmarine warfare officer on deck that day. "The big difference is that sonar uses pulses of sound to detect targets while radar uses electronic pulses. Sonar also provides audio simultaneous with the pulses whereby the sonar operator can actually listen to the return of the acoustic pulses."

At around 10:00 A.M. the *McCaffery* and a second ship, the USS *Cassin Young,* located a large metallic object that they determined was the platform. At least one ship tried to raise survivors trapped in the hull by using the underwater radio but they had no luck. Someone suggested that they try the sonar's transducer to tap Morse code. Again, they had no luck. Someone then suggested that they tap out the beat of an old favorite, "Shave and a haircut—two bits." (Today people use this rhythm to knock on doors—dot-di-di-dot-dot, with the reply—dot-dot.) With nothing to loose, the sonar operator on the *Mc-Caffery* pinged out the first part—*dot-di-di-dot-dot.* In what no doubt was an electrifying moment few would ever forget, over the headsets they heard the unmistakable cadence of the reply—*dot-dot.* The sonar operator on the USS *Cassin Young* tried the same message and received the same reply but only louder—*bang! bang!* "What we observed was so convincing to my seasoned operators that they became highly emotional," said Tiedmann. "The acoustic returns strongly suggested that there were men trapped in the tower."

The news spread through the ships like electricity. Some reported cheering among the sailors. The sonar compartment was soon besieged by sailors wanting to hear the tapping. The captain of the *Caissin Young* made his way down to restore some order, and then he listened. The sonar operator pinged the first half of the ditty. Back came the reply. *Bang! Bang!* Then, in the most hopeful message of all, from the bottom came the banging of the first part of the song—*dot-di-di-dot-dot*—to which the *Caissin Young* pinged back the answer—*dot! dot!* The excitement was such that men fumbled for words. The captain of the *McCaffery* said that the exchange "was a kind of coded message that could only come from men."

Miraculously, after more than fourteen hours, someone was still alive. The command ship *Wasp* processed the reports from the ships and passed the information on to the coast guard. At least four ships reported the tapping and each had come to the same conclusion: someone was inside the sunken hull. Said the message from the *Wasp*: "At 10:34 A.M. this morning the USS *McCaffery* heard tapping noises on sonar. They exchanged tapping signals. Now has heard what may be human voice over sonar. Definite possibility that survivors trapped in tower structure. Am attempting scuba dive."

AROUND THE TOWER the search continued and a second body was spotted in the ocean as it crested a wave. The destroyer USS *Norris* came alongside it but they were unable to pull it in. Remembered a seaman on the ship: "Our recovery crew made an attempt to recover a man dressed in civilian clothes. He was found floating facedown without a life preserver and when the recovery crew attempted to secure the body, it rolled over onto his back and whatever air there was keeping him afloat escaped from his body and it sank before recovery could be made. I'll never forget that sight, he was dressed in khaki work pants and a plaid shirt."

THE U.S. NAVY dive ship the USS *Sunbird* arrived on the scene on Monday evening with a full complement of navy divers. The ship was commanded by Lieutenant Commander A B. Crabtree. "There was a feeling on the part of some of us that there possibly was some life on the tower, even though it was submerged," said Crabtree in his testimony. "There have been many cases in the past of people living in submerged objects for some time."

Commander Crabtree launched a whaleboat to let his swimmers make their initial dives but then he backed his ship off to allow navy tugs to drag the ocean at different depths.

The swimmers faced a difficult dive. At the depth of 185 feet, Tower Four was well past the range of recreational divers and into a zone that could bring death in mere seconds. Bottom time would be limited to prevent the onset of nitrogen narcosis, and visibility would be so poor that there was a very real danger of becoming ensnared in the wreckage, perhaps fatally so. The team decided on a collaborative effort to map out the bottom. "Divers had depth gauges attached to their wrists," said Crabtree. "They were directed to certain parts at which time they took a depth reading and from this information we managed to piece together a picture of how the wreckage sat on the bottom. Two corners of the wreck were on the bottom [and] one piece of one caisson was intact, propping one corner off the bottom. The top of this caisson was attached to the wreck." Crabtree was describing something that looked like an enormous wedge with the top of the wedge held up by a length of severed leg 115 feet long.

Crabtree's teams were also trying to find where the tower had originally stood. "We still had the problem of locating the original site of the wreck. We did that by removing our anchor from our anchor chain and dragging the chain along the bottom steaming back and forth until the chain finally struck metal on the bottom at which time we dropped a buoy." Crabtree sent swimmers down to survey the bottom. "We found all three footings but the tangle of wreckage was such on the bottom that no one swimmer was in view of all three footings at the same time. It was like a junk pile on the bottom."

THE SEARCH INSIDE the platform took days. "We had much less difficulty getting into the wreckage than we at first anticipated," said Crabtree. "The windows were carried away and most, if not all of the external hatches were blown off."

But it was a tricky process. Not only were the divers going extremely deep but the platform was on its side, so anything that hadn't been bolted down had been tossed about during the collapse. A body could have been trapped by a sliding cabinet or sent reeling into a room where the force of the collapse may have caused a door to snap shut. "We sent many swimmers inside," said Crabtree. "In the process of looking for bodies the divers saw a good deal of what might be electronic gear. It's hard to say what they saw, some of it was test gear. We eventually recovered one body. It turned out to be the only body in the wreck. It was the body of a sergeant wearing a life jacket," meaning Master Sergeant Roald Bakke, the man sent inside by Phelan.

AKL-17 WAS RELEASED from the scene Monday evening. Mangual steamed through the night and docked in New Bedford at 8:59 A.M. on Tuesday, January 17. One by one the exhausted seaman dragged themselves ashore, their arms aching, their bodies spent from the ordeal. They had been at sea for six days. The news media surrounded them.

OTIS AIR FORCE Base sent a helicopter and brought Mangual and the New Bedford reporters to a press conference that they convened that afternoon. It was presided over by Lieutenant Commander Ernest J. White, commander of the 551st Distant Early Warning and Control Wing, Otis AFB. With him was Major Sheppard.

One of the first questions asked by a reporter was about the tapping. Colonel White responded by saying that there was a possibility that survivors were in the radomes that contained air. Someone else asked about air defense— what should America think of the "hole" now left in the early-warning radar line? White said that radar picket ships and airborne early-warning aircraft were already plugging the gap and that the nation was secure. More reassuring words could hardly be found, and *secure* would be repeated in the morning editions.

The press conference ended at 3:00 P.M.

ON THE COVER of the January 27 issue of *Life* magazine was a photograph of President John F. Kennedy's motorcade as it traveled down Pennsylvania Avenue in the aftermath of his inauguration as the thirty-fifth president of the United States. Kennedy is seated next to his wife, Jacqueline, who is smartly dressed in a pink suit with a matching pink pillbox hat.

The story of the tower's collapse appeared on page 75. There is a photograph of a lifeless body found inside the tower being hauled out of the sea.

DEFCON

ON JANUARY 1, 1962, Chrome Dome B-52s began carrying the Hound Dog air-to-surface nuclear missiles and four Quail decoys, thus becoming the first bombers to fly a mission fully configured for a strike against the Soviet Union.

CONTINGENCY PLANNING WAS an integral part of Strategic Air Command's DNA. If it could happen, SAC took it into consideration and tested outcomes. Such was the case in the postwar scenario and a program called the National Alternate Landing Sites. In the aftermath of a nuclear exchange, SAC air bases would no doubt be utterly destroyed or too contaminated to use. The unlucky survivors of Soviet airbursts would be tending to their wounds and doing what they could for others in the midst of the radiating wreckage and the smoldering ruins.

In this scenario, the small number of surviving bombers that were able to return to base would have no safe place to land. SAC had other ideas. Wrote one of their historians: "In September 1961, SAC initiated a formal study of unprepared natural areas for recovery and reconstitution of combat forces. Other types of natural alternate landing sites (NALS) existed, but the SAC study, nicknamed Dry Stone, involved investigation of dry lake beds. Over 300 dry lakes existed in the continental United States, primarily in the sparsely populated and remote regions of the Southwest. Of this number, 201 met the SAC minimum area criterion of three miles by one-half mile."

Determined as ever to fully study this option, in 1962 SAC actually authorized a series of flight tests. On March 6, a Strategic Air Command B-47 and a KC-135 tanker took off from their air base and made a landing on Bicycle Lake near Edwards Air Force Base, California. The two airplanes taxied to a halt, shut down their engines, and went on ground alert. Surrounded by the quiet of the desert, the crews stayed overnight and took off the next day.

In April, SAC initiated a second test and this time went all-out. B-47s and KC-135s landed on Mud Lake in Nevada and on Three Sisters Lake, West Lake, Hidden Hills Lake, and Silver Lake in California. All of the lake-bed aircraft immediately went on ground alert. Not limiting themselves to the medium bombers, SAC included the B-52s in these tests. For sixteen days SAC landed no less than fourteen B-47s, twelve B-52s, and twenty-six KC-135s on lake beds. All of the aircraft stood alert for two days and all were subjected to at least one no-notice klaxon requiring the crews to race to their airplanes, start engines, and check in by radio. On twelve occasions the lake-bed forces were actually launched. The average time to takeoff was eleven minutes. To prevent rutting, the takeoffs were flown as smoothly as a pilot could and most landings were made with little or no braking action.

According to declassified documents, the testing went so well that by July 1963, Strategic Air Command combat mission folders included at least one dry lake bed for every bomber as a recovery base of last resort. Not wanting to leave any detail up in the air, SAC even developed plans to refuel those bombers, regenerate their bomb loads, and to deliver new target folders to the crews for their next combat mission.

Fearful, however, that too much activity would reveal their intent and thus turn these rural landing sites into Soviet targets, once the flight tests were concluded and the supply logistics worked out, SAC ruled out further activity on the lake beds.

The best disguise for the alternate landing sites would be a lone wolf scrounging for food or dust billowing up into small clouds.

ACCORDING TO A 1962 SAC history, to pass an Operational Readiness Inspection all alert bombers in a bomb wing had to pass a flight test that included meeting their scheduled launch times, flying a navigation leg in accordance with their established war-plan routes, completing at least one air refueling, arriving at the H-hour control line as briefed, actuating their bomb-release system, and flying a precisely planned low-altitude maneuver designed for the delivery of the bulky MK-39 Mod 2 nuclear bomb or the lightweight parachute-retarded MK-28 RI nuclear bomb. If more than two out of eight bombers failed, the entire wing failed. If the failure was traced to an individual versus a mechanical failure, the consequences were swift.

In matters of the written tests, SAC simplified the process. If a member of a flight crew scored 100 percent, he passed. If he scored 99 percent, he failed.

* * *

SAC'S MISSILE CONTRACTORS were delivering missiles certified as operational when in fact many required further tests. This ran against the grain of SAC's culture. Said SAC: "We are faced with the prospect of having a system in the inventory, on EWO, with little probability of acquiring any measure of confidence in the capability of the system until many months have elapsed. Needless to say, this situation violates a basic doctrine of this command, i.e., SAC does not claim a capability which does not, in fact, exist."

"HOW IS A bomb to know if it was deliberately or inadvertently released from a plane?" wrote the authors of a paper on safety devices and nuclear weapons, a question that was hardly rhetorical. From experiences with crashes it was well known that the many unpredictable forces of an accident mimicked the forces that various sensors in a bomb were programmed to recognize as permissions to arm and fire a bomb. For instance, to a sensor, if a B-52 blew apart in the sky, the sudden release of the bomb would feel no different from a controlled release from the bomb bay, and that would close one firing gate. As the bomb fell through the air, the baroswitches would sense changes in the density altitude and that would close another. Thus it would continue as it had at Goldsboro, one gate after the other confirming a live release until the bomb hit the ground. The question was, what to do about it?

The answer was a series of weak links and strong links. A weak link associated with an arming device was supposed to fail before the arming device could perform. For instance, after a crash, a bomb that sat in burning jet fuel would not detonate because a low-heat capacitor holding the electrical charge would be melted by the heat, thus eliminating the charge. Strong links, on the other hand, were mechanical devices placed along the energy pathways that, unless properly activated and driven into position, would leave a gap and thus dud the bomb. Some or all of the strong links were activated by a pattern discriminator that had to receive a precise twenty-four-part signal pattern confirming twenty-four motions or "events." Because strong links were "single try" mechanisms, if the motion discriminator did not recognize the signal pattern that it received, the mechanism would lock.

At the Nevada Test Site, nuclear weapons were purposefully crashed into concrete walls, set on fire, dynamited, burned, dropped from aircraft, thrown into abnormal trajectories, and subjected to other abnormal forces in attempts to trigger a nuclear explosion.

It was through these tests that strong links and weak links were refined, further complicating the bomb's electronics package but further reducing the possibility of sensors misreading an accident as a mission.

FROM THE SOVIET perspective, the American doctrine of absorbing a first strike before retaliating was no more than a "passive anticipation of attack." A doctrine based on passive anticipation would, in their minds, lead to "a repetition of the Nazi invasion in 1941," the German Pearl Harbor, if you will.

Rather than risk that again, the Soviets came up with a concept called the "retaliatory-meeting strike." As one historian summarized his interviews with senior Soviet officials: ". . . the USSR defined a new kind of strike, a retaliatory-meeting strike whereby Soviet missiles were expected to pass American missiles in midair on the way to targets on U.S. territory."

The way it would work was as simple as it was logical. As soon as an American strike was confirmed, the Soviets would empty their silos rather than wait to absorb the attack. Said a senior Soviet official: "Our EW [Early Warning] satellites were able to detect a strategic missile attack upon launch, approximately 30 minutes from impact, but we did not consider the attack confirmed until our radar confirmed the trajectory to a target, approximately 14 minutes prior to the first splash. Yet our control system was so well prepared that this was more than enough time to launch a retaliatory strike, even if it took the leadership over 10 minutes to make a decision. It took just 13 seconds to deliver the decision from Moscow to all of the launch sites in the Soviet Union."

But one former Soviet official disagreed and would later say that the retaliatory-meeting strike concept wasn't in practice possible: ". . . [T]his is not realistic. We discuss considerably less complicated questions for hours. Do you really think it is possible in 10 minutes to make a decision based on the report of a general on duty looking at a radar screen, to push the button that may take millions of lives."

This didn't mean that the retaliatory-meeting strike wasn't planned to be used by the Soviets; rather, this official was speaking of the same problem Americans had. Could one make a decision in that slim margin of 15 minutes' warning?

"THIS COMMAND HAS been on alert since 1957," wrote an SAC historian. "No other military force in history has maintained the same level of operational readiness for so long a period of time, and there was little likelihood the requirement would lessen in the immediate future."

*   *   *

SAID SECRETARY OF Defense Robert McNamara in congressional testimony: "We are approaching an era when it will become increasingly improbable that either side could destroy a sufficiently large portion of another's strategic nuclear forces either by surprise or otherwise, to preclude a devastating blow."

In an interview with Stewart Alsop in the *Saturday Evening Post,* he called this "the balance of terror."

FOUR WARHEADS WERE lost during missile tests at the Pacific proving grounds. On June 4, 1962, a Thor missile was destroyed in flight. The warhead dropped into the Pacific and was never found. On June 20, a second Thor was destroyed in flight and its warhead was never found. In July a third Thor was destroyed on the pad, and in October a fourth Thor was destroyed in flight.

No further explanations were given about these warheads, although official reports claim that at least two of the four warheads were blown apart with their boosters and that one warhead fell into waters too deep to worry about.

IN JULY 1962, the army brought to the Nevada Test Site a jeeplike personnel carrier. Mounted on that jeep was a recoilless rifle with a four-inch tub into which was inserted a launcher to which was attached a fifty-one-pound atomic warhead. The rifle was fired, the warhead arced through the air, and a small mushroom cloud rose above the desert in an explosion that yielded .01 kilotons, a small atomic bomb but nonetheless an atomic bomb.

Among those in the observation stands was Attorney General Robert F. Kennedy.

More than two thousand Davy Crockett atomic recoilless rifles were built.

BY THE MIDDLE of 1962, SAC had completed 147,108 runs against radar-bomb scoring sites, a pace that would certainly eclipse the total of 213,718 runs scored for the entire year of 1961.

The three RBS Express railroad trains were averaging twenty-two hundred simulated attacks a month, almost all flown at low level. The FAA had approved twenty-seven new low-level oil-burner corridors for the trains.

B-52 bombers were now flying Chrome Dome routes steadily. There were eight bombers a day on the northern route and four on the southern route, plus two B-52s on the Thule Monitor route.

Chrome Dome bombers were now flying with two Hound Dogs under their wings and, in most cases, four H-bombs in their bomb bays. The Hound

Dogs, noted one report, increased drag sufficient to increase fuel consumption by 15 percent. Pilots didn't care for them.

Tankers were now scheduled to fly the Thule Monitor route if a B-52 aborted, a change in tactics that in time would be permanent.

The Emergency Rocket Communications System was tested. A new design called for the transmitters to activate two minutes after launch and to broadcast for twenty-seven minutes. Test launches remained disappointing, however.

The Airborne National Command Post grew in importance and in size. Five modified KC-135s were stationed at SAC headquarters and four each at three other air bases. There were thirty-six B-47 aircraft acting as airborne relay stations.

The Bomb Alarm System was now operational and entered full service.

And at midyear there were 942 bombers and tankers on alert—72 more than at the end of 1961.

And then came Cuba.

ON OCTOBER 14, 1962, Strategic Air Command U-2 spy planes found a medium-range ballistic-missile launch site near the Cuban town of San Cristobel. Soviet missiles could now strike targets in the United States, against which little if any strategic warning would be available. President Kennedy demanded that the missiles be removed. Soviet Premier Khrushchev demurred.

ON OCTOBER 19, SAC pulled out its bombers and tankers from Homestead, MacDill, and McCoy air force bases, all located in Florida. "This was done to accommodate the increased buildup of tactical and air defense (fighter planes) and army troops in these logical jumping off places for operations against Cuba. The disposed aircraft went to bases in Georgia, Texas and Michigan where they resumed alert."

ON OCTOBER 22, 1962, President Kennedy announced a naval blockade of Cuba. All ships entering the blockade zone would be boarded and inspected. Marines promptly reinforced the base at Guantanamo Bay and began amphibious operations in Puerto Rico. Navy jets began low-level reconnaissance flights over Cuba. Six army divisions were placed on alert, as was Strategic Air Command, which quickly dispersed its bombers to other air bases. Tactical Air Command, the fighter component of the air force, began to make plans to strike the Cuban missile installation.

SAC would strike the Soviet Union.

Said Kennedy in an address to the nation: "It shall be the policy of this nation to regard any nuclear missile launched from Cuba against any nation in the Western Hemisphere as an attack by the Soviet Union on the United States, requiring a full retaliatory response upon the Soviet Union."

MARVIN T. BROYHILL, Airman Second Class of Strategic Air Command's 308th Bomb Wing at Plattsburgh AFB, in upstate New York, remembered the day: "Kennedy wasn't kidding. We could see that for ourselves. All we had to do was look out the door to see our ramp covered with nuclear bombs. I'd never seen so many at one time . . ."

He went outside. "The base was a beehive of activity. Crews were speedily working on every plane. There were nuclear weapons all over the ramp. Everywhere I looked, planes were being uploaded."

ON OCTOBER 23, 1962, SAC's readiness posture was elevated to DEFCON 2. Over the next several days, every Emergency War Order sortie was fueled, bombed up, and manned by an alert crew. Every nook and cranny on every SAC base was overflowing with pilots, copilots, boomers, bomb-navs, and every other crew member needed to execute the war order. There were 1,436 bombers on fifteen-minute ground alert. The Chrome Dome bomber-stream routes were now pulsing with 75 B-52s. They required 150 aerial refuelings per day.

Reflex bombers overseas and the tactical aircraft of the European and Far East quick-reaction forces went on alert. Overseas bombers not on Reflex were flown back to their units and generated to alert. Bombers with bombs were dispersed to civilian airports and to non-SAC satellite bases. All available nuclear missiles—182 in total—went on alert. A total of 2,952 nuclear weapons had been loaded onto delivery vehicles and were ready to launch.

Sorties were continuously updated by SAC's battle staff, minor changes no doubt but with profound consequences on the targets in the Soviet Union. Three MK-28s on sortie 9 were upgraded to four MK-28s, and so on.

Computers as well as people were working overtime. More destruction was now poised to launch than ever before.

INDIVIDUAL WINGS WOULD write their own stories of the Cuban missile crisis, but even reading just one fully declassified report sheds light on the enormity of it all. The 307th Bomb Wing sent four of their bombers in their Emergency War Order configuration to Mitchell Field, Milwaukee, and eight bombers with weapons to Duluth Municipal Airport. Some of their aircrews were sent to the United Kingdom to man ground-alert B-47s there. All of the wing's remaining bombers were configured for war, and cocked.

The 4128th Strategic Wing juggled targets and weapons in their combat mission folders as if they were trading cards. Said a declassified portion of their activities during these days of the crisis: "Sortie 3 from 4 MK-28INs to 2 MK-15/2s; Sortie 82-4 add 2 MK-15/2s information; Sortie 11 from 2 MK-28RIs to 4 MK-28RIs; Sortie 82 from 2 MK-28RIs to 4 MK-28RIs; Sortie 1, third target changed; Sortie 9 from 4 MK-28INs to 2 MK-15/2s." More bombs here, fewer there; one target changed for a laydown delivery, one target changed to an airburst—and each change triggered another change and another change as the mission folders were undated for the more than fourteen hundred alert aircraft, causing one historian to note in their wing history that they simply ran out of the right bombs for each sortie.

BETWEEN OCTOBER 14 and November 8, 1962, SAC flew forty-three U-2 reconnaissance flights over Cuba. In roughly that same time period the navy flew fifty-four low-level flights and the air force flew another fifty-two.

On October 27, a frustrated Fidel Castro ordered his antiaircraft-missile batteries activated and shot down an SAC U-2. A navy reconnaissance flight was then shot up by ground fire but the pilot made it back to base. In a private letter to Castro, Khrushchev chastised him for these actions. In his response, Castro admitted impatience with the American overflights but conceded that he must show more restraint, lest a small incident result in a misunderstanding that would lead to a full-scale attack on Cuba by the United States.

ON OCTOBER 28, the Soviets agreed to remove ballistic missiles from Cuba.

On December 2, intelligence photos showed forty-two medium missiles on ships returning to the Soviet Union. Knowing full well that there were cameras in the sky above them, missiles on the ships in Cuban ports sat with their canvas coverings pulled back to reveal their classic silhouettes.

ON NOVEMBER 15, SAC resumed its ordinary 50 percent fifteen-minute ground alerts. Dispersed bombers returned to base. Defueling and offloading began. DEFCON 4 would be resumed on November 28, 1962, thus ending the Cuban missile crisis.

* * *

"WE GENERATED THE whole command," said General Power, speaking of SAC at the peak of the Cuban missile crisis, and he was indeed accurate. Some statistics have been released. All told, SAC put in 109,000 hours of flight time, including 2,088 B-52 Chrome Dome missions that required 4,076 aerial refuelings. Air-alert bombers flew more than 20 million miles without incident.

Including dispersal flights, reconnaissance flights, air alert flights, and movements among bases, between October 1 and December 31, SAC suffered just five significant accidents, an almost impossibly perfect safety record. Said LeMay many years before: "There is no substitute for time on the job. No substitute, ever, for experience." The rigorous, unforgiving training that was the hallmark of SAC in peacetime bore its fruits at the edge of war.

SAID AIR FORCE general David Burchinal, "We had such total superiority at that time that there was just no question, no contest . . . the Russians were so thoroughly stood down, and we knew it. They didn't make a move. They did not increase their alert; they did not increase any flights, or their air defense posture. They didn't do a thing; they froze in place." Perhaps as proof, at the worst possible moment, a U-2 pilot lost his bearings and accidentally flew into Russian airspace over Chukotski Peninsula. With heightened tensions, one could imagine the worst. But there was no response. "The Russians knew what was going on," said Burchinal. "There was no reaction on the Soviets' part, because they were stood down."

THE CUBAN MISSILE crisis did not entirely abate. By the end of the year SAC was largely back to normal, but "normal" represented one of its largest-ever peacetime commitments to alert. As the year came to an end, Strategic Air Command had 2,613 bombers and tankers, of which 942 were on ground alert with 12 more flying Chrome Dome.

There were now 224 ICBMs consisting of 142 Atlas missiles, 62 Titans, and 20 of the new Minuteman missiles. Forty-nine of those ICBMs were on alert.

From new documents we also know that the actual number of SIOP alert forces totaled 1,551 delivery vehicles—bombers, missiles, submarines, navy aircraft—with 3,382 megatons on hair-trigger readiness. There were 27,387 nuclear weapons in the national stockpile.

The Soviet stockpile numbered 3,322 bombs.

BEER CANS

THE ELECTRIC BOAT Division of General Dynamics designed an escape capsule which was placed on Tower Two and Tower Three in October 1962. New rules stipulated that all towers would now be evacuated whenever the forecasts called for fifty-knot winds or thirty-five-foot waves. Because of "complication occasioned by Soviet trawlers, which often loitered close by the towers," a seven-man security crew would stay behind. Said an official air force report: "Without a standby crew to keep guard, Soviet sailors might try to board a fully evacuated tower, then claim possession on grounds of salvage rights. If worse came to worse as regards tower stability during a storm, the seven-man standby crew could scramble into the survival capsule for protection."

DESPITE THE ADDITION of survival capsules, the collapse of Tower Four injected realism into the system, a sense of realism that said that the early-warning benefits were simply overwhelmed by the risks. Texas Tower Two was thus decommissioned on January 15, 1963, two years to the day after Tower Four collapsed. Salvage rights were sold to a scrap-metal company but Tower Two sank to the bottom when its legs were blown out from under it.

Tower Three was decommissioned two months later and was also sold for scrap, but, as a precaution, the scrap-metal company pumped its hull full of urethane foam. When the legs were blasted out from underneath it, the platform bobbed to the surface and was floated ashore.

Towers One and Five were never built.

WHAT HAPPENED TO Tower Four? The precise mechanism of its collapse is unknown and no investigation was undertaken. Explained the report of a United States Senate investigating committee: "A determination of the reasons for the collapse would have merit if the knowledge to be gained were

applicable to the remaining towers. However, since they are of differing design, it is doubtful if any information from such an analysis would have any
bearing."

Had the tower fallen over like a tree, the platform would have landed no
more than 250 feet from the caissons. Instead, the platform came to rest 600
feet away and was turned thirty-five degrees off-center to the north.

What could move a steel hull weighing millions of pounds so far? Many
believed it was the 133-foot wave that Professors Bretschneider and Reid
warned of. Indeed, the *Wasp* reported a rogue wave of considerable height that
may have continued through the Atlantic and finished off Tower Four.

Others noted that the legs were thin and that the lower halves were in fact
hollow and that the weight of the structure at some point might have caused
them to buckle. Robert G. Bea, PhD, a professor in the Department of Civil
and Environmental Engineering at the University of California, Berkeley,
studied Tower Four and tried to understand its collapse. Bea felt certain it
wasn't just wave motion, although that was part of it. Rather, Bea ran data that
suggested that the legs were overloaded and buckled like "beer cans trying to
support an elephant." Bea believed that the weight of the gravel and cement on
the platform, plus the force and weight of the waves, simply crushed the legs.
Wave motion would have completed the picture, powering the platform away
from where it stood as if it were a stone.

Interestingly, among the hundreds and hundreds of pages of testimony and
interviews conducted in the aftermath of the collapse, there appears an otherwise insignificant reference from Theodore Kuss that supports Bea's theory and
suggests that Kuss, too, recognized that the legs were overburdened. As the
January storm made up, Kuss recommended that they take the excess fuel oil
off the tower, although he didn't say why, only that he wanted to reduce the
burden on the tower. He also recommended deflating the radomes, thus reducing wind resistance. His recommendations were not ignored but it was apparent that the subtext was not fully understood by the airmen who carried them
out. They checked the fuel reservoirs and found sixty-five thousand gallons on
the platform, or roughly 260 tons of weight. Reducing the tower's weight
clearly didn't register with them; the airmen simply checked the tanks and
noticed that they were not full, which in their minds meant that there wasn't
any excess fuel to be jettisoned.

A BOARD OF Officers inquiry was opened by the air force under the Uniform Military Code of Justice. Three of Phelan's superior officers, including

Colonel Banks, were court-martialed for dereliction of duty with respect to the collapse of Tower Four. All three were acquitted.

Kuss's patent was cited in several other patent applications for newer deep-water oil-rig designs. One inventor called the Kuss tip-up method "slow, impractical, and hazardous." Another mentioned the collapse of Texas Tower Four. Said one applicant, the Kuss method left the men "in constant danger" as they maneuvered the platform onto the legs.

Such was the harsh competition in the offshore-oil industry.

Leon DeLong's work continued and his company grew. DeLong's name, while associated with the Texas Towers, was largely unblemished by the Tower Four tragedy. In 1965, his company, like many other military contractors, began work in Vietnam, installing DeLong piers in Cam Ranh Bay, Qui Nhon, Vung Tau, and Danang.

As it would happen, Curtis LeMay would have the final say in the matter of Texas Tower Four. In October 1961, secretary of the air force Eugene M. Zuckert wrote a letter to General Curtis LeMay, now air force chief of staff. Zuckert references the court-martial of Colonel William F. Banks, which held that he had no ongoing responsibility to stay abreast of the evolving situation on Tower Four and that he was found innocent of dereliction of duty. Zuckert asked LeMay if there wasn't a higher standard involved here. LeMay answered that there was: "It is my concept [of command] that a commander does have an affirmative duty to stay on top of any developing situation affecting his command. Any officer who does not accept this responsibility is not, in my opinion, a fit commander."

THE DEAD HAND

DESTROYING AN INCOMING enemy warhead was not as daunting as it might seem. For one, the task was greatly simplified by knowing where the missiles would land. Because each country knew their own highest-value ground zeros, air-defense forces were able to concentrate their firepower on significantly smaller segments of airspace. Helpful, too, were the enormous kill boxes of the nuclear-tipped surface-to-air missiles. Once an inbound trajectory was calculated and a solution computed, the intercept did not have to be precise, just close enough.

By 1963, the need for missile-penetration aids triggered a flurry of activity. Because of its sleek profile and low radar cross section, most engineers believed that the Minuteman warhead would be nearly invisible to Soviet radar, but as an added measure of comfort the nose cone was hardened to absorb a nuclear blast while in flight. Moreover, anticipating future improvements in Soviet defensive countermeasures, consideration was given to adding decoys and electronic countermeasures to the nose-cone package.

Penetration aids were also updated on Atlas and Titan by adding nose-cone packages that would eject decoys that were designed to confuse Soviet radars. By May 1964, Atlas and Titan ICBMs had flown twenty-one successful "penetration flights" down the Atlantic and Pacific missile ranges. The Atlas had been able to successfully pump out twelve midcourse decoys and eight reentry decoys while Titan ejected six midcourse decoys and eight reentry decoys. In yet another move to confuse Soviet radar operators, the main stage of the Atlas was to be "fragmented," presumably meaning that it would be blown up, so as to shower the Soviet air-defense tracking radars with a blizzard of spurious returns.

WROTE A STRATEGIC Air Command report, even 15 minutes was in some cases not enough time: "In 1963, SAC had provided each base covered by the Ballistic Missile Early Warning System (BMEWS) with the specific reaction time available for launch and survival. The command expected the aircraft alert force at each base to be capable of launching within the BMEWS reaction time available to that base. Reaction time available to continental U. S. bomber bases ranged from a minimum of 11 minutes, 40 seconds at Loring AFB [Maine] to 19 minutes, 33 seconds at Homestead AFB (Florida)."

At Loring, 15 minutes was now 11 minutes 40 seconds, a span of time during which the entire alert force had to be flushed before the first Soviet fireball flashed above the base.

WAS 15 MINUTES realistic? In 1963, a time-and-motion study was conducted to see if the president of the United States could in fact escape on the National Emergency Airborne Command Post KC-135s at Andrews AFB within the allotted fifteen-minute warning. From the first confirmed radar indication of a missile attack and the issuance of a warning, the warning would have to be confirmed by NORAD at a high enough confidence level to contact the president. The president would have to be found immediately, briefed, select a course of action, issue military orders, and begin an evacuation. This would consume six minutes.

The next seven minutes would be a blur of motion. The president's family would sprint to Marine One, the helicopter next to the White House, which would depart promptly and make its best speed to Andrews Air Force Base. On landing, the president would sprint across the tarmac and up into the waiting KC-135. Thirteen minutes would have elapsed.

The Night Watch jet would release its brakes and accelerate down the runway, but, according to the study, there would be "insufficient time for the NEACP to become airborne and get beyond the effective range of a weapon detonated over Andrews."

Of course, as the Soviets had already pointed out, making such a fateful decision in 360 seconds was decidedly a weak link in the plan. But even if that came to pass, the time-and-motion study concluded that, unlike the heroic escape of the NEACP jet in the movie *Independence Day*, this plane would not slip ahead of an ever-growing fireball and devastating blast wave. For the president at least, there were no 15 minutes.

SAID THE SECRETARY of defense: "Although we have an effective capability to sink enemy submarines in a protracted war at sea, we have no realistic prospect of being able to destroy a major part of deployed enemy SLBM forces in a sudden attack."

An SLBM was a submarine-launched ballistic missile.

THE LATEST PLAN for the Emergency Rocket Communications System called for the more reliable and far more powerful Minuteman booster to lift the transmitters into the sky. Six boosters were thus assigned to the program each with nose-cone packages modified to carry radio transmitters that for twenty-seven minutes would broadcast a prerecorded thirty-to-sixty-second Emergency Action Message over the length of its five-thousand-mile flight.

Although reports differ as to the precise routes, there is general agreement that three missiles would be fired. One missile would be launched toward the Mediterranean to communicate with the bombers flying the southern Chrome Dome routes and the alert forces holding at their H-hour control lines in that region. Another missile would be launched toward the Arctic to execute the bombers on the Thule Monitor routes, the bombers on the northern Chrome Dome routes, and the bombers holding at their HHCL positions. The third booster would be aimed toward the Pacific to activate the alert forces in Guam and the other forces holding in the east.

If the bombers did not directly pick up the transmissions from the ERCS missiles, SAC's Remote Ultra High Frequency network of seventeen radio repeaters would be activated and would broadcast the message. Commonly called the Green Pine System, Green Pine repeaters were located in Europe, Africa, Alaska, Greenland, Iceland, South America, and even on the island of Sardinia, with signal coverage of virtually all SAC SIOP sorties.

All of the ERCS missiles would launch from Whiteman Air Force Base, Missouri, well inside American borders. ERCS became fully operational in 1967, and by 1968 the network of underground launch-control centers were updated to receive its messages.

WHEN THE ERCS system became known to the Soviets it caused them alarm as it seemed to mirror a rocket system of their own, which the Soviets had designed for the final round of a general war. This in turn heightened suspicions that America might soon be on the offensive.

So well had their intelligence services operated that with perhaps a note of braggadocio, one Soviet officer noted many years later that the American system was called the "L-492 flying command centers" and that it "used the recorded voice of the president to activate launch commands."

The Emergency Rocket Communications System was in fact known as a 494L—close enough—but it was unlikely and entirely unnecessary that the president's voice be the one that played as a Minuteman streaked through the sky.

But it was not impossible.

THE CONCERNS TRIGGERED by the Emergency Rocket Communication System played into the Soviets' dead-hand scenario that used sensors to launch Soviet rockets that would transmit go codes to whatever missiles remained in their silos.

A senior Soviet official explained that the dead-hand system was part of what the Soviets called the "command-missile system." Describing a well-protected system that was linked to a predefined set of missiles, the official elaborated in extraordinary detail: "The basic command-missile system is comprised of a command missile or missiles deployed near, but not in, clusters of silos. The command missiles are well concealed, physically hardened well beyond the hardening of weapons launch platforms, and especially well hardened against damage from electromagnetic pulse. Each command missile is linked in its communications package with a specific set of launch platforms. Upon command, the missiles are launched into near space from which each missile transmits launch orders to that cluster of ICBMs to which it is linked.

"There are two means by which each command missile might be launched to transmit its message to the ICBMs. The first is under positive control from the central control system. The decision is taken to launch [if] the time before impact of the enemy's strike is seen to be insufficient to permit normal launch procedures.

"The second is the 'Dead Hand' launch mechanism. Under the 'Dead Hand' mechanism, the decision maker at the center unblocks the no-fire mechanism at the center, thereby releasing launch control [authority] to local automatic triggers associated with each command missile. The triggers, fed by numerous sensors, will launch its local command missile and, in turn, its associated cluster of ICBMs, once the sensors are excited by the light, or seismic shock, or radiation, or atmospheric density associated with an incoming nuclear strike."

Said the speaker: "It is important to understand that unblocking of 'Dead

Hand' assumes the scenario of a situation that is extremely threatening to the political and military leadership of the state. The basic expectation is that all decision makers are dead when the command missiles automatically fire."

Dead.

DETAILS OF THE Soviet defensive capabilities largely remained classified, making it nearly impossible to put criticism of SAC's massive retaliatory capability and nation-killing megatonnage into any meaningful perspective. Not so now, given newly declassified SAC histories. While there is no reason to take issue with the generality that there were eight hundred primary air-defense installations on the SIOP target list, the true air-defense gauntlet was far deadlier than ever before revealed. As one researcher explained, what the Soviets lacked in sophistication and cutting-edge technologies they made up in "brute force." This brute force, we now know, included remote land- and sea-based jamming sites designed to blind SAC bombers even before they entered Soviet airspace, more than ten thousand fighter jets, some two thousand radar sites, and some one thousand SAM sites. Bombing a Soviet target, LeMay knew, but could scarcely reveal to his critics, would take every skill and every bomb SAC had and then some.

By June 1964, SAC's intelligence directorate had identified 1,892 active Soviet radar sites and 5,985 operational radars. SAC also identified and mapped a Soviet distant-early-warning network similar to the American DEW Line, called Tall King, which had grown to 187 stations. A secondary early-warning line had also been identified and it now consisted of another 387 radars. The newest height-finding radars in the Soviet inventory had been added to 37 radar sites.

Controlled by those radar sites was an impressive array of deadly surface-to-air missiles. In 1964, Soviet missile defenses against SAC bombers consisted of 999 operational launch sites in 227 complexes, with another 251 sites in 39 complexes pending further analysis. The earliest SA-1 missiles still ringed Moscow in impressive numbers but they were now reinforced by the larger SA-2s and by the first of the new Soviet SA-3 low-altitude intercept missiles at 91 sites. The SA-3 was designed to shoot down SAC B-52s within a few hundred feet above the ground on their low-altitude penetration routes.

Just as troubling was a new type of missile battery. Air force intelligence had recently identified Soviet antiballistic missile launchers around Leningrad. Ninety launchpads had been charted, each configured with refire capability that would send four missiles per pad into the air, for a total of 360 interceptor missiles in one complex alone. No doubt there were similar installations around

Moscow, as well as key weapons-manufacturing facilities and weapons-storage areas, but the report is silent on this.

Complicating matters, SAC intelligence had also confirmed upgrades to missile warheads. In recent months, higher-yielding warheads had been added to the Soviet SAMs, although precise information remains classified.

The report called the Soviet fighter-interceptor force "formidable," and so it was. While America had some thirteen hundred fighters on twenty-three air-defense air bases, there were an estimated sixty-two hundred fighters in the Soviet Union and another five thousand fighters in the satellites and in China. Some of the fighters were now all-weather capable and many were equipped with guided air-to-air missiles, both nuclear and conventional, though most had just guns and unguided rockets and inadequate look-down radars. If not technologically sophisticated, however, the air-defense fighter force was nonetheless overwhelming in number, a chief tenet of Soviet military strategy.

Tying these defense assets together was a system similar to the American SAGE computers, called SADS—the Semi-automatic Air Defense System. SADS controllers now covered the breadth of the Soviet Union with centers that included remote centers in the satellite countries.

In addition to missiles and fighters, American intelligence had confirmed extensive placements of land- and sea-based sites packed with electronic countermeasures designed to blind penetrating American bombers. Based on the signal analysis of these jammers, SAC expected "severe interference" with their onboard bomb/navigation equipment.

THE DRUMBEAT TO speed up takeoffs was relentless, and yet another innovation was developed to further cut the reaction time of the ground-alert forces. One of the more time-consuming parts of takeoff was the time it took to start an engine. Engines required power and massive gulps of compressed air to reach the required RPMs to fire the engine igniters, which could take two minutes on a good day and twice that in winter. Tests were run to see if by using explosive-cartridge engines aircraft could be spun up to minimum RPMs in less than one minute. This became known as the Quick Start modification. It worked beautifully, SAC would later note, saying that all eight engines were going in "30-to-60 seconds, generally."

"It was quite a sight," said one pilot. "Basically, battery on, hit the starter button, push all eight throttles over the hump, turn on generators and you were up and running. Crew chiefs had to wear breathers for all the dense smoke each bomber made."

* * *

THE DEBATE BETWEEN missiles and manned bombers continued. In 1963, Secretary of Defense Robert McNamara reframed the argument when he spoke before the House Armed Services Committee. "Manned bombers present soft and concentrated targets," said McNamara, speaking of the Soviet ability to destroy them on the ground. McNamara went on to describe the protection provided by a hardened missile silo as well as the difficulty the Soviets would have killing silos spread across the hundreds of thousands of square miles of the missile ranges. Moreover, said McNamara, manned bombers were woefully vulnerable to ever-more-sophisticated Soviet air defenses, including surface-to-air missiles.

LeMay testified next. He was not against missiles per se but rather the tendency to see missiles as a one-for-one replacement for bombers. Missiles had a purpose but they had limitations. Missiles were inflexible. Once launched, they could not be recalled. Manned bombers gave commanders options. "With manned bombers you can maneuver and change bases," said LeMay. "You can fly them out so they can be seen on the radar or actually conduct some limited attacks if you wanted to."

For the time being, the committee was swayed by LeMay. It would be "a most dangerous course of action" to place emphasis on missiles at the expense of a modern fleet of manned bombers, said the committee. The committee was uncomfortable with "the push button war of long-range missiles." A manned bomber force, concluded the committee, "embraces the highly essential element—the judgment of man."

Judgment.

THE NUMBER OF bombs the Soviets would clandestinely place in American harbors grew from a single ten-megaton bomb detonated in New York Harbor, as estimated in 1956, to four one-hundred-megaton bombs detonated in four harbors, plus smaller bombs here and there for good measure, as written in 1964. "In the clandestine attack," wrote a current war plan, "448 megatons were utilized in the 23 cities . . . this attack employed four 100 MT devices lowered from neutral flag merchant ships to the harbor bottom in Boston, New York City, San Francisco, and Seattle. Seventy-six agents emplaced 33 one megaton weapons and one 15 megaton weapon [in Washington, D.C.] in the remaining 19 cities."

No doubt the column of water lifted by a one-hundred-megaton bomb would momentarily drain the harbors, while the collapse would trigger a base surge of radioactive mist and steam that would swallow whole the Golden Gate Bridge and the Empire State Building.

It was like that at Operation Crossroads. Operation Crossroads lifted up a base surge of radioactive mist that moved at astonishing speed across the surface of the lagoon and rose two thousand feet as it engulfed the ships—a bomb that was by comparison to 100 megatons a mere firecracker.

JOHN F. KENNEDY was assassinated on November 22, 1963. Jacqueline Kennedy wrote a letter to Khrushchev in which she said: "I know how much my husband cared about peace, and how the relationship between you and him was central to this care in his mind. He used to quote some of your words in some of his speeches—'In the next war the survivors will envy the dead.'

"I send this letter because I know so deeply of the importance of the relationship which existed between you and my husband, and also because of your kindness, and that of Mrs. Khrushchev in Vienna. I read that she had tears in her eyes when she left the American Embassy in Moscow after signing the book of mourning. Please thank her for that."

It was December 1, 1963. Cold war adversaries, yes, but still a tear for Jack.

DESPITE THE ARGUMENTS in budget meetings and the debates in the press, Strategic Air Command was inexorably becoming a missile force. As 1963 came to an end, there were 922 bombers and tankers on alert but there were also 631 ICBMs in silos, of which 426 were on alert.

At the end of 1963 the SIOP alert forces totaled 2,071 delivery vehicles with 3,976 megatons.

KILLING A SOCIETY

IT IS IMPOSSIBLE to imagine how anyone could dispassionately calculate the near-complete annihilation of humans living in two countries
the size of the United States and the Soviet Union, yet counting the dead
was a nearly annual event. In 1964, the National Security Council's Net
Evaluation Subcommittee prepared another estimate of the price of general
war. "In evaluating the results of these exchanges," they wrote, "fatalities
were used as the primary yardstick by which to measure the effect of these
exchanges."

Taking into account weapons, delivery systems, defenses, and populations
at Desired Ground Zeros, this report expected 93 million Americans to die
from an initial attack consisting of 409 Soviet weapons yielding 2,548 megatons. One hundred forty million Soviets would die in the American counterstrike. Missiles, noted the analysis, accounted for 20 percent of the forces but
would increase to more than half by 1968. In the war that followed, the United
States would be attacked by 1,213 Soviet weapons delivering 7,262 megatons.
The United States would retaliate with 3,774 weapons. In both countries, the
survivors would largely be involved with disposing of the dead.

Said the NET subcommittee of the devastation that would result from just
the first wave of bombs: "The alert force would be expected to kill 37 percent
of the population of the Soviet Union (and 55 percent of the urban population) . . . and to destroy 75 percent of the buildings as measured by floor space."

ON MARCH 15, 1964, for the first time in Cold War history, the number
of ICBMs on alert exceeded the number of manned bombers. A total of 620
missiles were on SIOP alert, as opposed to 619 bombers. With more than 400
Minuteman ICBMs due to arrive, and more than 300 B-47s due to retire, in
time the main element in the SAC deterrence force would be an ICBM.

The Minuteman.

* * *

MANNED BOMBERS WERE largely unnecessary in the age of missiles, argued Secretary McNamara, although he did see a unique reason to embrace a new low-level-strike bomber called the FB-111, an airplane developed under a program called the Advanced Manned Strategic Aircraft. Said McNamara, if a replacement requirement for a new bomber ever came about and if high-altitude bombing was favored, the lessons learned from the new Mach 3 SR-71 reconnaissance plane could be applied, but if low-altitude penetration was favored, the lessons learned from the FB-111 would be applicable. The FB-111, noted McNamara, could be used not only to drop bombs but also to "serve as an airborne missile platform."

Such was the fixation on missiles.

COMING IN OVER the Tonopah Test Range in Nevada was a B-52. The pilot was flying just a scant 150 feet off the ground and was going as fast as he could, perhaps some five hundred miles per hour. His mission was to demonstrate a new low-altitude-release system that could accurately hit a target without exposing the bomber to enemy antiaircraft fire. The trick was to stay low and to release the bomb from 150 feet. To make this possible without blowing the bomber out of the sky, the pilot would execute a maneuver called a PUP—a pitch-up followed by a quick push-over. If he went fast enough and timed his pitch-up to the second, this maneuver would allow him to punch out the nuclear bomb and escape the blast and heat without exposing himself to the increasingly lethal low-altitude antiaircraft defenses deployed by the Soviets.

The bomber bore down on the target and as planned the pilot pulled back on the yoke until his attitude indicator showed a slight 7.5-degree climb. After a count of five, the sling holding the bomb in the bomb bay was blown apart by explosive bolts and the nine-megaton eighty-eight-hundred-pound MK-53 laydown bomb popped free. The MK-53, still in use today on the bat-winged B-2, had five parachutes to slow its descent as the pilot did his pushover and turned-and-burned to the best of his ability to get out of there.

The test was a resounding success. The pug-nosed MK-53 bomb landed exactly twenty feet from the bull's-eye. So impressive was this accuracy that a picture was taken to immortalize the event, a picture that has survived more than fifty years. The MK-53 is in the ground like a lawn dart. It towers over three men who are standing beside it side by side with their arms stretched out to show the distance between the bomb and ground zero.

Pitch-up push-over—PUP—would become a standard maneuver for SAC pilots. SAC's MK-53 and the sleek MK-28RI would now be delivered from bombers flying at an altitude one could reach with a simple nine-iron. Men would again say that they were flying with their hair on fire.

It was May 1964.

SAC's OFT-STATED POSITION in the 1950s was that a nuclear bomb was a conventional weapon and that "conventional" iron bombs could better be delivered by commands other than SAC. This, however, gave way to the new reality, which was that if SAC didn't learn how to drop conventional iron bombs it would lose its relevance. "During the first six months of 1964," wrote an SAC historian somewhat stiffly, "the command also carefully examined and validated the non-nuclear capability of its strategic aircraft."

In March 1964, SAC B-47s and B-52s went back to the bombing ranges at Eglin Air Force Base, Florida, to practice, well, bombing. At the location where years before they had conducted the stockpile-to-target tests for thermonuclear bombs, they were now experimenting with conventional bombs. In fact, they were testing their ability to release a long stream of bombs, called "sticks." In one test a B-52 successfully dropped fifty-one conventional 750-pound bombs, twenty-four of which had been carried externally under its wings using a new, specially designed bomb rack. As if to underscore the transformation at hand, these new bomb racks were attached to the very same hard points that before had been used by the alert bombers as the attach points for their nuclear-tipped Hound Dog air-to-surface missile.

Such were the changing times.

THE SECRETARY OF defense wrote to the president and in his memorandum defined certain terms related to war. "Assured destruction," said the secretary, "[is] the capability to destroy both the Soviet Union and Communist China as viable societies, even after a well planned and executed surprise attack on our forces."

McNamara elaborated: "Assured destruction is the very essence of the whole deterrence concept." America must have the capability "to deter deliberate nuclear attack[s] upon the United States and its allies by maintaining a highly reliable ability to inflict an unacceptable degree of damage upon any single aggressor, or combination of aggressors, even after absorbing a surprise first strike."

McNamara continued: "What amounts and kinds of destruction we would have to be able to deliver in order to provide this assurance cannot be answered precisely, but it seems reasonable to assume that the destruction of, say, 25 percent of its population (55 million people) and more than two-thirds of its industrial capacity would mean the destruction of the Soviet Union as a national society. Such a level of destruction would certainly represent an intolerable punishment to any industrialized nation and thus should serve as an effective deterrent."*

Assured destruction gave rise to a term not used by McNamara but popularized. *Mutually assured destruction*—often abbreviated as MAD.

"Mutually assured destruction" thus entered the language of the Cold War.

A PARALLEL CONCEPT to assured destruction was called Damage Limitation. Damage Limitation was a counterforce strategy—that is, to destroy the enemy's military weapons—to disarm them before their weapons are used on America. It was, of course, a cousin to preemptive strikes and thus was a gray area. Said the secretary of defense: "Damage Limitation, [is] the ability to reduce the weight of an enemy attack . . . and to provide protection for our population against the effects of nuclear detonations."

The United States should be prepared to attack before fireballs burst over American cities. Said McNamara, damage limitation was a "hedge against the possibility that we may be presented with an opportunity to destroy at least some of the Soviet offensive forces before they are launched; and this means we must include in our strategic offensive forces some capability for that purpose."

In combination with assured destruction, this, said McNamara, was a "balanced defense."

GENERAL LEMAY OBJECTED to McNamara's concept of killing a society. Said LeMay: "Our problem is not one of killing our opponents. Our problem is to keep our opponents from killing Americans and our allies." Killing the enemy, LeMay said, was easy. Killing their military forces took a good deal more effort but was the only sure way to protect Americans.

---

* "Assured destruction" remains as defined by McNamara—to destroy an aggressor as a viable society. See USAF Intelligence Targeting Guide, 1998.

* * *

PETER SELLERS STARRED in a new movie satirizing the military and their use of nuclear bombs. *Dr. Strangelove or: How I Learned to Stop Worrying and Love the Bomb* was released in 1964. Much fun was made of fail-safe; in fact, the movie treated accidental nuclear war as an inevitability. It was nominated for four Academy Awards, including one for its director, Stanley Kubrick. Most thought it was a wonderful commentary on the Wild West attitude of those at SAC who toyed with the bomb.

A more somber side of Kubrick was later quoted as saying: "I suspect that few planets survive their nuclear age."

CRASHES CONTINUED. A winter storm caught a Chrome Dome B-52 en route to its home base in Georgia. It crashed near Cumberland, Maryland, in near blizzardlike conditions, killing three of the five crewmen and badly damaging the two nuclear bombs it carried.

A Minuteman's retro-rocket attached to the warhead-reentry vehicle inadvertently fired inside the silo, all but destroying the warhead.

During a December storm that had all but shut down Grissom Air Force Base, in Peru, Indiana, a surprise ORI began, during which a B-58 was blown off an icy taxiway and collapsed onto its fully fueled centerline pod and five nuclear bombs.

"The high explosives in all five weapons detonated," said the accident report. "The aircraft and weapons wreckage burned for two hours." During the recovery operations, which began the next day, the secondary of one of the MK-43s burst into flames. It was extinguished but then it happened again. "The next day, when this secondary was moved, it ignited again and was extinguished with sand."

It was as if the bombs *wanted* to explode.

A COMMERCIAL WAS created to support the candidacy of President Lyndon Baines Johnson for reelection by portraying hard-line conservative Republican Barry Goldwater as willing to start a nuclear war. It came to be known as Daisy Girl. In this commercial, a young girl is seen picking off the petals of a summer daisy, and as she picks the petals she counts, ". . . one . . . two . . . three." The image, however, is transformed into a countdown clock for a nuclear weapon and reverses: ". . . three . . . two . . . one . . ." The picture of the girl is replaced by the explosion of an H-bomb, a juxtapositioning entirely intended by its creators.

Said Johnson in a short and rather bleak voiceover: "To make a world in which all of God's children can live. Or to go into the dark. We must love each other, or we will die."

The commercial aired only once but it is widely credited with playing an important role in Johnson's landslide election victory.

As 1964 came to an end, Strategic Air Command had 464 bombers and 701 missiles on fifteen-minute alert. The actual number of SIOP alert forces totaled 2,689 alert delivery vehicles with 5,835 megatons.

FOREVER LAMED

SAID STRATEGIC AIR Command general Joseph J. Nazzaro, SAC's fourth CINCSAC: "Faced with the militant threat of world Communism, the Free World cannot afford to base its plans for survival on wishful thinking or hopes for a better world. Instead . . . SAC operates from a strategy of deterrence . . . while our opponents are the only men in the world who know what level of superiority will deter them, to date our decisive—if not overwhelming—capability has prevented a nuclear confrontation."

SAID A FORMERLY top secret "Memorandum of Conversation" summarizing the comments made during a joint meeting of senior officials from the Department of Defense and the Department of State, including Secretary of Defense Robert McNamara, Secretary of State Dean Rusk, and McGeorge Bundy, President John F. Kennedy's special assistant for national security: "[Mr. McNamara] went on [to] describe the crashes of U.S. aircraft, one in North Carolina and one in Texas, where by the slightest margin of chance, literally the failure of two wires to cross, a nuclear explosion was averted. He concluded that despite our best efforts, the possibility of an accidental nuclear explosion still existed . . ."

It was January 1963.

As of 2010, no document has been declassified that discloses the crash of a U.S. aircraft in Texas that came as close to exploding as the now-well-known crash in North Carolina.

SAID PRESIDENT JOHNSON: "Our experts tell us today that a full-scale nuclear exchange between the East and the West would kill almost 300 million people around the world, and in the midst of that terror and tragedy we would expect that weapon after weapon would soon engulf a portion of mankind. A cloud of deadly radiation would drift and destroy, menacing every

living thing on God's earth, and in those unimaginable hours unborn generations would forever be lamed."

Forever lamed.

STRATEGIC AIR COMMAND reluctantly entered the Vietnam War.
Thirty B-52 bombers converted to carry conventional iron bombs were flown
to Andersen Air Force Base, Guam. On June 18, 1965, twenty-seven of these
bombers flew to Vietnam and bombed areas suspected of being Vietcong staging areas.

Two were lost when they had a midair collision en route.

The thermal-reflective white paint that protected the underside of a B-52
from the heat effects of a nuclear blast was painted over in black so that a
bomber would be less visible from the ground when it flew over Vietnam.

Aircrews that once proudly wore white ascots and carried the most technologically advanced weapon now used "clip-in" racks to haul tons of "dumb"
bombs over Southeast Asian rice paddies.

This was the first use of SAC bombers in Vietnam.

Some compared using the B-52 against guerillas in sandals to "swatting
flies with a sledgehammer."

The term *carpet bombing* joined the language of war.

LIEUTENANT COLONEL DANTE Bulli's B-52 is identified by a sign
along a road in Maine. The sign says B-52 CRASH SITE—6.9 MILES. One of the
structural problems in the B-52 was somewhere in the tail, and tail failures
were causing crashes. To understand the problem, Bulli was tasked to fly his
B-52 on a low-level flight along the ridges of Maine's Elephant Mountain to
purposefully expose his bomber to severe updrafts, downdrafts, and cross-
winds. It was more than he bargained for—those wind forces cleanly snapped
off his tail. The giant bomber plowed into the side of the mountain.

Said one report: "The people of Greenville watched helplessly as the fire
from the crash lit up the distant mountainside. Working side by side, townsfolk
and military rescue crews used dog sled, snowmobiles, and a new Scott Paper
Co. bulldozer to claw their way up through 5 feet of snow to the crash site."

As recently as 2006, the mountainside was still littered with shards of the
fuselage, sections of the landing gear, and the tail-gunners' bay "tilted against
a tree trunk," as one report described it. Dotting the crash sites were American
flags planted in cracks and crevices by respectful visitors. One girl, brought
there by her parents, picked up a small piece of wiring harness.

* * *

THE NEED TO continue the airborne-alert program was questioned by McNamara: "The [airborne alert] was proposed and approved in an environment in which bombers were our primary strategic weapons, and their survival on the ground or ability to get airborne during an attack was questionable.

"Missiles are now our primary strategic retaliatory weapons, and strategic missiles presently in inventory have greater survivability and much faster reactions than bombers (even airborne bombers).

"Can we discontinue the practice of maintaining 12 B-52s on continuous (airborne) alert and thereby reduce the B-52 flying hour program by 65,000 hours and save the associated costs?"

The answer to the obviously rhetorical question was yes. And no.

In November 1965, McNamara informed SAC that effective July 1966 air alert would be canceled; however, using a procedural process, SAC was able to delay the action by requesting a reevaluation. Rather than cancel air alert altogether, SAC proposed a reduction in alert, but this, too, was met with opposition. In a memorandum to the Joint Chiefs, McNamara argued that because of Minuteman, air alert was "no longer necessary" and that air alert was "no longer the way to get maximum effectiveness out of the bomber force."

AT THE END of 1965, SAC was flying some 300 sorties a month in South Vietnam. It was reported that General Westmoreland wanted to increase that number to 450 a month at the beginning of 1966, and then to 600 during April through June, and to sustain it at 800 sorties per month thereafter.

The SIOP requirements for SAC bombers remained in the war plan, but against each bomber removed from the attack timeline for duty in Vietnam was a notation that the sortie had been "degraded."

THE FIFTEEN-MINUTE GROUND-ALERT forces now heavily favored missiles. As 1965 came to a close, there were just 336 bombers on ground alert plus 12 flying Chrome Dome. This compared to 829 ICBMs on alert.

The actual SIOP megatonnage for 1965 has not been released.

COMPLETE WEAPONS

SAC, FOR ALL its flying, had yet to suffer a major incident on foreign soil. All that changed in 1966.

Thirty thousand feet above the southern coast of Spain, a Chrome Dome B-52 bomber neared the halfway point of its twenty-hour alert mission. Waiting to refuel it was a Texas-based KC-135 tanker flying out of an air base in Spain. The B-52 was scheduled to take on gas before it would coast out over the Atlantic for the return leg home to its air base in the United States. The B-52 carried four MK-28 hydrogen bombs.

The tanker flew a racetracklike pattern, trailing the refueling boom. The boom operator—the man who would navigate the connection between the tanker and the B-52—lay facedown, watching the bomber approach through a window in the tail of the tanker. The skies were crystal clear.

THE ACCIDENT HAPPENED in an instant. As the B-52 maneuvered in toward the boom, it lurched forward and up, striking the tanker. Like a matador lancing a bull, the refueling boom lanced the B-52 behind the wing, and hit a key member of the jet's structural spine called a "longeron," thereby dealing the bomber a fatal blow. Sections of the skin began to ablate as cracks ripped through the fuselage. The bailout horn rang and the red lights spun up and down the cabin. Men punched out even as sections of the bomber tore away. One pilot climbed through the navigators' hatch and pushed himself into the sky, dodging a blizzard of jagged fragments from the disintegrating B-52.

The tanker, too, was dealt a fatal blow. For a brief moment, it glided through the sky in eerie silence, a hidden ignition source racing toward the fuel tank until with a muted *whoosh!* it exploded. All four crew members were killed instantly.

From the sky, engine pods, sections of the wings, landing gear assemblies, sheets of burning fuel, and four MK-28FI nuclear bombs—all this debris slammed down to the ground around the coastal village of Palomares, Spain.

All but one bomb.

ON JANUARY 19, 1966, a pair of United Press International reporters picked their way down the rocky hillside toward the village of Palomares and while turning down a dirt road they came face-to-face with an engine from the KC-135 tanker. They drove farther, only to come upon a section of an airplane's landing gear. They ran into men in yellow coveralls moving through the fields in a line-abreast formation.

And with that, they had a story.

That evening, the UPI put out a wire story claiming that an American B-52 had exploded over Palomares, Spain, and that nuclear bombs had been involved. The air force responded with a vaguely worded press release about unarmed nuclear armaments, but SAC was a nuclear-bombing force and it had gone to great lengths to make that clear to the world.

Soviet trawlers promptly made their way to Palomares.

THE AIR FORCE poured men and equipment into Palomares. Search teams moved in line-abreast formations across the arid hills. Barrels were filled with sand and topsoil. Helicopters thumped above, moving men to and from search sites, often dropping plastic tubes with classified communiqués down to the teams. U.S. Navy ships dotted the horizon. Since Palomares was littered with mine shafts, a detachment of mine experts arrived from the Bureau of Mines in Colorado.

Questions poured into the United States State Department, the embassy, and the air force. As yet, it was only a tragic midair collision, but there was too much going on to be explained by the simple removal of wreckage. On January 22, 1966, the air force reluctantly acknowledged that nuclear bombs had been on board the stricken B-52 and that one of those bombs was missing.

The reaction was immediate and harsh. Angry Spaniards surrounded the American embassy in Madrid and protested the presence of nuclear weapons in their skies and on their soil. American allies offered little consolation: it was well known that SAC had airborne bombers, but few knew those bombers were flying over their countries with nuclear bombs on board.

THE SEARCH FOR the missing bomb continued for three agonizing months. Protestors ringed American embassies the world over. Anti-American sentiment poured out in the streets of capitals and violence occasionally erupted.

The search turned to the sea, but that was hampered by a deep undersea trench. It was not until March 15, 1966, that the experimental submersible *Alvin* found the missing H-bomb. Groping through the darkness, the bomb suddenly appeared in the cone of light from the submersibles' searchlights. It was perched on a ledge at a seventy-degree slope 2,850 feet beneath the sea.

Alvin snagged the bomb's parachute but then it fell free and for another two weeks the submersible probed the trench until the bomb again appeared in its beam of light. Said one observer of what might be better thought of as good luck than skill, finding the bomb was akin to "filling the Grand Canyon with coffee, tossing in a golf ball, and retrieving it."

ON APRIL 7, 1966, the bomb was pulled out of the water and laid on the deck of the USS *Petrel*. The navy pulled back the tarpaulin. "The world's eyes may see that the bomb has been found," said Admiral Wetherby Hill. Cameras snapped the first pictures ever taken of a thermonuclear bomb. The next day, the most secret weapon in America's arsenal was reproduced on the front pages of newspapers around the world.

The Joint Committee on Atomic Energy promptly called for hearings.

THE JOINT COMMITTEE on Atomic Energy gaveled hearings to order and began calling witnesses. One of those witnesses was W. J. "Jack" Howard, assistant secretary of defense for atomic energy. Congressman Chester Holifield, chairman of the Joint Committee, asked Howard if there were any other lost bombs. As the committee knew, there was one. On December 5, 1965, a navy A-4 Skyhawk jet fell off the deck elevator of the aircraft carrier USS *Ticonderoga* with an MK-43 nuclear bomb under its wing and sank in the ocean. Neither the jet nor the pilot nor the bomb was ever recovered. The loss had occurred just after the *Ticonderoga* had ported, which if made public would have made it impossible to deny that U.S. ships were bringing American nuclear weapons into foreign countries. The accident was, of course, classified and not a word of it had leaked to the press.

Mr. Howard, who was under oath, was then asked if there were others. Howard was unsure. "Mr. Howard," the chairman said icily, "please respond to this committee in writing and list all accidents involving nuclear weapons where the weapon has been lost."

Howard, one of the most senior officials in the Department of Defense with respect to atomic bombs, left the hearings and began his research.

On April 22, 1966, Jack Howard wrote that there were four incidents resulting in *five* lost bombs—two that were complete bombs with capsules and three that did not have capsules. One of the complete bombs was the one ejected by Howard Richardson near Savannah, Georgia. The other was the A-4 that fell off the *Ticonderoga*. The bombs without capsules were the two bombs ejected into the Atlantic off the coast of New Jersey by the C-124 transport, and the bomb released by the navy P5M that was forced to ditch off Whidbey Island, Washington.

There is no indication how the committee reacted but it was probably mild—all these accidents had been previously disclosed to them. And yet, long after the Cold War was over, few documents would be as controversial as this two-page letter.

IN 2000, HOWARD Richardson and Bob Lagerstrom were sent copies of the letter written by Jack Howard as well as copies of the letters sent to the Joint Committee by General Loper. Both pilots strenuously disagreed with Jack Howard's contention that the bomb they ejected near Savannah was armed. Both men insisted that the bomb was without a capsule and thus was not a complete weapon.

"They told us the bomb was unarmed when we signed for it," said Richardson.

Not surprisingly, they were even more adamant about the statement General Loper made in his first letter to the Joint Committee, saying that the pilots had unsuccessfully attempted to land three times. "Nonsense," said Lagerstrom. "Howard was too good of a pilot for that." Said Richardson: "I landed on the first pass."

On that point, the official air force crash report states that Howard Richardson indeed landed on the first attempt.

RENEWED INTEREST IN the Savannah bomb led to demands that it be found and removed. The air force agreed to study the matter and in 2001 held a press conference in Savannah. At that press conference they released the results of what they called a thorough study of the incident and concluded that the bomb was without a capsule and that there was no risk to the population. Because of that, no effort would be taken to recover it.

The report, however, left much to be desired, at least if accuracy mattered.

For instance, the media did not notice that in the report the air force authoritatively repeats the long-discredited statement that Howard Richardson attempted three landings.

THE FIRST MK-15 nuclear bomb was a removable capsule variant that would be formally called the MK-15 Mod 0. The MK-15 Mod 0 was tested on Bikini Atoll on May 13, 1954, as the code-name Nectar shot of Operation Castle. It yielded 1.69 megatons—the explosive equivalent of 3.4 billion pounds of TNT. War-ready MK-15 Mod 0s went into production in April 1955 and were placed in the nuclear stockpiles that summer, three years before Howard Richardson's flight.

The Mod 2 variant was developed in the summer of 1956. It featured a contact fuse in the nose cone and improved batteries. The MK-15 Mod 2 began arriving at the stockpiles in March 1957.

Visually, the bombs were identical. Each was eleven feet long and three feet in diameter, cylindrical in shape, and weighed seventy-six hundred pounds. Each had a tail section with four steel fins, although the Mod 2 had a small parachute that would retard its descent.

Furthering the potential for confusion, during the transition from the Mod 0 to the Mod 2, the MK-15 Mod 0 underwent field conversions. Upgrade kits were sent out to SAC bases and to the stockpile sites to convert the Mod 0 to the Mod 2. Still, from the outside, it was all but impossible to tell one from the other.

UNDERSECRETARY OF DEFENSE Dave Oliver expected to bring the issue of the Savannah bomb to a close when he wrote to Georgia congressman Jack Kingston (with copies to Senators Max Cleland and John Warner and Representatives Floyd Spence and Ike Shelton), refuting Jack Howard's 1966 letter.

Said Mr. Oliver: "Our research of both classified and declassified records show that it was not possible for the Savannah weapons to be anything but a MK-15 Mod 0. The pilot of the B-47 signed for a MK-15 Mod 0 and a 'simulated' capsule. We have discussed this letter and our conclusions with Mr. Howard. He now agrees with this letter and the conclusion that the 1958 Savannah nuclear weapon accident should have been classified as a 'weaponless capsule.'"

But this explanation created renewed doubts. If the crew had signed for a simulated capsule they would have been given a simulated capsule, and it would have been inside the "birdcage," the complicated contraption that looked like an hourglass but stood more than two feet tall and weighed more than sixty pounds.

Said Oliver: "The pilot of the B-47 signed for a MK-15 Mod 0 and a 'simulated' capsule."

But the pilots disagreed.

"We didn't carry a capsule on the plane," said Richardson.

Lagerstrom remembered it the same way: "We didn't have the cap."

This leaves unanswered the original question triggered by a letter written under oath in 1966: Is the bomb armed and thus dangerous to the residents of Savannah, or is it without a capsule? And if without, why did the pilots sign for a capsule they didn't receive?

That any of this matters is of course worthy of consideration. In a democracy, the public must believe that a government carries out the policies it says it has, and if necessary the public needs to verify that it does. Equally, the public must also know that they can rely on the integrity of the information that the government provides.

THE SITUATION WITH the Palomares bomb was no less awkward. In the aftermath of the Palomares crash, SAC canceled all airborne-alert sorties, but only for a day. Somewhat incredibly, on January 18, SAC resumed Chrome Dome flights including the flights over Spain, but as local protests mounted and anti-American sentiment grew, the government of Spain had a change of heart and notified the United States that overflights of aircraft carrying nuclear weapons were no longer authorized.

Grudgingly, SAC suspended flights on the southern route but worked up two alternate proposals for the Spanish government to consider, one that would allow armed nuclear bombers to use Spanish airspace in emergencies and the other to continue as before but to refuel over the Atlantic.

A dumbfounded air staff read these proposals and declined to present them to Spain. They advised Strategic Air Command that the "current atmosphere at Washington level is definitely not favorable to any proposal for resumption of Spanish overflights with weapons." Nor was the air force willing to support negotiations for emergency-landings rights. Said an SAC historian, "the air force recommended one of two courses: continue the stand-down of the southern route until various options could be evaluated, or fly B-52s without nuclear weapons on the southern route."

Instead of accepting the rather meaningless option of flying empty bombers, SAC removed the southern Chrome Dome route from its air alerts altogether.

PRESS TARGETS

THE ESTIMATED FATALITIES resulting from a general nuclear exchange were again calculated, this time for a war taking place in 1966. Secretary of Defense Robert McNamara's staff depicted two scenarios—the first scenario calculated the number of deaths in the event of a surprise attack for which American forces had no warning; the second, the number of deaths from an attack with 15 minutes' warning. Because as yet there was no national fallout-shelter system for civilians, and because military deaths were such a small percentage of the total fatalities in a general war, the death toll was largely unaffected by the amount of warning, which, in either case, would kill seventy-five million Americans in the initial Soviet attack.

In terms of retaliation, the American response was again near annihilation. The 1966 alert force would successfully launch aircraft and missiles directed at 1,607 aiming points. Two hundred urban-industrial targets would be hit by 510 warheads, 300 air-defense facilities would be targeted with 976 warheads, while targets in 240 European satellites would be hit with 450 warheads. There would be sixty-five million Soviet dead.

If the navy's Polaris missiles were launched, they would kill another thirty million Soviets. Preferably they would remain in their tubes and be held in reserve for "war termination bargaining."

Bargaining.

ON FEBRUARY 15, 1966, during hearings before the Appropriations Committee, Secretary McNamara explained his final position on air alert: "At present we have alert (12 planned, 8 actual) aircraft in the air constantly, essentially as a training measure. That provides us only a small capability, and it has become particularly small in relation to our huge and growing missile force. So, there is no need to carry on that program."

* * *

Two Minuteman II ICBMs were launched simultaneously from Vandenberg Air Force Base, California. Their exhaust trails etched parallel lines of smoke as they arced across the sky. The two contrails demonstrated that a "salvo" launch was feasible—that is, the countdown and launch of multiple missiles under combat conditions.

It was February 1966.

To some, atomic bombs weren't the point. The point was winning a war. In the end, how one died scarcely mattered. "Nothing new about death, nothing new about deaths caused militarily," said LeMay from the comfortable repose of retirement. "We scorched and boiled and baked to death more people in Tokyo on that night of March 9–10 than went up in vapor at Hiroshima and Nagasaki combined."

Scorched. Boiled. Baked. Vaporized.

An Air Defense Command fighter pilot remembered: "I was the leader of a section of F-4s that intercepted two Bears east of Gibraltar. We knew they were coming many hours in advance and the rules were to make the intercept at exactly one hundred miles from the ship and not one mile more or less. The only rule of engagement was that we were not to lock on with the radar. After the intercept, I tucked in under the Bear's wing and got about as close to his outboard prop as I was comfortable. Those pilots were smooth as silk and favored us with the courtesy of head signals preceding course and power changes. They gradually descended and flew directly over the ship and began their climb heading north. On the way out, I moved in close to the large Plexiglas blister close to the Bear's tail. There was a guy in the blister manning the kind of old tripod camera with a hood. He gave me a series of hand signals to position me for some photos. When I complied he gave me a couple of sharp thumbs up and dived under the hood. I sure hope he got a medal for those photos."

Said an SAC history: "During the first months of bombing missions in Vietnam authority for strikes was centralized at the highest levels of government—the President, Defense, State, and JCS."

SAC had neither a voice in the targeting nor any real interest in the politics behind the decisions, but it did understand what it was doing, particularly when it was ordered to bomb Laos. Said a newly declassified 1966 SAC history: "B-52s were not confined to the territorial limits of South Vietnam during the first part of the year. Almost 400 sorties were flown against infiltration points on the Ho Chi Minh Trail in Laos. These were . . . 'covered' each time by a three bomber strike against a valid target in South Vietnam."

That SAC grasped the ramifications of what it was doing was evident. "It will be recalled that the first Laos mission in December 1965 had been announced as taking place within South Vietnam. During the early months of 1966, whenever a Laotian target was struck, another target in South Vietnam was struck at the same time. The latter one was the only one announced. Although these came to be referred to as 'press targets,' they were valid targets and not contrived just for that purpose. This arrangement seems to have worked, at least no political problems developed as a result."

SAC also understood the politics behind its orders, however uninterested they were in the debates. "The use of B-52s in Laos no matter how close to the South Vietnam border, could be interpreted as an escalation of the war on the part of the United States, thus it was sensitive politically. Missions during the first six months of 1966 were not announced to the press, nor were they cleared beforehand with the neutralist premier of Laos, (Prince) Souvanna Phouma."

The magnitude of secret Laotian operations was already significant. What began modestly in December 1965 had in the first six months of 1966 grown to a total of 399 missions against targets in Laos with some twelve bombers per mission, or about forty-eight hundred B-52s dropping bombs on Laos.

They were covered, of course, with press targets.

S A C   W A S   A S unhappy about its involvement in Vietnam as it continued to be with the unwelcome transition to missiles. It didn't entirely believe in missiles and Vietnam was a distraction. "Although less than 15 percent of SAC's B-52s and KC-135s resources, and none of its B-58s, were actively engaged in contingency operations, the effects of the war in Vietnam permeated every activity. Most particularly, the increasing demand for pilots in Southeast Asia caused a steady drain upon the aircrew resources of all strategic aircraft units.

"At the end of June, 15 B-52 alert sorties were off alert . . . because of bomber crew shortages and seven tankers were off alert because the bombers had been degraded for crew shortages."

"Contingency operations" was SAC-speak for bombing Vietnam.

V I E T N A M   P R O P E L L E D   S T R A T E G I C   Air Command into the limelight far more than it desired. However, in 1966, SAC was assigned a Vietnam mission for which it wanted no publicity at all. The mission was developed by the secretive research group with the office of the secretary of defense (OSD) called ARPA, the Advanced Research Project Agency. Details about this mission have been classified for more than forty years and remain obscure even to this day. Said the command's historian: "What must be counted as one of the most unusual uses made of B-52s in South Vietnam came in late February when MACV asked SAC to deliver incendiary bombs in a test of the feasibility of destroying the jungle cover.

"This particular test was under the overall direction of an Advanced Research Projects Agency (OSD) unit in Vietnam. The plan was to first dry out the jungle by applying a chemical defoliant and then set it ablaze with an incendiary raid. By early March the defoliant had been applied and the foliage thought sufficiently dry for ignition. There had been no rain for five days and the weather was forecast to remain dry. MACV ordered the 15 B-52 strikes for 3 March. On the day of the raid, however, with the bombers already on their way, the weather in the target area unexpectedly worsened. Thunderstorms were forecast. The mission was then cancelled and the aircraft, now four hours out of Guam, returned to base. The mission was rescheduled for 11 March. With the weather cooperating, this time it was accomplished. In Hot Tip I and II seventeen B-52s . . . each dumped twenty-seven 750 pound M-35 incendiary clusters (172 tons) in the target area and returned to base. The Advanced Research Projects Agency termed the test an '. . . outstanding operational success but [a] qualified technical success pending further evaluation.'" SAC had been on time and on target but the qualification came because "heavy flames were not observed and fire storms did not develop."

"The nature of the test was not announced to the press. It was feared that the press would give the test attention out of proportion to its actual significance."

In fact, this was part of Operation Rose, which was terminated precisely because the fires did not develop but which would evolve and in time become a defoliation project that would years later be better known for the health effects of a compound called Agent Orange.

A s   t h e   y e a r   came to a close, the substitution of missiles for bombers continued. Strategic Air Command now had just 275 bombers on ground alert and 951 ICBMs. Chrome Dome had been reduced to just 8 solitary B-52s circumnavigating North America, a pitiful force that carried at most 32 bombs. With the reduction of ground-alert bombers, the need for runways decreased. Five SAC bases were closed.

VIETNAM

SAC CONTINUED TO divert forces to Vietnam. "The conflict in Southeast Asia was not only instrumental in reducing the number of required SAC alert sorties, it was also responsible for most of the degradations in the programmed posture."

There were sixty-three B-52 ground-alert sorties degraded from the SIOP forces all "directly or indirectly from the demands of the war in Vietnam."

ON JUNE 31, 1967, the Department of Defense instructed SAC to reduce the ground-alert forces from 50 percent of manned bombers to forty percent. On July 1, SAC reported that it had 212 B-52s and 32 B-58s on alert with 233 tankers.

CHROME DOME FLIGHTS were reduced to just four B-52 sorties daily. Two sorties continued to monitor the Thule BMEWS site. No doubt SAC itself had to wonder. At best, air alert counted for between just eight and sixteen bombs.

DURING THE FIRST half of 1967, SAC received the last of its one thousand Minuteman missiles. For the first time in more than ten years there were no new silos under construction. For the first time in more than thirty years there were no new heavy bombers on the drawing boards.

SAC was now equipped as it would be for the remainder of the decade.

SAC TRIED TO make the most of the unwanted decline in manned bombers, writing that although there were many more missiles on alert, the alert missiles carried less megatonnage than did the alert bombers, and the alert bombers continued to shoulder a disproportionate share of the total alert megatonnage that would be delivered in the SIOP plan. Moreover, said SAC, bombers were the only follow-on forces available to the United States if fol-low-on forces were needed. Said SAC: "Despite the steady decline in the im-portance of bombardment aircraft in the SIOP, the B-52s were still programmed to deliver more than one-half of the megatonnage represented by the SAC nu-clear alert forces. Another factor which should be considered is the significant follow-on capability of the aircraft forces—sorties which could be placed on alert status in a period of extreme tension. The total number of B-52s targeted in SIOP-4B was 528 (212 alert), and the total B-58 capability was 75 (32 alert). On the other hand, the missile alert commitment represented the total ICBM force targeted in the SIOP."

The math said that 359 bombers were available for follow-on strikes—and zero missiles.

In truth, SAC seemed unwilling to admit that it was now a missile com-mand with bombers, not a bomber command with missiles.

As the year drew to a close, Strategic Air Command had 219 bombers and 928 ICBMs on alert.

Needing even fewer runways for alert takeoffs, three more bases were closed.

13.8 MINUTES

"IT IS NOT necessary to discuss at length the strategy considerations which resulted in the decisions to place less reliance on the manned bomber as a strategic weapons system, and correspondingly, to place more emphasis on the deterrent qualities of the ballistic missile," wrote an SAC historian, albeit with some bitterness. "Secretary of Defense McNamara's decision to retire the early B-52s had been made several years earlier. It is necessary, however, to mention the effect of this decision on the forces available to SAC." The writer went on to describe the reduction of B-52 bombers available to SAC, but that was not entirely the point. "It was not then in consideration of total numbers of bombers in the inventory that one gained the best appreciation of the changing character of the SAC forces, it was rather in the alert forces committed to the Single Integrated Operational Plan. There were at the end of June 150 B-52s and 32 B-58s on alert."

Less than ten years earlier there were 1,769 bombers. And no missiles.

MORE THAN ONE hundred of SAC's five hundred B-52s were now assigned to Vietnam. The conventional-bombing sortie was now called an Arc Light mission. Said an SAC historian: "The Vietnam War continued to frustrate efforts to maintain a high [level of] ground alert aircraft. The contingency sortie rate was increased from 1200 to 1800 a month."

SAC wore Vietnam like a hair shirt.

SO FAR HAD the world moved away from nuclear bombers and to the high-technology world of missiles that when an SAC bomber crashed it was more than jolting, it was somehow intrusive, and offensive. On January 21, 1968, a B-52 from Plattsburgh Air Force Base, New York, was circling Thule on the Thule Monitor route when fire broke out. Smoke and flames quickly filled the cabin. The captain hit the Bailout button. Red lights spun inside the fuselage as men pulled their ejection handles. One by one, the ejection seats fired crew members into the icy cold sky over Greenland until the bomber was empty.

From the tower at Thule Air Base, controllers watched as the B-52 turned through the night back toward the base, a finger of flames trailing it until it slammed into the ice cap over North Star Bay. Plumes of billowing flames surged into the sky. One by one, the four H-bombs exploded.

Bombs were once again down on foreign soil. Greenland. Which was part of Denmark.

THERE WERE NO committees. There were no hearings. There didn't need to be any. And it took less then twenty-four hours. Said an internal air force memorandum: "On January 22, 1968 SAC terminated the carrying of nuclear weapons aboard airborne alert aircraft indoctrination level missions. No publicity is being given this fact." The memo was written by Brigadier General Marshall B. Garth, deputy director of operations at the National Military Command Center in Washington, D.C.

Seven days later, on January 29, 1968, Strategic Air Command removed nuclear weapons from all its alert bombers.

The term *cocked bombers* would now fade from use.

ON MAY 1, 1968, a KC-135 tanker took the place of the B-52s on the Thule Monitor flights.

SAID A 1968 memo to the president: "We deter a rational enemy from launching a first strike against us by maintaining a strong and secure ability to retaliate under any circumstance. We measure our second strike ability in terms of Assured Destruction—the capability to inflict unacceptable damage, calculated under extremely conservative assumptions, on the USSR after sustaining a surprise Soviet first strike. I believe that our ability to kill from one-fifth to one-fourth of the Soviet people, including at least two-thirds of the people and industry in their large cities, is enough to deter the USSR from launching a first strike against the U.S. even in extreme situations." The Soviets would now be killed by missiles sitting silently in silos sunk into the ground across the heartland of America.

The term *push-button war* and the chant *ban the bomb* could be heard on college campuses and in Washington alike.

* * *

ALL THE EMERGENCY command posts and evacuation procedures might be for naught. "The more closely we are approaching an emergency," said an assistant to the president in a letter to the secretary of defense, "the more necessary it is for the president to be in Washington."

Then again, so instant would push-button war be that it would end only because there would be nothing left: "Following a heavy nuclear exchange," said a National Security memorandum, "effective war termination capabilities [would be] marginal."

FIFTEEN MINUTES CAME to an end. The proliferation of Submarine Launched Ballistic Missiles (SLBMs) put the network of Airborne National Command Posts and the NEACP EC-135s at risk. Wrote the WSEG: "Under current conditions, ABNCPs are vulnerable to SLBM attack. They are under 15-minute ground alert but all bases are within 13.8 minutes flight time of the SS-N-6 launch locations."

SS-N-6 was a class of Soviet submarines.

AS 1968 CAME to an end, Strategic Air Command had 105 bombers bombing Vietnam and 182 bombers on ground alert, without bombs. Chrome Dome flights had come to a complete end. There were 59 Titan ICBMs and 967 Minuteman missiles, all on alert.

ON SEPTEMBER 27, 1991, President George H. W. Bush ordered Strategic Air Command to stand down their alert forces. On June 1, 1992, Strategic Air Command was dissolved.

AS OF SEPTEMBER 2010, the United States Air Force nuclear bombing force consisted of 96 B-52s, 66 B-1B bombers, and 20 B-2s. There were 450 Minuteman IIIs. The F-15, F-16, and F-22 fighters were nuclear capable.

EPILOGUE

THE COLD WAR is over, but there is much left to examine. We can look back and see the complex ecosystem of offensive forces, defensive radars and fighters, atomic and nuclear weapons, overseas and domestic bases, missiles and bombers and countless changes in tactics, all of which had at their core the threat of massive retaliation. But what do we make of it?

Citing more than a dozen flash points between the Soviet Union and the United States since World War II, Cold War historian John Lewis Gaddis said that without the atomic bomb, and without the fear of a retaliation, those incidents "in almost any other age, and among almost any other antagonists, would sooner or later have produced war." But they did not.

Columbia University professor and international relations expert Kenneth Waltz agreed with Gaddis: "Never since the Treaty of Westphalia in 1648 . . . have great powers enjoyed a longer period of peace than we have known since the Second World War." This "happy condition," said Waltz, came about because of the unacceptable consequences of using the bomb.

Despite the admonition of Stanley Kubrick, we have survived our nuclear age, or at least the *first* nuclear age, as Schell would put it, and for this, General Curtis LeMay deserves a share of the credit. Yes, LeMay had a well-known tendency to say the wrong thing—*we should nuke the bastards*—and, yes, LeMay no doubt left his legacy in tatters by becoming the running mate on the presidential ticket of George Wallace, the Alabama governor and avowed segregationist most famous for standing in the schoolhouse doors to halt the integration of public schools. But, given LeMay's demanding job—containment, deterrence, massive retaliation, flexible response—he was the exemplary general. Not for the thinnest fraction of a second did Washington or Moscow ever doubt that his SAC would do what it said it could do—never did Truman, Eisenhower, or Kennedy have to question SAC's abilities, readiness, or will to carry out its mission. "SAC does not claim a capability which in fact does not exist," and Curtis LeMay's inextinguishable war machine *was* the perfection of deterrence.

IT IS PERHAPS impossible for the reader not to ask the obvious question: if deterrence had failed, what gain would have come from the exchange of nuclear weapons? It is a good question, indeed. "Instead of one side winning and one side losing it is as though all human beings lost and the weapons won," wrote Schell, and that appears to be the case. There is no evidence that either country intended to occupy the other, no evidence of a Soviet military force prepared to take over America or an American force prepared to take over Russia. We are struck; we strike back. There it would end. The two countries would largely have expended themselves, two powerless nations with no nuclear weapons, no bombers, no submarines, no air bases, no air-defense installations, no ships, no ports, no central governments, no communications systems, no factories that could make engines or airframes or automobiles, no Washington, D.C., or New York or Boston, no Chicago, Dallas, St. Louis, Seattle, Omaha; no London or Guam or Bermuda or Labrador or Greenland or the Azores or any of the other bases we needed to move bombers overseas; even my hometown of Louisville, Kentucky, would have been destroyed by a fireball, because all this would have happened when the world was on the gold standard and Fort Knox held our gold. Perhaps former secretary of defense Robert McNamara said it best: "Nuclear weapons serve no military purpose whatsoever. They are totally useless . . . except to deter one's opponent from using them."

And if that failed, annihilation was the sole consequence.

THE KLAXONS ARE silent now, the moleholes are empty; the winds sweep over those herringbone stubs with blowing sands that scour the paint down to concrete. No more disks of light trace a silent path across a winter's night sky; no more clusters of tankers hold a silent vigil waiting for an RB-47 to blink its lights as it emerges from behind Banana Island in the Barents Sea; no more radar stations spray their sinister beams from stations in the Arctic. It is over.

The Cold War was played out on oil burner routes, on ORIs and Chrome Domes and airborne and ground alerts and emergency rocket communications systems and dead-hand systems just as surely as if it had played out in foxholes with bullets and bombs. It was a war fought with simulators, computers, think tanks, generals and politicians who debated the data that spoke of cities destroyed, fatalities, casualties, fireballs, megatons, sorties, ground zeros, clobber factors, H-hour control lines, fail-safe, off-continent fallout, bonus effects, and machines firing the last salvo against machines.

Except so few knew it that way.

But now we do.

It is common enough to see a list of abbreviations before or after a history such as this one; of course, whether or not they're read is an entirely different matter. I, for one, dislike them, but not this time. The Cold War generated a language of its own, laced with abbreviations and acronyms that were themselves brisk packets of data that communicated so much in just one utterance. Words like *fail-safe, CINCSAC, doomsday, TNs,* and *ICBMs* were part of that language and used in ordinary conversation. But in writing a history such as this, I think terms slow a reader down so I largely avoided them in this book.

That said, these abbreviations tell a story of their own, a Strategic Air Command story that you now know, which begins with a surprise attack on America by the Soviets, covers the launch of SAC's alert bombers and tankers, and ends with surviving bombers limping home to the contingency plans no one wanted to consider. With the dogmatism of brevity, here is the language of the Cold War.

AAF/AF　Army air forces. Prior to 1941, the army air forces were called the army air corps. Between 1941 and 1947, the official name was the army air forces. In 1947, the word *army* was dropped as the United States Air Force came into being.

ABNCP　Airborne National Command Post. This was the KC-135 tanker that remained airborne for more than thirty years as a hedge against a Soviet surprise attack. The ABNCP was a postattack airborne command post for Strategic Air Command. The assumption behind it was that a Soviet nuclear attack would destroy all the nation's high-value command-and-control centers, such as the Pentagon, the White House, and even SAC's own headquarters in Omaha, Nebraska. In the postattack environment, the ABNCP would be the surviving senior command post and thus the cornerstone of a new airborne communications network that could send messages to and from SAC elements as well as the similarly named aircraft, the National Emergency Airborne Command Post (NEACP), which hopefully would have the president onboard. The ABNCP KC-135 initially sat on fifteen-minute ground alert but was later elevated to continuous airborne status.

AC&W   Aircraft Control & Warning, the formal name for air-defense radar stations.

ADC   Air Defense Command.

ADIZ   Air Defense Identification Zone. An imaginary line surrounding the United States through which no aircraft could fly without positive identification. Often called the Air Defense Intercept Zone.

ADS   Aviation Depot Squadron. Through at least the late 1950s, a fully certified bombs-on-base Aviation Depot Squadron had to be able to load a bomb on a nuclear bomber in less than two hours.

AEAO   Airborne Emergency Action Officer. The SAC general officer who flew aboard the Airborne National Command Post. If the AEAO visually confirmed that a nuclear bomb had hit SAC headquarters, this officer would take over as the commander in chief of SAC. At that point he would have the authority to issue the "go" code to the nuclear forces.

AEC   Atomic Energy Commission.

AEW&C   Aircraft Early Warning & Control. Airborne early-warning aircraft patrolled the Atlantic and Pacific approaches to the United States. They were augmented by the Texas Tower radar stations erected in the Atlantic.

AFB   Air Force Base.

AFS   Air Force Station.

ANGELS   An aircraft's altitude expressed in thousands of feet—as in "angels twenty" for twenty thousand feet.

AFSWP   Armed Forces Special Weapons Project. This was a joint army, navy, and air force command to oversee nuclear-weapons' testing, development, and assembly, military exercises, military requirements for new weapons, and radiological safety. This command absorbed the military portions of the Manhattan Project.

ALERT   Alert aircraft. This refers to bombers and tankers loaded with gas and bombs and prepositioned on the ground, ready for immediate takeoff. This also refers to bombers flying racetrack patterns around the North American continent on what was known as airborne alert. From at least 1958, ground- and air-alert bombers carried war-ready bombs.

ASM   Air-to-Surface Missile. This generally refers to the nuclear-tipped Hound Dog missiles carried by SAC bombers to help them penetrate Soviet defenses. ASMs were previously known as GAMs, or ground attack missiles, and thus early models of some of the missiles used GAM and a number to identify the model, such as GAM-77 or GAM-44, etc.

ATC Air Target Chart. This is the highly classified chart provided to an SAC bomber crew to find and attack their desired ground zero. The ATC was an essential part of the crews' combat mission folders.

BAS Bomb Alarm System. A network of passive sensors that were erected around major cities and critical military bases. The BAS was programmed to "recognize" a nuclear flash and alert SAC that a bomb had gone off.

BDA Bomb Damage Assessment.

BMEWS Ballistic Missile Early Warning Station. A chain of three long-range radar stations that could detect incoming Soviet missiles and provide SAC 15 minutes' warning before impact.

BOB Bombs-on-Base. A Strategic Air Command program to ready its bases to receive and otherwise take control of atomic weapons. This occurred during a period when atomic weapons began to move from centralized storage facilities out to the strategic forces. In a historical context, bombs-on-base was but one round in the tug-of-war that eventually saw the transfer of control of atomic bombs from the civilian AEC to the military.

BRL Bomb Release Line. The release point for a nuclear weapon.

CAS Complete Assembly for Strike. This was a bomb prepared for an atomic strike and loaded into a bomber's bomb bay. Inspectors would rate the CAS work of technicians against protocols that would indicate whether the bomb when dropped would explode or be a dud.

CEP Circular Error Probable. The distance between a desired ground zero and the actual impact point of a warhead or bomb, expressed in feet. During training missions, CEP was used to measure the accuracy of a bombing crew. CEP was also an accuracy variable in the calculation used by war planners to estimate the likelihood that a given target would be destroyed by a given number of bombs of a given yield detonating a given CEP from the desired ground zero.

CINCSAC Commander in Chief Strategic Air Command.

CLOBBER To evaluate the likelihood that a bomber would reach its target, attrition factors were applied to all penetration routes. Because many routes were over unmapped territory, consideration was given to the probability that a bomber would fly head-on into an unmarked obstacle such as a high power line, a smokestack, or some other unknown obstacle. This dreadful prospect was called "the clobber factor."

CMF Combat Mission Folder. The combat mission folder specified the targets that an SAC bomber was assigned and contained all the necessary navigation charts and radar-identification aids to get there and accurately hit the desired ground zero. Included in the combat mission folders were the high-altitude navigation charts for the flight across the Atlantic, the low-altitude operational navigation chart that covered the egress into the target, target-identification aids such as the air-target chart, and a chart with "Radar Significant Power Lines and Locations" to help identify radar-visible aiming points; visual images of the target called basic-target graphics and seasonal-target graphics and hard-target graphics—all with specific delivery tactics, air-defense installations, and other threats on the route clearly indicated on a timeline that included a specific time-over-target, a bomb-release line, and so on. The combat mission folder was sometimes called a crew mission folder.

COCKED   A bomber was called a "cocked" bomber when it was fueled up and loaded with its bombs and certain other preflight shortcuts had been completed. Cocked bombers were also alert bombers.

CONUS   The forty-eight contiguous states.

COUNTERFORCE   The targeting of an enemy's military assets (versus civilian or industrial areas).

COUNTERVALUE   Targeting an enemy's industrial areas to eliminate their manufacturing base and thus the enemy's ability to support a war effort.

DBL   Destroyed Before Launch. A factor added to the war plan to account for the SAC forces destroyed on the ground.

DEAD HAND   Also "Dead Man." A last-resort Soviet mechanism to communicate go codes to missiles in the event that the entire chain of command had been killed. In what would presumably be their own final act, launch controllers would open a switch that would transmit the go codes if external sensors picked up the thermal or light signature of a bursting bomb. See SWESS.

DI   The Intelligence Directorate. This was SAC's internal intelligence operation. A vast, highly classified directorate that had its own facilities and staffers, the DI operated SAC's main warning center, which continuously updated the CINCSAC on enemy activities and processed CIA-generated target photography, electronic intelligence, and all other data inputs that would be used to help aircrews identify Soviet targets and Soviet air defenses. The DI generated tens of thousands of target charts and planning aids that were used by SAC's bomber crews. Basically, the DI generated the combat mission folders.

DGZ   Desired Ground Zero (or "designated" ground zero).

DOD   Department of Defense.

DOE   Department of Energy.

EAM   Emergency Action Message. As portrayed in movies, this was the "go" code. When authenticated, it authorized the offensive forces to execute their war orders.

ECM   Electronic Countermeasures. ECMs included frequency jammers, chaff, flares, and even shapes that would confuse search radars. ECMs were carried by aircraft but they were also inside missile warheads and even in the nuclear bomb itself.

E-HOUR Execute Hour. This would be the Cold War version of D-day.

ERCS Emergency Rocket Communication System. Modified Minuteman ICBMs that would be shot on intercontinental trajectories during which they would broadcast the "go" code to SAC bombers and missiles. A last-ditch option.

EWO Emergency War Order. Because the word *plan* seemed open-ended and thus subject to discussion, the word *plan* was changed to the word *order,* as in EWO.

EWP Emergency War Plan. The plan of attack. There were several types of EWPs. The master EWP integrated all nuclear attackers and deconflicted individual sorties. EWPs were also specific to individual air wings, groups, squadrons, and individual aircraft. Tankers as well as bombers had EWPs. LeMay would famously—and unexpectedly—land at an air wing, step out of his jet, and say, "Execute your war plan!"

FERRET SAC's secret but nonetheless daring intelligence-gathering flights along the edges of, and sometimes over, the Soviet Union. Ferrets collected the radar frequencies of Soviet air-defense radar stations, the frequencies used by tracking radars attached to surface-to-air missiles, and other intelligence that would be used to map Soviet defenses.

FINDER Ferret Intelligence Data Evaluator. A computer program that processed electronic intelligence gathered by the ferret flights.

HACK Slang for a point on a timeline signifying a predefined event.

HE High Explosives. The chemical explosives wrapped around the fissile capsule inside a nuclear bomb.

HHCL H-Hour Control Line. An imaginary line outside Soviet air-defense radars through which SAC bombers could not proceed without an authenticated EAM.

ICCT Initial Contact Control Time. Used by air-refueling tankers as the initial time hack from which they would coordinate their scheduled refueling hook-ups with their assigned bombers.

IFI In-flight Insertion. The process of inserting a ball of fissile material into the pit of a nuclear bomb after takeoff or before landing. This was a safety measure to preclude the possibility of an accidental nuclear explosion if a plane crashed on takeoff or landing. IFI was at first a manual process completed inside the bomb bay. In time, IFI would become automatic. Automatic IFI allowed jets to carry nuclear bombs under their wings. After takeoff, a mechanical screw would push the ball into the pit of a bomb.

IP   Initial Point. Once past the HHCL, a pilot would execute a pushover, drop to low altitude, and at IP begin his high-speed bomb run at the target.

JCS   Joint Chiefs of Staff.

KT   Kiloton. The explosive equivalent of one thousand tons of TNT.

LABS   Low Altitude Bomb System. A method of tossing or lobbing a nuclear bomb. By flying in an arc similar to that of an underarm softball toss, a jet would initiate a rapid pull-up and near the top of the pull-up release the bomb. The bomb could be tossed forward or over the shoulder of the jet, depending on the point of release. LABS deliveries were used by fighter aircraft. The maneuver allowed them time to escape the bomb blast.

LADDS   Low Altitude Drogue Delivery System. A method of releasing a nuclear bomb from a bomber flying as low as 150 feet. The pilot would pitch up the bomber into a slight climb, release the weapon, and then, relying on a series of parachutes contained in the after-body of the bomb—and perhaps delayed burst fuses—use the ensuing time interval to escape the blast.

LASL   Los Alamos Scientific Laboratories.

LAYDOWN   A laydown bomb was a bomb that was fused for a delayed burst. Laydown bombs could stay on the ground for seconds or hours before bursting. Most laydown bombs were parachuted into a target and had shock-absorbing spikes or collapsing nose cones.

LCC   Launch Control Center (or Complex), the underground bunker from which a complex of missile silos was controlled.

LCO   Launch Control Officer. The launch controller in an LCC.

LFP   Launch Fix Point. A geospatial point used to fix the current position in the guidance system of a Hound Dog air-to-surface missile. The Hound Dog was carried by the B-52.

MACV   Military Assistance Command Vietnam. The in-country controlling military apparatus for the Vietnam War.

MITO   Minimum Interval Takeoff. A swarming, intense takeoff technique practiced by SAC that released one jet after another onto the runway with a slim fifteen seconds of spacing between aircraft. Pilots would talk about "busting out" or being "flushed" from alert bunkers onto runways darkened by the black engine exhausts of departing aircraft.

MLC   Military Liaison Committee. DOD committee that transmitted to the AEC the military requirement for a specific bomb, including their desired characteristic (yield, burst height, weight, etc.).

MPE   Maximum Permissible Exposure. The maximum amount of accumulated radiation exposure for personnel at a nuclear test. In a much-abused practice, an

MPE could be adjusted upward depending on an individual's importance to the completion of the test.

MT   Megaton. The explosive equivalent of one million tons of TNT.

NALS   National Alternate Landing Sites. In the aftermath of a nuclear exchange, SAC bases would either be gone or be too contaminated for continued operations. NALS was a tested and approved end-of-the-world plan to use dry lake beds as landing sites for returning aircraft. Essentially, dry lake beds would become SAC's air bases of last resort.

NAS   Naval Air Station.

NEACP   National Emergency Airborne Command Post (pronounced "kneecap"). A converted KC-135 tanker designed to evacuate the president from Washington, D.C. The NEACP was on continuous fifteen-minute ground alert at Andrews AFB. Once airborne, it had all the equipment the president would need to issue orders and communicate with the ABNCP and other command centers.

NORAD   North American Air Defense Command.

NSC   National Security Council.

NSS   National Stockpile Sites. These were the first nuclear weapons' stockpile sites, of which there were six. The six National Stockpile Sites were dispersed around the nation and were near but not part of operating SAC bases. The location of a stockpile site was a well-guarded secret.

NSTL   National Strategic Target List. A master list of targets approved by the Joint Chiefs and culled from the navy target inventory, the air force target inventory, SAC's, and those of other services that had atomic missions. The NSTL was the first step toward an integrated plan of attack that would minimize overbombing and reduce the possibility of friendly-fire casualties.

OAP   Offset Aim Point. Many Soviet targets were "no-show" targets—that is, targets that were not readily visible through a bomb scope (such as a missile silo). In such cases, a radar-visible reference point such as a bend in a river would become an aiming point from which a navigator would begin an offset heading to the bomb-release point.

ORI   Operational Readiness Inspection. A realistic and unforgiving test to determine an air wing's capability to execute their EWO. (See EWO.)

OSD   Office of the Secretary of Defense.

OSS   Operational Storage Sites. Additional nuclear weapons' storage sites similar to NSS but built on operating military bases. There were seven OSS and six NSS, for a total of thirteen sites in the United States that stored bombs. This overly centralized system would yield to the less-time-consuming plan to store bombs on bases.

PACCS   Post Attack Command Control System. A network of remote command centers and airborne aircraft to relay messages to SAC forces nationwide. The ABNCP was part of PACCS.

PCTAP   Positive Control Turn Around Point. The mandatory turnaround point for all SAC bombers if no Emergency Action Message was received. This was the "fail-safe" concept—that is, this was the method of halting an attack without directly communicating with a bomber. If the "go" code was not received, the crew turned around at their PCTAP (pronounced "pic-tap").

POL   Petroleum, Oil, and Lubricants. As in, the first bombs were targeted against the enemies' POL sites.

PUP   Pitch-Up-Pushover, a maneuver employed by SAC bombers to release a nuclear weapon at extremely low altitudes by briefly pulling the bomber up and "pitching" a parachute-retarded bomb toward a target, then pushing over for the escape. This maneuver kept a bomber below enemy fire but allowed for a LADDS or "laydown" delivery.

RAVENS   The RB-47 was a B-47 bomber converted for intelligence gathering. The bomb bay of the RB-47 was fitted with a special pod that had room for three intelligence-gathering specialists and their signal-gathering equipment. Because these were secret missions, which were often called "black" operations, the specialists in the pod were called Ravens.

RBS   Radar Bomb Scoring sites. RBS sites were ground-based installations that used telemetry and radar equipment to electronically map the fall of a bomb from an SAC bomber. These data were used to score an aircrew's bombing accuracy. To minimize the advantage of familiarity with an RBS site, in time RBS sites were mounted on railroads and moved to unusual locations. Railroad-based RBS sites were called the RBS Express.

SIMCOM   Simulated Combat Mission. This was a realistic simulation of an aircrew's EWO sortie. It was flown across American airspace. Pilots on SIMCOMs were usually "attacked" by Air Defense Command fighter interceptors. SIMCOMs were also called Unit Simulated Combat Missions (UCSM). SIMCOMs were generally flown with bombs.

SIOP   Single Integrated Operational Plan. The master plan of atomic attack incorporating bombers, missiles, navy aircraft, and so on. The first SIOP was effective in 1962 and was called SIOP-62. SIOP replaced the EWO.

SORTIE   SAC combat missions were called sorties and were generally numbered, as in sortie 15 or sortie 21-B. By following the combat mission folder, a bomber would arrive over a designated target with a specified bomb load at a specified time on the flight plan that included escape options and alternate air bases to land and refuel.

SPECIAL WEAPONS   The term for all atomic or nuclear weapons.

SSS   Strategic Support Squadrons. "Triple-S" air-cargo squadrons were air squadrons dedicated entirely to the transport of atomic bombs and atomic bomb parts. The early SSS flew the C-124 cargo plane. Two bombs ejected from an SSS C-124 remain lost off the coast of New Jersey.

STS   Stockpile-to-Target-Sequence. This was a detailed, step-by-step map of the sequence of events in the movement of an atomic bomb from storage, onto a bomber, through the air, to the bomb-release line, ending with the drop and the ultimate explosion. The STS examined the physical forces on the bomb across this entire sequence to determine if the bomb would actually survive and detonate as planned. An Operational Suitability Test was a live test of the STS using the actual bomb, the actual bomber, and a full release over a test range, including the detonation of that bomb but without the nuclear capsule.

SWESS   The Special Weapons Emergency Separation Switch. This was a switch installed on the B-52 bombers that when activated by the aircrew would automatically release the bomb if it sensed that the bomber was falling through the sky. This was a dead man's switch.

TDI   Target Data Inventory. Similar to the NSTL, but a larger and more inclusive list of all enemy targets, including Soviet, Chinese, and satellite countries.

TN   Thermonuclear bombs.

TOT   Time over Target. The arrival of a bomber over a desired ground zero.

USAF   United States Air Force.

USCM   Unit Simulated Combat Mission. Same as SIMCOM.

VN   Vulnerability Number. A factor index applied to each target to indicate its vulnerability to nuclear weapons of various yields.

WSA   Weapons Storage Area. Bombs on military bases were stored in these areas.

ZI   Zone of the Interior, used to mean CONUS air bases plus Ernst Harmon Air Force Base, Newfoundland, Kindley Air Force Base, Bermuda, and Ramey Air Force Base, Puerto Rico. All other SAC bases were "overseas" bases.*

---

*   What constituted the ZI varied. Goose Bay Air Base, Labrador, for instance, is sometimes included as a ZI air base. *History of Strategic Air Command* January–June 1962, Historical Study No. 91, FOIA, p. 296.

SOURCES

"2009 USAF Almanac Structure of the Force," *Air Force* Magazine, May 2009, pp. 24–57.

307th Bomb Wing B-47/KC-97 Association, "History of the 30th Bombardment Wing (Medium): Lincoln AFB, Nebraska, 1954–1965," 2000, http://www.307bwassoc.org/ (accessed June 2010).

3084th Aviation Depot Squadron, Stony Brook Air Force Station, "A History of a Cold War Mission," http://www.3084adg.us/ (accessed 6/10).

7th Bomb Wing B-36 Association, "Histories of the 7th and 11th Bombardment Wings (Through 1958)," http://www.7bwb-36assn.org/index.html (accessed June 2010).

_____, "Reflections," http://www.7bwb-36assn.org/index.html (accessed June 2010).

Abbott, Don, e-mail messages to the author regarding Texas Towers, 1998–2009.

Abella, Alex, *Soldiers of Reason: The Rand Corporation and the Rise of the American Empire*, Orlando, Harcourt, 2008.

Adams, Chris, *Inside the Cold War: A Cold Warrior's Reflections*, Maxwell Air Force Base, Alabama, Air University Press, 1999.

Air Defense Command, *Report of a Board of Officers—Loss of Texas Tower 4*, March 1961, Washington, D.C., Government Printing Office.

Air Policy Commission, *Survival in the Air Age: A Report by the President's Air Policy Commission*, January 1, 1948, Government Printing Office.

Alexander, Sigmund, *B-47 Aircraft Losses*, June 2008, San Antonio, Texas.

Alsop, Joseph and Stewart Alsop, "We Accuse!" *Harper's*, October 1954, pp. 24–25.

Ambrose, Stephen. *D-Day, June 6, 1944: The Climactic Battle of World War II*, New York, Scribner, 1995.

America's Atomic Bomb Tests, VHS set, Avion Park Productions, 2004.

Arkin, William A., Robert S. Norris, and Joshua Handler, "Taking Stock: Worldwide Nuclear Deployments 1998," Washington, D.C., Natural Resources Defense Council.

Atomic Energy Commission, "Daily Diary—Bikini Atoll, 11 January 1954–11 May 1954," DOE/NV.

———, "Proposed Safety Rules for B-47 and B-52 Aircraft," August 1, 1960, Scott Sagan Collection, National Security Archive, Washington, D.C.

———, "Proposed Air Force Safety Rules for the N-47 and B-52 Aircraft with the MK-43 Weapon," April 4, 1961, Scott Sagan Collection, National Security Archive, Washington, D.C.

———, "Proposed Changes to Certain USAF Weapon System Safety Rules," August 12, 1961, Scott Sagan Collection, National Security Archive, Washington, D.C.

———, "Proposed Air Force Safety Rules, Proposed Safety Rules for the B-47, B-52/ MK-28 FI Weapon System," August 24, 1962, Scott Sagan Collection, National Security Archive, Washington, D.C.

Atomic Veterans.org, "The Atomic Experience," http://www.atomicveterans.org/ atomic_experience.htm (accessed June 2010).

Austin, Diane, Bob Carriker, Tom McGuire, Joseph Pratt, Tyler Priest, and Allen G. Pulsipher, *History of the Offshore Oil and Gas Industry in Southern Louisiana Volume I: Papers on the Evolving Offshore Industry,* 2004, New Orleans, U.S. Department of the Interior.

Austin, Diane, and Tom McGuire, *History of Offshore Oil and Gas Industry in Southern Louisiana, Interim Report, Volume III: Samples of Interviews and Ethnographic Prefaces,* 2004, New Orleans, U.S. Department of the Interior.

Baldwin, Hansen W., "Are We Safe from Our Own Bombs?" *The New York Times,* March 16, 1958.

Baldwin, Robert D., "Staff Memorandum: Experiences at Desert Rock VIII," March 1958, Washington, D.C., Department of the Army, DOE/NV.

Bartholomew, Frank H., "SAC's 'Fail Safe' Keeps False Alarms from Turning into War," *St. Louis Post-Dispatch,* n.d., National Archives, CIA-RDP62B00844 R000200200027-2.

Bierbaum, R. L., J. J. Cashen, T. J. Kerschen, J. M. Sjulin, and D. L. Wright, "DOE Nuclear Weapon Reliability Definition: History, Description, and Implementation," April 1999, Albuquerque, Sandia National Laboratories, DTIC.

Boren, Paul, to John A. Kapral, memorandum, "Internal Dose Assessment for Rongerik Weather Unit, Operation Castle," May 31, 1985, Washington, D.C., Defense Nuclear Agency, provided to author by Kapral family.

Boyne, Walter J., *Beyond the Wild Blue: A History of the United States Air Force 1947–1997,* New York, St. Martin's Press, 1997.

———, *Silver Wings: A History of the United States Air Force,* New York, Simon & Schuster, 1993.

Brinkley, Douglas, and Dean Acheson, *The Cold War Years 1953–1971,* New Haven, Yale University Press, 1994.

Brode, Harold L., and Richard D. Small, "Fire Damage and Strategic Targeting," Washington, D.C., Defense Nuclear Agency, 1983, DTIC.

Broyhill, T. Marvin, *A Peaceful Profession,* an unpublished book manuscript provided to author, 2009.

Buderi, Robert, *The Invention That Changed the World: How a Small Group of Radar Pioneers Won the Second World War and Launched a Technological Revolution,* New York, Simon & Schuster, 1996.

Builder, Carl H., "The Future of Nuclear Deterrence," a paper, Santa Monica, The RAND Corporation, 1991.

Burr, William, "Newly Declassified Documents on Advance Presidential Authorization of Nuclear Weapons Use," August 30, 1998, National Security Archive, Washington, D.C.

_____, ed. "Launch on Warning: The Development of U.S. Capabilities, 1959–1979," April 2001, National Security Archive, Washington, D.C.

_____, ed. "First Declassification of Eisenhower's Instructions to Commanders Predelegating Nuclear Weapons Use, 1959–1960," May 18, 2001, National Security Archive, Washington, D.C.

_____, ed. "First Strike Options and the Berlin Crisis, September 1961," September 25, 2001, National Security Archive, Washington, D.C.

_____, ed. "It Is Certain There Will Be Many Firestorms? New Evidence on the Origins of Overkill," January 14, 2004, National Security Archive, Washington, D.C.

_____, ed. "The Creation of SIOP-62: More Evidence on the Origins of Overkill," July 13, 2004, National Security Archive, Washington, D.C.

_____, ed. "Consultation Is Presidential Business: Secret Underpinnings on the Use of Nuclear Weapons, 1950–1974," July 1, 2005, National Security Archive, Washington, D.C.

_____, ed. "How Many and Where Were the Nukes? What the U.S. Government No Longer Wants You to Know about Nuclear Weapons During the Cold War," August 18, 2006, National Security Archive, Washington, D.C.

_____, ed, "Special Collection: Some Key Documents on Nuclear Policy Issues, 1945–1990," June 15, 2007, National Security Archive, Washington, D.C.

_____, ed. "How Much Is Enough? The U.S. Navy and Finite Deterrence. A Moment in Cold War History when the Fundamentals of the U.S. Nuclear Posture Were at Stake," May 1, 2009, National Security Archive, Washington, D.C.

Burr, William, and Svetlana Savranskaya, eds., "Previously Classified Interviews with

Former Soviet Officials Reveal U.S. Strategic Intelligence Failure Over Decades," December 11, 2009, National Security Archive, Washington, D.C.

Burton, H. C., to Commander Joint Task Force Seven, "Historical Installment Number 3 of the History of Operation Castle," n.d., DOE/NV Record 79980.

_____, to Commander Joint Task Force Seven, "Historical Installment Number 4 [final installment] of the History of Operation Castle, Period 8, April through 15 May 1954," n.d., DOE/NV.

Center for Defense Information, "U.S. Nuclear Weapons Accidents: Danger in Our Midst," *The Defense Monitor,* volume 10, no. 5 (1981).

Central Intelligence Agency, "Utilization of the U-2 Reconnaissance Fleet," n.d., National Archives, CIA-RDP74J00828R000100200021-6.

_____, "Situation Estimate for Project Chalice Fiscal Years 1961 and 1962," March 14, 1960, National Archives, CIA-RPD63-00313A000600050012-8.

_____, "Memorandum for Deputy Director of Central Intelligence, Strategic Air Command, Use of TALENT Materials," National Archives, CIA-RDP61S00750 A000200090070-2.

_____, "Some Animadversions Regarding the Matter of the 'Missile Gap,'" memorandum, National Archives, CIA-RDP85G00105R000100110001-4.

Chairman Joint Chiefs of Staff to Secretary of Defense, "SAC Maneuver of Sealed Pit Weapons," memorandum, December 24, 1958, Department of Defense, FOIA Reading Room.

Chairman's Staff Group, Memorandum for Admiral Radford, Appendix, "Actions and Results Under Conditions of Strategic Surprise," November 1, 1956, Department of Defense, FOIA Reading Room.

Chrestensen, Louis B., "Island Evacuation," n.d., DOE/NV Record 410480.

Christensen, Wayne J., "Operation Castle. Blast Effects on Miscellaneous Structures," July 1955, Armed Forces Special Weapons Project, DTIC.

Clark, John C., "We Were Trapped by the Radioactive Fallout," *The Saturday Evening Post,* July 20, 1957.

Clearwater, John, "U.S. Nuclear Weapons in Canada," quoted in "How Many and Where Were the Nukes?" edited by William S. Burr, National Security Archive, August 18, 2006.

Cockburn, Andrew and Leslie, *One Point Safe,* New York, Anchor Books, 1997.

Coffey, Thomas M., *Iron Eagle: The Turbulent Life of General Curtis LeMay,* New York, Avon Books, 1986.

Compton, Arthur H., to Mr. George Harrison, Memorandum on "Political and Social Problems from Members of the Metallurgical Laboratory" of the University of

Chicago, June 12, 1945, http://www.mtholyoke.edu/acad/intrel/feros-pg.htm (accessed 6/10).

Commanding Officer USS *Bairoko* to Commander Task Group 7.3, memorandum, "Radioactive Contamination; Summary of Period 1–8 March 1954," DOE/NV Record 410504.

Condit, Kenneth W., *The Joint Chiefs of Staff and National Policy* volume II, 1947–1949, Washington, D.C., Office of Joint History, 1996.

_____, *The Joint Chiefs of Staff and National Policy* volume VI, 1955–1956, Washington, D.C., Historical Office, 1992.

Conrad, Robert A., MD, Eugene P. Cronkite, MD., Victor P. Bond, MD., James S. Robertson, MD., and Stanton H. Cohn, MD., "Fallout Radiation: Effects on Marshallese People," DOE/NV.

Cooper, Edward H., *Radiation Fallout: My Story,* unpublished manuscript provided to author, 1999.

Department of Defense, "Narrative Summaries of Accidents Involving U.D. Nuclear Weapons 1950–1980," Department of Defense, FOIA Reading Room.

Defense Nuclear Agency, "Handbook of Underwater Nuclear Explosions," volume 2, part 2, March 1972, Washington, D.C., DTIC.

_____, "Castle Series 1954 United States Atmospheric Nuclear Weapons Tests, Nuclear Test Personnel Review," Washington, D.C., DOD.

Devlin, John C., "Radar Tower Is Lost at Sea in Turbulent Storm. $21-Million Ocean Radar Station Built Like Drilling Rigs Off Coast, *The New York Times,* January 17, 1961.

Doomed: Tower at Sea, VHS, Our Town Films, History Channel Home Video, 2009.

Dow, James, *The Arrow,* Toronto, James Lorimer & Company, 1997.

Drake, Philip, "What It Was Like," *The Wetokian,* spring 2001.

Dulles, Allen W., "The Soviet Challenge," speech, Yale University, February 3, 1958, National Archives, CIA-RDP70-00058R00100110022-4.

Eden, Lynn, *Whole World on Fire: Organizations, Knowledge, and Nuclear Weapons Devastation,* Ithaca, New York, Cornell University Press, 2004.

Elwood, Noah J., and John W. Gaythwaite, "The DeLong Pier Repair Project: The Unique Challenges of Designing Repairs to a 1950 Vintage Marine Structure in the Arctic," conference proceeding paper, *American Society of Civil Engineers,* 2007.

Fairchild, Byron R., and Walter S. Poole, *The Joint Chiefs of Staff and National Policy* volume VII, 1957–1960, Washington, D.C., Office of Joint History, 2000.

Farquhar, John Thomas, *A Need to Know: The Role of Air Force Reconnaissance in War Planning, 1945–1953,* Maxwell Air Force Base, Alabama, Air University Press, 2004.

Federation of American Scientists, "USAF Intelligence Targeting Guide, Glossary of References, Abbreviations, Acronyms, and Terms, Air Force Pamphlet 14-210 Intelligence," February 1998, http://www.fas.org/irp/doddir/usaf/afpam14-210/part14.htm (accessed 1/2010).

Fehner, Terrence R., and F. G. Gosling, "Origins of the Nevada Test Site," Washington, D.C., Department of Energy, 2000.

Fenton, John H., "First Man-Made Radar Island Launched; 30 to Stand Offshore to Warn of Attacks," *The New York Times,* May 21, 1955.

_____, "Radar Tower Launched in Maine," *The New York Times,* June 27, 1967.

Fermi, Rachel, and Esther Samra, *Picturing the Bomb: Photographs from the Secret World of the Manhattan Project,* New York, Abrams, 1995.

Fifteenth Air Force, "History Fifteenth Air Force July–December 1955," SAC200118970000, FOIA.

_____, "History Fifteenth Air Force January–June 1956," SAC200118980000, FOIA.

_____, "History Fifteenth Air Force January–June 1958," AFHRA.

_____, "History the 4128th Strategic Wing, 1–28 November 1962," n.d., Scott Sagan Collection, National Security Archive, Washington, D.C.

_____, "Fourteenth Strategic Aerospace Division, Cuban Crisis Annex," n.d., Scott Sagan Collection, National Security Archive, Washington, D.C.

_____, "Twenty-sixth Strategic Aerospace Wing 20–29 October 1962," n.d., Scott Sagan Collection, National Security Archive, Washington, D.C.

Foster, John, notes dictated at the request of John T. Conway, "Accident of B-52, January 24, 1961, 12½ miles North of Seymour-Johnson Air Force Base," February 7, 1961, National Archives, RG340.2, Records of the Secretary of the Air Force.

Franks, Kenny A., and Paul F. Lambert, *Early Louisiana and Arkansas Oil: A Photographic History 1901–1946,* College Station, Texas A&M Press, 1982.

Fursenko, Aleksandr, and Timothy Naftali, *Khrushchev's Cold War: The Inside Story of an American Adversary,* New York, W. W. Norton, 2006.

Futrell, Robert Frank, *Ideas, Concepts, Doctrine: Basic Thinking in the United States Air Force 1907–1960,* Maxwell Air Force Base, Alabama, Air University Press, 1989.

_____, *Ideas, Concepts, Doctrine: Basic Thinking in the United States Air Force 1961–1984,* Maxwell Air Force Base, Alabama, Air University Press, 1989.

Gaddis, John Lewis, *Strategies of Containment: A Critical Appraisal of Postwar American National Security Policy,* New York, Oxford University Press, 1982.

Gibson, Elizabeth, *It Happened in Nevada,* Guilford, Connecticut, Twodot Books, 2001.

Gibson, James N., *Nuclear Weapons of the United States: An Illustrated History,* Atglen, Pennsylvania, Schiffer, 1996.

Glasstone, Samuel, and Philip J. Dolan, *The Effects of Nuclear Weapons, Third Edition*, Washington, D.C., DOD and DOE, 1977.

GlobalSecurity.org, "B-52 Safety Statistics," March 2001, www.globalsecurity.org/wmd/systems/b-52-safety.htm (accessed May 2009).

Goetz, J., et al., "Analysis of Radiation Exposure—Service Personnel on Rongerik Atoll Operation Castle—Shot Bravo," July 9, 1987, Defense Nuclear Agency, DOE/NV Record 410409.

Gramling, Robert, "Oil in the Gulf: Past Development, Future Prospects," 1995, New Orleans, U.S. Department of the Interior.

Grant, C. L., *The Development of Continental Air Defense to 1 September 1954*, USAF Historical Studies: No. 126, n.d., Maxwell Air Force Base, Alabama, Air University, USAF Historical Division, AFHRA.

Graves, Alvin C., and P. W. Clarkson, "Memorandum for Record, BRAVO Shot, Operation CASTLE," April 12, 1954, Joint Task Force Seven, DOE/NV.

Greene, Warren E., "The Development of the SM-68 Titan," Historical Office Air Force Systems Command, August 1962, AFHRA.

Haggerty, James J., "Rehearsal for Mission No. 1," *Collier's* magazine, reprint, n.d.

Hansen, Chuck, *The Swords of Armageddon*, DVD, San Jose, Chucklea Publications, n.d.

———, appendix, "Typical U.S. Nuclear Weapons Accidents, 1950–1981," in *U.S. Nuclear Weapons: The Secret History*, Dallas, Aerofax/Orion, 1988.

Haver, Sverre, "A Possible Freak Wave Event Measured at the Draupner Jacket January 1, 1995," Stravenger, Norway, Marine Structures and Risers, 2003.

Headquarters Strategic Air Command, "The Development of Strategic Air Command January–June, 1954," n.d., Scott Sagan Collection, National Security Archive, Washington, D.C.

———, "History of Strategic Air Command, 1 July 1954–30 June 1956," Historical Study no. 66, FOIA.

———, "History of Strategic Air Command, 1 January 1957–30 June 1957," Historical Study no. 68, FOIA.

———, "History of Strategic Air Command, 1 July 1957–31 December 1957," Historical Study no. 69, FOIA.

———, "History of Strategic Air Command, 1 January 1958–30 June 1958," Historical Study no. 73, volume I, FOIA.

———, "History of Strategic Air Command, 1 January 1958–30 June 1958," Historical Study no. 73, volume II, FOIA.

———, "History of Strategic Air Command, July 1958–July 1959," Historical Study no. 76, volume I, FOIA.

_____, "History of Strategic Air Command, July–December 1960," Historical Study no. 83, volume I, FOIA.

_____, "History of Strategic Air Command, January–June 1961," Historical Study no. 86, volume I, FOIA.

_____, "History of Strategic Air Command, July–December 1961," Historical Study no. 88, volume I, FOIA.

_____, "History of Headquarters Strategic Air Command, 1961," Historical Study no. 89, FOIA.

_____, "History of Strategic Air Command, January–June 1962," Historical Study no. 91, volume I, FOIA.

_____, "History of Strategic Air Command, January–June 1962," Historical Study no. 91, volume II, FOIA.

_____, "History of Strategic Air Command, January–June 1964," Historical Study no. 95, volume I, FOIA.

_____, "Reconnaissance, History of SAC, January–June 1965," FOIA.

_____, "History of Strategic Air Command, January–June 1966," Historical Study no. 102, volume I, FOIA.

_____, "History of Strategic Air Command, January–June 1967," Historical Study no. 106, volume I, FOIA.

_____, "History of Strategic Air Command, January–June 1968," Historical Study no. 112, volume I, FOIA.

_____, "History of Strategic Air Command, January–June 1968," Historical Study no. 112, volume II, FOIA.

_____, "History of Strategic Air Command, January–June 1968," Historical Study no. 112, volume III, FOIA.

_____, "Strategic Air Command Weapon Systems Acquisition 1964–1979," Historical Study no. 177, volume I, FOIA.

_____, "Strategic Air Command Weapon Systems Acquisition 1964–1979," Historical Study no. 177, volume II, FOIA.

_____, "Strategic Air Command Weapon Systems Acquisition 1964–1979," Historical Study no. 177, volume III, FOIA.

_____, "Strategic Air Command Weapon Systems Acquisition 1964–1979," Historical Study no. 177, volume IV, FOIA.

_____, "Alert Operations and the Strategic Air Command, 1957–1991," Offutt Air Force Base, Nebraska, December 7, 1991, DTIC.

_____, "The Development of Strategic Air Command, 1946–1976," Offutt Air Force Base, Nebraska, March 12, 1976, AFHRA.

_____, "The SAC Alert Program, 1956–1959," Historical Study no. 79, March 21, 1976, National Security Archive, Washington, D.C.

Herbert, H. Joseph, "Report Lists 29 Accidents Involving Nuclear Weapons," Associated Press, April 9, 1992.

HMR-362, "Operation Castle 'Easy' Report," report of marine helicopter operations during Castle, DOE/NV.

Hill, Mike, John M. Campbell, and Donna Campbell, *Peace Was Their Profession, Strategic Air Command: A Tribute,* Atglen, Pennsylvania, Schiffer, 1995.

Hillyard, W. L., and J. O. Cobb, memorandum to Holders of J.C.S 2019/348 (SAC Maneuver of Special Munitions report), December 29, 1958, Department of Defense, FOIA Reading Room.

_____, memorandum to Holders of J.C.S 2019/351 (SAC Maneuver of Special Weapons), report, January 13, 1959, Department of Defense, FOIA Reading Room.

Historical Division, Air Force Special Weapons Center, "History of Task Group 7.4 Participation in Operation Castle," November 8, 1954, DOE/NV.

Holl, Jack M., and Roger M. Anders, introduction, "Atoms for Peace: Dwight D. Eisenhower's Address to the United Nations," Washington, D.C., National Archives and Records Administration, 1990.

Holloway, David, *Stalin and the Bomb: The Soviet Union and Atomic Energy 1939–1956,* New Haven, Yale University Press, 1994.

Houghton, Karl H., "Memorandum for the Record, Personnel Overexposures Post BRAVO," April 26, 1954, DOE/NV Record 76549.

_____, "Memorandum for the Record, Evacuation of Rongerik After Shot Bravo, Operation Castle," April 11, 1954, DOE/NV Record 58875.

House, R. A., "Memorandum for the Record, Final Weather and Radsafe Check, 0430, 1 March 1954," DOE/NV.

_____, "Tab B, Radsafe, Narrative Sequence of Events," attached to memorandum for Record, Bravo Shot Operation Castle, Joint Task Force Seven, April 12, 1954, DOE/NV Record 410804.

_____, "Radsafe Office Operations for Critical Times," Joint Task Force Seven, DOE/NV Record 125473.

Hunter, Mel, *Strategic Air Command,* Garden City, New York, Doubleday, 1961.

Isaacson, Walter, and Evan Thomas, *The Wise Men: Six Friends and the World They Made,* New York, Touchstone, 1986.

James, Michael, "U.S. Starts Work on 'Islands' for Radar Chain in Atlantic," *The New York Times,* August 12, 1954.

Jenkins, Dennis R., *Magnesium Overcast: The Story of the Convair B-36,* North Branch, Minnesota, Specialty Press, 2001.

Johnson, Lyndon Baines, "Daisy Girl," TV commercial in support of his candidacy, www.youtube.com (accessed June 2010).

_____, "Remarks in Seattle on the Control of Nuclear Weapons," September 16, 1964, Public Papers of the Presidents, Lyndon Baines Johnson.

Johnson, Stephen B., *The United States Air Force and a Culture of Innovation 1945–1965,* Air Force History and Museums Program, 2002, AFHRA.

Joint Chiefs of Staff, "Emergency Action Procedures of the Joint Chiefs of Staff, Volume I, General," Washington, D.C., Joint Chiefs of Staff, Department of Defense, FOIA Reading Room.

_____, "The Evaluation of the Atomic Bomb as Military Weapons," June 30, 1947, Truman Papers, http://www.mtholyoke.edu/acad/intrel/feros-pg.htm (accessed 6/10).

Joint Task Force Seven, "Operation Castle Radiological Safety, March–May 1954," DOE/NV Record 410195.

_____, "Operation Castle, Report of Commander, Task Group 7.1," June 1954, DOE/NV.

_____, "History of Operation Castle," 1954, DOE/NV.

_____, "Operation Castle, Commander Task Group 7.3 Final Report," DOE/NV Report 41818.

_____, "Operation Castle, Report of Commander Task Group 7.1," n.d., DOE/NV Record 410488.

_____, "History of Task Group 7.4 Participation in Operation Castle 1 January 1953–26 June 1954," DOE/NV 76890.

_____, "Radiological Safety, Final Report, Volume I," spring 1954, DOE/NV Report 0051031.

_____, "Radiological Safety, Final Report, Volume II," spring 1954, DOE/NV Report 51072.

Junger, Sebastian, *The Perfect Storm: A True Story of Men Against the Sea,* New York, W. W. Norton, 1997.

Kennan, George, "The Sources of Soviet Conduct," *Foreign Affairs,* 65, volume no. 4 (1987), reprint of same authored by "X."

Kepler, George W., "Reflections of George W. Kepler, Air Policeman at Stony Brook Air Force Station, 3084th Air Police Squadron," 2004, http://www.3084adg.us/Reflections%20of%20AP%20Kepler.pdf (accessed 5/10).

Kohn, Richard H., and Joseph P. Harahan, eds., "Strategic Air Warfare: An Interview with Generals Curtis E. LeMay, Leon W. Johnson, David A. Burchinal, and Jack Catton," Office of Air Force History, 1988.

Kunsman, David M., and Douglas B. Lawson, "A Primer on U.S. Strategic Nuclear Policy," Albuquerque, New Mexico, Sandia National Laboratories, 2001.

Kurson, Robert, *Shadow Divers: The True Adventure of Two Americans Who Risked Everything to Solve One of the Last Mysteries of World War II,* New York, Random House, 2004.

Lashmar, Paul, *Spy Flights of the Cold War,* Annapolis, Naval Institute Press, 1996.

Laurence, William L., "Airborne H-Bomb Exploded by U.S. Over Pacific Isle," *The New York Times,* May 21, 1956.

LeMay, Curtis E., "The Operational Side of Air Offense," Remarks to the USAF Scientific Advisory Board at Patrick Air Force Base, Florida, May 21, 1957, Department of Defense, FOIA Reading Room.

_____, to secretary of the air force Eugene Zuckert, memorandum regarding Colonel Banks, October 13, 1961, National Archives, RG340.2, Records of the Secretary of the Air Force.

LeMay, Curtis E., with MacKinlay Kantor, *Missions with LeMay: My Story,* New York, Doubleday & Company, 1965.

Lemmer, George F., "The Air Force and the Concept of Deterrence 1945–1950," USAF Historical Division Liaison Office, 1963, AFHRA.

_____, "The Air Force and Strategic Deterrence 1951–1960," USAF Historical Division Liaison Office, 1967, AFHRA.

Library of Congress, Wringer Collection, Air Intelligence Information Report, http://lcweb2.loc.gov/frd/wringer/wringerhome.html (accessed 6/10).

Lindsay, C. Richard, "Material Programming and War Planning Guidance," letter to the assistant for production programming, USAF, April 19, 1956, Scott Sagan Collection, National Security Archive, Washington, D.C.

Lloyd, Alwyn T., *A Cold War Legacy: A Tribute to Strategic Air Command 1946–1992,* Missoula, Montana, Pictorial Histories Publishing, 1999.

"Log of the U.S.S. Bairoko Commanded by Emmet O'Beirne, Captain Attached to Commander Task Group 7.3, U.S. Pacific, Commencing 0000, 1 March 1954, Bikini Atoll, Marshall Islands," National Archives, RG340.2, Records of the Secretary of the Air Force.

Love, Kenneth, "Hope for Radar Men Ends; Tapping from Hulk Stops," *The New York Times,* January 17, 1961.

Madden, R. F., report, "Commander Task Group 7.3 History of Operation Castle Installment Number 2, Period Ending 24 January 1954," February 1954, DOE/NV.

Maggelet, Michael H., and James C. Oskins, *Broken Arrow: The Declassified History of U.S. Nuclear Weapons Accidents,* www.Scribd.com.

McCool, W. B., "Statement in Nuclear Weapons Accidents by General Loper Before JCAE on May 7, 1958," May 25, 1958, National Archives RG340.2, Records of the Secretary of the Air Force.

McNamara, Robert S., to Senator John Stennis, memorandum, "Answers to Questions Prepared by the Preparedness Subcommittee, 3 November 1961," National Archives RG340.2, Records of the Secretary of the Air Force.

_____, to President John F. Kennedy, "Appendix I: To the memorandum for the President: Recommended Long Range Nuclear Forces 1963–1967," memorandum, September 23, 1961, Department of Defense, FOIA Reading Room.

_____, to President John F. Kennedy, "Recommended FY 1964–1968 Strategic Retaliatory Forces," November 21, 1962, Department of Defense, FOIA Reading Room.

_____, to President Lyndon Johnson, "Memorandum for the President: Recommended FY 1966–1970 Programs for Strategic Offensive Forces, Continental and Missile Defense Programs, and Civil Defense," December 3, 1964, Department of Defense, FOIA Reading Room.

_____, *The Essence of Security: Reflection in Office,* London, Hodder & Stoughton, 1968.

"Memorandum of Telephone Conversation between General Grooves and Lieutenant Colonel Rea, Oak Ridge Hospital, 9:00 A.M., 25 August 1945," http://www.mtholyoke.edu/acad/intrel/feros-pg.htm (accessed 6/10).

Miller, Jay, *Convair B-58 Hustler: The World's First Supersonic Bomber,* Leicester, England, Aerofax, 1985.

Mola, Robert A., "This Is Only a Test," *Air & Space Magazine,* March 1, 2002.

Moody, Walton S., "Building a Strategic Air Force," Air Force History and Museums Program, 1995, AFHRA.

Mosley, Leonard, *The Battle of Britain,* Alexandria, Virginia, Time-Life Books, 1977.

Nalty, Bernard C., "The Air Force Role in Five Crises 1958–1965," U.S. Air Force Historical Division Liaison Office, June 1968, Air Force Historical Research Agency.

_____, "USAF Ballistic Missile Programs 1962–1964," USAF Historical Division Liaison Office, April 1966, AFHRA.

_____, "USAF Ballistic Missile Programs 1965," USAF Historical Division Liaison Office, March 1967, AFHRA.

_____, "USAF Ballistic Missile Programs 1967–1968," Office of the Air Force History, September 1969, AFHRA.

_____, ed. "Winged Shield, Winged Sword: A History of the United States Air Force Volume II 1950–1997," Washington, D.C., Air Force History and Museums Program, 1997.

National Security Archive, "Air Force Histories Released through Archive Lawsuit Show Cautious Presidents Overruling Air Force Plans for Early Use of Nuclear Weapons," April 30, 2008, Washington, D.C.

_____, "National Security Agency Releases History of Cold War Intelligence Activity," November 14, 2008, Washington, D.C.

Narducci, Henry M., "Strategic Air Command and the Alert Program: A Brief History," Offutt Air Force Base, Nebraska, Office of the Historian, 1 April 1988.

National Security Archive, "The Cuban Missile Crisis, 1962: The 40th Anniversary, Chronologies of the Crisis," 2002, Washington, D.C.

National Security Council, "'U.S. Objectives with Respect to the USSR to Counter Soviet Threats to U.S. Security,' NSC 20/4," 23 November 1948, http://www.mtholyoke.edu/acad/intrel/feros-pg.htm (accessed 6/10).

Natural Resources Defense Council, "Global Nuclear Stockpiles, 1945–2006," *Bulletin of the Atomic Scientists,* July/August 2006.

Nazzaro, Joseph J., "SAC: An Instrument of National Policy," *Air University Review,* January–February 1968.

Nemitz, Bill, "Crash Site Tells of Cold War History," *Maine Today,* August 30, 2006, Reprint.

Neufeld, Jacob, "The Development of Ballistic Missiles in the United States Air Force 1945–1960," Office of Air Force History, 1990, AFHRA.

_____, ed., "Technology and the Air Force: A Retrospective Assessment," Air Force History and Museums Program, 1997.

Newport, Curt, "Broken Arrow," *Air & Space Magazine,* October/November 1990, pp. 24–27.

Office of the Secretary of Defense (Atomic Energy), "History of the Custody and Deployment of Nuclear Weapons, July 1945 Through September 1977," February 1978, Department of Defense, FOIA Reading Room.

_____, "History of the Custody and Deployment of Nuclear Weapons, July 1945 Through September 1977," Chapters 1–8, with handwritten notes, February 1978, Department of Defense, FOIA Reading Room.

Ogden, Robert, Oral history regarding transfer of bombs to Europe, http://www.aero-web.org/specs/boeing/b-50d.htm (accessed 2/2010).

Olsen, Jan M., "Possible Link Between U.S. Crash and Illness," Associated Press, January 20, 1995.

_____, "Greenland Says U.S. Withheld Facts on Bomber Crash," Associated Press, February 2, 1995.

O'Keefe, Bernard J., *Nuclear Hostages,* Boston, Houghton Mifflin, 1983.

Operations Evaluation Group, Office of the Chief of Naval Operations, "Some

Factors Affecting the Feasibility of Very Long Range Bombing from North American Bases," July 12, 1949, DTIC.

Patrick, Rayford P., "Nuclear Hardness and Base Escape," March 31, 1981, Offutt Air Force Base, Nebraska, Strategic Air Command, DTIC.

Pearson, David E., "The World Wide Military Command and Control System Evolution and Effectiveness," Maxwell Air Force Base, Alabama, Air University Press, June 2000.

Place, W. M., Colonel F. C. Conn, and Lieutenant Colonel C. G. Defferding, "Palomares Summary Report, 15 January 1975," Kirtland Air Force Base, New Mexico, Defense Nuclear Agency Technology and Analysis Directorate.

Plummer, David W., and William H. Greenwood, "The History of Nuclear Weapon Safety Devices," *American Institute of Aeronautics and Astronautics,* 1998, DTIC.

Polakor, Melvin, Dudley Squire, F. Hobbs, and George E. Lucas, "Operation Castle, History of Task Group 7.4 Provisional for the Month of March 1954," n.d., DOE/NV.

Ponturo, John, "Analytical Support for the Joints Chiefs of Staff: The WSEG Experience, 1948–1976," Arlington, Virginia, Institute for Defense Analysis, July 1979.

Poole, Walter S., *The Joint Chiefs of Staff and National Policy Volume IV 1950–1952,* Washington, D.C., Office of Joint History, 1998.

Pratt, Joseph A., Tyler Priest, and Christopher J. Castaneda, *Offshore Pioneers: Brown & Root and the History of Offshore Oil and Gas,* Houston, Gulf Publishing Company, 1997.

Preston, M.A., to Major General William P. Fisher, "Briefing by the Honorable Herbert Loper," June 4, 1958, RG340.2, Records of the Secretary of the Air Force.

Project 1-M-54, "Report of Project 1-M-54 on Thirty Service Men Exposed to Residual Radiation at Operation Castle," July 1954, Washington, D.C., Department of the Army, from the Kapral family, author's collection.

Radomes.org, Air Defense Radar Museum, documents, papers, and first-person accounts related to the Texas Towers, http://www.radomes.org/museum/ (accessed 6/10).

RAND Corporation, "Special Memorandum, Vulnerability of U.S. Strategic Air Power to Surprise Enemy Attack in 1956," April 15, 1956, DTIC.

_____, "Implications of Large-Yield Nuclear Weapons," July 10, 1952, DTIC.

Randolph, John, "Russian Fighters Buzz USS Kitty Hawk," posted Thursday, December 14, 2000, Newsgroups: rec.aviaton.military (accessed 1999).

Ray, Thomas W., "A History of Texas Towers in Air Defense 1952–1964," Air Defense Command Historical Study No. 29, March 1965.

_____, "A History of the Dew Line 1946–1964, June 1965," Air Defense Command Historical Study No. 31, Scott Sagan Collection, National Security Archive, Washington, D.C.

Reese, H. L., "DoD Nuclear Mishaps," Armed Forces Radiobiology Research Institute, n.d., DTIC.

Rhodes, Richard, *Dark Sun: The Making of the Hydrogen Bomb,* New York, Touchstone, 1995.

Richardson, Howard, "Mid-Air Collision: B-47 and F-86H, 5 February 1958," unpublished, personal papers of Howard Richardson provided to author, September 26, 1997.

Richelson, Jeffrey T., *Spying on the Bomb: American Nuclear Intelligence from Nazi Germany to Iran and North Korea,* New York, W. W. Norton, 2007.

Robinson, Fellie F., "Rongerik Incident," March 27, 1954, DOE/NV Record 76554.

Rosenberg, David Alan, "A Smoking Radiating Ruin at the End of Two Hours," *International Security,* volume 6, no. 3 (winter 1981/82), pp. 8–23.

Rosenberg, Max, "USAF Ballistic Missiles 1958–1959," USAF Historical Division Liaison Office, July 1960, AFHRA.

Ross, Steven T., *American War Plans: 1945–1950,* London, Frank Cass & Co., Ltd., 1996.

Sagan, Scott D., *The Limits of Safety: Organizations, Accidents, and Nuclear Weapons,* Princeton, Princeton University Press, 1993.

Scarpino, G., "Statements of [Gerald Scarpino] Concerning Experiences on 'Operation Castle' Bikini Atoll 1953–1954," December 15, 1970, DOE/NV Record 403174.

Schaffel, Kenneth, "The Emerging Shield: The Air Force and the Evolution of Continental Air Defense 1945–1960," Office of Air Force History, 1991, AFHRA.

Schnabel, James F., *Volume I The Joint Chiefs of Staff and National Policy 1945–1947,* Washington, D.C., Office of Joint History, 1996.

Schnabel, James F., and Robert J. Watson, *The Joint Chiefs of Staff and National Policy Volume III 1950–1951 The Korean War Part One,* Washington, D.C., Office of Joint History, 1998.

_____, *The Joint Chiefs of Staff and National Policy Volume III 1951–1953 The Korean War Part Two,* Washington, D.C., Office of Joint History, 1998.

Schell, Jonathan, *The Fate of the Earth,* New York, Knopf, 1982.

Schwartz, Stephen I., ed., *Atomic Audit: The Costs and Consequences of U.S. Nuclear Weapons Since 1940,* Washington, D.C., Brookings Institution Press, 1998.

Shambroom, Paul, *Face to Face with the Bomb: Nuclear Reality After the Cold War,* Baltimore, Johns Hopkins Press, 1992.

Sharp, Robert, and William H. Chapman, "Operation Castle—Project 4.1 Addendum, Report to the Scientific Director, Exposure of Marshall Islanders and American Military Personnel to Fallout," March 1957, DOE/NV Report 410283.

Shaw, Frederick L., ed., "Locating Air Force Base Sites: History's Legacy," Air Force History and Museums Program, 2004, AFHRA.

Shaw, Jr., Frederick J., and Timothy Warnock, "The Cold War and Beyond: Chronology of the United States Air Force, 1947–1997," Air Force History and Museums Project, 1997, GPO.

Sheehy, Bill, "Memorandum for Mr. Borden, Re: The B-36 Crash," National Archives, RG340.2, Records of the Secretary of the Air Force.

Smith, Richard K., "Seventy-Five Years of Inflight Refueling: Highlights, 1923–1998," Air Force History and Museums Program, 1998, AFHRA.

Society of the Strategic Air Command, Inc., *Strategic Air Command*, Paducah, Kentucky, Turner, n.d.

Sontag, Sherry, and Christopher Drew with Annette Lawrence Drew, *Blind Man's Bluff: The Untold Story of American Submarine Espionage*, New York, PublicAffairs, 1998.

Spray, Stanley D., "History of U.S. Nuclear Weapons Safety Assessment: The Early Years," n.d., Albuquerque, New Mexico, Sandia National Laboratories, DTIC.

Stapp, John A., "Eniwetok-Rongerik Experiences," *The Wetokian*, volume 1, issue 1, winter 2000.

(Strategic Air Command), "Strategic Air Command, SAC and the Cuban Crisis," n.d., Scott Sagan Collection, National Security Archive, Washington, D.C.

Sturm, Thomas A., "The Air Force and the Worldwide Military Command and Control System, 1961–1965," USAF Historical Division Liaison Office, August 1966, AFHRA.

Time magazine, "New Bomber," May 9, 1960.

_____, "The Safety Catch on the Deterrent," April 26, 1958.

_____, "Operation Powerhouse," December 31, 1956.

_____, "What Red Airpower?" July 9, 1956.

_____, "Bye, Bye Bombers," September 10, 1945.

_____, "The Supersonic Shield," December 20, 1954.

_____, "Looking Outward," February 18, 1946.

_____, "How Close Is War?" October 4, 1948.

_____, "No Time for Delusion," April 10, 1950.

_____, "Plain Words," January 29, 1951.

_____, "The Brutal Truth," March 23, 1953.

_____, "Bombs for Everybody," October 5, 1953.

_____, "What Price Survival," November 23, 1953.

_____, "Distorted Commentary," April 5, 1954.

_____, "The Road Beyond Elugelab," April 26, 1954.

_____, "The Oilmen & the Sea," July 5, 1954.

_____, "Islands for Defense," August 23, 1954.

_____, "Islands to Order," September 9, 1957.

_____, "Power on the Side," February 16, 1959.

The New York Times, "Danger Signs in North: Increasing Soviet Air Activity Is Seen," July 21, 1952.

_____, "Atomic Discord Lingers," October 11, 1953.

_____, "Texas Tower Afloat: Weather Prevents Tilting of Base into Position," *The New York Times,* July 6, 1957.

_____, "Soviet Progress in Air: Russians Making Big Strides in Jets," July 17, 1951.

_____, "Texas Tower in Position, Platform for Warning Unit Is Installed at Sea," July 8, 1957.

_____, "Europe's View of Bomb Mingles Fear and Hope," February 5, 1950.

_____, "Military Air Toll 5,000 in 5 Years: 18,000 Accidents Cost U.S. 3 Billion Figures Show," March 29, 1959.

_____, "The Looking Glass, Through," August 5, 1990.

"Texas Tower Failure Suit Settled," *Engineering Record,* December 17, 1964, contained in reel #31613, AFHRA, Texas Tower 4 documents, Record 1012570.

United Press, "New Superbombs Indicated by A.E.C. as Result of Tests: Report Hints at Missile Triple Hydrogen's Weapons Force," *The New York Times,* January 30, 1955.

United States Air Force, "Information Plan, 58-A-9; Annex G to WSEG Test Plan No. 3—The Phase I Evaluation Exercise, dated 4 June 1958," National Archives, RG340.2, Records of the Secretary of the Air Force.

_____, "Air Force Search & Recovery Assessment of 1958 Savannah, GA B-47 Accident," Washington, D.C., AF Nuclear Weapons and Counterproliferation Agency, April 12, 2001.

_____, "USAF Flight Mishap History, CY47-CY06," Kirtland Air Force Base, New Mexico, www.afsc.shared/media/document/AFD-080407-052.pdf (accessed June 2010).

_____, "Soviet Capabilities to Interfere with US Delivery of Atomic Weapons to Targets in the USSR," March 9, 1951, National Archives, CIA-RDP79R01012 A0008000300001-8.

_____, "Final Report, Operation Castle, Task Group 7.4, July 1953–June 1954," DOE/NV Record 76918.

United States Air Force Historical Research Center, "U.S. Air Force Oral History Interview, Lt. Gen. William J. Campbell," Washington, D.C., Office of Air Force History, December 19, 1985 AFHRA.

United States Patent and Trademark Office, "Patent # 2,586,966, Theodore Kuss and Ralph D. Russell," filed August 8, 1949.

U.S. Congress, Senate Committee on Armed Services, *Inquiry into the Collapse of Texas Tower No. 4,* 87th Congress, 1st session, May 17, 1961, Washington, D.C., Government Printing Office.

_____, *Report on the Collapse of Texas Tower No. 4,* 87th Congress, 1st session, June 15, 1961, Washington, D.C., Government Printing Office.

_____, *Supplemental Report on the Collapse of Texas Tower No. 4, Discharge of Command Responsibility,* 87th Congress, 2nd session, March 25, 1962, Washington D.C., Government Printing Office.

U.S. Congress, Senate unnamed committee, questions that were answered by General Curtis E. LeMay in open hearings, 84th Congress, 2nd session, April 30, 1956, FOIA, AFHRA.

U.S. Department of Energy, "United States Nuclear Tests, July 1945 through September, 1992," National Technology Information Service, DOE/NV-209-REV15.

_____, Nevada Test Site, "Civil Defense Effects Tests," March 2001, DOE/NV.

U.S. Department of State, Office of the Historian, *Foreign Relations of the United States, 1961–1963,* volume VI, Kennedy-Khrushchev Exchanges, http://history.state.gov/historicaldocuments/frus1961-63v06 (accessed 6/10).

Universal-International Newsreel, "A New Moon Is in the Sky," 1957, www.youtube.com (accessed June 2010).

_____, "May Day Parade 1961," www.youtube.com (accessed June 2010).

Wachsmuth, Wayne, *B-36 Peacemaker,* Carrollton, Texas, Squadron/Signal Publications, 1997.

Wainstein, L., C. D. Cremeans, J. K. Moriarty, and J. Ponturo, "The Evolution of U.S. Command and Control and Warning, 1945–1972," June 1975, Arlington, Virginia, Institute for Defense Analysis.

Weapons System Evaluation Group, Enclosure "E" to WSEG Report no. 43, "The Relationship of Public Morale on Information about the Effects of Nuclear Warfare," n.d., Department of Defense, FOIA Reading Room.

Weapons System Evaluation Group, WSEG Report no. 23, "The Relative Advantage of Missiles and Manned Aircraft," May 6, 1957, DTIC.

Weisgall, Jonathan M., *Operation Crossroads: The Atomic Tests at Bikini Atoll,* Annapolis, Naval Institute Press, 1994.

Welsome, Eileen, *The Plutonium Files: America's Secret Medical Experiments of the Cold War,* New York, Delta, 1999.

Western Union, "Bomb Alarm Display System 210-A," http://coldwar-c4i.net/index.html (accessed June 2010).

Wilson, Stewart, *Vulcan, Boeing B-47 & B-52: The Story of Three Classic Bombers of the Cold War,* Fyshwick, Australia, Aerospace Publications, 1997.

Winkler, David F., "Searching the Skies, The Legacy of the United States Cold War Defense Radar Program," Headquarters Air Combat Command, June 1997, DTIC.

Wise, Charles E., "History of the Weather Central Element, Provisional and The Task Force Weather Central, Book II, 'Operational Phase' Instalment no. 2, 1 March 1954 to 31 March 1954," Historical Offices, Joint Task Force Seven, April 30, 1954, DOE/NV.

Witkin, Richard, "Collisions Worry Air Force: Strategic Air Command Says Hundreds of Near Misses Occurred This Year," *The New York Times,* November 9, 1955.

Wohlstetter, A. J., F. S. Hoffman, and H. S. Rowen, *Staff Report: Protecting U.S. Power to Strike Back in the 1950's and 1960's,* September 1, 1960, Santa Monica, RAND Corporation, www.albertwohlstetter.com (accessed 2/2010).

Wylie, Evan McLeod, "Tragedy on Tower Four," *Reader's Digest,* condensed from *True, the Man's Magazine,* April 1962, pp. 95–102.

Young, David L., United States Air Force Oral History Program, "Interview of Lt. General Edgar S. Harris, Jr.," Maxwell Air Force Base, Alabama, USAF Historical Research Center, 1985.

Zuckert, Eugene, to Curtis E. LeMay, "Texas Tower No. 4 Court Martial Proceedings," National Archives, RG340.2, Records of the Secretary of the Air Force.

[Unknown], "Briefing for the President on SAC Operations with Sealed-Pit Weapons," 1958, National Security Archive, Washington, D.C.

[Unknown], "Custody of Atomic Weapons: Historical Summary of Principal Actions," n.d., Department of Defense, FOIA Reading Room.

INDEX